Information Modelling for Archaeology and Anthropology

This book contains multiple diagrams expressed in ConML. See www.conml.org for more information on ConML. This book also makes extensive reference to the Cultural Heritage Abstract Reference Model (CHARM). See www.charminfo.org for more information on CHARM. ConML and CHARM are research outcomes of Incipit CSIC (www.incipit.csic.es) and can be used freely under a Creative Commons Attribution 4.0 International License (https://creativecommons.org/licenses/by/4.0/).

Most of the many examples used throughout this book have been made up by the author to better illustrate the different modelling techniques. No particular statements or views on the world should be assumed from them.

Interior photographs correspond to Praza das Praterías in Santiago de Compostela, Spain; excavation at 95 George Street, Sydney, Australia; the National Museum of China in Beijing, China; a river mill in Begonte, Lugo, Spain; and Maes Howe in Orkney, Scotland. They were taken jointly by the author and Isabel Cobas.

This book was prepared by the author using Microsoft Word 2016 for editing and layout, and Microsoft Visio 2016 for the figures. The ConML diagrams were composed by using the Visio stencil at http://www.conml.org/Resources_Templates.aspx.

There is a Spanish language edition of this book, titled "Modelado de Información para Arqueología y Antropología: Principios de Ingeniería de Software para Patrimonio Cultural", and with ISBN 978-1537766706.

Cesar Gonzalez-Perez

Information Modelling for Archaeology and Anthropology

Software Engineering Principles for Cultural Heritage

 Springer

Cesar Gonzalez-Perez
Incipit, CSIC
Santiago de Compostela, A Coruña
Spain

ISBN 978-3-319-89193-4   ISBN 978-3-319-72652-6   (eBook)
https://doi.org/10.1007/978-3-319-72652-6

Printed on acid-free paper

This Springer imprint is published by Springer Nature
The registered company is Springer International Publishing AG
The registered company address is: Gewerbestrasse 11, 6330 Cham, Switzerland

To the memory of my father, for his curiosity, idealism, and passion.

Preface

This book is the result of over 20 years of research and practice in the interdisciplinary area of information technologies and cultural heritage. In the 1990s, we had not heard yet of the "digital humanities", but we were aware that archaeology, anthropology and other areas in the humanities desperately needed proposals to help manage the increasing amounts of information that they were generating, and sustain the associated knowledge-generation practices. Today, this trend has only intensified, and the application of solid, high-quality engineering principles to the construction of information systems and knowledge-generation approaches in the humanities is paramount. In particular, research in the humanities depends very much on the information that is managed, how it is shaped and structured (i.e. "modelled"), and how knowledge is generated from it through interpretive processes. In the absence of a rigorous approach, we may end up being unable to use our valuable information for the intended goals.

The software and knowledge engineering disciplines have been using conceptual modelling for a while and exporting it to other fields such as biomedicine or business organization. However, robust applications of conceptual modelling to the humanities are scarce. In this book, we apply proven principles and techniques from the software and knowledge engineering fields to the problems of cultural heritage. Also, we show how these principles and techniques have been adapted and extended to cope with the peculiarities of the humanities and, specifically, archaeology and anthropology.

This book is primarily aimed at students and teachers of data management, information modelling and related areas in any field related to cultural heritage, such as archaeology, anthropology, art, museology, geography, history, architecture, archival science, literature, and even sociology or soil sciences. Other specialists in cultural heritage such as researchers, heritage managers or heritage professionals working in industry can also use this book in a self-paced manner to learn about the topic.

This book assumes no previous exposure by the reader to information technologies and no knowledge whatsoever of conceptual modelling, ontologies or other topics in software or knowledge engineering. Technical detail is kept low or moderate, and special technical asides used to provide highly specialized or complex details only when needed are marked "Technical". You can safely skip these sections if not interested in the philosophical or engineering underpinnings of things. Specific words or phrases being discussed are shown in double quotes, like "this". Single quotes, like 'this', are used to refer not to the words but to the underlying concepts. Bibliographic references mentioned in the text are indicated by numbers in brackets, like this [15]. There is a reference list at the end of each chapter. In addition, most of the chapters in this book end with a summary of the contents presented, as well as some exercises that you can use to verify how well you have understood them. Solutions to the exercises are provided at the end of this book.

This book is organized into five parts of increasing complexity. First, a general philosophical introduction to conceptual modelling is provided, to develop a contextual feel of the approach and a better understanding of the technical issues that are described later. Secondly, the basics of conceptual modelling are introduced, using the ConML (www.conml.org) language as an infrastructure, and employing examples from everyday life and, as often as possible, cultural heritage. Then, advanced topics in conceptual modelling are presented, in order to fully cover the necessary aspects of ConML that will allow the reader to develop and understand complex conceptual models. After this, a proposed conceptualization of cultural heritage is presented, using the Cultural Heritage Abstract Reference Model (CHARM, www.charminfo.org) as a reference, so that conceptual models of cultural heritage can be easily constructed. Finally, various usage scenarios and applications of cultural heritage modelling are described, giving practical tips on how to use different techniques to solve real-world problems. You are free to read only the first few parts if you are only interested in an overview of the topic, or jump to the last parts if you are already familiar with it. If you are learning about conceptual modelling in cultural heritage for the first time and you are interested in obtaining a comprehensive view, then I suggest that you read this book cover to cover.

Finally, I would like to acknowledge the contributions that many people have made to the materials presented in this book. Most specially, the ConML modelling language has benefited from the input of Charlotte Hug and Patricia Martín-Rodilla. Parts of Chap. 19 have been co-written with César Parcero-Oubiña, and his input, as well as David Barreiro's, has been crucial to the whole chapter. The definitions of culture, cultural heritage, cultural value and heritage value that are discussed in Part IV have been refined from the results of a series of internal workshops at Incipit CSIC (www.incipit.csic.es), with contributions by Ana Ruiz-Blanch, A. César González-García, César Parcero-Oubiña, Cristina Sánchez-Carretero, David Barreiro, Felipe Criado-Boado, Joan Roura-Expósito, Juan Castro-Cal, Patricia Martín-Rodilla and Ruth Varela. In turn, the initial version of the Cultural Heritage Abstract Reference Model (CHARM) was developed by a core team led by the author plus Alejandro Güimil-Fariña, Camila Gianotti, César Parcero-Oubiña, Charlotte Hug, Patricia Martín-Rodilla, Pastor Fábrega-Álvarez and Rebeca

Blanco-Rotea, with additional input from Cristina Mato-Fresán, Lucía Meijueiro and Rocío Varela-Pousa. The whole manuscript was revised by Isabel Cobas.

In addition, my co-workers at Incipit CSIC have been courageous enough as to not only accept a stranger between them, but also provide a challenging and exciting environment where truly transdisciplinary research can be carried out. My collaborators at the *Centro de Investigación en Métodos de Producción Software* (PROS) of the *Universitat Politècnica de València*, the *Centre de Recherche en Informatique* (CRI) of the *Université Paris 1—Panthéon-Sorbonne*, and the Centre for Object Technology Applications and Research (COTAR) of the University of Technology, Sydney, have opened many doors and shaped the results of my research very significantly. Also, the community around the Computer Applications and Quantitative Methods in Archaeology (CAA) association and annual conference has also been an endless source of inspiration and problems waiting to be solved. The users of ConML and CHARM, including the students of our regular postgraduate courses at the University of Santiago de Compostela and elsewhere, have also provided very useful feedback. And, last but not least, the boundless conversations with my dear Isabel have delivered both uncompromising support and powerful insights into the conceptual modelling of cultural heritage like nobody else's. Thank you all.

Santiago de Compostela, Spain   Cesar Gonzalez-Perez

Contents

About the Author

Cesar Gonzalez-Perez is a Staff Scientist at the Institute of Heritage Sciences (Incipit, www.incipit. csic.es), Spanish National Research Council (CSIC), where he leads a co-research line in software engineering and cultural heritage. The ultimate goal of his work is to develop the necessary theories, methodologies and technologies to help understand how meaning is constructed in relation to cultural heritage. Previously, Cesar has worked at a number of public and private organizations in Spain and Australia, both in industry and academia, and in the fields of conceptual modelling, metamodelling and situational method engineering. He has started three technology-based companies, is active in the international standards community through ISO and AENOR, is an elected member of the steering committee of the Computer Applications and Quantitative Methods in Archaeology (CAA) association and has authored or co-authored over 80 publications.

Part I
Introduction to Conceptual Modelling

This part provides a straightforward philosophical introduction to the modelling of information and knowledge. Some premises and linguistic connections are discussed, and the benefits of using conceptual modelling are described.

Chapter 1
What Is Conceptual Modelling?

Abstract In this chapter, we describe what modelling is from a general perspective. We start by explaining that models represent something in the world in a simplified manner, so that we can reason on the model and then apply the conclusions back to the modelled subject. We define the notions of model *scope* and *purpose* and describe how they work as guides to decide what to keep and what to discard when modelling. Then we move on to explain what conceptual models are, and the fact that they are composed of concepts rather than physical things. These concepts can be of two kinds: the *individual* entities in the world, as well as the *categories* that we use to organize them. In this manner, conceptual models work as ontologies of the world.

We all build and use models. We do it in many different contexts, from the most sophisticated technical settings to our daily routine. We create mental models of the world in which we live, we sketch something on a piece of paper to explain an idea to someone else, and we use our hands to signal how large or small something is. In the specific field of cultural heritage, we also build and use models for technical reasons. For example, we use maps to locate sites or other relevant places, we construct Harris matrices to describe stratigraphic sequences, and we record information in databases for later use. Sketches, maps, Harris matrices and database records are models, because *they purposefully represent something of interest to us*.

Every model has three interesting properties:

- It represents something. For example, a map represents a portion of the territory.
- It simplifies the represented subject. For example, the lines and shapes on a map are much simpler than the real territory.
- It allows us to reason on the representation and then apply the conclusions back to the modelled subject. For example, we can carry out measurements on a map and then we expect that they will hold on the terrain.

Models can represent anything. Whatever is supposed to be represented by a model is called its *scope*. Architects sometimes make cardboard models of the buildings they plan to construct or modify. A map is a model of the territory.

© Springer International Publishing AG 2018

C. Gonzalez-Perez, *Information Modelling for Archaeology and Anthropology*,
https://doi.org/10.1007/978-3-319-72652-6_1

A table listing data about pottery fragments in a report is also a model. The scopes of these models are the buildings to be constructed, the territory and the pottery fragments, respectively. Also, and in all these cases, the models are physical things, being made of cardboard, lines and shapes on a sheet of paper, or letters printed or displayed on screen. Models like these are very convenient because, being physical, they can be perceived and interacted with by us with little effort. However, sometimes they fall short of satisfying some of our needs. For example, very abstract things may be difficult to represent physically. Also, and more importantly, a model that is purely physical is difficult to verbalize and describe to someone else; for example, giving directions to someone by using a map as a reference is no much simpler than giving the same directions by using the actual terrain as a reference. For these reasons, models are more convenient if they are strongly grounded on our linguistic ability and, in consequence, on our cognitive mechanisms. A model that is made of ideas or concepts instead of physical things is called a *conceptual model*.

Technical

There is some debate in the conceptual modelling community as to whether conceptual models are models made of concepts (as proposed in this book) or models about concepts. A discussion on this topic can be found in [1].

As any other model, conceptual models possess the three properties described above. In particular:

- A conceptual model represents something by using concepts.
- It does so in a simplified manner, so that only the relevant details are captured in the model, and the others discarded.
- By doing so, we or others can reason on the representation and then apply the conclusions back to the modelled subject.

There are a few things that need further exploration. First, when we say "by using concepts" this includes various possible situations. Sometimes, conceptual models represent the ideas held by a particular individual; some other times, they represent the ideas shared and agreed upon by a group. In this sense, "concepts" may refer to the concepts of a particular individual or to concepts shared by a group. As we will see throughout this book, both scenarios are common and extremely useful.

Second, and since a model is necessarily simpler than the modelled subject, a conceptual model keeps only the relevant details and discards the rest. But, relevant for what? You may remember that we defined "model" above as something that purposefully represents something else that is of interest to us. The words "purposefully" and "interest" point to the fact that a model always has a *purpose*. When we create a model, conceptual or otherwise, we need to have a clear goal in mind. This goal will guide us in the decision process of what to keep and what to discard. For example, an architect creating a model of a small village in order to study its urban configuration will probably record the distances between buildings and the materials they are made of, but will probably discard details such as the names of the house owners or the folk tales associated to particular buildings. However, an anthropologist trying to learn about the social practices of the villagers is likely to include the folk tales but perhaps discard the distances and materials. Having a clear purpose is crucial when constructing models, and we will come back to this idea regularly. Similarly, knowing the purpose that the model creator had in mind when they built it is important when using a model. The statistician George Box is usually credited as having said "all models are wrong; some models are useful". This means that all models are significantly different to the reality they aim to represent (and, hence, "wrong"); still, many may still be useful since we can reason on them and apply the results back to the represented subject.

Third, conceptual models are about knowledge. By using concepts in our minds, we can represent what we know in quite sophisticated ways. A conceptual model can represent statements about the world at various abstraction levels, notably describing what entities we believe to exist in the world, what properties they have and how they are organized. Being made of concepts, conceptual models are abstract things in our heads. We can draw them on a piece of paper or describe them in words, but the lines on the paper or the words that we speak are simply representations of the conceptual model in our head, and not the model itself. In other words, conceptual models are purely mental constructs and, as such, not communicable but through other models which are physical and thus perceivable, such as drawings or textual descriptions.

Fourth, the fact that conceptual models are about knowledge places them quite high up in the Ackoff hierarchy [2]. This hierarchy proposes a conceptualization where *data* lies at the bottom, as the simplest and most primary form of contents that we can find; *information* exists on top of data; *knowledge* is based on information; and *wisdom* is at the top, based on knowledge. Although this hierarchy involves a substantial simplification of the relationships between these notions, it is still useful to delineate significant differences between them. By using the Ackoff hierarchy, we would say that conceptual models consist of knowledge rather than information or data. This contrasts with other forms of representation oriented towards data or information, such as linked data or other approaches related to the semantic web. These approaches work at a lower level of abstraction than conceptual modelling and, in fact, are better considered mechanisms for data encoding rather than information modelling. Consequently, they do not describe the world in terms of knowledge, but organize and record data with a given structure.

Technical

According to most sources, data consists of simple, isolated and uninterpreted quantities or qualities such as numbers, texts or images. In other words, data is about naked symbols that have the potentiality to be interpreted. Information, in turn, is composed of data but also involves a sender and a meaning to be conveyed; in other words, information is about telling others about things by using data, and for this reason it entails a particular interpretation of the underlying raw quantities or qualities.

In turn, knowledge is usually defined as *justified true belief* [3, "The Analysis of Knowledge"]. This is a classical definition dating back to Socrates and Plato, which requires that something is believed by someone is true and is justified by the holder in order to constitute knowledge. On the first requirement, someone must believe something before we can call it knowledge; that is, knowledge cannot exist outside a mind. Secondly, knowledge must be true; a false statement cannot constitute knowledge even if we believe it. For example, we should not say that "I know it's raining" if it is not raining. This classical definition of knowledge, though, is disputed by some philosophers, although there is no consensus on a better definition. In particular, some works in cultural heritage, such as [4], have challenged the idea that knowledge must be true. Finally, knowledge must be justified; that is, the holder must be able to explain why or how they believe it, in order to rule out lucky coincidences and other uncommon situations.

It is also worth noting that knowledge can be encoded as information in order to be communicated. Since knowledge is a mental process, it cannot be perceived by anyone but its owner; the only way we have to communicate knowledge to others is, precisely, to encode it as information and let others interpret this information to construct knowledge in their own heads that, hopefully, will resemble our own. We do this when we speak, write or draw diagrams on a whiteboard.

Fifth, not every collection of concepts in our mind constitutes a conceptual model. A conceptual model needs to be simple, created with a clear purpose, and be expressed in such a way that is easy to convey to others. This means that concepts in conceptual models must be simple, crisp and neatly organized, showing something that we will call *formality* in Chap. 2.

Finally, conceptual models allow us or others to reason on the model and then apply the conclusions back to the modelled ideas. This means that we can use a conceptual model as a surrogate of whatever is being represented, and then apply the consequences of our reasoning back to the modelled subject. We do this, for example, when we construct a spatial model in a geographical information system, carry out some analysis on it and then apply our findings to the real landscape.

Technical

Modelling, as such, is an old concept. For a brief introduction to modelling and model theory, see [3, "Model Theory"].

Conceptual modelling, as a discipline, originated around the 1980s within the field of software engineering. However, its connection to software is only historical, and conceptual modelling has since been applied to various areas such as business organization or genomics. A good introduction to conceptual modelling in software engineering is [5].

We must also realize that not all ideas are of the same kind. A very basic distinction can be made between ideas about *particulars* and those about *universals*. This is an old and usually accepted way to describe the ontology of the world, dating back to ancient Greece. According to this distinction, particulars are concrete things, usually situated in space and time. The chair I am sitting on as I type this, the computer I am using, the word processor software that it is running, and the company who developed this software are all particulars. Universals, on the other hand, are abstract concepts that describe the common properties shared by a set of particulars. For example, the concept of 'chair' in my mind is a universal, as it captures the properties that something must have for us to call it a chair. In other words, the chair I am sitting on, plus the identical chair next to me, plus any other chairs I remember having seen or can imagine are all particulars of the 'chair' universal.

Usually, we say that particulars refer to things, whereas universals refer to categories. This is easily seen through language use. When we point, physically or mentally, to a chair and say "that chair" or "the chair that was in your room last Sunday", we are referring to particulars. However, when we speak about chairs in general, saying for example "chairs give me back ache" or "some chairs have armrests", we are referring to a universal.

Technical
The difference between particulars and universals dates back to Plato and Aristotle. A more recent treatment is that of the type versus token distinction originally made by Peirce in the late nineteenth century, under which a token model is one representing particulars, and a type model is one representing universals. See [3, "Types and Tokens"] for a detailed account.

Even more recently, the issue has received attention in the conceptual modelling community, and three (rather than two) ways of representing have been defined: isotypical (corresponding to tokens), prototypical and metatypical (corresponding to types). See [6] for more details.

The words "particular" and "universal" are common in philosophy, but in conceptual modelling in general, and in this book in particular, we prefer to use "entity" and "category". Both pairs of words mean the same thing: a particular is an entity, and a universal is a category. The distinction between entities and categories is relevant to conceptual modelling because, as we will see in detail, some conceptual models represent entities while others represent categories. In other words, some models focus on the specific things that exist in the world, while others describe the world in terms of what kinds of things there are. Although entities and categories can be mixed together in the same model, this is not very usual.

Conceptual modelling has been linked to philosophy, and to ontology in particular, in many ways. In fact, the word "ontology" is often seen in the software engineering and computing literature as a close synonym for "conceptual model". This usage is quite different to the typical usage of "ontology" in philosophy, where it is almost always used in singular and refers to the branch of philosophy concerned with being. In computing, however, "ontology" is often used in plural and refers to a shared conceptualization of the world. If you have heard of ontologies in the sense of computer representations of a portion of reality, then you have probably heard about conceptual models. Works like those of Partridge [7] provide an excellent take on how conceptual models work as ontological stances on the world.

Technical

In the computing literature, an ontology is usually defined as "a formal specification of a conceptualization", following Gruber's seminal work [8].

The similarities and differences between ontologies and conceptual models are a subject of debate. They are probably very similar things, but conceptual models originated within the software engineering discipline whereas ontologies started in the artificial intelligence field. A good summary of commonalities and differences can be found in [9].

Summary

Conceptual models **represent** something by using concepts in our minds.

They do it in a **simplified** manner, so that only the relevant details are captured.

Conceptual models are determined by their **scope** (the portion of the world being modelled) as well as the **purpose** for which they are constructed.

We can **reason** on a model and then apply the conclusions back to the modelled subject.

Conceptual models can represent the **entities** in the world as well as the **categories** that we use to organize them.

In this manner, conceptual models work as **ontologies** of the world.

Chapter 2
Premises and Foundations of Conceptual Modelling

Abstract This chapter starts by presenting the ontological (in the philosophical sense) premises for conceptual modelling. These involve agreeing that reality can be discretized into separate entities, and that these entities can be organized into categories. Then we move on to describe the connections between conceptual modelling and natural language, and how by using conceptual models we can express different linguistic constructs, including existence ("there is a person"), identity ("Isabel is my wife"), predication ("Isabel is tall"), classification ("Isabel is a person") and subsumption ("A dog is an animal"). Finally, we explain that models are usually expressed by using *modelling languages*, such as ConML (www.conml. org), which are quite formal, comprising very strict lexical, syntactical and semantic rules, and even affecting the way in which we conceptualize the world.

This chapter presents the ontological (in the philosophical sense) premises for conceptual modelling, the connections between conceptual modelling and natural language and the need for formality.

Premises

In order for conceptual modelling to work, we need to commit to two basic ontological premises. Without this commitment, we would not be able to create or use conceptual models.

> **Premise 1**
> Reality can be discretized into separate things.

This premise means that reality, in whatever way we understand it, can be "cut up" into separate things. In other words, we don't conceive reality as a continuous, uninterrupted phenomenon, but as something made of distinct things.

© Springer International Publishing AG 2018

C. Gonzalez-Perez, *Information Modelling for Archaeology and Anthropology*,
https://doi.org/10.1007/978-3-319-72652-6_2

This premise does not mean that everyone cuts reality along the same seams, or that we must always cut it up in the same manner; in fact, different people, especially when they come from different cultures, usually organize reality into things by cutting it along different seams, and even the same individual may want to consider different "cutting" approaches at different moments and for different purposes. This premise only means that reality can be cut up, in whichever ways, as opposed to being a single monolithic and continuous thing.

Also, the fact that we perceive reality in the form of separate things does not mean that these things cannot be interconnected. As we will see, they often are.

The things that we perceive as distinct, arising from this cutting up of reality, are called *entities* in Chap. 1, and roughly correspond to the particulars of classical philosophy.

Premise 2
Things can be categorized in a meaningful way.

This premise means that the things that we perceive as making up reality can be assigned to categories according to some reason. In other words, things can be classified into kinds, types or whatever other groupings, so that we can describe the world in terms of categories instead of the specific things that make it up.

A direct consequence of this is that things must have properties that allow us to decide what category to assign each to at any given moment. That is, our understanding of the things that we perceive as making up the world must be such that meaningful categories can be used to organize things.

Like in the previous case, this premise does not mean that everyone assigns the same things to the same categories, or that everyone assigns one thing to the same category all the time. In fact, different people categorize things differently, and even the same person may categorize something in different manners depending on purpose or other factors. This premise only means that things can be categorized, in whichever way.

The groupings that we use to arrange entities are called *categories* in Chap. 1, and roughly correspond to the universals of classical philosophy.

Technical
The emphasis on categories comes from the fact that categorization is often agreed to be a natural and unavoidable phenomenon in the human mind. The linguist George Lakoff pointed out that "There is nothing more basic than categorization to our thought, perception, action, and speech" [10].

Linguistic Connections

We mentioned the connection between language and conceptual modelling in Chap. 1, in relation to the distinction between particulars and universals. This connection is also strong with regard to the basic kinds of facts about entities and categories that we can express when we speak. There are five of them:

- **Existence**. We can state that something exists. For example, "There is a person". This allows us to state what entities exist and are relevant to us.
- **Identity**. We can state that two things are the same one. For example, "Isabel is my wife". In this example, "Isabel" and "my wife" refer to the same entity. This allows us to express what constitutes a distinct entity that is different to any other, and detect those cases where multiple words or descriptions refer to the same entity.
- **Predication**. We can assign a property to an entity. For example, "Isabel is tall". In this example, we are assigning the property 'tall' to the entity referred to by "Isabel". This allows us to characterize entities by describing their features.
- **Classification**. We can assign a category to an entity. For example, "Isabel is a person". In this example, the 'Isabel' entity is said to belong to the 'person' category. This allows us to classify entities according to whatever scheme we may find useful.
- **Subsumption**. We can state that a category subsumes another category. For example, "A dog is an animal". In this example, the 'dog' category is said to be subsumed by the wider encompassing 'animal' category. This allows us to organize categories into meaningful structures.

Interestingly, these five kinds of statements are expressed by using the verb "to be" in English, and the equivalent verbs in many other languages. Conceptual models, however, allow us to represent these kinds of statements by using very different mechanisms, as we will see in Part II.

Conceptual Modelling Languages

Natural language is powerful and intuitive. We can express all sorts of things in English, French or any other language, with little effort and great flexibility. However, natural language is also highly ambiguous. Or, rather, we should say that meaning is highly underspecified in natural language. This means that the meaning of a sentence like "I don't think her parents should come over for dinner" resides not only in the words that we use (lexicon), and the ways in which we inflect and combine them (grammar), but also in other contextual elements, such as the particular situation where the sentence is uttered, the tone employed or the backgrounds and expectations of the speaker and listeners. The fact that meaning in natural language is highly underspecified is a valuable resource; thanks to it, we can make shortcuts and speak very economically, and we can write literature that suggests and evokes. However, it also means that understanding this kind of language entails great complexity. Our minds can cope most of the time, and since most spoken language is used in interactive settings, we can always ask for clarifications when something is ambiguous. However, written sources are more difficult to interpret, since usually we cannot ask the author if something is unclear.

As we mentioned in Chap. 1, models must be simpler than the reality that they represent. Also, models are usually expressed in some form of writing rather than orally, so meaning must be clear from the start in order to minimize ambiguity. For these reasons, expressing a model in natural language is rarely a good idea. If we expressed a conceptual model in natural language, the inherent ambiguity would add complexity to the model, which would be a contradiction. For this reason, conceptual models (and most models in general) are usually expressed in special languages called, precisely, *modelling languages*.

A modelling language is an artificially constructed language that is much simpler than a natural language. But, like a natural language, a modelling language has a lexicon, a syntax and some semantics. The lexicon is the set of "words" or basic language units that we can use. The syntax is the set of rules that we must obey when putting lexicon elements together in order to compose meaningful "sentences". And the semantics is the collection of relationships between these "words" and the things in the world they refer to. Most modelling languages are extremely simple as compared to natural languages, having at most a few dozen "words" and very straightforward syntactic rules. Also, modelling languages are usually, but not always, depicted in graphical form, through diagrams or icons, instead of sequences of characters like we do for natural languages.

Also as a consequence of greater simplicity and the need of as little ambiguity as possible, modelling languages are highly *formal*. This means that their lexicon, syntactic rules and semantics are usually specified with great detail and must be mandatorily followed. With a natural language, we can get poetic and create new words, use awkward constructions or, in general, play with the language to express irony or provoke others. With a formal language, however, what elements exist is absolutely fixed, the meaning of each element is very clear and must be respected, and the manners in which they can be combined are strictly established. There is no room for wordplay. This is the price we pay to remove complexity.

Technical

You may have heard of the Unified Modeling Language (UML). This is a well-known modelling language in the software engineering community, which has been standardized by the Object Management Group (OMG) and by ISO as ISO/IEC 19505. Although some people use UML for conceptual modelling, it is heavily oriented towards the specification of computing systems rather than conceptual modelling, so we won't be discussing it much in this book. If you are interested in UML, you can start by looking at [11]. The technical specification can be found in [12].

Finally, we must bear in mind that a modelling language, very much like a natural language, allows us to *express knowledge* encoded as information. In other words, by using a modelling (or natural) language we can represent the concepts in our mind and put them to paper or screen so that others can read and understand. Like the sentences we utter, the diagrams that we draw constitute information. When we write a sentence or draw a diagram on a piece of paper, we are encoding the concepts in our head as information, and conveying this information with the hope that someone else (or even ourselves), by reading and interiorizing what we've written or drawn, can reconstruct in their mind some concepts that are as similar to the ones in ours as possible. If we attain this, we have communicated successfully. Also like natural languages, modelling languages influence the way in which we can conceptualize things; in other words, whatever modelling language we "speak", it will certainly introduce a bias in the way in which we discretize and categorize the things in the world.

Technical
The fact that the language that one speaks affects the manner in which they conceptualize the world has been called *linguistic relativity* and is often linked to the work by linguistic anthropologists Sapir and Whorf in the early and mid-twentieth century. See [3, "Culture and Cognitive Science"] for a brief introduction to linguistic relativity.

Figure 2.1 shows the major elements and relationships that are involved in conceptual modelling. According to the figure, we first perceive the entities in the world that fall within a given scope, and then we conceptualize them informally, perhaps for a particular purpose. A conceptual model is then created in our mind by formalising our conceptualizations, this time with a clear purpose in mind. Then, models can be depicted as diagrams or other information forms for communication or visualization purposes.

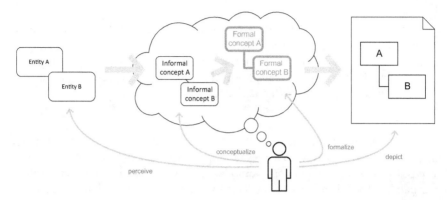

Fig. 2.1 The process of conceptual modelling. The large grey arrows indicate representation processes

What Are Conceptual Models Made Of?

Conceptual models are made of discrete but interconnected *model elements*. A model element is a formal construct that corresponds to a particular part of the modelling language being used, very much like a word in English (such as "book" or "run") is a lexical unit that corresponds to a particular part of speech (such as nouns or verbs). Like the English language, through its syntax, establishes how words may be combined to compose meaningful sentences, a conceptual modelling language establishes how model elements of different kinds may be combined to produce meaningful models. Part II describes the major types of model elements that we will use throughout this book.

Summary

In order to do conceptual modelling, we need to accept that reality can be discretized into separate **entities**.

We also need to accept that the resulting entities can be organized into **categories**.

Through conceptual modelling, we can express **existence**, **identity**, **predication**, **classification** and **subsumption**.

We can communicate conceptual models by "writing them down" using a particular **modelling language**.

Modelling languages are quite **formal**, since they comprise very strict lexical, syntactical and semantic rules.

Modelling languages, in addition to dictating how we may depict things in diagrams, also influence how we may conceptualize reality.

Conceptual models are composed of **model elements**, each of them corresponding to a given construct in the associated modelling language.

Chapter 3
Benefits and Applications of Conceptual Modelling

Abstract In this chapter, we explain why conceptual modelling should be used, what interest it has for archaeology and anthropology, and benefits can be derived from using it. First, we explain how conceptual modelling can help us to *explore* areas of the world that we do not understand very well, that is, we can try to model a small part of the world in various manners and explore which one makes more sense. In this regards, conceptual models can help us to "organize our minds". Then we explain that conceptual modelling can also help us to *document* the world for later reference. Instead of taking notes in English or other natural language, or carrying out any other form of informal recording, we can create a conceptual model as a way to document a part of the world, with the aim that others, or even ourselves, will use this information in the future to learn about what was described. This is particularly relevant, for example, when the documented entities are to be destroyed, like with many archaeological interventions. After that, we explain that conceptual modelling is useful to *communicate* our ideas to others. We can sketch formal diagrams on paper or a whiteboard, or we can use a computer-stored conceptual model, as a way to disseminate information or share our ideas. Given the formal nature of conceptual modelling, this is especially useful when trying to communicate with specialists from very different backgrounds. Then we explain that conceptual models can work as guidelines to *design* tools or methodologies. For example, a conceptual modelling that is shared within an organization can be easily employed as the basis to develop a company-wide database system or a common fieldwork methodology. Finally, we conclude the chapter by explaining that conceptual modelling can help us to make our information *interoperate* with other sources. By establishing shared conceptual frameworks of reference, databases and data sets can be interpreted by external agents with less effort.

You may be wondering why you should use conceptual modelling after all. Is it useful for cultural heritage? What benefits can you obtain by using it? In this chapter, we describe the major advantages of conceptual modelling in five areas:

- **Exploring** areas of the world that are not well understood.
- **Documenting** things or phenomena for later reference.

© Springer International Publishing AG 2018   17
C. Gonzalez-Perez, *Information Modelling for Archaeology and Anthropology*,
https://doi.org/10.1007/978-3-319-72652-6_3

- **Communicating** information to others.
- **Designing** tools and techniques for your work.
- **Interoperating** between data sets or information sources.

The following sections describe each of these in detail.

Exploration

Cultural heritage is a complex phenomenon, and we often struggle to understand it to its full extent. Whether you are an archaeologist digging up a site, a historian trying to explain some events, or an anthropologist putting together an interpretation, you are likely to be faced with vague ideas that resist pinning down and connections between things that are too complex to handle.

Conceptual modelling can help you explore a relevant fragment of the world by letting you state the ideas that are clearest in your mind with the most precision, while staying uncertain about others. You can even try various approaches to express the same ideas and see how well each one works, for example, by selecting different details to capture in the model. Very often, when you start modelling a tricky situation, you will notice that the modelling process helps you "organize your mind" and adds a lot of clarity to your thoughts. This is a consequence of using a modelling language, which, as we discussed in Chap. 2, is necessarily simple; it removes complexity from the subject of your cognition and makes reasoning about things much easier and more efficient.

Some examples of conceptual modelling being used to explore a research field can be found in [13–16].

Documentation

We often want to document things or phenomena because we need to come back to them later. Sometimes, it is because policies or standards at work expect us to do it. Sometimes, as usual in anthropology, it is because what we are documenting constitute ephemeral processes that will not leave much tangible trace by themselves if not properly described. And even sometimes, like very often in archaeology, you need to document something because you are destroying it by the very process of studying it, so the information that you record is the only thing that will survive.

Conceptual modelling helps you document anything in a precise, accurate and efficient way. Since any model needs a scope and a purpose (see Chap. 1), you will need to decide (and often write down clearly) what the purpose of your work is, and this will guide you to select which details of the modelled subject are going to be included in the model and which ones are going to be discarded. Since you will be a using a modelling language, its low ambiguity and high simplicity will help you state what you want to state in an extremely clear fashion, so that you will easily understand what you meant when you come back to your model months or years later, and others will understand what you mean when you are not there to explain. Also, the model will serve as a perfect source of information for further reasoning, computer processing or any other kind of elaboration.

Communication

We rarely work alone. More and more, we tend to work in teams, often composed of people from different disciplines and backgrounds, and collaborate with other teams in even more distant fields. We need to be able to discuss complex ideas not only with our colleagues but also with specialists in chemistry, mathematics, sociology, soil science or astronomy. In addition, some of us need to teach students at various levels about cultural heritage, providing a clear and affordable view of the key concepts and phenomena.

Conceptual modelling can help you bridge the gap between the different mindsets and working styles of the different disciplines, by establishing a *lingua franca* that everyone can understand. This does not mean that everyone must agree on the same ideas; it means that everyone will be able to speak the same language when discussing ideas, even if it is to defend different points of view. Using conceptual modelling to interact in a heterogeneous group is like using English to interact at an international gathering; you may or may not agree with other people's ideas, but you can understand them and make yourself understood, regardless of everyone's native tongue. This is especially valuable in multidisciplinary settings where you must understand and be understood by specialists in other areas, and also in educational settings, where conceptual models of cultural heritage (or a subset of it) can work as crucial resources when designing lesson plans.

Some examples of conceptual models being used for communication between professionals of different backgrounds can be found in [17, 18]. A good example of conceptual modelling being used in an educational setting can be found in [19].

Design

No matter how good our conceptualizations of cultural heritage are if the tools that we use to record and manage information are misaligned with them. For example, we often use forms that we fill up in the field to document things, and reports that we generate, manually or through a computer, to summarize relevant data. Methodological tools like these need to be in sync with our conceptualizations; by being in sync, we mean that the tools we use must be designed to record and report the details that we are interested in, avoid other details that we do not consider relevant, and express information at the appropriate level of abstraction. If our tools do not work well, the recorded or reported information will not be properly understood and will probably be incomplete or even contain errors.

Conceptual modelling can help you design tools that are optimally adapted to the way you work. For example, a conceptual model can work as a guide to develop a survey form, helping you decide which fields need to be included, what kinds of answers are possible for each one, and how they relate to each other. Similarly, a conceptual model would make a perfect foundation for the construction of a database, no matter how simple or how complex. Having a good model in place will help you determine what tables and columns you need, and how they must be interconnected.

An example of a cultural heritage conceptual model being used to guide the design of a software system can be found in [15].

Interoperability

We may be able to explore, document, communicate and design successfully but, at some point, unexpected needs will come up for the information that we have been gathering. It is impossible to think in advance of every possible situation that involves sharing our information, comparing it to the information from other sources, or integrating our information with that of others. Also, we tend to express ourselves in the manner that is best adapted to the task at hand when we work; for example, when we design a database to store and manage information, we usually design it so that it is specifically fit for the task at hand. This makes a lot of sense, but also makes it very unlikely that other teams, working elsewhere and unknown to us, express their information in a similar fashion and following similar information structures; in turn, this means that your data and theirs will most certainly be of a different shape and incompatible. And, still, it is possible that we will need to collaborate with them.

Conceptual modelling helps you by making sure that everyone can discuss your information in a meaningful way. Similarly, you will be able to understand and reason about information expressed by others, following conceptualizations that are unfamiliar to you. In this manner, you will be able to compare and relate your information to other sources much more easily. You will also be able to reconcile the conceptual discrepancies between different databases or other sources in a simpler way, and with a greater degree of certainty that what you are understanding from the data is what the authors actually intended to state.

A good example of a conceptual model that is often used for interoperability in cultural heritage is that of the CIDOC Conceptual Reference Model (CRM) [20], also known as ISO 21127 [21]. Some application examples of CIDOC CRM can be found in [22, 23]. Also in this regard, see [24] and Part IV.

Summary

Conceptual modelling can help us to **explore** areas that we do not understand well.
It can also help us **document** reality for later reference.
Conceptual modelling is also useful to **communicate** our ideas to others.
Also, conceptual models can work as guides to **design** tools or methodologies.
Finally, conceptual modelling can help us make our information **interoperate** with other sources.

Part II
The Basics of Conceptual Modelling

In this part, we introduce the basic concepts and language elements for conceptual modelling, using ConML (www.conml.org) as an infrastructure. Examples from everyday life and cultural heritage are used throughout. Objects, classes, attributes, enumerated types, associations and generalizations are described and explained.

Once you finish this part, you will be able to create and understand simple conceptual models of cultural heritage.

Chapter 4
Objects

Abstract In this chapter, we introduce the notion of *objects*, which are elements in a conceptual model which represent relevant entities in the world. We describe the key ideas of object identifier, which works as an arbitrary proper name, and object category, which classifies the object. Then, we move on to describe how the characteristics of an entity can be expressed in a model by using *values* within an object. Each value is expressed as a name plus contents, such as in *Age = 37*. If no contents exist for a particular value, the special word *null* must be used, such as in *Description = null*. After that, we explain how objects can be connected in a model by using *links*, in order to describe how entities are interrelated in the world. Each link is labelled with a name, such as *BelongsTo* or *IsLocatedIn*. We close the chapter by explaining that a collection of interrelated objects with their values and links constitute an *instance model*. Instance models can be used to represent sets of relevant entities, their characteristics and the connections between them.

In previous chapters, we said that conceptual models can represent both entities and categories. We start in this chapter by looking at how entities are represented, and Chap. 5 and the following will look at the representation of categories.

In Chap. 1, we said that entities, or particulars, as they are known in philosophy, are concrete things, usually situated in space and time. Also, we said in Chap. 2 that entities correspond to the chunks that we make out of reality. Since we have accepted that our perceived reality is not continuous but discrete and that portions of it can be delimited, each of these portions is an entity. Note that the concept of entity is extremely abstract; it encompasses *anything* that we can point to, literally or metaphorically; it also includes both real and imaginary things. The most evident kinds of entities are physical things such as books, buildings, hammers or trees. But immaterial things are entities too, including songs, laws or beliefs. People are entities too, and processes and events, such as wars, rituals or earthquakes, are also entities. Fictional things such as Excalibur or Atlantis are also entities. Actually, anything that we can think of is an entity.

© Springer International Publishing AG 2018
C. Gonzalez-Perez, *Information Modelling for Archaeology and Anthropology*,
https://doi.org/10.1007/978-3-319-72652-6_4

Technical

Since everything is an entity, you may argue that categories are entities too. And, according to many authors, you would be right. Although in previous chapters we have defined entities and categories as two separate kinds of things, categories can in fact be considered to be a specific type of entity, albeit immaterial and abstract. This may make them *abstract objects* in the philosophical sense, which would mean that they cannot cause effects in the world.

Still, and for practical purposes, we will keep discussing entities and categories as separate and somehow opposed kinds of things.

Objects

In order to represent an entity in a conceptual model, we use an *object*. An object is a formal construct that stands for an entity. The word "object" is very common in its dictionary sense, and different fields of knowledge assign different nuances to its meaning. For example, an archaeological object is something very specific in the mind of most archaeologists. But the objects we are talking about here are different. In conceptual modelling, an object is a special kind of concept having two properties: first, it is formal; that is, it is defined according to the strict rules of conceptual modelling; second, it represents an entity in a non-ambiguous way.

Technical

Objects are what give name to the *object-oriented paradigm*, a popular approach to conceptual modelling and computer programming. Object-orientation is a particular way to conceive information systems in terms of objects and their features. A classic text on object-oriented modelling is [25]. Other approaches are possible for conceptual modelling, although not as common.

We define an object as follows:

Definition

*An **object** is the formalization of an entity that is relevant to the model.*

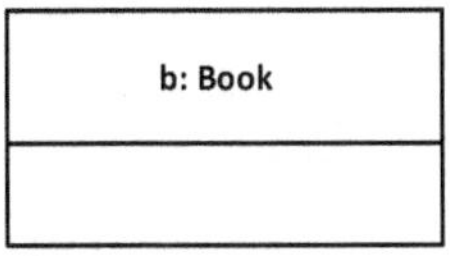

Fig. 4.1 Diagrammatic
representation of an object
named *b* of category *Book*

b: Book

Let us imagine that we want to represent this book as an object in a model. We can draw the object like in Fig. 4.1. Here, the rectangle (or "box", as we usually call it) stands for an object. The upper section of the rectangle contains a line of text of the following form:

identifier: Category

As a convention, identifiers are written in lower case and categories with an initial capital. To separate both, we use a colon. In our example in Fig. 4.1, the object depicted has *b* as identifier, and *Book* as category. The *identifier* of an object works as a proper name, or unique label, that we give an object in order to distinguish it from any other in the model. In our example, we have chosen to label our object *b*, but we could have called it *xyz*, *ab123*, or anything else that works for us, as long as it is different from any other object identifier in the model.

You may recall from Chap. 2 that conceptual models allow us to express, among other things, existence, identity and classification. Existence is expressed by the mere fact of having included an object in our model. In the context of conceptual modelling, existence must be understood in a very ample sense; for example, imaginary entities such as Atlantis or the sword Excalibur do exist, and we can definitely represent them in a model.

Technical

Contemporary philosophers disagree on whether existence is a property of things like their colour or weight. Some like Russell believe it is not, whereas others like Meinong claim it is, and there are existing as well as non-existing entities. A summary of current positions on existence can be found in [3 "Existence"].

In any case, existence in conceptual modelling is rather informal. We say that something exists if we can discuss it and we find it relevant to our models.

Identity, in turn, is expressed, precisely, by the object's identifier; we could add a second object to the model, like in Fig. 4.2, giving it a different identifier to signal that it represents a different entity in the world. In Fig. 4.2, each object depicted has a different identifier. This means that each object represents a different entity in the world. If two boxes were labelled with the same identifier, we should assume that

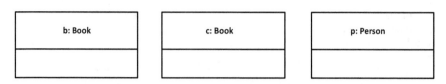

Fig. 4.2 Diagrammatic representation of three objects. Each object has a different identifier

both of them refer to the same entity in the world. In the example, our model represents three entities named *b*, *c* and *p*.

Also, bear in mind that object identifiers are *arbitrary*; that is, they do not convey any meaning about the underlying entity. In terms of philosophy of language, they designate without describing. We are not supposed to infer any information from an object's identifier, no matter how informative it may look to us. If we want to convey an actual description of the entity, we must use values, as explained in the next section.

Technical
Object identifiers are what philosophers of language would call *rigid designators*; they are able to "pick out" one object without providing any descriptive information about it. A comprehensive view on rigid designators can be found in [3 "Rigid Designators"].

The *category* of an object, finally, is what we use to express classification. When we say in Fig. 4.2 that object *b* has *Book* as category, we are saying that *b* is a book. Similarly, *c* is a book too, and *p* is a person. We can name categories as we please, using a conceptualization that makes sense to us and helps with the purpose of the model.

Both identifier and category are crucial pieces of data about an object; they declare how we refer to it, and how we have classified it. However, both are properties that we assign to the object as a concept in our mind, rather than being properties of the represented entity. In other words, entities in the world do not have identifiers or categories; it is us, during the conceptualization and formalization processes, who assign these to the entities.

We must make a very important note here. Note that the boxes shown in Figs. 4.1 and 4.2 are not objects, but graphical representations of objects. As we said in previous chapters, conceptual models reside in our minds, since they are made of concepts. Objects are a particular kind of concepts, and therefore, they are intangible and not perceivable outside our own mind. In order to remember or communicate objects, we can draw diagrams like those in the figures. We can informally talk about "the object *b* in the figure" as a short cut for "the object in my mind represented by the box labelled *b* in the figure" as long as we remember that the diagrams are not conceptual models, but just a visual representation of them.

Values

Objects like those in Fig. 4.2 say very little about the entities that they represent. In fact, they say nothing, since the only information that they carry is the identifier and the category, both of which pertain to the objects themselves rather than the represented entities. In order to actually capture properties of the represented entity, we need to use *values*. We define a value as follows.

> **Definition**
> *A **value** is the formalization of an atomic characteristic of an entity that is relevant to the model.*

By "atomic characteristic" we mean a simple property of the entity, such as its name, colour or weight. How simple something must be in order to be modelled as a value is a matter of judgment. As a rule of thumb, a property that can be given as a single number or piece of data should be approachable as a value. However, there is no hard rule on this. For example, we can express the colour of something as a simple piece of data, such as in "sky blue" or #3399FF in RGB notation. But we could also express the same colour as separate pieces of data for the red, green and blue channels; if we wished to do so, each of the colour channels would be modelled as a separate value. Similarly, a long description of something may constitute a value too, despite the fact that it may contain multiple sentences.

We can use values to represent the properties of an entity. Figure 4.3 shows our example from Fig. 4.2 with some values added. In Fig. 4.3, each value is depicted as a line of text inside the lower section of the object boxes. For example, object *b* (a book) has values *Title = "Cathedral"* and *Year = 1983*. Values take the following form:

$$Name = Contents$$

The value *name* is a word or phrase that tells us what the value is about. By convention, it is written with an initial capital and, if composed of multiple words, no spaces are left between them and initial capitals are used for all, like *GivenName*.

Fig. 4.3 Values have been added to the objects from Fig. 4.2. Each value is displayed as a line of text inside the corresponding object box

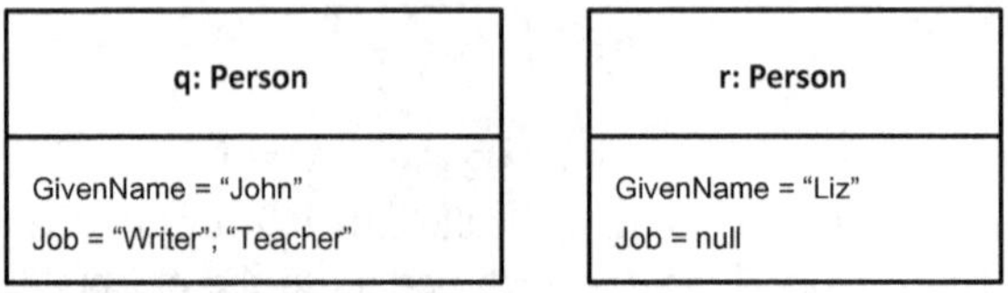

Fig. 4.4 Two person objects
showing different options for
the *Job* value. Person *q* has
two jobs, whereas person
r has none

q: Person
GivenName = "John"
Job = "Writer"; "Teacher"

r: Person
GivenName = "Liz"
Job = null

In the example, we have captured the title and year of each of the books, and the family name, given name and nationality of the person. After the value name, and separated by an equal sign, we write the value *contents*. The contents express the data corresponding to the value. For example, the book *b* in our example has the text "Cathedral" as title, and 1983 as year. As a convention, texts are written in double quotes, but numbers are not.

In Chap. 2, we said that conceptual models allow us to express predication among other things. Precisely, values constitute the mechanism by which we can predicate properties on entities. In our example, we are stating that book *b* has "Cathedral" as title and 1983 as year, by placing these values inside its box. In this manner, we can describe the entities represented by the objects in as much detail as we want, depending on the purpose of the model.

Sometimes, the entities that we are modelling are such that multiple values exist with the same name. For example, we can have a house made of multiple materials, or a person with multiple phone numbers. Also, sometimes entities lack a value altogether. Figure 4.4 shows examples of both situations. In Fig. 4.4, person *q* shows two quoted texts as contents for *Job*, separated by a semicolon: "Writer" and "Teacher" . This means that person *q* is both a writer and a teacher. Each of the two quoted texts actually constitutes a separate value, but we do not write them in two lines repeating the value name; rather, we string them together as shown in Fig. 4.4 for greater simplicity.

Object *r* in Fig. 4.4 shows a different situation; here, the word *null* appears in place of the value contents for *Job*. The word *null* is a special word, and it means that no contents exist for a value. That is to say, person *r* in our example has no job. You can use *null* anytime that you wish to express the fact that an entity lacks a property where one would be expected. You may argue that a simple way to capture this fact would be to omit the *Job* line altogether from the diagram. However, we did include it for person *q*, so we should also include it for other person objects for the sake of consistency.

Technical
The consistency rule that makes us include a *Job* line even if there is no job for some person objects is given by the fact that we must describe every object of the same category through the same list of values. That is, it is impossible to represent a person having values for *GivenName* and *Job*, and another person having values for *GivenName* and *Age*, for example.

> Whatever values we decide to express, we must stick to them for all objects of the same category. We explain why at the end of Chap. 6.

Note that *null* indicates that *no fact exists* about the corresponding value. For example, *Job* = *null* means that there is no job for this person. It does not mean that we do not know what the job is but that there is no job at all. If we knew that the person has a job but and we did not know about it, then there would be a fact, and we would ignore it. These are very different situations; we describe how to deal with unknowns in Chap. 14.

Finally, remember that we said in Chap. 1 that a model always has a purpose and that this purpose works as a guide to decide what details we should keep in the model, and which we should discard. The details to which we refer in saying so are, among other things, the values that we include in our objects. Depending on our purpose, we may decide to capture the given name, family name and job of persons if we were constructing a model to assist us with project-management, for example. But if we were designing a model for the management of a library, we would probably discard the job value and keep instead the nationality or birth date. Ultimately, you document what you want; a clear purpose will guide you to consistent and useful models.

Links

So far, we have learnt how to represent entities in a model by using objects, and how to describe their characteristics by using values. But this is not enough. Entities do not exist in isolation, but are connected to each other in a multitude of ways. In order to represent the connections that exist between entities, we use *links*. We define a link as follows:

> **Definition**
> A **link** is the formalization of a connection between two entities that is relevant to the model.

We may want to connect entities for many different purposes. For example, we may want to show in our model that a person is reading a book, that a person has written a book or that a book is stored in a particular library. In any case, a link always connects two entities, so in order to capture a link in our model, we need to capture the two involved entities first. Figure 4.5 shows our example from earlier sections with some added links.

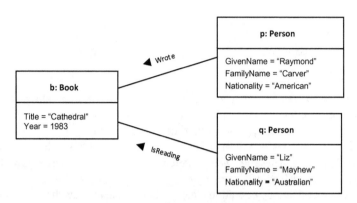

Fig. 4.5 Model of two persons connected to the same book; person *p* wrote the book, and person *q* is reading it now

In Fig. 4.5, each link is shown as a line that connects the corresponding object boxes. For example, there is a line connecting person *p* and book *b* to indicate that these two entities are related. Furthermore, the line is labelled *Wrote*, and a small black arrowhead points in the intended reading direction, to indicate that it is Raymond Carver who wrote *Cathedral*, rather than *Cathedral* who wrote Raymond Carver (which would be nonsense). Similarly, there is a line between person *q* and the book to indicate that Liz is reading the book now. The text on each line is called the link *name*. You can write anything as a link name as long as it fits the model purpose. Like with value names, link names are written without space between words and with initial capitals for each word.

Instance Models

An *instance model* is a collection of related objects, values and links. An instance model, therefore, represents a set of relevant entities, their characteristics and the connections between them. We can use instance models, for example, to represent, describe and document specific material or immaterial entities, agents, events or ideas.

Instance models are abstract constructs in our minds, as any other kind of conceptual model. In order to visualize and communicate them, we often depict instance models as object diagrams, such as those shown in the figures in this chapter. However, instance models can grow potentially very large, with object counts in the range of thousands or even millions. For this reason, and for practical purposes, we rarely draw instance models in the form of diagrams if they are too big. For very large instance models, a database or other software-based tool does a better job than diagrams on paper or screen. Still, bear in mind that an instance model stored in a database is still an instance model, so everything you have read in this chapter still applies. Chapter 34 introduces the construction of databases and related tools.

Summary

Objects model elements that represent relevant entities.

Every object has an **identifier**, which works as an arbitrary proper name, plus a **category**, which classifies the object.

The characteristics of the entity can be captured in the model by using **values**.

Each value is expressed as a **name** plus **contents**. The contents consist of one or more pieces of data.

If no contents exist for a particular value, the special word *null* must be used.

The connections between entities can be captured in the model by using **links**.

Each link is labelled with a **name**.

Instance models can be used to represent sets of relevant entities, their characteristics and the connections between them.

Exercises

1. Find a picture of the painting *Automat* by Edward Hopper on the Web. Imagine you want to describe the painting to someone who does not know about it. Draw a diagram showing three objects that represent entities in the painting. Do not forget to give the objects meaningful identifiers and categories.
2. Complete the objects from Exercise 1 by adding some values to them. Focus on values related to the appearance of the entities in the painting. You can make up some characteristics if you want. Remember that objects of the same category must be described having the same list of value names.
3. Further complete the previous model by adding links between the objects. You may add as many links as needed. Focus on the physical and spatial relationships between entities in the painting.

Chapter 5
Classes

Abstract In this chapter, we move the focus from individuals to categories. Here, we introduce the notion of *classes*, which are model elements that represent relevant categories of things. We explain that classes have a name, which differentiates the class from others, such as *Building* or *Person*, as well as a definition, usually in the form of "genus plus differentia". In relation to class definitions, we introduce the two complementary mechanisms to characterize classes: invariants, corresponding to the criteria that every member of the category must fulfil, plus variables, corresponding to the aspects that pertain to every member of the category, but which may take different quantities or qualities. Then, we describe how class variables can be formalized in a model as *properties* within a class. We explain that every property has a name that distinguishes it from others of the same class, such as *Age* or *Description*, as well as a cardinality, which establishes how many things may exist for the property for each individual entity. We finish the chapter by establishing a connection between classes and objects (introduced in the previous chapter): classes are the types of objects, and objects are instances of classes.

The previous chapter looked at how entities are represented in a conceptual model. In this chapter, we will introduce how categories are captured. Subsequent chapters will explore category modelling in further detail.

You may wonder why it is so important to represent categories in our models, and why we can't simply represent entities, since entities constitute the most direct and simple piece of evidence that we can have about the world. This is true, but it is also true that categorization, at least in part, is an innate mechanism in our minds, as described by Harnad [26] or Lakoff [10]. This means that we organize the world and are able to reason about things through inductive generalization. For example, once we have interacted with a few dogs as children, we know what to expect from the next dog we come across: if all the dogs we have found are friendly and nice, we will assume that any other entity that resembles a dog will also be friendly and nice. We can do this because we categorize some entities in the word as dogs, and by doing so we assign common properties to them. This does not always work, of

© Springer International Publishing AG 2018

C. Gonzalez-Perez, *Information Modelling for Archaeology and Anthropology*,
https://doi.org/10.1007/978-3-319-72652-6_5

course, and we continuously revise our category systems as we gather more knowledge about the world.

By representing categories in our models, we can express what the world is like in terms of general concepts instead of specific examples. For example, by using categories in a model we can say that, in general, dogs are four-legged furry friendly animals, without the need to describe any particular dog.

Classes

In order to represent a category in a conceptual model, we use a *class*. A class is a formal construct that stands for a category. Like in the case of objects, the word "class" is very wide in its dictionary sense, and different people may understand different things by "class". The classes we are discussing here have no other special connotation than being formal, that is, defined according to the strict rules of conceptual modelling, and representing a category in a non-ambiguous way.

We define a class as follows:

> **Definition**
> A **class** is the formalization of a category that is relevant to the model.

Let us imagine that we want to represent the concept of books in our model. We are not referring to a particular book, but to the overall category of books, or *bookness*, if you wish. We can draw this class like in Fig. 5.1. Here, the box stands for a class. The upper section of the box contains a line of text with the class name. This notation is very similar to that for objects; however, we can tell apart a class from an object because objects carry a two-part text in the top section, composed of the identifier plus the category, whereas classes carry a simple text expressing the class' name. The *name* of a class works as a unique label that allows us to find and identify the class within a model; for this reason, we cannot have two classes in a model with the same name. As a convention, class names are written without spaces (if they consist of more than one word) and with initial capitals.

Class names must be chosen carefully. A class name should always be a countable noun in singular form. It must be a noun because it designates a category, and nouns are the kinds of words that we use to designate things. It must be

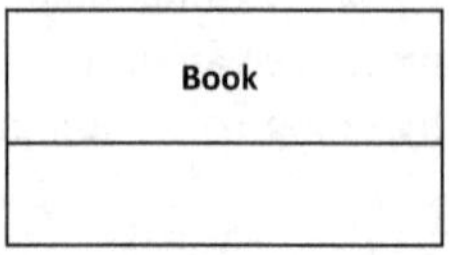

Fig. 5.1 Diagrammatic representation of a class named *Book*

countable because the existence of a category, by definition, implies that there are things that belong to that category, and therefore each of these things would be named with that word, and a collection of these things, with the plural form of the word. For example, the *Book* class is called "Book" because there are books in the world, we can refer to each book through expressions like "a book" or "that book over there", and we can refer to collections of books with expressions such as "a few books" or "all the books in the library". Finally, it is conventional to write class names in singular.

As a rule of thumb, a class name is good if you can plug it into the following sentence:

This is a ___, and these are a few ___s.

Words such as "Book", "Building" or "Song" are good class names, whereas words such as "Time", "Soil" or "Heritage" are bad class names. You may argue that we can use these words in plural as, for example, in "different soils were found", but uses like this are quite metaphorical, really meaning "different types of soil were found".

Also, class names convey the conceptualization of the world that we make. For example, we can use "Person" as a class name, but we could use "Individual" as well. Whether we choose one over the other is a matter of accuracy, familiarity and personal preference. As opposed to object identifiers, which are arbitrary labels, class names are meant to be interpreted by people looking at our model and thus carry powerful semantics. Do not choose your class names lightly.

Finally, and like we did in the case of objects, we must make the point here that the boxes in diagrams such as Fig. 5.1 are not classes, but pictures of classes. The classes, like the objects, are purely conceptual and reside in your mind. We informally talk about "the *Book* class in the figure", but we must understand that the *Book* class is actually in your mind, and the figure only shows a convenient graphical representation of it.

Definition

A class name, if well chosen, conveys a lot about the class it designates. However, a class cannot be fully characterized through its name alone; a definition is needed. The *definition* of a class is a full sentence specifying the membership criteria of the underlying category. For example, take the *Book* class. What criteria should we use to determine whether something is a book or not? This question should be answered by the class definition.

A class definition is usually constructed through an approach called *genus plus differentia*. According to this approach, a definition has two parts:

- The **genus**, i.e. a part that states of what kind this category is. "Genus" is Latin for "kind" or "type". For example, we could say that "a book is a document". In this example, "document" is the genus of "book".
- The **differentia**, i.e. a part that states how the category differs from other categories of the same genus. "Differentia" is Latin for "difference". For example, we could say that books are documents "composed of a collection of leaves fastened together at one side"; this would be the differentia, distinguishing books from other kinds of documents such as letters or leaflets.

In general, we can think of a class definition as a sentence with the following form:

A Class *is a* Genus *that* Differentia

where *Class* stands for the class being defined, *Genus* for its genus and *Differentia* for its differentia. For example,

A book is a document that is composed of a collection of leaves fastened together at one side.

Or, possibly,

An archaeological site is a spatial region having an abnormally high density of primary entities that are considered to be relevant.

In the previous definition, the *ArchaeologicalSite* class is defined as being of the "spatial region" genus and "having an abnormally high density of primary entities that are considered to be relevant" being its difference. As mentioned above, the difference lets us distinguish between archaeological sites and other spatial regions that are not sites, such as administrative regions or natural places. It does not matter if you agree or not with our definition of archaeological site; we are only trying to illustrate how class definitions work.

The genus plus differentia approach is not the only one you can use to define categories. For example, you can use an approach based on similarity and contrast, according to which you define a category as being similar to another, but having some divergence from it. For example:

A bicycle is like a motorbike, but has no engine and uses pedals and a chain to propel itself.

This approach works by using sentences with the following form:

A Class *is like a* SimilarClass *but* Contrast

Although this approach can produce some practical definitions, it is much more limited than the previous one, so we do not recommend it for general use.

When you create a conceptual model containing classes, you should write down their definitions for future reference. Definitions can be a bit long, so they are not included in the diagrams that we draw. You should use a separate document to keep a list of class names and their definitions.

Invariants and Variables

Class definitions are useful not only to determine what things belong to the category being represented. They also work to provide a foundation for *class structure*. This means that definitions are an excellent starting point to explore a deeper characterization of classes, especially in two aspects:

- The class **invariants**, i.e. those characteristics of a category that never vary regardless of which category member we look at.
- The class **variables**, i.e. those characteristics of a category that are always present, but may take different qualities depending on which category member we look at.

Consider the previous definition of *Book*:

A book is a document that is composed of a collection of leaves fastened together at one side.

According to this, we can expect every book:

- to be a document and
- to be composed of a collection of leaves fastened at one side.

These are the *invariants* of the *Book* class. If you read them carefully, you will see that they make up a condensed and "essential" form of the class definition, since they capture the criteria that anything needs to satisfy in order to be a member of the underlying category. For this reason, we can say that class invariants comprise the *canonical definition* of a class, that is a definition from which nothing can be removed without significantly changing its meaning. When we said above that class definitions are not shown in diagrams but are often recorded as text in a separate document, we were referring to these canonical definitions.

In addition to invariants, the class definition also alludes to some characteristics that are not fully specified. In our example:

- Each book will have leaves, but how many is not said.
- The pages of each book will be fastened at one side, but the particular side of the fastening is left unsaid.

These are the *variables* of the *Book* class. They correspond to aspects of variability of the category; we know that every book has pages, but the definition allows for a varying quantity. Similarly, we know that every book is fastened at one side, but which side may also vary.

Class variables can often be inferred from the definition, like we did in our example. There may be other variables "hidden" in the definition, and we are free to be creative with regard to which ones to elicit depending on our modelling purpose.

For example, if we were constructing a model to describe a second-hand book seller's business, we may want to consider one more variable:

- The pages of each book will be fastened at one side, but the particular kind of fastening (glued, spiral, stitched, etc.) is unsaid.

In any case, class variables constitute the starting point for the modelling of *properties*.

Properties

We said above that class invariants, taken as a canonical definition of the class, are not shown in diagrams but separately documented. Variables, on the other hand, are shown in diagrams in the form of properties. A property is a formal construct that stands for a characteristic of a category. Like in previous occasions, the word "property" can be interpreted in quite a number of ways; the meaning that we use here has no other special connotation than being formal, that is, defined according to the strict rules of conceptual modelling, and representing a characteristic of a category in a non-ambiguous way.

We define a property as follows:

> **Definition**
> A **property** is the abstract formalization of a characteristic of a category that is relevant to the model.

Let us retake the previous example of the *Book* class, and let us assume that we want to represent some relevant characteristics of books in our model. What characteristics are relevant and which are not, again, is given by the model's purpose. If we imagine that the purpose is the cataloguing of books in a library, we could draw the *Book* class as shown in Fig. 5.2. Here, we can see the same *Book* class as in Fig. 5.1, but this time we have added some properties. Each property is depicted as a line of text inside the lower section of the class box. For example, the *Book* class has properties such as *Title: ?* and *Author: ?*. Properties take the following form:

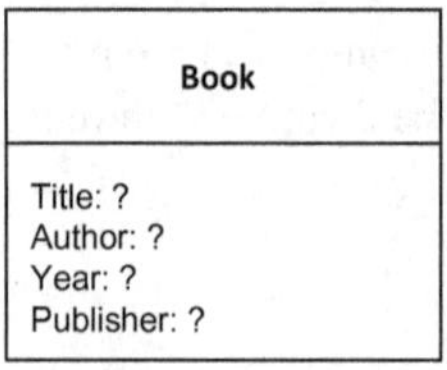

Fig. 5.2 Diagrammatic representation of the *Book* class containing properties *Title, Author, Year* and *Publisher*

Book
Title: ? Author: ? Year: ? Publisher: ?

Name: ?

The property *name* is a word or phrase that tells us what characteristic the property is representing. By convention, it is written with an initial capital and, if composed of multiple words, no spaces are left between them and initial capitals are used for all, like in previous occasions. In the example, we have captured the fact that the title, author, year and publisher are relevant characteristics in our model. Please bear in mind that we are representing the category of books rather than any particular book, so this statement merely means that, in general, books have these four characteristics, and we are interested in them.

After the property name, and separated by a colon, we write a question mark. This means that we have not decided yet how to fully express the property. For example, Fig. 5.2 shows the fact that we are interested in documenting the author of books, but we have not decided yet whether we will just record author names, or perhaps names and nationalities, or even perhaps a full author record with lots of personal details for each one. In this regard, and as stated in the definition, properties are abstract features; that is, they provide only some details and defer some decisions to a later moment (which we will discuss in Chap. 6).

Finally, we must notice that a property always belongs to a particular class. In Fig. 5.2, properties *Title* or *Author* belong to the *Book* class, and in consequence, they are shown inside the corresponding box. It does not make sense to talk about a property without putting it in the context of its owner class, since a property represents a characteristic of some given category. In order to provide this context, we often write the property name prefixed by the class name and using a dot as separator when we quote the property in text, for example *Book.Title* or *Book. Author*. A class cannot have two properties with the same name; however, a property in a different class may have the same name as a property in this class, and perhaps mean something very different. For example, *Book.Title* and *Person.Title* mean very different things.

Cardinality

Properties are useful to describe what characteristics we are interested in for a class. So far, we have seen that properties refer to the represented characteristic by their name, such as *Book.Title* or *Book.Author*. However, properties can (and should) be described with more detail. A crucial aspect that we can add to properties is that of their *cardinality*. The cardinality of a property describes how many things can exist for this property for each individual entity. For example, the cardinality of *Book. Title* specifies how many titles there may be for any given book. Similarly, the cardinality of *Book.Author* specifies how many authors a book may have.

Sometimes, expressing how many things may exist for a given property is very easy; in our example, we could probably agree that only one title may exist for any given book, although you may argue that some books could have multiple titles, and even that some books have no title at all. This logic can be useful in some scenarios, but since the purpose of our sample model is to catalogue books in a library, we can safely assume that every book will have one and only one title. Hence, the cardinality of *Book.Title* is one. Regarding authors, we can probably agree that every book will have at least one author, and some books will have multiple authors. You may argue here that some books are anonymous and therefore no author is known. However, the fact that we do not know who the author is does not mean that the book lacks an author, as we said in Chap. 4 when discussing values. Ontologically, a book always has an author, since a book is an intentional product that someone must have written. However, we cannot easily set an upper limit for how many authors a book may have. In situations like this, we use a range to express that books have a minimum of one author and a maximum of many authors. This is expressed as follows:

$$1..*$$

The previous expression is read as "from one to many". The number 1 corresponds to the minimum cardinality, and the asterisk, meaning "many" or "multiple", corresponds to the maximum cardinality. Minimum and maximum cardinalities are separated by two consecutive dots.

Using this rule, we can easily add cardinalities to the previous example, like in Fig. 5.3. Here, we can see the same *Book* class as in Fig. 5.2, but this time we have added cardinalities. Notice that cardinalities are written right before the question mark for each property. In this manner, each property line takes the following form:

$$Name: Cardinality\ ?$$

Note also that cardinalities may be expressed as a single value when a specific number of things can be established for a property, or as a range when not. For example, we agreed that there can be one title only for any given book, and therefore, *Book.Title* has a cardinality of 1. Similarly, *Book.Year* has cardinality 1 too, since any book has been published in a particular year, whatever it is. The cardinality of *Book.Author*, on the other hand, is 1..*, because there must be at least one author, and potentially many. Finally, the cardinality of *Book.Publisher* is interesting; note that a range of 0..1 is used for this property in Fig. 5.3. This means that zero publishers can exist for a book, or 1 publisher as a maximum. In other

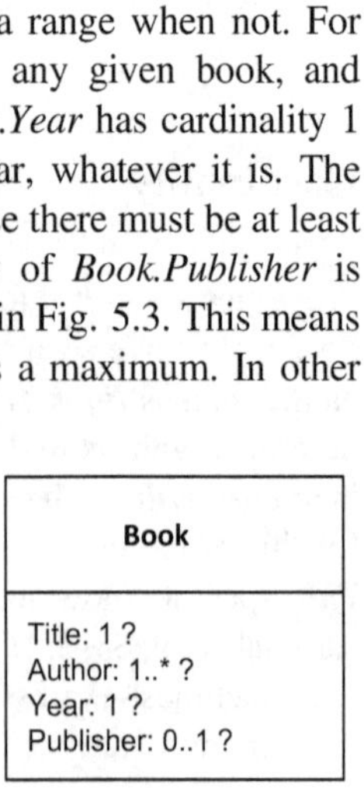

Fig. 5.3 Diagrammatic representation of the *Book* class containing properties *Title, Author, Year* and *Publisher*. Cardinalities are shown

Book
Title: 1 ? Author: 1..* ? Year: 1 ? Publisher: 0..1 ?

words, we are stating that each book will necessarily have either no publisher or one publisher at most.

Properties like *Book.Publisher*, which have a minimum cardinality of zero, and no matter what their maximum cardinality is, are called *nullable properties*, because they leave the door open to null values as we described in Chap. 4 when discussing values. In other words, a nullable property allows situations where there is no fact to be represented at all.

Limitations of Classes

Classes constitute a powerful mechanism through which we can represent the categories that are relevant to us, and in this manner describe the world in terms of categories instead of individual entities. We will see over most of the sections in this book that classes, in fact, comprise the core notion for conceptual modelling.

However, classes also have some limitations. To start with, a class represents a category, but one that can be named through a noun. As we said at the beginning of this chapter, a class must always be named with a countable noun in singular form. This allows us to model classes representing all sorts of things, but representing categories related to, for example, actions, becomes much more difficult. For example, we can easily conceptualize actions such as walking or running. But we should not have a *Walking* class or a *Running* class in our model, because these words are not countable nouns. Please remember the rationale behind this rule: a countable noun is needed because, since a class represents a category, we are expected to be able to name the members of that category by using the same noun. Thus, a *Book* class allows us to point to individual *books*. But a *Running* class does not work because we cannot point to individual "runnings".

Representing actions or other things that are usually linguistically expressed through verbs is possible in an indirect manner. For example, we could have a *RunningSession* or *RunningActivity* class in our model, if this fits its purpose. Still, you should assume that conceptual modelling, at least the conceptual modelling variant that is described in this book, is eminently geared towards representing noun-things rather than verb-things.

A second limitation of classes relates to the fact that classes usually cannot represent concepts that we refer to through mass nouns. A mass noun, or uncountable noun, is one that refers to things without differentiated units. Examples are "water" or "time". We can say things like "water is scarce", but we cannot refer to "one water" or "those waters", as we do with nouns such as "chair" or "song". For this reason, we should not have classes such as *Water* or *Time* in a model. Again, this is due to the fact that categories represented by classes are supposed to have instances, and mass categories such as 'water' or 'time' do not possess instances.

You may argue that nouns such as "water" or "time" can indeed be used as countable nouns, like in "there was a time…" or "this water is better than that one".

However, these uses correspond to different meanings of the words. In "there was a time", we are using "time" to mean "moment" or "period" rather than 'the continuous flow of existence'; similarly, in "this water is better than that one", we are using "water" to mean "water type" or "amount of water" rather than 'the substance with chemical formula H_2O'. We may have a model with a *Moment* or *Period* class, or a *WaterType* or *WaterAmount* class, but not *Time* or *Water*. Be aware of overloaded semantics, and always try to use the most precise terminology that you can find.

Finally, classes can represent only *classical categories*. A classical category is one that is defined by a set of criteria; the things that fulfil the criteria are considered to be members of the category, whereas things that do not are left out. Following this, the invariants of a class specify the class' definitional criteria. This is very convenient and works very well in most occasions. However, not all the categories that we use in our daily lives are classical. For example, Lakoff [10] describes *radial categories*, which cannot defined by a set of shared criteria but constructed through similarities between their members. An example used by Lakoff is that of 'mother'. We use the word "mother" to refer to biological mothers, foster mothers, adoptive mothers, stepmothers, surrogate mothers, etc. All these fall into the category of 'mother', but there is no single set of criteria that is common to all of them. Lakoff argues that the 'mother' category started with the basic concept of mother, probably a biological mother, and was later and gradually extended through the incorporation of related concepts such as foster mother or stepmother, each one being closely related to the previous, but with no overall shared criteria. Since a class needs a definition based on common criteria (its invariants), classes cannot successfully represent radial categories.

We can still have a *Mother* class in our model if needed. However, we must be aware that this class does not stand for the complex and encompassing radial category of 'mother' as Lakoff describes it, but to a more reduced conceptualization which, perhaps, includes only biological mothers or some other kinds of mothers. Class names and definitions must be chosen always carefully, and more especially so when radial categories are involved, in order to avoid ambiguity.

Technical

A definition that specifies a category through a set of shared criteria is called an *intensional definition* (not "intentional" but "intensional"). This is opposed to an *extensional definition*, which specifies a category by enumerating each of its members. Some authors, such as Partridge [7], highlight the importance of extensional definitions in conceptual modelling and point out that classes must be extensionally defined. This can be philosophically elegant and would definitely allow us to represent radial categories in conceptual models, but entails significant problems when trying to define classes in a brief and convenient manner. For the sake of feasibility, most conceptual modelling approaches, including the one in this book, use intensional definitions of categories.

Also, an extensional definition of a category alludes to what philosophers of language, and especially Frege [3, "Gottlob Frege"], would call the *reference* of the category name, that is the actual entities in the world pointed at by the name. Contrarily, an intensional definition, being based on the characterization of the member entities through criteria, which are dependent on the model's purpose, alludes to the *sense* of the category name in Fregean terms. See [27, Chap. 1] for a good introduction to these concepts and the differences that they entail.

Objects as Instances of Classes

In Chap. 4, we described objects as formal representations of relevant entities in the world. We also said that an object is always characterized through an identifier plus a category. Now that we have learnt about classes, we can add some information about the connection between classes and objects. In fact, classes and objects are closely related in multiple ways. To start with, *an object's category is a class*. In other words, the category that we assign to an object, and which we display in a diagram as a short text after the object's identifier, actually refers to a class name. See Fig. 5.4 for an example. In Fig. 5.4, object p is connected to the *Person* class in two ways. First, the class name "Person" appears as part of the object's characterization in the top section of the box. Secondly, there is a line connecting the object box to the class box. Note that this line bears an open arrowhead that points from the object to the class. This arrow represents an *instantiation* relationship, which stands for the fact that object p is an instance of the *Person* class. "Instance" means "particular case" or "example"; in fact, an object's category is the particular piece of information that, as we said in Chap. 4, implements the classification mechanism.

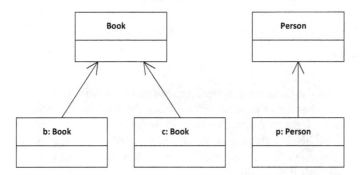

Fig. 5.4 Objects and their classes. Objects b and c are instances of class *Book*; object p is an instance of class *Person*. The arrows are read as "is an instance of"

The inverse of "instance" is "type". That is, we can say that the type of object *p* in Fig. 5.4 is *Person*. This is the same as saying that object *p* is an instance of *Person*, but expressed the other way around.

There are two rules about instantiation that are very important. First, every object has one, and exactly one, class as its type. This means that an object cannot lack a type class or have multiple type classes. If we want to describe something that looks like two or more things at once, we cannot do it by saying that this thing is an instance of two or more classes; rather, we would need to create a class in the model that captures this special hybrid situation. For example, a calculator-watch cannot be modelled by an object that is an instance of both *Calculator* and *Watch*. Rather, it should be modelled as an instance of a *CalculatorWatch* class.

Second, the type class of an object cannot vary over time. Once an object is created as an instance of a particular type class, this relationship is forever. Classes are supposed to capture essential categories in the world, and objects are supposed to describe entities in terms of their essential characteristics, rather than accessory or accidental ones. For these reasons, moving an object from one type to another is rarely needed if the model is good. If you find the need or the potentiality, revise your classes and your overall conceptualization of the model scope.

Finally, and as shown in Fig. 5.4, objects *b* and *c* are both instances of the *Book* class, so each of them shows its own instantiation arrow. Notice that the instantiation arrow and the class name inside the object box are redundant. That is, they both express the same thing. For this reason, they must be in sync; it would be an error to draw a diagram having an object *b*, for example displaying the class name "Book" inside its box, but at the same time connected to the *Person* class by an instantiation arrow. You need to be consistent. In practice, you will rarely see diagrams where objects and classes are shown together, unless for educational purposes or to emphasize the fact that objects are instances of classes. Most usually, classes are depicted in class diagrams, and objects in object diagrams. When we do so, the redundancy disappears and the only mechanism that we can (and must) use to describe an object's type is to use the class name as part of the object's characterization in the top section of the object box.

You may be wondering about values and links, and whether they are related to classes. They are, and we will go into the details over the next few chapters.

Summary

Classes are model elements that represent relevant categories of things.

Every class has a **name**, which differentiates the class from others.

Class names must be countable nouns in singular.

A class also needs a **definition**, usually in the form of genus plus differentia.

A class definition can be simplified by removing non-essential parts, thus giving the class' **canonical definition**.

A canonical definition is composed of the class' **invariants**, that is the criteria that every member of the category must fulfil.

A class also may have **variables**, that is aspects that pertain to every member of the category but which may take different quantities or qualities.

Variables can be formalized in a model as **properties**.

A property belongs to a class.

Every property has a **name** that distinguishes it from others of the same class.

Also, every property has a **cardinality**, which describes how many things may exist for the property for each individual entity.

Classes are the **types** of objects; objects are **instances** of classes.

Exercises

4. Imagine that you want to study how buildings are organized to make up towns. Draw a diagram showing two or three classes that describe this situation. Give the classes good names, and define them. Add some properties to the classes to represent the relevant characteristics.

Chapter 6
Attributes

Abstract In this chapter, we explain that properties (from the previous chapter) corresponding to atomic and simple characteristics can be developed in a model in the form of *attributes* within a class. We explain that every attribute has a name that distinguishes it from others of the same class, as well as a cardinality, which describes how many things may exist for the attribute for each individual entity. We also introduce the fact that every attribute has a type, which describes what kind of quantities or qualities may be used to express the corresponding values. Then, we move on to explain that the type of an attribute is expressed as a *data type*, and there are five pre-defined data types: Boolean, Number, Time, Text and Data. Boolean attributes only admit true or false values. Number attributes admit any number, whatever their magnitude or sign. Time attributes admit any expression of time, regardless of its precision. Text attributes admit text values of any length. Finally, Data attributes admit any other kind of data that is not contemplated by the previous data types. We finish the chapter by linking back to the concept of object and explaining that the values in an object, how many there are, and the kinds of their contents, are determined by the attributes of the corresponding class.

In the previous chapter, we learnt how to use properties to represent characteristics of a category in a model. Properties, as we discussed, are abstract features, and provide only some details about the characteristic being described, deferring some decisions to a later moment. This means that, at some point, properties need to be resolved into concrete features. The way to accomplish this varies depending on what kind of characteristic we are trying to model.

Some characteristics are simple and describe the associated category through atomic quantities or qualities, such as numbers or text strings. This is the case, for example, of a book's title (a simple text) or a person's age (a number). Other characteristics are more complex and describe the associated category by associating it to other categories. This is the case, for example, of a person's mother (another person) or a building's location (a place). In this chapter, we discuss the former, and in Chap. 8, we discuss the latter.

© Springer International Publishing AG 2018

C. Gonzalez-Perez, *Information Modelling for Archaeology and Anthropology*,
https://doi.org/10.1007/978-3-319-72652-6_6

Attributes

In order to represent a simple and atomic characteristic in a conceptual model, we use an *attribute*. An attribute is a formal construct that stands for an atomic characteristic of a category.

We define an attribute as follows:

> **Definition**
> An **attribute** is the formalization of an atomic characteristic of a category that is relevant to the model.

You may recall the *Book* example in the previous chapter, reproduced here as Fig. 6.1. Some of the properties depicted in Fig. 6.1 may be developed into simple, atomic features. Let us consider each in turn.

- A book's title is usually provided as a text string. This qualifies as simple and atomic.
- A book's author (or authors) may be given as a name (such as "Raymond Carver"), but it may also be given by pointing to a full record of the author including, for example, their name, nationality, place of birth and biographical notes. In the former case, a book's author would qualify as simple and atomic, but not in the latter case.
- A book's year of publication is often given as a simple number, which clearly qualifies as simple and atomic.
- Finally, a book's publisher may be given as a text (such as "Oxford University Press"), or as a record with full details of the publisher, for example, its name, location and contact details. Like in the case of the book's author, the publisher would qualify as simple and atomic in the former case but not in the latter.

For the sake of illustration, let us assume that we wish to represent publishers as simple texts, but authors through complete records containing various pieces of information. According to this, we may reach a model like that depicted in Fig. 6.2. Note that properties and attributes are shown together inside the lower section of the class box. Each attribute is depicted as a line of text, very much like a property.

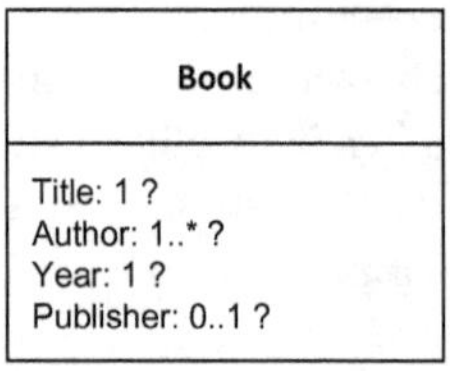

Fig. 6.1 Diagrammatic representation of the *Book* class containing properties *Title, Author, Year* and *Publisher*. This is identical to Fig. 5.3

Book
Title: 1 ? Author: 1..* ? Year: 1 ? Publisher: 0..1 ?

Fig. 6.2 Diagrammatic
representation of the *Book*
class containing attributes
Title, *Year* and *Publisher*, as
well as property *Author*

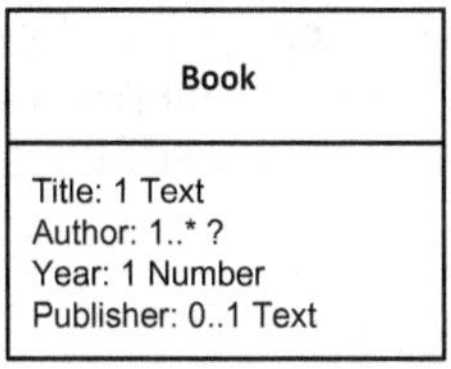

Book
Title: 1 Text Author: 1..* ? Year: 1 Number Publisher: 0..1 Text

However, the form of attribute lines is different. For example, the *Book* class in Fig. 6.2 has attributes such as *Title: 1 Text* and *Year: 1 Number*. Attributes take the following form:

Name: Cardinality Type

The attribute *name* is a word or phrase that tells us what characteristic the attribute is representing. By convention, it is written with an initial capital and, if composed of multiple words, no spaces are left between them and initial capitals are used for all, like in previous occasions. In the example, we have captured the fact that the title, year and publisher are relevant atomic characteristics in our model and modelled them as attributes. The author has been left as a property.

After the attribute name, and separated by a colon, we write the attribute's *cardinality*, following the same rules we described for properties. In our example, every book must have one title and one year, as indicated by the 1 cardinalities, and may have a publisher or not, as indicated by the 0..1 cardinality.

After the cardinality, and instead of the question mark that we used for properties, we write the attribute's *type*. This indicates what kind of quality or quantity may be used for this attribute to describe instances of the associated class. For example, we said that a book's title is usually given as a text string, and that is why we write *Text* for the *Book.Title* attribute. Similarly, we write *Number* for the *Book. Year* attribute because years are usually given as simple numbers. What we can write in a diagram as an attribute's type is limited to a few options, which are described in the next section.

Even though it is not reflected in the diagram, every attribute must have a *definition*. An attribute's definition helps you and others understand what the attribute is meant to represent. Do not trust the attribute name as the only source of information. For example, look at the *Book.Year* attribute in Fig. 6.2. Is it supposed to mean the publication year or the writing year of the book? What if the book has been published at different times in different countries? You need to clarify issues like these through the attribute definition. For example, you could write something like "Book.Year: The year of the earliest publication of the book, in any country." You should keep attribute definitions on a separate sheet of paper or document for easy reference.

Finally, we must note that attributes are quite similar to properties, with the major difference that attributes have a type whereas properties do not. This is a consequence of the fact, which we already discussed, that properties constitute deferred features for which a suitable implementation has not been devised yet, while attributes are fully specified features. Also like properties, a class cannot have two attributes with the same name.

Data Types

As we said in the previous section, we cannot write anything as an attribute's type, but are constrained to a few options that we describe below, and which we call *data types*.

We define a data type as follows:

> **Definition**
> A *data type* is a specification of what kind of quantities or qualities may be used to represent atomic values.

The pre-defined base data types are the following:

- **Boolean**. Values may only be *true* or *false*.
- **Number**. Values are numbers; integer or not; positive, zero or negative. For example, *17, 0.061* or *−321.87*.
- **Time**. Values are time points of any precision, and not limited to the usual scheme of days, months, years, hours, minutes and seconds. For example, *8 June 1917 at 17:30, May 2012* or *late 12th century*.
- **Text**. Values are character strings of any length, including zero. For example, "John Horton Conway", "PX127", or "".
- **Data**. Values are raw, uninterpreted data of any length, including zero. See below for examples.

The following sections describe each data type in turn.

Boolean

Boolean attributes may only take the values *true* or *false*. These two words are special keywords and can be used with Boolean attributes only. A Boolean attribute always represents a characteristic that may be true for some instances of the class, and false for others. For example, the attribute *Person.IsMarried* would be Boolean, since it may only take true or false values.

Please note that not all attributes that involve two mutually exclusive values are Boolean; for example, an attribute such as *Person.Gender*, assuming that only male and female genders are considered, would not be Boolean, since "male" and "female" are different to true and false. Only attributes for which true and false are the only possible answers should be modelled as Boolean.

> **Technical**
> The word "Boolean" is taken from Boolean algebra, which is named after George Boole. In Boolean algebra, the values that variables may take are restricted to *true* and *false*.

Values of Boolean attributes are written with no quotations and in lower case, simply as *true* or *false*.

Number

Number attributes may take any number as value, whether it is integer or decimal, and whether it is positive, zero or negative. For example, *Person.Age* or *Building. Height* should be modelled as of type Number, since a person's age or the height of a building are commonly given as numbers. Most number attributes fall within the following categories:

- Counts, such as *Building.NumerOfFloors* or *Book.NumberOfPages*.
- Measures, such as *Artefact.Weight* or *Building.Orientation* (expressed as an angle).
- Time spans, such as *Process.Duration* or *Meeting.Length*.

In general, only characteristics on which we perform mathematical operations such as addition or division should be modelled as of the Number type. For example, phone numbers or social security numbers are usually composed of figures, but this does not mean that we should model *Person.PhoneNumber* or *Person. SSN* as numbers. This is so because we never carry out additions, multiplications or other mathematical operations on phone numbers or social security numbers. Even though they are made of numbers, they lack a mathematical nature, and for this reason, we should model them as texts. In fact, non-numeric characters such as letters could perfectly be part of phone numbers or social security numbers and they would still work. This is not the case with counts, measures or time spans.

Values of number attributes are written with no quotations, using figures, the minus sign if applicable, and a decimal separator if needed. All the following are valid number values:

- *17*
- *0.061*
- *−321.87*
- *0*

Time

Time attributes may take time points of any precision as values. This means that we are not limited to the usual scheme of days, months, years, hours, minutes and seconds to express a point in time. In fact, any expression of a point in time, regardless of its precision, works as a time value. For example, we should model *Building.ConstructionDate* or *Person.DateOfBirth* as of type Time.

Values of time attributes are written with no quotations, using the necessary characters to express the time point. All of the following are valid time values:

- *8 June 1917 at 17:30*
- *May 2012*
- *The 1950s*
- *Late 12th century*
- *First millennium BCE*

Text

Text attributes may take any text string as value, of any length, including zero length. For example, *Person.Name* or *Book.Summary* should be modelled as of type Text, since a person's name or the title of a book is commonly given as texts. Most text attributes fall within the following categories:

- Labels, such as *Person.Name* or *Book.Title*. They are short and non-discursive. They are often useful to identify the thing that they describe.
- Facts, such as *Person.Address* or *Building.Style*. They are usually longer than labels, also non-discursive, and descriptive. They do not identify the thing that they describe.
- Narratives, such as *Book.Summary* or *Site.Description*. They can be very long, composed of free text, and usually involving multiple sentences.

The Text data type is the most common, since it can easily represent a wide range of characteristics. As we mentioned above in relation to the Number type, characteristics that are given as numbers but lack a mathematical nature (such as phone numbers) should also be modelled as of the Text type.

Values of text attributes are written in double quotation marks. Any characters, except double quotation marks, are allowed between the quotation marks. All the following are valid text values:

- "John Horton Conway"
- "PX127"
- "The theory is based around the purported empirical observation that it is possible to think about something…"
- ""

Data

Data attributes take raw and uninterpreted data of any length as values, including zero-length data. This means that they can hold anything at all. For this reason, the Data data type is the most flexible and generic of all. However, its usage is rare, being only employed for those cases where none of the other data types can be applied. The Data type can be used, for example, to represent images, sound clips or other multimedia entities that we usually store as computer files and cannot be easily described as either Boolean, Number, Time or Text. For example, *Person. Photo* or *Interview.AudioRecording* should be modelled as of type Data.

Due to their nature, values of data attributes can rarely be written down. We usually employ an ellipsis to stand for them: …

Values as Instances of Attributes

At the end of Chap. 5, we explained that objects are instances of classes, and we finished on a mysterious note by saying that further chapters would describe how values and links are also related to classes. Now that we have learnt about attributes, we can state that *values are instances of attributes*. In other words, values, which we introduced back in Chap. 4, are directly related to attributes through the classification mechanism. See Fig. 6.3 for example. Figure 6.3 is an elaboration of Fig. 5.4, with attributes and values added. Note how, in Fig. 6.3, the values of objects follow

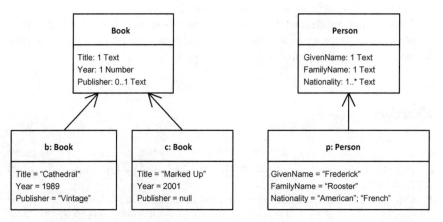

Fig. 6.3 Objects and their classes. Objects *b* and *c* are instances of class *Book*; object *p* is an instance of class *Person*

the pattern established by the attributes of the corresponding classes. For example, object *b*, of class *Book*, has values named *Title*, *Year* and *Publisher*, as dictated by the attributes of its class. The number of values for each attribute is also controlled by the corresponding cardinalities. For example, the cardinality for *Book.Title* is 1, meaning that every book must have exactly one title. There could not be a *Book* object in the diagram with *null* for a title. Similarly, the cardinality for *Person. Nationality* is 1..*, meaning that every person must have at least one, but possibly more nationalities. Object *p*, a *Person*, has two, which is compatible with this.

Note also that *Book.Title* is of type Text, and therefore, the contents of its values are texts and shown in double quotes. The type of *Book.Year* is Number, and values are therefore numbers and shown without quotes.

In summary, every object must obey the attribute names, cardinalities and types expressed by its class.

Summary

Properties that pertain to atomic, single characteristics can be developed in a model as **attributes**.

An attribute belongs to a class.

Every attribute has a **name** that distinguishes it from others of the same class.

Also, every attribute has a **cardinality**, which describes how many things may exist for the attribute for each individual entity.

Every attribute also has a **type**, which describes what kind of quantities or qualities may be used to express the corresponding values.

The type of an attribute is expressed as a **data type**.

There are five pre-defined data types: **Boolean**, **Number**, **Time**, **Text** and **Data**.

What values there are in an object, how many, and the kinds of their contents, are determined by the attributes of the corresponding class.

Exercises

5. Look again at the diagram you created for Exercise 4, and convert as many properties as possible into attributes. Use the best data types and rethink the cardinalities.
6. Draw a diagram showing some objects instantiated from the classes in the previous exercise for some particular town that you are familiar with.

Chapter 7
Enumerated Types

Abstract In this chapter, we continue working with data types and introduce the notion of *enumerated types* as model elements that comprise collections of enumerated items. An enumerated item, in turn, is a label with specific semantics, such as *France* or *Green*. We explain that enumerated types allow us to specify lists of semantically related labels that can be used to characterize entities, and that, consequently, an attribute of an enumerated type is restricted to taking the values given by the associated enumerated items. We also explain that the enumerated items within an enumerated type may be arranged hierarchically to represent subtyping or aggregation. For example, a *Colours* enumerated type may have items Red, Green and Blue, and then *NavyBlue* as a subtype of *Blue*.

In Chap. 6, we said that only five data types are available: Boolean, Number, Time, Text and Data. Each of these data types establishes the rules to apply to the value contents of attributes; for example, an attribute of type Number means that only numbers can be used for this attribute in any instance of the associated class. Data types, however, are open, in the sense that a Number attribute, for example, may take any number, and a Text attribute may take any text. In other words, by using these simple data types we cannot restrict the range of possible values that an attribute may take. Imagine an attribute *Building.Style* of Text type. Being a text, we can assign any textual value to this attribute for any instance of the *Building* class. Some texts may make sense, such as "Gothic" or "Neoclassical", but some others would not, such as "Light red" or "All human beings are born free and equal in dignity and rights". Enumerated types can help to mitigate this problem.

© Springer International Publishing AG 2018

C. Gonzalez-Perez, *Information Modelling for Archaeology and Anthropology*,
https://doi.org/10.1007/978-3-319-72652-6_7

Enumerated Types and Enumerated Items

In order to represent a list of possible values in a conceptual model, we use an *enumerated type*. An enumerated type is a formal construct that contains a list of well-known *enumerated items* or possible values that an attribute of this type may take.

We define an enumerated type as follows.

> **Definition**
> An **enumerated type** *is a data type that defines a list of named items that can be associated to a value of this type.*

Enumerated types, in contrast with the simple data types described in the previous chapter, are "smart" data types capable of specifying what individual values are valid for the associated data. These individual values are determined by enumerated items.

We define an enumerated item as follows.

> **Definition**
> An **enumerated item** *is a unique name within a given enumerated type.*

We can easily extend the *Book* example from previous chapters to illustrate enumerated types. Let's consider that the books we are interested in may be of any of the following genres: short story, crime, satire and memoir. We would like to add an attribute to the *Book* class that allows us to describe a book's genre, and guarantee that whatever value it takes, it will always be one of the above. To do this, we follow a two-step process:

1. First, we define an appropriate enumerated type that will hold the necessary enumerated items.
2. Then, we add an attribute to the class of the enumerated type created above.

For the first step, we would define an enumerated type named, for example, *BookGenres*, having the following enumerated items:

```
BookGenres:     ShortStory
                Crime
                Satire
                Memoir
```

Note that the names of enumerated types and enumerated items follow the same rules that we discussed for other names: they are phrases of one or more words, avoid spaces between words and use initial capitals for each word.

Fig. 7.1 The *Book* class containing attributes *Title, Year, Genre* and *Publisher*

Book
Title: 1 Text Year: 1 Number Genre: 0..* enum BookGenres Publisher: 0..1 Text

Once this is done, we would add the necessary attribute to the *Book* class, as shown in Fig. 7.1. In Fig. 7.1, the *Genre* attribute is shown as being of type *enum BookGenres*. You may recall from the previous chapter that attributes are written by using the following form.

Name: Cardinality Type

In the case of attributes of enumerated types (rather than simple data types), the special word *enum* is written followed by the name of the enumerated type. This clearly conveys the message that the attribute is of a type that has been created by us as part of the model, rather than a pre-defined simple data type such as Number or Text. In Fig. 7.1, the *Genre* attribute captures the fact that a book may have no, one or multiple genres (according to the 0..* cardinality), and that each of the genres is a value taken from the list given by the *BookGenres* enumerated type. This allows us to control with great precision what genres we want to consider and which we do not. Consider the example in Fig. 7.2. This example shows two *Book* instances; book *b* is a short story, and book *c* is a crime and satire work. Note that enumerated items, unlike texts, are shown without quotes.

Fig. 7.2 The *Book* class and two of its instances, *b* and *c*

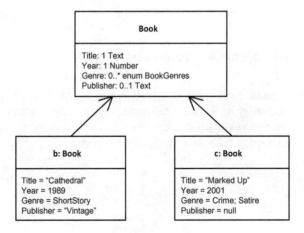

The definition of an enumerated type and its associated enumerated items is not shown in the diagrams. You will need to write them down in a separate document, perhaps together with the definitions of your classes and other additional material. Still, the keyword *enum* in the diagrams makes clear that an attribute is expected to take a controlled range of values which are listed elsewhere.

Also, note that an enumerated type can be reused by multiple attributes. For example, imagine that we add a *Movie* class to our model, and this class has a *Genre* attribute as well. We may rename our *BookGenres* to simply *Genres* and make *Book.Genre* and *Movie.Genre* both of the *enum Genres* types.

Finally, bear in mind that the name of an enumerated item may not be unique in your model. For example, object *c* in Fig. 7.2 shows *Crime* as a genre. Since this model is very simple, we can safely assume that every time that we mention *Crime* we are referring to the enumerated item named "Crime" within the *BookGenres* enumerated type. However, there may be another enumerated type in the model, say, for types of unlawful acts, like this.

```
UnlawfulActs:    Crime
                 Contraband
                 Misdemeanour
```

If the two enumerated types coexist in the same model, mentioning *Crime* is not clear anymore, since we may be referring to crime as an unlawful act or crime as a book genre. To resolve ambiguities like this, we often prefix the enumerated item name with the name of the enumerated type, using a dot as separator. We would have:

- *BookGenres.Crime* refers to the crime genre.
- *UnlawfulActs.Crime* refers to the crime unlawful act.

Hierarchical Enumerated Types

We said in the previous section that an enumerated type contains a list of enumerated item. This is a half-truth. Actually, the items in an enumerated type may be arranged as a list but can also be hierarchically arranged, which is much more interesting. Consider the following example.

```
BookGenres:      Fiction
                     ShortStory
                     Crime
                     Comic
                         Comedy
                         Satire
                 NonFiction
                     Memoir
                     TextBook
```

Here, enumerated items are arranged so that some of them are nested under others. For example, *ShortStory*, *Crime* and *Comic* are nested under *Fiction*, and *Comedy* and *Satire* are nested, in turn, under *Comic*. Items that are not nested are called *root items*, and items having no nested items are called called *leaf items*. Root items are said to be at *depth* 0, items nested under them are at depth 1 and so on. In our example above, the hierarchy established by the nesting reflects the types and subtypes of book genres that are familiar to us. In fact, both comedies and satires are considered to be subtypes of comic works, and comic works, in turn, are considered to fall inside fiction.

Technical

Enumerated types exist in other modelling languages, such as UML, as well as in many programming languages such as Java, Python or C#. However, enumerated types in mainstream languages are always linear rather than hierarchical. The ability to define and use hierarchical enumerated types is a peculiarity of the conceptual modelling approach that we present in this book.

Another example of a hierarchical enumerated type is the following.

```
WorldRegions:    Europe
                    France
                    Germany
                    Spain
                        Galicia
                            Lugo
                            Pontevedra
                        Andalusia
                 Asia
                    China
                    Japan
```

In this example, world regions are arranged according to their location, and nesting indicates which regions are located within others.

We can use hierarchies in enumerated types for two major purposes.

- To represent types and subtypes, like in the example with book genres. This constitutes a particular case of subsumption, of the major linguistic devices introduced in Chap. 2.
- To represent containment or aggregation, like in the example with world regions.

In either case, an object described in terms of an enumerated item can also be described in terms of its parent item, albeit at a higher abstraction level. In other words, the higher the depth, the more specific an item is, and the lower its depth, the more abstract it is. For example, a place having *Region = China* (depth 1) can also be described as being in *Asia* (depth 0), since *China* is nested under *Asia* in our example.

We can refer to enumerated items in a hierarchy in two ways. If there is no chance of ambiguity, we may use the enumerated item name, as in *China* or *Lugo* in the previous example. However, sometimes there may be a chance of ambiguity. For example, consider the following enumerated type.

```
Colours:        Red
                    Light
                    Dark
                Blue
                    Light
                    Dark
```

A reference to *Red* would be clear, but a reference to *Dark* would not. Are we referring to dark red or dark blue? To resolve this, we employ the enumerated item's *absolute name*, which is composed of its name prefixed with the absolute name of its parent item, if it has one, and using a slash as separator. For example, *Red* has no parent item, so its absolute name coincides with its simple name: *Red*. However, the *Dark* item under *Red* has a parent item, so its absolute name is *Red/Dark*. A reference to *Red/Dark* would be unambiguous. Absolute names can be used even if they are not strictly necessary. For example, we can refer to *Lugo* in our previous example as simply *Lugo* (since there is no chance of ambiguity), or as *Europe/Spain/Galicia/Lugo* if we wish to be clearer. Bear in mind that the enumerated type name can be added at the front, as we described in the previous section, if needed: *Colours.Red/Dark* or *WorldRegions.Europe/Spain/Galicia/Lugo*. This is exemplified in Fig. 7.3.

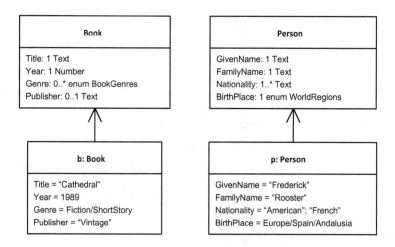

Fig. 7.3 The *Book* and *Person* classes and two of their instances, *b* and *p*, using absolute names for enumerated items

Finally, consider the statement that we made at the beginning of this section. We said that items in an enumerated type may be organized as a list or as a hierarchy. In fact, there is no difference between both options: a list is just a hierarchy having a single level. Enumerated types are hierarchical by nature, and we are free to use nesting to express subtyping or aggregation if we wish.

Summary

Enumerated types are model elements that comprise collections of **enumerated items**.

Enumerated types can be used to express attribute types, very much like simple data types.

An **attribute** of an enumerated type is restricted to taking the values given by the associated enumerated items.

Enumerated items within an enumerated type may be arranged **hierarchically** to represent subtyping or aggregation.

Exercises

7. Look back at the diagram you created for Exercise 6 and add an attribute to describe the style of the buildings, if you do not have it yet. Use an enumerated type for this attribute, and update the corresponding values. Document the enumerated items separately.

Chapter 8
Associations

Abstract In this chapter, we focus on the fact that classes do not exist in isolation, but are semantically connected. We explain that class properties corresponding to complex and relational characteristics can be developed in a model in the form of *associations*. An association is composed of two *semi-associations*, which are inverse of each other. Every semi-association belongs to a class, called the *participant class*, and connects it to the *opposite* class. We also explain that every semi-association has a name that distinguishes it from others of the same class, such as *LivesIn* or *BelongsTo*, as well as a cardinality, which describes how many instances of the opposite class may exist for the semi-association for each instance of the participant class. Finally, we explain that a semi-association may have a role, which works as an alternative name for the opposite class in the context of the association, such as *Residence* or *Owner*. Then, we move on to two particular association cases. The first is that of whole/part semantics and explain that some associations represent the fact that some things are composed of others. This is the case, for example, of a forest and its trees, or a town and its houses. The second case is that of self-associations, that is, associations that connect a class with itself, representing situations where things of the same type are connected to each other. This is the case, for example, of a person and his/her children (who are also persons), or a land division and its subdivisions (which are also land divisions). We close the chapter by linking back to the concept of object and explaining that the links that an object may have, how many, and to which other objects, are determined by the associations of the corresponding class.

In Chap. 5, we learnt how to use properties to represent characteristics of a category in a model. Properties, as we discussed, are abstract features, and provide only some details about the characteristic being described, deferring some decisions to a later moment. As we said in Chap. 6, this means that, at some point, properties need to be resolved into concrete features. The way to accomplish this varies depending on what kind of characteristic we are trying to model. Some characteristics are simple and describe the category through atomic quantities or qualities, such as numbers or text strings; in this case, they become attributes. But other characteristics are more complex, and describe the category by associating it to other categories, like in the case of a person's mother (another person) or a building's location (a place). In this chapter, we discuss these situations.

Associations and Semi-Associations

In order to represent a complex and relational characteristic in a conceptual model, we use an *association*. An association is a formal construct that stands for a relational characteristic of a category.

We define an association as follows.

> **Definition**
> An **association** is the formalization of a structural connection relationship between categories that is relevant to the model.

In other words, an association relates a class to another class. You may recall the *Book* example in Chap. 6, reproduced here as Fig. 8.1. The *Author* property was not modelled as an attribute because we said that a book's authors should be represented through complete author records containing various pieces of information, rather than a simple text. Now we can turn the *Author* property into an association. Look at Fig. 8.2. Here, the line connecting the two classes stands for an association. Associations are always binary, that is, they have two ends. This means that an association can be seen from either of them. In our example, we can describe the association from the perspective of the *Book* class or from the perspective of the *Person* class. It is the same association, but seen from different viewpoints. Each of these viewpoints or perspectives corresponds to a *semi-association*. We define a semi-association as follows.

> **Definition**
> A **semi-association** is the description of an association from the viewpoint of one of the classes that participate in it.

Fig. 8.1 Diagrammatic representation of the *Book* class containing attributes *Title*, *Year* and *Publisher*, as well as property *Author*. This is identical to Fig. 6.2

Book
Title: 1 Text Author: 1..* ? Year: 1 Number Publisher: 0..1 Text

Fig. 8.2 The *Book* and *Person* classes, connected by a *Wrote* association

Fig. 8.3 The association in Fig. 8.2, as seen from *Book*. The large grey arrow, which is not part of the model, can be read as "Every"

Let's describe the association in Fig. 8.2 from each of its two viewpoints. From the perspective of *Book*, we can say that every book has been written by someone, perhaps multiple people. Look at Fig. 8.3. By following the large grey arrow, it is easy to read that "every book was written by one or more persons". Note that the sequence of words in this sentence matches the sequence of elements in the diagram: first the *Book* class, then the name "WasWrittenBy", then the cardinality 1..*, and finally the *Person* class. A small black arrowhead is added to the name in order to make the reading direction clear. In the context of this semi-association, *Book* is called the participant class, and *Person* is called the opposite class.

Let's now look at the same association but from the opposite end. From the perspective of *Person*, we can say that every person may have written any number of books. Look now at Fig. 8.4. Again, by following the large grey arrow, we can read that "every person wrote zero or more books". Like in the previous case, note that the sequence of words in this sentence matches the sequence of elements in the diagram: first the *Person* class, then the name "Wrote", then the cardinality 0..*, and finally the *Book* class. A small black arrowhead is added to the name in order to make the reading direction clear. And also like in the previous case, in the context of this semi-association, *Person* is the participant class, and *Book* is the opposite class.

The "WasWrittenBy" and "Wrote" names in the figures are *semi-association names*. They convey the semantics of each semi-association, very much like a class name conveys the meaning of a class. Semi-association names follow the usual rules for names: they are written with initial capitals and no spaces between words.

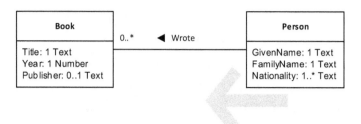

Fig. 8.4 The association in Fig. 8.2, as seen from *Person*. The large grey arrow, which is not part of the model, can be read as "Every"

Semi-association names, as opposed to class names, are not nouns but verbal phrases. This is a consequence of the fact that an association represents a connection relationship, and these are usually described in language as verbs or verbal phrases. For example, "Owns", "HasWritten" or "IsLocatedOn" are good semi-association names, whereas "In" or "Owner" is not. Make sure you use good semi-association names that contain a verb for the sake of clarity in your models. Like in the case of properties and attributes, a class cannot have two semi-associations with the same name. And, like in the case of properties and attributes, we often write semi-association names prefixed by the participant's class name and using a dot as separator when we quote the semi-association in text; for example, *Book.WasWrittenBy* or *Person.Wrote*.

In addition to its name, each semi-association also has a *cardinality*. Like in previous cases, this indicates how many things may exist for each instance of the corresponding class. In the particular case of semi-associations, cardinalities indicate how many objects of the opposite class there may be linked to an object of the participant class through the semi-association. For example, Fig. 8.3 shows that there may be from one to many persons linked to a book through the *WasWrittenBy* semi-association, and Fig. 8.4 shows that there may be from zero to many books linked to a person through the *Wrote* semi-association.

Like in the case of attributes, and even though it is not reflected in the diagram, every semi-association must have a *definition*. A semi-association's definition helps you and others understand what the semi-association is meant to represent. Do not trust the semi-association name as the only source of information. For example, look at the *Person.Wrote* semi-association in Fig. 8.4. Since it is expressed in past tense, should we assume that only books written in the past are to be considered? What if someone is currently writing a book? Can't we describe that situation with this semi-association? You need to clarify issues like these through the semi-association definition. For example, you could write something like "Person. Wrote: Indicates the books written by the person in the past". You should keep semi-association definitions on a separate sheet of paper or document for easy reference.

Two inverse semi-associations together comprise a complete association. By *inverse*, we mean that the participant class of one is the opposite class of the other, and the other way around.

If you look back at Fig. 8.2, you will see that cardinalities for both semi-associations are shown on the association line, each on the corresponding end. Only one name is shown, however. We could have shown both, one in each direction, but very often only one is depicted, especially when the inverse name is easily inferred, like in our example. In situations like this, the semi-association that is easier to remember or has a clearer meaning is used to name the whole association and is called the *primary semi-association*. The inverse is called the *secondary semi-association*.

Remember that reading associations is easy if you follow these rules. First, look at the small black arrowhead in the association name to determine which is the reading direction for the primary semi-association. Then start at the class behind the arrowhead and construct a sentence as follows.

1. Begin your sentence with "Every".
2. Add the name of the class you are starting at; in our case, "person".
3. Add the semi-association name, "wrote".
4. Follow the black arrowhead and add the cardinality, "zero to many".
5. Finish with the name of the opposite class, in plural if needed; "books".

Note that the cardinality next to the starting class is not used when reading an association like this. This makes sense; you would use it when reading the association backwards, that is, from the inverse viewpoint.

1. Begin your sentence with "Every".
2. Add the name of the class you are starting at; in our case, "book".
3. Infer the secondary semi-association name from the name shown; we could say "was written by" as a linguistic inverse of "wrote".
4. Going against the black arrowhead, add the cardinality, "one to many".
5. Finish with the name of the opposite class, in plural if needed; "persons".

Remember that we said at the beginning of this section that associations are always binary. This means that there cannot be associations with three or more ends; if we wanted to connect three classes together, for example, we would need to find a way to use multiple binary associations to achieve it. For example, imagine that we want to represent the fact that people participate in projects that carry out archaeological excavations. It seems that three classes are involved here: *Person*, *Project* and *Excavation*, and that the three of them are inextricably connected, as shown in Fig. 8.5. The way to resolve cases like this is to use two or more associations, bearing in mind that you do not need to connect every class to every other. Figure 8.6 shows a possible solution. Note that, in Fig. 8.6, there is no association between *Person* and *Excavation*; in other words, there is no direct way to know who participated in a particular excavation or to what excavations a particular

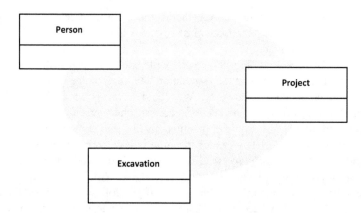

Fig. 8.5 The *Person*, *Project* and *Excavation* classes need to be connected together

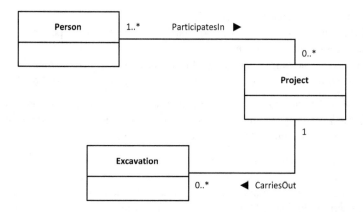

Fig. 8.6 The *Person*, *Project*, and *Excavation* classes connected together by two associations

person contributed. You can get most of this information indirectly, because you can know what projects someone participated in, and which excavations these projects carried out. Still, you may need to add a third association, between *Person* and *Excavation*, to address some specific needs. For example, the solution in Fig. 8.6 does not allow us to know whether a given person was at an excavation or not; we can know what excavations were carried out by the projects this person was in, but that's all. If we wanted to address this specific need, a third association would be needed.

Finally, bear in mind that multiple associations can exist between any number of classes, even between a given pair of classes. Consider the example in Fig. 8.7. Here, two different associations connect *Book* and *Person*, since two different facts need to be represented in the model: the fact that people write books and the fact that people read books. Each needs a separate association. At the same time, a third association connects *Book* and *Publisher*, representing the fact that books are

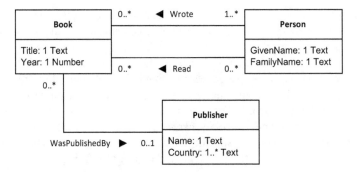

Fig. 8.7 Classes *Book*, *Person* and *Publisher* interconnected by multiple associations

published by publishers. Complex models can easily have dozens or hundreds of classes interconnected in large meshes by numerous associations.

Roles

As we just described, a class may participate in multiple associations. Figure 8.7, for example, shows the *Person* class having two associations to *Book*. Each of these has different meanings; in one case, we are representing the persons who write books, and in another case, we are representing those people who read books. We can say, in fact, that a person may play different roles in relation to books: you can be the author of a book, which is represented by the *Wrote* association; and you can be the reader of a book, which is represented by the *Read* association. This can be formalized as shown in Fig. 8.8. Here, roles are explicitly shown in the diagram. The *role* of a semi-association is a label that provides a specific name for the opposite class in the context of the semi-association. For example, the *Person* class can be referred to as *Author* whenever we are discussing the *Book.IsWrittenBy* semi-association. That is to say, the person who wrote a book is called its author. Similarly, the book written by a person is called their work, which is captured in the diagram by the *Work* role next to *Book*. Finally, the person who reads a book is

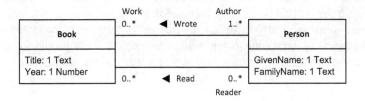

Fig. 8.8 Classes *Book* and *Person* interconnected by two associations, and showing roles *Work*, *Author* and *Reader*

called a reader. Note that not all semi-associations carry roles; you should only write roles for those semi-associations where a role name comes up easily and adds information to the model. For example, the book being read by a person does not receive any particular name, so we have not added a role here.

When you do use roles, please bear in mind the following. First of all, roles follow the same rules as other names: they are written with initial capitals and without spaces between words. Second, they must be phrased as countable nouns in singular form, very much like class names, since they are, after all, alternative names for classes in the very specific context of an association. Third, roles are written in the diagram next to the class that they refer to. In Fig. 8.8, for example, *Author* and *Reader* are placed next to *Person*, signalling that they are alternative names for *Person* in specific contexts.

Also, note that roles can be easily incorporated into the semi-association reading mechanism that we described in the previous section. For example, if we look at the *Wrote* semi-association in Fig. 8.8, we can read it as "every person wrote zero to many books, which are their works" or, alternatively, "every person wrote zero to many works, which are books". Finally, bear in mind that roles cannot be duplicated within any given class, very much like semi-association names.

Roles provide additional information to your models. In general, you do not need to use them for every semi-association, but you need to choose good role names if you want to use them. If you do not find a good role name, leave it out; no role is better than a poorly named one.

Technical

Some modelling languages do not differentiate between attributes and associations. If you have used UML, you will have noticed that in UML an attribute of a class is, in many respects, considered to be an association from that class to the corresponding data type. For example, an attribute such as *Book.Title: 1 Text* would be indistinguishable from an association from *Book* to a *Text* class. Similarly, if you are familiar with the CIDOC Conceptual Reference Model (CRM) [20], you will have noticed that in CIDOC CRM classes only have "properties", which may be connections to other classes or to data types such as *E26 String* or *E60 Number*.

Mixing together attributes and associations may seem to produce a simpler modelling language, but it has serious drawbacks. Conceptually, a class represents a category that is relevant to the model, and therefore will make sense in the specific domain of discourse that you are dealing with, such as French medieval poetry or Iron Age settlements. Data types, contrarily, are independent of the domain being modelled, being universally valid for all of them: text is text in any domain, and numbers are numbers in any domain too.

A language that mixes both together must necessarily use the same modelling primitive (such as "properties" in UML or CIDOC CRM) for both, producing a suboptimal solution. In this book, we use different modelling mechanisms for different things, each one finely adjusted to its needs.

Whole/Part Semantics

So far, we have learnt that associations represent structural connections between classes, and that these connections can mean anything, depending on the names that we use. For example, we can have an association *Wrote* between *Person* and *Book*, or an association *WorksFor* between *Person* and *Organization*. If you do a lot of modelling, you will observe that the range of meanings for associations is very large. However, there is one particular meaning that keeps reappearing very often, that of *aggregation*, also called *whole/part*. A whole/part (or aggregation) association means that something, called a *whole*, is composed of *parts*. For example, consider the situation depicted in Fig. 8.9. Here, the *IsComposedOf* semi-association has whole/part semantics; that is, it means that books are composed of pages. In this model, *Book* is a whole, and *Page* defines the parts that make up this whole. You can usually identify whole/part associations because they have names like "IsComposedOf", "ConsistOf" or "Contains". Sometimes, the association may be named from the opposite viewpoint, and names may be similar to "IsPartOf" or "BelongsTo". In either case, whole/part semantics are very common, because representing reality in terms of things and their parts is a very natural approach to us. You can find many situations where whole/part associations appear:

- A city and its buildings.
- A community and its members.
- A wall and the stones that make it up.
- A text and its sentences, or words.

Since whole/part associations are so common, we can use a specific notation to depict them in a more compact form, as shown in Fig. 8.10.

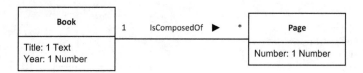

Fig. 8.9 Classes *Book* and *Page* connected by an association with whole/part semantics

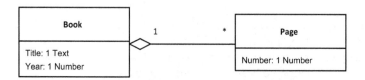

Fig. 8.10 Classes *Book* and *Page* connected by a whole/part association. This is equivalent to the diagram in Fig. 8.9, but here the "whole" notation is used

In Fig. 8.10, the plain association line that we usually employ has been replaced by a line with a small diamond shape on one end. Note that the diamond is placed next to the whole class, *Book* in our example. This diamond indicates that this is a whole/part association, and therefore the association name may be omitted, since its meaning can be readily inferred from the diamond.

Whole/part associations are asymmetric by nature: one class is the whole, and the other is the part. This means that we cannot have diamonds on both ends of a line; that would mean that one thing is composed of another, and this is, at the same time, composed of the former, which is impossible.

> **Technical**
> The study of whole/part relationships in general is the concern of the science of *mereology*. For more information, see [3, "Mereology"].

Self-Associations

At the beginning of this chapter, we said that associations are binary, that is, they always have two ends. So far, all the associations that we have shown connect two classes, but this does not need to be the case. We can easily have associations that, while having two ends, connect a class to itself. They are called *self-associations*. Consider the example in Fig. 8.11. Here, *Person* has an association that loops back to itself. The association still has two "ends", but both are attached to the same class. Let's observe what this association means.

Fig. 8.11 Class *Person* connected to itself by a self-association

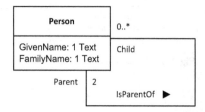

- Reading in the primary direction, "every person is a parent of zero to many children, which are persons".
- Reading in the secondary direction, "every person is a child of 2 other persons, who are called the parents".

As you can see, self-associations are useful to describe relationships between instances of the same class, in our case, persons. This does not mean that one particular person will be parent of themselves; what it means is that one person will be parent of some other persons.

> **Technical**
> An association that permits that one thing is related to itself is called *reflexive* in mathematics. For example, you can brush someone else's hair, but you can brush your own hair too; *Person.BrushesHairOf* would be reflexive. However, this is not what self-associations are about. Self-associations may or may not be reflexive, and there is no way to indicate this in our diagrams. What makes self-associations special is that *they connect things of the same type*, rather than things of two different types. From a mathematical point of view, self-associations correspond to *binary relations*.

Self-associations are very common. For example:

- A village may be visible from other villages.
- A person may be friends, or family, to another person.
- An author may influence other authors.

Except for the fact that self-associations involve only one class, they work exactly like regular associations. They are composed of two semi-associations, each one with a name and a cardinality. Role names, in this case, are highly recommended, since they help in distinguishing the different parts that the only class involved plays in each direction.

Also, self-associations exhibit a very interesting property. Look again at Fig. 8.11. According to it, every person has two parents. Take any person you like; he/she will have two parents. But each of these parents is also a person, so he/she must have two parents too. And each of them will have two parents in turn. And so on and so forth. This infinite regress is caused by the recursive nature of self-associations. In our example, the regress cannot be stopped, since our model states that every person must have two parents. Note that this does not happen in the inverse direction: every person may have zero or more children. For any person that you take, he/she may have children. Each of these children is a person too, so he/she may have children in turn, and so on and so forth. But note the "may" word; it allows us to stop the regression at any point, because, eventually, someone will not have any children. The "may" word in the sentence, and the possibility to stop the regression, are caused by the fact that the self-association has a zero minimum

Fig. 8.12 Class *Region*
connected to itself by a
whole/part self-association

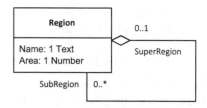

cardinality in this direction. A zero minimum cardinality allows us to have no things connected, and hence stop. However, the cardinality in the opposite direction is 2, so we are always obliged to have two persons connected as parents to any person we pick. In summary, minimum cardinalities greater than zero in self-associations mean that there will be an infinite regress. Sometimes this is reasonable, like in our *Parent* example, because it represents a genuine character-istic of the world that we are describing. However, dealing with infinite regress is tricky, and for this reason you should think twice before defining a minimum cardinality greater than zero in a self-association. Avoid them if not strictly necessary.

A self-association may have whole/part semantics too. This is not infrequent. Look at the example in Fig. 8.12. Here, the *Region* class is connected to itself by a whole/part association. This association represents the fact that every region is composed of zero or many subregions, and every region, in addition, may belong to a super-region. Note that minimum cardinalities are zero in both directions, which avoids an infinite regress.

Links as Instances of Associations

At the end of Chap. 5, we explained that objects are instances of classes, and in Chap. 6, we described how values are also instances of attributes. Now that we have learnt about associations, we can state that *links are instances of associations*. In other words, links, which we introduced back in Chap. 4, are directly related to associations through the classification mechanism. See Fig. 8.13 for an example. In Fig. 8.13, classes *Book* and *Person* are shown connected by a *Wrote* association. This means that instances of *Book* and instances of *Person* must be connected by links as dictated by the corresponding cardinalities. In other words, any book must have one or more connected author persons, and each person may have any number (including none) of connected books. The example shows *b*, a book, connected to two people, *p* and *q*. The diagram may perfectly show a person that is not connected to any book, since this would be permitted by the zero minimum cardinality on the side of *Book*. However, the diagram could not show a book with no connected

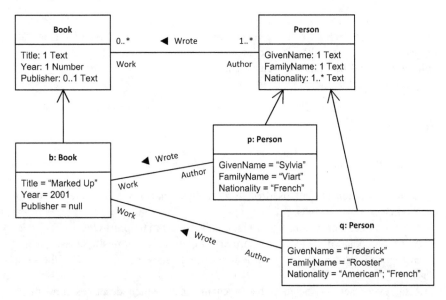

Fig. 8.13 Some objects connected to their classes. Links are shown for the association between the classes

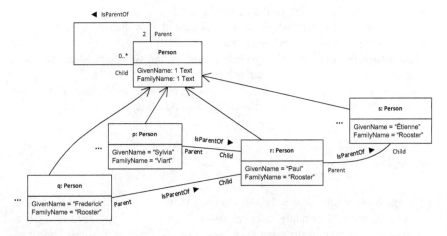

Fig. 8.14 Some objects connected to their class. Links are shown for the self-association

authors, since the cardinality on the *Person* side indicates that there must be one at least.

It is worth showing how self-associations get instantiated. Consider the example in Fig. 8.14. Here, four instances of *Person* are shown. Objects *p* and *q* are parents of object *r*, and object *r* is a parent of object *s*. As we said above, self-associations involve different objects of the same type; here, each instance of the *IsParentOf* association involves two *Person* instances. Note also that, according to the cardinality on the *Parent* side of *IsParentOf*, two parent objects should appear in the diagram for each person; however, this is impossible because of the infinite regress issue we described in the previous section. In Fig. 8.14, we have used ellipses to signal that missing objects should appear.

Summary

Properties that pertain to complex, relational characteristics can be developed in a model as **associations**.

Each association is composed of two **semi-associations**, which are inverse of each other.

A semi-association belongs to a class, called the **participant class**.

A semi-association connects its participant class to the **opposite class**.

Every semi-association has a **name** that distinguishes it from others of the same class.

Also, every semi-association has a **cardinality**, which describes how many instances of the opposite class may exist for the semi-association for each instance of the participant class.

A semi-association may have a **role**, which works as an alternative name for the opposite class in the context of the association.

Some associations have **whole/part** semantics; that is, they represent the fact that some things are composed of others.

Self-associations relate a class to itself, representing situations where things of the same type are connected to each other.

What links an object may have, how many, and to which other objects, are determined by the associations of the corresponding class.

Exercises

8. Look back at the classes in the diagram that you created for the previous exercise and add as many associations between them as you need in order to represent the relationships between buildings and other entities. Use adequate names, cardinalities and roles. Use plain associations or whole/part associations if needed.
9. Working on the previous model add an association to represent the fact that some buildings can be seen from other buildings.
10. Take the model from Exercise 9 and draw some objects that instantiate the classes in it for a town you are familiar with. Include the necessary values and links, as dictated by the attributes and associations.

Chapter 9
Generalization and Specialization

Abstract In this chapter, we deal with the complex problem of category subsumption and describe how it is implemented in conceptual modelling. To do this, we introduce *generalization* relationships between classes, which can be used in a model to represent subsumption relationships between categories. The inverse notion of generalization is *specialization*. Both words refer to the same relationship, but from opposite perspectives. We describe that classes can be arranged in specialization hierarchies of multiple levels, to represent how some categories in the world are subtypes of other categories. For example, this is the case of *Building*, having subtypes *House*, *Barn* and *ShoppingMall*. The criteria that we use to decide what subclasses exist for a given class are called a *discriminant*. In our example, the discriminant would be *Function*. We also connect the notion of generalization to class definitions, as the definition genus of subclasses makes a reference to the superclass in the generalization. As a consequence, everything that we may say about a class also applies to all its subclasses. We explain that this is called the *rule of inheritance*: a class inherits all the properties, attributes and semi-associations from its superclass, and this happens recursively in a specialization hierarchy. We further explain that a consequence of the rule of inheritance is that an object that is an instance of a class can be described in terms of an ancestor class through abstraction. We also explain why a class cannot have multiple specializations and introduce the notion of abstract classes, which may be used in a model when they are not intended to be instantiated directly. We finish the chapter by explaining how a collection of inter-related classes with their attributes and associations make up a *type model*. Type models can be used to represent sets of relevant categories, their features and the connections between them.

So far, we have learnt how to represent categories by using classes and how to characterize these categories through attributes and associations. In particular, associations allow us to represent, at the type level, the many ways in which entities can be related to one another. Categories, in addition, can themselves be related through a very different mechanism, which we mentioned back in Chap. 2: that of subsumption. In common language, we often say things like "an orange is a fruit" or "a hillfort is a particular type of construction". Of course, in these sentences, we

© Springer International Publishing AG 2018
C. Gonzalez-Perez, *Information Modelling for Archaeology and Anthropology*,
https://doi.org/10.1007/978-3-319-72652-6_9

are not referring to a particular orange, which happens to be a fruit, or a particular hillfort which happens to be a construction. On the contrary, we are stating the fact that all oranges are also fruits, and all hillforts can also be considered constructions. We are, in a nutshell, generalizing from a more concrete category ('orange', 'hillfort') to a more general one ('fruit', 'construction').

Generalization/Specialization Relationships Between Classes

In order to represent a subsumption relationship in a conceptual model, we use a *generalization relationship*. This is a formal construct that stands for a subsumption relationship according to some specific criteria. The opposite of generalization is *specialization*; both words refer to the same thing, but seen from opposite perspectives. If a concept generalizes another, then the latter specializes the former. For example, since "fruit" generalizes "orange", then we can say that "orange" specializes "fruit".

> **Technical**
> In linguistics, a word or phrase subsumes another if the semantic field of the latter is included in that of the former. The subsuming word or phrase is called a *hypernym*, and the subsumed one is called a *hyponym*. The generalization relationship that we describe here is very similar and linguistically equivalent.

We define a generalization relationship as follows:

> **Definition**
> A *generalization* is the formalization of a subsumption relationship between two categories that is relevant to the model.

Since subsumption occurs between categories, generalization occurs between classes in a model. Consider the situation depicted in Fig. 9.1. Here, *Person* is connected to *Building* and *House* through two different associations. On the one hand, the model states that people may have visited buildings; on the other hand, that people live in houses. Note, however, that the *Building* and *House* classes are not explicitly related in any manner. But our knowledge about the world tells us that houses are a particular type of buildings or, in other words, *Building* subsumes or generalizes *House*. We can show this fact in the model by adding a generalization/specialization relationship, as shown in Fig. 9.2.

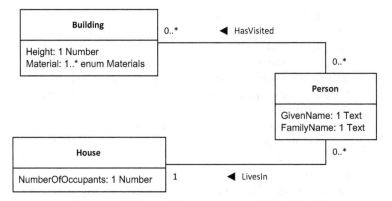

Fig. 9.1 Classes *Building and House* connected to *Person* through two associations

Here, a generalization/specialization relationship has been added from *House* to *Building* by drawing an arrow from the more concrete class (*House*) into the more general one (*Building*). The arrow has a white triangular arrowhead, which can be read as "is a kind of". Note that the arrow flows from the more concrete to the more general, that is, in the direction of the generalization. Specialization occurs in the opposite direction, that is, against the arrow.

In the context of a generalization/specialization relationship, the general class is often called the *superclass*, and the concrete class is called the *subclass*. In our example, *Building* is the superclass of *House*, and *House* is a subclass of *Building*.

Note that, whereas associations represent connections between entities of specific categories, generalization/specialization relationships represent relationships between categories themselves. In Fig. 9.2, for example, the *HasVisited* association represents the fact that some persons have visited some buildings, rather than the (non-sensical) fact that the *Person* class has visited the *Building* class. To

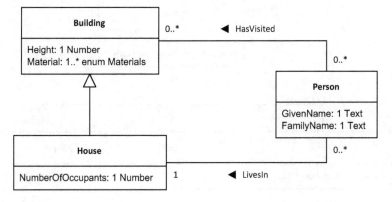

Fig. 9.2 Classes *Building and House* connected to *Person* through two associations. A generalization/specialization relationship has been added between *Building* and *House*

the contrary, the generalization/specialization relationship in the diagram represents the fact that the *Building* class subsumes the *House* class, not the (non-sensical) fact that some buildings subsume some houses. Generalization/specialization happens between categories (or classes), not between entities.

We know that other kinds of buildings exist in addition to houses, such as barns or shopping malls. We can add them to the model, as shown in Fig. 9.3. Note how the generalization arrows going out each of the subclasses are merged into a single arrowhead connected to the superclass. This is because the three merged arrows, all of them, correspond to one generalization/specialization relationship, not three. In this example, the generalization/specialization relationship has one superclass and three subclasses, but there could be other numbers.

Also, generalization/specialization relationships can happen in multiple levels. For example, there are different types of houses, such as bungalows, farm houses or villas. We can easily add them to the model too, as shown in Fig. 9.4. Class structures such as this one are called *specialization hierarchies*, since they usually have one "root" class (the one at the top), and branch out as a "tree" of subclasses, sub-subclasses, etc., until the terminal or "leaf" classes. In practice, you can have specialization hierarchies as deep as you want. Usually, we draw the root class at the top, like in the previous figures, so that specialization extends downwards, but this is a convention only, and you can arrange specialization hierarchies in any way you like as long as they are meaningful and you keep a neat and tidy diagram.

All the classes that are "upstream" from a given class, following generalization relationships, are called its *ancestors*, and the classes that are "downstream" from a given class, following its specialization relationships, are called its *descendants* its *descendants*. For example, the ancestors of *FarmHouse* in Fig. 9.4 are *House* and *Building*; the descendants of *Building* are all the classes in the diagram except for *Building* itself.

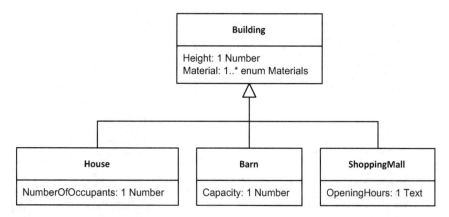

Fig. 9.3 Class *Building* plus subclasses *House, Barn* and *ShoppingMall*, connected through a generalization/specialization relationship

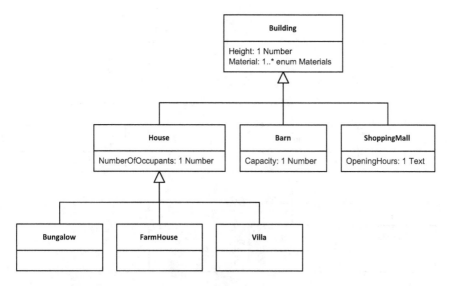

Fig. 9.4 Class *Building* plus subclasses *House*, *Barn* and *ShoppingMall*. *House*, in turn, has subclasses *Bungalow*, *FarmHouse* and *Villa*. Two generalization/specialization relationships connect the classes into a specialization hierarchy

Discriminants

In the previous example (see Fig. 9.4), we said that there are three types of buildings: houses, barns and shopping malls. This may make sense, but it would also make sense to say that there are four types of buildings: existing, in construction, planned for construction and destroyed, or that there are two types of buildings: heritage protected and not protected. All of these specialization schemes make sense, but they obey different purposes and rationales. In the first case (and in Fig. 9.4), we are using the building's function to determine the subclasses. In the second case, we are using the building's existence status, and in the third case we are using the building's heritage protection level. The criterion that help us determine what subclasses may exist is called a *discriminant*, because it refers to the characteristic that allows us to discriminate instances of a superclass and assign them to one subclass or another.

When we construct a specialization hierarchy, we must decide on a single discriminant for each generalization/specialization relationship and be systematic about it. The discriminant that we use for each level must be shown next to the corresponding arrowhead in the diagram, as shown in Fig. 9.5. Here, the *Building* class is first specialized according to function, which yields classes *House*, *Barn* and *ShoppingMall*. This captures the fact that we should look at a building's function in order to classify it as a house, a barn or a shopping mall. Then, *House* is specialized according to structure, which gives *Bungalow*, *FarmHouse* and *Villa*.

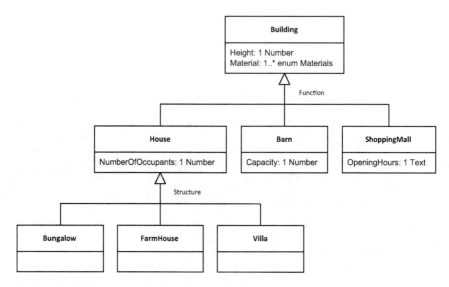

Fig. 9.5 Specialization hierarchy based on the *Building* class. Discriminants are shown for each generalization/specialization relationship

Like before, this captures the fact that we should look at a house's structure in order to classify it as a bungalow, a farm house or a villa. Discriminants are named like attributes, that is, with an initial capital and no spaces between multiple words.

In addition, note that the subclasses for any generalization/specialization relationship in the hierarchy represent categories with no overlaps. In other words, the "sibling" subclasses in any generalization/specialization relationship in the hierarchy are mutually exclusive. For example, if a building is a house, then it cannot be a barn or a shopping mall, and if a house is a farm house, then it cannot be a bungalow or a villa. This is good, because it helps us to cleanly delimit the semantics of each class in the hierarchy. Using clear discriminant with precise semantics helps to achieve this, and vague or ill-defined discriminants, such as "type" or "variety", hinders it. If you are not careful with your discriminants, you can end up with very awkward models. Look at the example in Fig. 9.6. Here, no clear discriminant has been used and, consequently, the subclasses that arise keep no relation to each other. The three of them are, technically speaking, genuine subclasses of *Building*, but they do not work as a family, because they do not help us organize buildings into clean separate categories. It is perfectly possible that a particular building is, at the same time, a house, an ancient building and a protected building, and this is not something we want in a model. Remember that we said at the end of Chap. 5 that every object has one and exactly one class as its type; if we had overlapping sibling classes like in Fig. 9.6, we may find an object that is, at the same time, an instance of multiple subclasses, which is a contradiction. In summary, avoid overlapping subclasses and avoid vague discriminants.

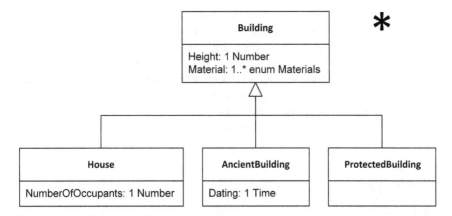

Fig. 9.6 Generalization/specialization relationship rooted on the *Building* class and without a clear discriminant. The asterisk indicates that this is a very poor model

Generalization and Class Definitions

Generalization/specialization relationships are extremely useful to organize classes in a model. In addition, they relate strongly to discussion on class definitions back in Chap. 5. We said there that a class is usually defined through genus plus differentia; the genus determines of what kind the class is, and the differentia distinguishes the class from others of the same kind. For example, when we define a *Book* as "a document that is composed of a collection of leaves fastened together at one side", the word "document" refers to the genus and the rest of the phrase to the differentia. Now that we have learnt about generalization, we can state that *the genus in a class definition constitutes a potential superclass*. This means that we may use the genus in a class definition to find a superclass for the class we are defining. For example, since a *Book* is defined as "a document that is composed of a collection of leaves fastened together at one side", we can introduce a *Document* class in our model and make it *Book*'s superclass.

This also works the other way around: when we are trying to define a class, we can look at its superclass and the overall generalization involved in order to obtain the genus in its definition. For example, since *House* specializes from *Building* in Fig. 9.5, we could start the definition of *House* with "a building that..." and complete it with some differentia that distinguishes houses from instances of other sibling classes such as *Barn* and *ShoppingMall*. This difference should relate to the discriminant being used for the associated generalization/specialization relationship. For example, we could say that a *House* is "a building designed for people to live in" and define *Barn* as "a building designed to keep livestock and store farm-related goods".

In summary, generalization/specialization relationships are closely related to class definitions, as the genus in the definition of a class refers to the same concept as its superclass. Of course, some classes in your model will be defined in terms of a genus that does not appear in the model at all; this is why we said above that the genus in a class definition is a *candidate* superclass. The genus suggests a super-class, but we are not obliged to introduce it into the model. If we did it, we would be entering into an infinite regress, since each new class in the model would be defined, and its genus would suggest a new class to be added, and so on and so forth. You should expect that some classes, those that pertain to very abstract categories, probably relating to common concepts that can be easily understood by most people or are too abstract for the model scope, will not have a superclass, becoming roots of a specialization hierarchy, like *Building* in Fig. 9.5.

Inheritance

The connection between class definitions and generalization relationships has a very interesting consequence. Look again at Fig. 9.5 and consider the definition that "a house is a building designed for people to live in". When we say that "a house is a building", we are, in fact, expressing the core idea of generalization/specialization and asserting that every house that we may observe or imagine is also a building. In other words, *if* x *is a house, then* x *is also a building*. We can express this, formally, as follows:

$$x{:}\,House \rightarrow x{:}\,Building$$

Now think of any characteristic of buildings. This can be anything that we agree that applies to buildings. For example, all buildings are made of some materials, or all buildings create an interior space. Anything that is a building will have this characteristic. Let's call this characteristic B. We can say then that *if* x *is a building, then* x *will have characteristic* B. Formally,

$$x{:}\,Building \rightarrow B(x)$$

Now, let's combine both formal expressions and apply some logic.

$$\frac{\begin{array}{c} x{:}\,House \rightarrow x{:}\,Building \\ x{:}\,Building \rightarrow B(x) \end{array}}{x{:}\,House \rightarrow B(x)}$$

By using a classic hypothetical syllogism on the two premises discussed above, we conclude that houses will have the characteristic of buildings too. Note that our reasoning is abstract, so that it applies to anything (represented by x above) that happens to be a house and also to any characteristic of buildings that we can think of (represented above by B). Also, we may replace any other two categories related by a generalization relationship for *House* and *Building*, and the reasoning would still hold. In simple English, we can state that:

Rule of inheritance
Anything that we may say about a class also applies to all its subclasses.

This is called the rule of inheritance because, through specialization, a class "inherits" everything from its superclass. And when we say "everything", we mean the following:

- The definition of a class also applies to its subclasses. For example, if we agree to define *House* as "a building designed for people to live in", and we have *Bungalow* as a subclass of *House*, then this definition also applies to *Bungalow*. In fact, a bungalow is also a building designed for people to live in.
- The properties and attributes of a class also apply to its subclasses. For example, if we have a *Building* class with attributes *Materials* and *Height*, then these attributes should also make sense for *House*, *Barn* or *ShoppingMall*. And they do make sense.
- The semi-associations of a class also apply to its subclasses. For example, look back at Fig. 9.2; the semi-association *Building.HasBeenVisited* (inferred from *Person.HasVisited*) also applies to *House*. In other words, if buildings can be visited, so can houses.

Technical
The rule of inheritance is strongly based on Liskov's substitution principle [28], which states that *if S is a subtype of T, then objects of type T may be satisfactorily replaced with objects of type S*. The word "subtype" here is equivalent to "subclass" in our discussion.

Liskov's substitution principle makes a lot of sense in the real world. It means that if you ask me for a fruit and I give you an apple, you cannot complain.

Inheritance is invisible. That is, we do not show it in diagrams, but we must assume it is there, flowing in the opposite direction to generalization arrowheads. Look at the example in Fig. 9.7. Here, the *House* class (as well as *Barn* and *ShoppingMall*) inherits all the attributes from its superclass, *Building*. This means that *House* will have the following attributes:

- *Height: 1 Number*, inherited from *Building*.
- *Material: 1..* enum Materials*, inherited from *Building*.
- *NumberOfOccupants: 1 Number*, defined by *House* itself.

Also, if *Building* had an association to another class, *House* would inherit it too. This may seem counterintuitive or difficult to grasp, because in the diagram, after all, the *House* class is drawn with only one attribute inside the box. However, it has

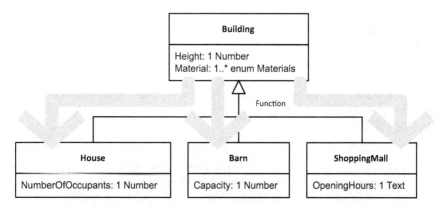

Fig. 9.7 The *Building* class with three subclasses. The thick grey arrows, which are not part of the model, represent the flow of inheritance

three. You will become used to "reading inheritance" automatically after you have worked with conceptual models for a short while.

Also, bear in mind that inheritance happens recursively in specialization hierarchies with multiple levels. For example, in Fig. 9.5, *House* inherits all the attributes from *Building*, and *Bungalow* then inherits all the attributes from *House*, including those that *House* got from *Building*. In other words, we can say that a class inherits every feature from all its ancestors and, together with its own, propagates them down to all its descendants.

Inheritance is automatic and immediate. We do not need to do anything or show anything special in a diagram to make it work. Since it is a logical consequence of specialization, it simply works, whether we like it or not.

Abstraction

An additional consequence of subsumption is *abstraction*. This is the phenomenon by which we can discard details and focus only on what is essential. In particular, remember the statement that *if something is a house, then it is also a building*, or more generically, everything that can be described in terms of a class can also be described in terms of its superclass. For example, if we agree that something is an apple, and describe it in terms of the *Apple* class, then we should agree that it is also a fruit and be able to describe it as such. Of course, using a more abstract class to describe something of a more concrete class means that some details are lost, since a specialized class, by definition, adds details to its superclass (via the differentia in its definition). As another example, look again at Fig. 9.7. Here, an object of type *Barn* would be described as having a height, one or more materials and a capacity. We could also describe this object as a building, without particularizing on what kind of building it is; but in this case, the object would only be described as having a height and a set of materials. No capacity could be possibly given, since buildings, according to the model, do not have a capacity. This removal of details when we use a class that is more general than needed constitutes abstraction.

You may wonder why abstraction is useful, since we can always describe things in terms of the most concrete class possible. But this is not always the most convenient thing to do. Depending on purpose and context, we often decide to describe things at higher abstraction levels. For example, a town council planning department would probably employ very detailed classes to describe the relevant buildings for preservation purposes. However, we rarely use such a large amount of detail; we do not point at a building and say "look what a beautiful Queen Anne, corner-towered, red brick detached house". We simply say "what a beautiful house". Being able to abstract gives us the opportunity to be more economical when describing things.

Generalization and Objects

In previous chapters, we explained that objects are instances of classes, that is, the structure of classes dictate the shape and contents of objects. How do generalization/specialization relationships between classes affect this? Essentially, you need to bear in mind two important things.

- Specialization hierarchies work at the class level, and they have no counterpart in the world of objects.
- Inheritance means that instances of a class will be regulated by that class plus all its ancestor classes.

To start with, and as we described in a previous section, generalization/ specialization relationships pertain to classes, that is, they describe how categories relate to each other. This is different to associations, which are also modelled between classes, but describe how instances of those classes relate to each other. Secondly, and as a consequence, class hierarchies get "flattened out" when we take instances. Consider the case depicted in Fig. 9.8. Here, object h of type *House* is a simple object like any other; the fact that its type is a subclass of another class is not visible by looking at the structure of the object. In fact, if we had a single class named *House* with attributes *Height*, *Material* and *NumberOfOccupants* instead of the specialization hierarchy in Fig. 9.8, object h would look exactly the same. Also, note the consequences of inheritance. Object h has values for three attributes: one comes from its direct type class, *House*, and the other two are inherited by *House* from *Building*. Again, we know this because we are looking at the class diagram, but this fact is unrecognizable in the object h itself.

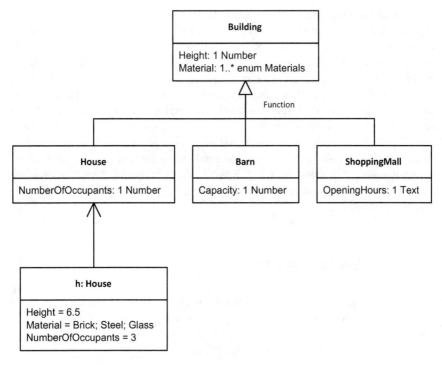

Fig. 9.8 A simple specialization hierarchy and one instance of a leaf class

The Is-A Confusion

We need to make a parenthesis here. You may have heard of Is-A relationships. Especially in the 1980s, a lot was written about them in the artificial intelligence and knowledge engineering literature. Basically, an Is-A relationship is one where the phrase "is a" is used to link two things, like in the sentence "Sydney is a city". However, using the Is-A terminology can be very confusing. As pointed out by Guarino [29] and many others, Is-A mixes together different kinds of relationships that we must distinguish if we want to construct useful conceptual models. For example, consider the following statements:

- Sydney is a city
- A city is a human settlement

In the first case, "is a" means classification: Sydney is an entity that we classify as being of the city category. In the second case, "is a" means subsumption: every city is also a human settlement. Classification and subsumption are two of the five linguistic devices that we discussed back in Chap. 2, and they should not be mixed up. In conceptual modelling, we represent them through very different mechanisms: instantiation in the first case and generalization in the second.

Do not use the Is-A terminology.

Avoiding Multiple Specialization

You may wonder whether a class may be specialized multiple times, using different discriminants. Look at the example in Fig. 9.9. As you can see, the figure shows an asterisk, which means that it is illegal (or, in some cases, legal but not recommended). A class can have at most *one* specialization; in other words, a class cannot be specialized multiple times. The reason for this is the same as in the previous case: if we allowed models like the one in Fig. 9.9, we may find an object that is an instance of one class from the *Function* specialization and, at the same time, an instance of one class from the *ProtectionLevel* specialization. Think, for example, of a protected barn; it would be an instance of *Barn* and also of *ProtectedBuilding*. As we said above, and also at the end of Chap. 5, every object has one and exactly one class as its type; if we had models like the one in Fig. 9.9, we would be entering into a contradiction.

Can't we express then the fact that buildings are organized in terms of function and also protection level? We can, but we need to take the following approach. First, we need to decide which of the two (or more) discriminants is more relevant for the model, or establishes a clearer and more prominent divide between types of buildings, and specialize *Building* according to this discriminant. Then, we can specialize the resulting subclasses, one by one, according to the second discriminant. Figure 9.10 shows the result.

You may think that this model is too cumbersome, because we have three specializations at the second level having the same discriminant and too many classes. However, this is the best way to model a double specialization of buildings. In addition, diagrams like this can usually be simplified through the following mechanisms. First of all, you may not need every specialization. For example, perhaps you need to distinguish between protected and non-protected houses, but you do not need that for shopping malls. In that case, you would omit the two subclasses of *ShoppingMall*, simplifying the model.

Second, it is often possible to replace a specialization with a Boolean or enumerated attribute. For example, instead of having *ProtectedHouse* and

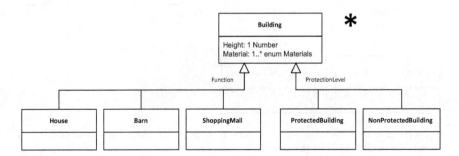

Fig. 9.9 The *Building* class with two parallel specializations. The asterisk indicates that this is an illegal model

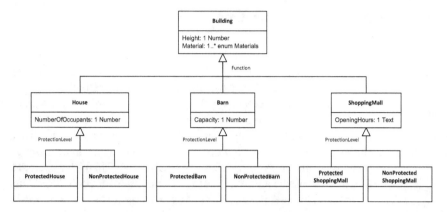

Fig. 9.10 The *Building* class with two consecutive specializations, first on *Function*, and then on *ProtectionLevel*. This is perfectly valid

NonProtectedHouse as separate classes, your model may work perfectly by replacing them with an extra attribute in *House* to represent the difference. Figure 9.11 shows the two options. In this case, the subclasses of *House* capture the fact that a house may be protected or not. This can easily be represented, in a more economical way, through a Boolean attribute. If you have three or more subclasses, or two subclasses that did not refer to a yes/no status, you would need an enumerated rather than Boolean attribute. Also, note that the attribute solution is much simpler than the one based on specialization, but it will not let you represent specific characteristics of instances of the subclasses. For example, if you wanted to add some attributes to *ProtectedHouse* in order to describe how a house is protected, you would need to keep the two separate subclasses *ProtectedHouse* and

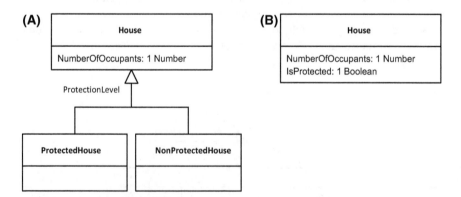

Fig. 9.11 In **A**, the *House* class has two subclasses. In **B**, the subclasses have been replaced by a Boolean attribute to represent the same distinction

NonProtectedHouse instead of the Boolean attribute. Use attributes like this only when you can treat all instances in the same manner, regardless of their type.

In summary, classes cannot have multiple specializations; you need to specialize them one discriminant at a time. However, classes can have multiple generalizations, as we will discuss in Chap. 12.

Abstract Classes

In a specialization hierarchy, the root class is the least specific. This is so because each level that we travel downstream, class definitions add details through their differentiae, so that the more we part from the root class, the more details will be contained in a class definition. Consider the example in Fig. 9.12.

Now consider the following definitions.

- A structure is a place with material boundaries that distinguish it from its surroundings.
- A building is a structure that is intentionally produced for some particular function.
- A house is a building designed for people to live in.

Fig. 9.12 A specialization hierarchy with four levels. *Structure* is the least specific class, and *Villa*, the most specific

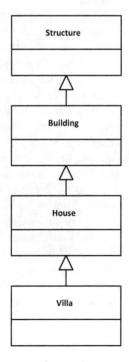

- A villa is a house for the residence of upper-class people and located in the country.

Do not pay much attention to whether you agree or not with the definitions. The point here is that each definition builds on top of the previous one, adding more detail. In fact, we could replace the genus in each definition with its complete definition to highlight how the level of detail keeps growing. For example,

- A structure is a place with material boundaries that distinguish it from its surroundings.
- A building is a [place with material boundaries that distinguish it from its surroundings], and that is intentionally produced for some particular function.
- A house is a [[place with material boundaries that distinguish it from its surroundings], and that is intentionally produced for some particular function], and designed for people to live in.
- A villa is a [[[place with material boundaries that distinguish it from its surroundings], and that is intentionally produced for some particular function], and designed for people to live in], specifically for the residence of upper-class people and located in the country.

We have used square brackets above to signal the replaced fragments. As you can see, the classes at the bottom of the hierarchy are much more specific, whereas the root class is very open-ended in its definition. For this reason, specialization hierarchies establish a *specificity gradient*, from the least at the top to the most at the bottom.

Classes that are very unspecific are rarely useful to represent the world in practical terms. For example, we do not go around pointing at houses and saying "look, what a nice structure". The concept of a structure, even if it is known and more or less clear in our mind, is too vague for practical purposes. We tend to describe our immediate reality in terms of more specific concepts, such as 'house' or perhaps 'building', which constitutes the well-known "basic level" categorization mechanism described by Rosch [30]. This means that, sometimes, the top-most classes in a specialization hierarchy are useful to provide structure to the model, rather than as practical representations of anything. In these situations, we can mark them explicitly as such. A class that is not meant to be used for direct representation, that is, instantiated, is called an *abstract class*. In turn, the classes that are meant to be instantiated and thus represent our world directly are called *concrete classes*. Look at the example in Fig. 9.13. Here, the *Building* class is marked with an A in parenthesis after its name. This is called an *abstract marker*, and means that *Building* is an abstract class, and thus not intended to be instantiated. The classes on the "leaves" of the tree are not marked, so they are considered concrete classes and intended for instantiation. The model in Fig. 9.13 allows us to create objects of type *House*, *Barn* or *ShoppingMall*, which have an appropriate level of detail. However, we could not possibly create an object of type *Building*. If we wanted to describe a

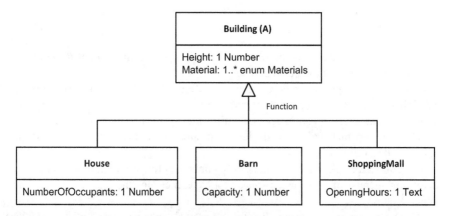

Fig. 9.13 A specialization hierarchy with an abstract root class

building entity that is not a house, a barn or a shopping mall (for example, a factory), we would need to add a new class to the model.

Often, all classes in a specialization hierarchy are abstract except for the leaf ones. This is more restrictive than leaving most classes as concrete. In your models, mark as abstract only those classes that are clearly too vague or open-ended as to be useful for the direct description of entities.

Type Models

A *type model* is a collection of related classes, generalization/specialization relationships, properties, attributes and associations. A type model, therefore, represents a set of relevant categories, their characteristics and their connections to one another. We can use type models, for example, to represent, describe and document the major categories of material or immaterial entities, agents, events or ideas.

An instance model, in turn, always conforms to a type model. This is to say, an instance model is always based on a particular type model, in the sense that the objects in the instance model are instances of classes in the type model, and links in the instance model are instances of associations in the type model. You cannot create an instance model that is not based on an existing type model.

Type models, like instance models or any other kind of conceptual models, are abstract constructs in our minds. In order to visualize or communicate them, we often depict them as class diagrams like those in this and previous chapters.

Since type models work at the category instead of entity level, they rarely grow too large to handle and usually stay in the range of dozens or hundreds of classes at most. Still, using some automated tools can be useful to manage and depict large type models. Some chapters in Part V deal with the use and application of tools like these.

Summary

Generalization relationships between classes can be used in a model to represent subsumption relationships between categories.

The inverse of generalization is **specialization**. Both words refer to the same relationship, albeit from opposite perspectives.

Classes can be arranged in **specialization hierarchies** of multiple levels.

The criterion that we use to decide what subclasses exist for a given class is called a **discriminant**.

Generalization relationships are closely connected to class definitions, since the definition genus of subclasses makes a reference to the superclass in the generalization.

As a consequence, everything that we may say about a class also applies to all its subclasses; this is the rule of **inheritance**.

A class inherits all the properties, attributes and semi-associations from its superclass, and this happens recursively in a specialization hierarchy.

An object that is an instance of a class can be described in terms of an ancestor class through **abstraction**.

A class cannot have **multiple specializations**. It may have one or none.

Classes may be marked as **abstract** in a model when they are not intended to be instantiated directly.

Type models can be used to represent sets of relevant categories, their features and the connections between them.

Exercises

11. Create a type model containing an *ArchaeologicalSite* class plus classes to represent tumuli, hillforts and villages. Use generalization relationships with the necessary discriminants.
12. Add attributes to the previous model to represent the sites' coordinates and the estimated population for hillforts and villages. Remember the rule of inheritance.
13. Draw an instance model with some objects for the *Village* class in the previous type model. Give them the necessary values.

Part 2
Recap of Part II

This is the end of Part II. So far, we have explored the basic mechanisms of conceptual modelling, learning how to create models that represent the world at two different levels: instance models to represent specific entities and their characteristics, and type models to represent categories and their features. We have also discussed a large number of concepts such as object, class, attribute, association, generalization and inheritance; we have learnt how to depict models in the form of diagrams by using a precise and rich notation.

The collection of concepts that we have introduced, as well as the graphical notation that allows us to represent them, are part of the ConML conceptual modelling language. ConML is a simple and affordable modelling language that was designed with the humanities and social sciences in mind. It is oriented towards people with no previous experience in information technologies or software engineering, and our experience tells us that it can be successfully learnt and applied in fewer than five days of full-time study [31].

ConML is defined semi-formally by using a metamodel, that is, a technical specification of the language elements and how they can be combined. If you are interested, you can find the complete metamodel in the ConML Technical Specification [32], and you are encouraged to visit www.conml.org for additional information and resources.

Part III
Advanced Conceptual Modelling

In the previous part, we introduced the basic mechanisms of conceptual modelling. In this part, we complete the previous one by presenting some advanced concepts and language elements in ConML (www.conml.org) and conceptual modelling in general. Real-world examples in cultural heritage are used. Known concepts such as enumerated types and attributes are enriched with new information, and new concepts and techniques, such as multiple generalization and feature redefinition, are described and explained. Also, we dedicate a few chapters to the discussion of "soft" issues such as vagueness, temporality and subjectivity.

This part is significantly more challenging than the previous one, so be prepared. Once you finish it, you will be able to create and understand rich and complex conceptual models of cultural heritage.

Chapter 10
Advanced Enumerated Types

Abstract This chapter elaborates on enumerated types (introduced in an earlier chapter) and describes the fact that an enumerated type can specialize from another enumerated type. The specialized enumerated type inherits all the items from its generalized type. We also explain why specialized enumerated types cannot introduce root items, in order to preserve the semantics of the generalized type.

In Chap. 7, we introduced enumerated types. Remember that an enumerated type defines a list of named items that can be associated to a value of this type. We explained that these types are very useful in those occasions when we want to provide a controlled list of options for an attribute. We also said that the items in an enumerated type can be arranged in a hierarchy, in order to represent subsumption or aggregation relationships.

In this chapter, we complete the discussion of enumerated types with some advanced topics; in particular, we discuss the fact that, like classes, enumerated types can participate in generalization/specialization relationships, which results in the inheritance of items.

Generalization/Specialization Relationships Between Enumerated Types

Imagine that we are creating a model for the classification of books. We want to describe each book in terms of its genre, and we also want to describe the library sections according to what genres of books they will contain. For example, we want separate areas in the library for large genre categories such as biography, reference or fiction. At the same time, we want to describe the genre of each book with more detail, for example, as science fiction or dictionaries. In summary, we need to classify both library sections and books, the latter with much greater detail than the former. We can use two separate enumerated types for this, as shown in Fig. 10.1.

© Springer International Publishing AG 2018   101
C. Gonzalez-Perez, *Information Modelling for Archaeology and Anthropology*,
https://doi.org/10.1007/978-3-319-72652-6_10

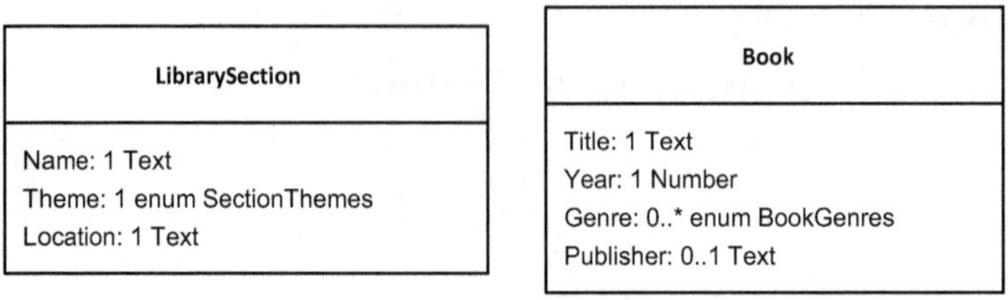

LibrarySection
Name: 1 Text
Theme: 1 enum SectionThemes
Location: 1 Text

Book
Title: 1 Text
Year: 1 Number
Genre: 0..* enum BookGenres
Publisher: 0..1 Text

Fig. 10.1 Library sections and books are classified according to different enumerated types

Here, the *LibrarySection* class uses the *SectionThemes* enumerated type to classify library sections. This enumerated type could look something like this:

```
SectionThemes:    Fiction
                  Biography
                  Reference
```

At the same time, the *Book* class uses the *BookGenres* enumerated type to classify books. This enumerated type could look something like this:

```
BookGenres:       Fiction
                     Crime
                     Fantasy
                     ScienceFiction
                     Historical
                  Biography
                     Autobiography
                  Reference
                     TextBooks
                     Dictionaries
```

Note that, since we need to match book genres to library sections, the top-level enumerated items in *BookGenres* coincide with the items in *SectionThemes*. For example, a book described as *Genre = Fantasy* would go into the library area described as *Theme = Fiction*. However, this approach presents two shortcomings. First of all, and although we can quickly determine what books go into which library sections by looking at their descriptions and the enumerated types, this is not evident from a formal point of view. That is, the *SectionThemes.Fiction* and *BookGenres.Fiction* enumerated items, despite both being named "Fiction", are different enumerated items, and the fact that their names are equal should not be taken as indicative that their semantics are equal too; in fact, we may have enumerated items with similar or equal names and very different semantics, as discussed in Chap. 7 in relation to the *Light* and *Dark* colours. Secondly, if we modify one of the two enumerated types at any time, for example by adding, renaming or deleting items, we will need to manually make sure that the changes are correctly applied to the other enumerated type. For example, if we wanted to add *AudioBooks* to *SectionThemes*, then we would need to add a similar item to *BookGenres*. This manual synchronization is tedious and error-prone.

In order to avoid these issues, we can use a *generalization/specialization relationship* between the enumerated types. You may recall from Chap. 9 that a generalization relationship between classes is the formalization of a subsumption relationship between the underlying concepts, and a specialization is the opposite relationship. These relationships can occur for enumerated types, too. In our example, we can see the book genres as a specialization of section themes, because book genres build on top of section themes and add extra detail to them without altering their original meaning. Following this, we can reformulate the two independent enumerated types that we illustrated above as follows:

```
SectionThemes:    Fiction
                  Biography
                  Reference

BookGenres (specialized from SectionThemes):
                  Fiction (inherited)
                     Crime
                     Fantasy
                     ScienceFiction
                     Historical
                  Biography (inherited)
                     Autobiography
                  Reference (inherited)
                     TextBooks
                     Dictionaries
```

Now, *BookGenres* specializes *SectionThemes*. This has several consequences. First of all, *BookGenres* inherits all the items in *SectionThemes*. Inheritance works like we described in Chap. 9 in relation to classes: everything that we say about an enumerated type applies also to all its subtypes. In our case, this means the collection of items; that is why *BookGenres* contains items inherited from *SectionThemes*. In addition, *BookGenres* is adding extra items and placing them under the inherited ones. Very importantly, note that the *Fiction* item in *BookGenres* (or any of the other inherited items) is the same thing as the *Fiction* item in *SectionThemes*. We do not mean that they have the same name, but that they are one same thing. This means that now we can formally infer that a book categorized, say, as *Fantasy*, should go into the *Fiction*-themed section. In addition, altering items is much easier now. For example, if we added an *AudioBooks* item to *SectionThemes*, it would automatically appear as an inherited item in *BookGenres*. This means that no manual synchronization is necessary.

In general, generalization/specialization of enumerated types is useful when you want to construct an enumerated type that is more detailed than, but similar to, another. Bear in mind that the generalized enumerated type *subsumes* the specialized one, and, as a consequence, everything that we can say about the generalized type also applies to the specialized one. Also as a consequence, anything described in terms of the specialized one can also be described, with higher abstraction, in terms of the generalized one. Going back to our previous example, a book having *Genre = Fantasy* can be abstractly described as simply *Fiction*, using *SectionThemes* instead of *BookGenres*.

There is an important rule that you need to bear in mind when using this feature. An enumerated type that specializes from another cannot have root items of their own; all the items that they introduce must be subitems of others. If we allowed specialized enumerated types to introduce new root items, we would be breaking the possibility for abstraction, since an object described in terms of the specialized type could potentially take values corresponding to the new root items which cannot be abstracted out into items of the generalized types. For example, imagine we could add a root *AudioBooks* item to *BookGenres*. A book having *Genre = AudioBooks* could not be possibly described in terms of *SectionThemes*, since SectionThemes would contain no reference whatsoever to audio books, and *AudioBooks* would not be a subitem of any other item.

Summary

An enumerated type can **specialize** from another enumerated type.
A specialized enumerated type **inherits** all the items from its generalized type. Specialized enumerated types cannot introduce root items.

Exercises

14. Imagine that you need to develop an urban planning model for a town council. In the council, overall, buildings are simply categorized as residential, commercial or industrial. However, the council planning department needs additional detail, having types such as detached house, factory, mall or apartment block. Create two enumerated types linked by a generalization/specialization relationship and having the necessary items. Add extra items that you can think of if you wish.

Chapter 11
Advanced Features

Abstract In this chapter, we elaborate on the ideas of properties, attributes and semi-associations, all of them introduced in earlier chapters and collectively called *features*. We introduce some additional characteristics of features, such as the idea that features which must preserve the order of their instances may be marked as *sorted* in a model. We also explain that semi-associations that connect a class to another that is mentioned on its definition should be marked as *strong*, to capture the fact that a definitional dependency exists between the classes. Then, we deal with the awkward but common phenomenon that some self-associations involve a single role and therefore a single semi-association; we explain that these are called *symmetric* self-associations and present a special notation for them. Finally, we explain that associations with overall semantics of "contains", "shares" or "refers to" can be depicted through a compact notation, which results in tidier diagrams.

Throughout various chapters in Part II, we described the concepts of property (Chap. 5), attribute (Chap. 6) and semi-association (Chap. 8). Despite being very different, these three concepts have a lot in common:

- All three belong to classes; that is, a class may have properties, attributes and semi-associations.
- All three are identified by a name and further described through a definition.
- All three have a cardinality.

Given these commonalities, it makes sense to treat properties, attributes and semi-associations from a common point of view for some purposes. The word that we will use to refer to the three of them together is *features*. Thus, we can say that classes possess features, which have a name and a cardinality, and there are three kinds of features: properties, attributes and semi-associations.

In this chapter, we introduce and discuss additional details about features, some of which apply equally to all three kinds.

© Springer International Publishing AG 2018

C. Gonzalez-Perez, *Information Modelling for Archaeology and Anthropology*,
https://doi.org/10.1007/978-3-319-72652-6_11

Sorted Features

Imagine that you want to represent the fact that a book may have multiple authors. You can use an association between *Book* and *Person* with a cardinality 1..*. This is a good start, but it does not allow us to represent the order of the authors in the book. The authors of a book have a meaningful order, and we should not change it. This is not so in other cases; for example, the trees of a forest or the houses in a town do not have a clear and precisely defined order. In those cases where a collection of things must be represented with a strict order, we can mark the corresponding feature as *sorted*. See the diagram in Fig. 11.1. Here, the "^" sign (called a circumflex accent or, informally, a caret) next to the cardinality of the *Person* class signals the fact that authors of a book are sorted. In other words, a book with three authors would have a first author, then a second and then a third one, and this order is meaningful. Similarly, the "^" sign after the cardinality for the *Person.FamilyName* attribute indicates that a person's family names have a meaningful order: there is a first family name and then a second family name.

Evidently, sorted features have always a maximum cardinality greater than one, because it would not make sense to sort a single item. Sorted features are not very common, and sometimes, you can employ alternative ways to model them which are more readable or elegant. For example, see the model depicted in Fig. 11.2.

Fig. 11.1 In this model, the authors of a book are sorted, as indicated by the "^" sign next to the *Person* cardinality. Also, a person's family names are sorted too

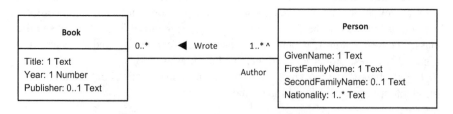

Fig. 11.2 In this model, the sorted *Person.FamilyName* attribute from Fig. 11.1 has been replaced by two separate attributes for the first and second family names

Here, we have replaced the sorted *Person.FamilyName* attribute from Fig. 11.1 with two separate attributes for the first and second family names. This allows us to be more expressive in the model and distinguish more readily between first and second surnames. Of course, this strategy would not be an option if the maximum cardinality were higher than two, because we should not add too many attributes to a class, especially if a maximum is not clearly known.

Strong Semi-Associations

In Chap. 8, we described how associations help us represent the connections between categories in a model. Sometimes, associations correspond to connections between well differentiated categories that have autonomous existence; some other times, however, associations represent connections that tie together parts of a complex or aggregate concept. The association in Fig. 11.2, for example, is of the first type: books and persons are very different things, and the *Wrote* association represents a connection between these very different things. Consider now the example in Fig. 11.3. This represents the fact that monuments may undergo different changes over their lifetime. The *Change* class has a *Date* attribute to capture when a change has occurred and a *Description* attribute to describe the change. Also, *Change* is associated with *Monument* so that we can know which changes affect which monuments. The short arrow with a circular base next to *Change*, in addition, indicates that the semi-association in this direction is *strong*; that is, the definition of *Change* relies strongly on *Monument*. For example, we could have a definition as follows.

A change is an event that modifies one or more monument in a significant manner.

Note that the definition of *Change* directly mentions *Monument*. Without a clear idea of what a monument is, the concept of change would remain poorly defined. To reflect the fact that *Change* depends so much on *Monument*, we say that the semi-association representing which monuments are affected by a change is a strong one. In other words, we can say that a strong semi-association, despite being a semi-association as any other, binds the two classes together in an especially tight fashion; in our example, *Monument* is almost part of *Change*. You may think that

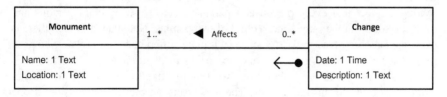

Fig. 11.3 The short arrow with a round base next to *Change* indicates a strong semi-association

this is counter-intuitive and that it is *Change* what is part of *Monument*, since common sense tells us that "monuments have changes". However, we are defining classes here, rather than objects, and therefore, we must describe things at the category (rather than entity) level. It is true that "monuments have changes", but from a category perspective, it is the *Change* category which "has", or mentions, the *Monument* category and hence the strong semi-association from *Change* to *Monument*.

The concept of strong semi-association is similar, but different, to that of whole/part association that we described in Chap. 8. In both cases, classes are tightly related to each other. However, whole/part associations denote a structural dependency by which instances of one class, the part, contribute to making up instances of the other class, the whole. This is the case, for example, of a forest and its trees, or a town and its buildings. Note that the fact that a structural relationship of aggregation exists does not mean that we need to define one class in terms of the other, which is what strong semi-associations are about. And, conversely, a class that is defined in terms of another (and, therefore, has a strong semi-association to it) does not need to be an aggregate, as shown by the example in Fig. 11.3. Having said this, you can have whole/part associations which, at the same time, are strong. Also, you cannot have an association where both semi-associations are "whole", but you can have an association where both semi-associations are strong. However, this would result in two tightly coupled classes, since each of them would be defined in terms of the other.

In any case, a strong semi-association usually entails a very clear consequence: instances of the "source" class do not make sense in the absence of accompanying instances of the "target" class. In our example of Fig. 11.3, an isolated change does not make sense; it necessarily needs an accompanying monument to provide the required context. Use strong semi-associations sparingly, since they introduce very tight couplings between classes, which may be detrimental to model quality as we will describe in Chap. 31.

Symmetric Self-Associations

In Chap. 8, we introduced the concept of self-associations, that is associations which connect a class to itself. Figure 11.4 illustrates two of these associations. Diagram A in Fig. 11.4 depicts a well-formed and meaningful association, representing the fact that every person is a parent of zero to many child persons and every person is, at the same time, a child of two parents. Note that, although there is only one class involved in the association, it plays different roles in relation to each semi-association. In other words, and according to diagram A in Fig. 11.4, each conceivable person instance will have two sets of linked persons: one for his/her children and one for his/her parents. These two sets are mutually exclusive: if one person is my child, then this person cannot possibly be my parent, and vice versa. For this reason, self-associations like this are called *asymmetric*.

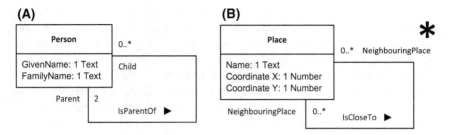

Fig. 11.4 Two self-associations. In **A**, an asymmetric self-association with two distinct roles. In **B**, a symmetric self-association with the same role on both ends. The asterisk indicates that this is an illegal model

See now diagram B in Fig. 11.4. Here, we are trying to represent the fact that every place may have a number of neighbouring places, or places which are close to it. How we define "close to" or "neighbouring" is irrelevant to this example. Note that, in this case, the roles played by the class are identical for both ends, because if a place is close to another, then this second place must necessarily be close to the original one. That is, each conceivable place instance will have a single set of linked places, namely its neighbours. For this reason, self-associations like this are called *symmetric*. The model in part B of Fig. 11.4, however, is illegal, as marked by the large asterisk next to it, because a class cannot have multiple semi-associations with identical role names. Fortunately, ConML provides a specific way to represent symmetric self-associations. Before we describe it, let us bear in mind what a symmetric self-association means. First of all, and by definition, the two semi-associations of a symmetric self-association look identical to each other: they have the same role, the same cardinality and even the same name and definition. For example, you need to describe both semi-associations of the self-association in part A of Fig. 11.4 if you want to provide its complete details and semantics; one semi-association will provide details in one direction, and its inverse will describe the other. However, you only need to describe the association in part B of Fig. 11.4 in one direction to achieve similar results, because the description in the inverse direction would be identical. For this reason, the two semi-associations of a symmetric self-association are, in fact, only one, which is an inverse of itself. See Fig. 11.5.

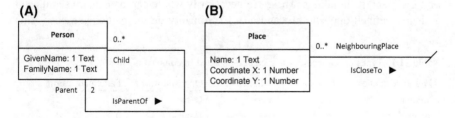

Fig. 11.5 Using Fig. 11.4 as a starting point, we have now redefined part **B** by using an asymmetric self-association

Here, the line going out of the *Place* class and ending in a slanted segment represents a symmetric self-association. Note that a single name, cardinality and role are depicted, meaning that only one semi-association is involved. In this manner, part B in Fig. 11.5 represents the fact that every place may be close to zero or more other places, which are called its neighbours.

Symmetric self-associations are quite common. Think, for example, of an archaeological site and all the sites that are visible from it, or an author and his/her co-authors, or a person and his/her spouse. All these cases correspond to symmetric self-associations.

> **Technical**
> Interestingly, UML is unable to model symmetric self-associations, because UML requires that associations have at least two "ends" and that each "end" has a different "name" or role. If you use UML, there is no way in which you can represent this kind of associations in your models.

Compact Notation for Associations

So far, we have been using lines in our diagrams to represent associations, as shown, for example, in Fig. 11.3. This is convenient and conveys very well the idea that an association represents a connection between two things. However, diagrams can grow very intricate if we use lines to depict every association, especially in the case of classes that are connected to many others. Think, for example, of a *Location* class that is used by many other classes in the model to describe the location of something, be it a site, a town, an artefact or an event. Having lines from all these classes to *Location* would result in a messy and unreadable diagram.

For this reason, ConML offers the possibility to use a *compact notation* for very common types of associations that usually occur for classes that are connected to many others. There are three particular cases, described in Table 11.1.

The first kind of association that can be depicted in compact notation corresponds to "contains" associations. These occur whenever instances of a class contain or aggregate instances of the related class, for example a forest and its trees, or a town and its buildings. These are necessarily whole/part associations and need a clearly defined opposite role and a 0..1 cardinality on the participant class. This

Table 11.1 Types of associations that can be depicted in compact notation

Overall semantics	Keyword	Whole/part	Opposite role	Participant cardinality
Contains	*con*	Yes	Defined	0..1
Shares	*sha*	Yes	Defined	0..*
Refers to	*ref*	No	Defined	0..*

(A)

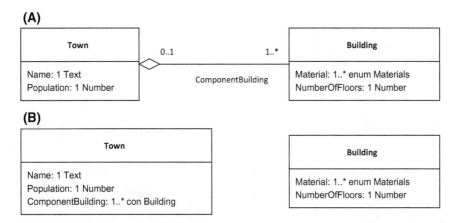

(B)

Fig. 11.6 A "Contains" association expressed in expanded (regular) notation in **A** and in compact notation in **B**. The two diagrams are completely equivalent, but we save one line in **B**

means that the contained object is exclusively "owned" by the container. See Fig. 11.6. In part B, note that the "contains" association is depicted as an extra line of text inside the lower section of the *Town* class box. Evidently, this shows the association from the perspective of only one class; as shown in part B of Fig. 11.6, only the *Town* class shows signs of its association to *Building*. We have chosen *Town* instead of *Building* because it is towns which contain buildings, rather than the other way around. A "contains" association in compact form takes the following form:

OppositeRole: Cardinality *con* OppositeClassName

The opposite role is, precisely, the role that we have defined for the opposite class in the association. The cardinality is whatever cardinality the opposite class has in the association, *con* is a special word in ConML to indicate a "contains" association in compact form, and the opposite class name indicates which other class is involved in the association. The cardinality of the participant class (*Town* in our example) is omitted, because it is always 0..1 for "contains" associations, as shown in Table 11.1, indicating exclusive containment.

The second kind of association that can be depicted in compact notation corresponds to "shares" associations. These occur whenever instances of a class contain or aggregate instances of the related class in a shared manner, for example a group of people and its members, or a house and its inhabitants. Like in the previous case, these are necessarily whole/part associations and need a clearly defined opposite role and a 0..* cardinality on the participant class. This means that

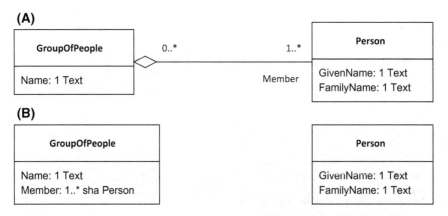

Fig. 11.7 A "Shares" association expressed in expanded (regular) notation in **A** and in compact notation in **B**. The two diagrams are completely equivalent, but we save one line in **B**

the contained object is not exclusively "owned" by the container, but potentially shared among many of them. Consider Fig. 11.7. In part B, note that the "shares" association is depicted as an extra line of text inside the lower section of the *GroupOfPeople* class box. As in the previous case, this shows the association from the perspective of only one class; as shown in part B of Fig. 11.7, only the *GroupOfPeople* class shows signs of its association to *Person*. We have chosen *GroupOfPeople* instead of *Person* because it is groups which contain people, not the other way around. A "shares" association in compact form takes the following form:

OppositeRole: Cardinality *sha* OppositeClassName

The opposite role is, precisely, the role that we have defined for the opposite class in the association. The cardinality is whatever cardinality the opposite class has in the association, *sha* is a special word in ConML to indicate a "shares" association in compact form, and the opposite class name indicates which other class is involved in the association. The cardinality of the participant class (*GroupOfPeople* in our example) is omitted, because it is always 0..* for "shares" associations, as shown in Table 11.1, indicating shared aggregation.

The last kind of associations that may be depicted compactly corresponds to "refers to" associations. These occur when instances of a class refer to instances of the related class, for example a building and its location, or a change and the monuments to which it applies. These associations are never whole/part and, like in the previous case, need a clearly defined opposite role; the cardinality on the participant class is always 0..*. See Fig. 11.8.

(A)

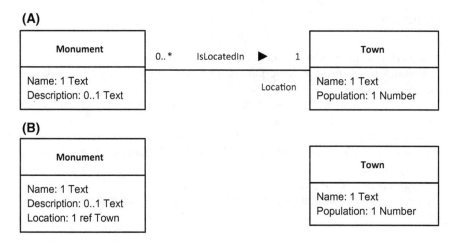

(B)

Fig. 11.8 **A** "refers to" association expressed in expanded (regular) notation in **A** and in compact notation in **B**. The two diagrams are completely equivalent, but we save one line in **B**

In part B, note that the "refers to" association is depicted as an extra line of text inside the lower section of the *Monument* class box. Like in the previous case, this shows the association from the perspective of only one class, *Monument* in our example. Again, we have chosen *Monument* instead of *Town* because it is monuments which refer to towns in order to express their locations, rather than the other way around. A "refers to" association in compact form takes the following form:

OppositeRole: Cardinality *ref* OppositeClassName

Like in the previous case, the opposite role is the role that we have defined for the opposite class in the association, and the cardinality is whatever cardinality the opposite class has in the association. The special word *ref* indicates a "refers to" association in compact form, and the opposite class name indicates which other class is involved in the association. Also, like in the previous case, the cardinality of the participant class (*Monument* in our example) is omitted, because it is always 0..* for "refers to" associations, as shown in Table 11.1.

Compact notation for associations can save you from drawing many lines in a diagram, thus resulting in a tidier and more readable diagram. However, be aware that compact notation "buries" associations inside classes, which may hinder the visibility of the overall structure of the model. Also, bear in mind that the role of the participant class or the names of the semi-associations cannot be shown when using compact notation, which may be a serious drawback sometimes. Use your judgement to decide whether to use compact or expanded notation for associations that permit it.

Summary

A **feature** is either a property, an attribute, or a semi-association.

Features which must preserve the order of their instances must be marked as **sorted** in a model.

Semi-associations that connect a class to another that is mentioned on its definition should be marked as **strong**.

Some self-associations involve a single role and therefore a single semi-association; they are called **symmetric self-associations**, and there is a special notation for them.

Associations with overall semantics of "contains", "shares" or "refers to" can be depicted through a **compact notation**, which results in tidier diagrams.

Exercises

15. Create a type model to represent the concept of 'person', including a person's phone numbers and jobs. Bear in mind that a person may have multiple phone numbers such as home, work, etc. Also consider that a person may have, at most, a primary job and a secondary job. Use sorted features where you see fit.
16. Create a type model to represent the fact that heritage elements may be assessed over time by different people, each assessment being about one particular heritage element. Include in your model classes for heritage elements, assessment and people. Mark which semi-associations are strong.
17. Imagine that you are studying a group of artists and their works. Some artists may have met others during their life; also, some artists may have studied under other artists. Create a type model for the concept of 'artist' and include associations for the two situations described above. Use symmetric self-associations where suitable.
18. Imagine that you are surveying an area and recording archaeological sites and the associated material. Each archaeological site is located at a particular place, and each find corresponds to a particular site. Draw a diagram for this situation, including classes to represent sites, places and finds. Use compact notation for associations where appropriate.

Chapter 12
Advanced Generalization

Abstract In this chapter, we elaborate on the notions of generalization and specialization, already introduced in earlier chapters. First, we explain that a class may not have multiple specializations, but it can have multiple generalizations. We describe how classes participating in multiple generalizations inherit features via all of them simultaneously, and how the concept of *dominant* generalization plays a major role in this mechanism. We also describe some scenarios where classes may be deemed illegal as a consequence of their place in a specialization structure, especially due to feature name clashes.

In Chap. 9, we introduced generalization/specialization relationships and described how they work as the basis to organize classes in meaningful specialization hierarchies. We said that a class may be specialized or not but, if it is, then it can have only one specialization (usually with multiple specialized classes) according to a well-known discriminant. In other words, a class cannot be specialized multiple times. However, and as we mentioned in passing, a class may have multiple generalizations. In this chapter, we explain what this means and what consequences it entails. We also discuss some special situation that can appear when constructing complex specialization hierarchies.

Multiple Generalization

Imagine that we want to create a model to represent the concept of 'feature' in archaeology, and that we have arrived to the following definition for the *Feature* class:

> *A feature is a place having boundaries with material properties that distinguish it from its surroundings and, also, a material entity that shapes the space where it is located, influencing visibility and/or mobility over it.*

© Springer International Publishing AG 2018

C. Gonzalez-Perez, *Information Modelling for Archaeology and Anthropology*,

https://doi.org/10.1007/978-3-319-72652-6_12

115

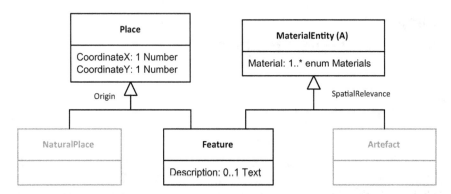

Fig. 12.1 The *Feature* class has two superclasses, which means that it is involved in two separate generalization relationships

You may or may not agree with this definition, but let us assume it is acceptable for the sake of argument. Note that the definition has two parts:

- "…a place having boundaries with material properties that distinguish it from its surroundings…"
- "…a material entity that shapes the space where it is located, influencing visibility and/or mobility over it".

Each of these two parts is in genus plus differentia form. The first part states that a feature is a kind of place, and the second says that a feature is a kind of material entity. Remember from Chap. 9 that the genus in the definition of a class refers to the same concept as the class' superclass. This means that *Feature*, having a two-part definition, must have two superclasses. Look at Fig. 12.1. Here, the *Feature* class participates in two separate generalization relationships. On the one hand, it is a subclass of *Place* according to *Origin*, together with its sibling class *NaturalPlace*, because natural places are not human made, whereas features are human made. On the other hand, *Feature* is a subclass of *MaterialEntity* according to *SpatialSignificance* together with its sibling *Artefact*, since features are spatially mediated whereas artefacts are not. Again, the point here is not whether this conceptualization is good or not, but to focus on the fact that a class, *Feature*, is defined through a double generalization.

Note that, because of the double generalization, the rule of inheritance that we introduced in Chap. 9 applies to *Feature* through both of its superclasses. The rule says that anything that we may say about a class also applies to all its subclasses. As a consequence, *Feature* in our example inherits simultaneously via two paths: it inherits the *CoordinateX* and *CoordinateY* attributes from *Place*, and also the *Material* attribute from *MaterialEntity*. This makes sense since, according to its definition, a feature is both a place and a material entity and, as such, is expected to have coordinates (as any other place) and be made of matter (as any other material entity).

Technical

Multiple generalization is often named "multiple inheritance" in the conceptual modelling and object-oriented programming literature. Although it is true that multiple generalization entails multiple inheritance, they are not the same thing. Generalization is a structural relationship between classes, whereas inheritance is a phenomenon that occurs as a consequence of generalization. For this reason, we think that the term "multiple generalization" is more expressive, since it points to the root issue rather than one of its consequences. If you are not a purist, then you can assume that, for practical matters, both "multiple generalization" and "multiple inheritance" mean the same.

In our example above, *Feature* is defined as a blend of two things, and as a consequence, it has two separate generalization relationships. In theory, it is possible that a class has an even larger number of generalizations, although this is very rare. Even classes like *Feature* here, with a double generalization, are uncommon. In addition, it is often possible to argue that a class with double or multiple generalization can better be modelled through aggregation. Consider the example depicted in Fig. 12.2. In this example, the same situation has been modelled in two different manners: through multiple generalization, and through aggregation. In Fig. 12.2A, we can see the same solution as in Fig. 12.1. In B, however, the generalization relationships have been replaced by whole/part associations with a cardinality of 1. The difference is crucial: in A, we are saying that a feature is a kind of place and also a kind of material entity. As such, *Feature* inherits everything from its superclasses. In B, on the other hand, we are saying that a feature contains, or is composed of, a place and a material entity. In consequence, *Feature* does not inherit anything from *Place* and *MaterialEntity*. A hybrid solution where *Feature* would have a single generalization towards either *Place* or *MaterialEntity*, plus a whole/part association with the other, is also possible; in this case, we would be saying that a feature is a kind of place and contains a material entity (or the other way around). Also, solutions where plan associations, instead of whole/part associations, are used, are also possible. Which solution is best depends on the semantics of the particular classes involved, the purpose of the model, and its overall structure. When trying to decide, look at how we refer to the involved concepts in spoken language; does it make sense to say that "a feature is located in a place"? Does it make sense to say that "a feature is a material entity"?

Multiple generalization is a very powerful technique that can solve very specific situations when needed. However, try not to overuse it.

Fig. 12.2 Multiple generalization and aggregation. In **A**, *Feature* is defined as being a kind of place and also a kind of material entity. In **B**, *Feature* is defined as being composed of a place (its location) plus a material entity (its materiality)

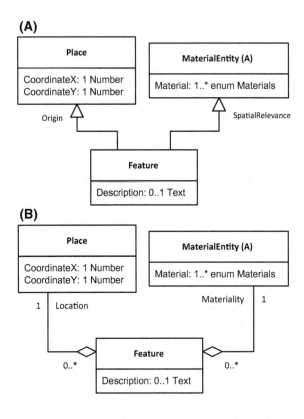

Dominant Generalizations

The fact that a class may have multiple superclasses opens the door to a number of potential issues. For example, look at the situation in Fig. 12.3.

Here, our running example has been extended to include a top-level class, *ArchaeologicalEntity*, bearing an *Id* attribute to represent the fact that we want to assign a unique identifier to any archaeological entity that is recorded. This may seem an innocent move, but consider the following. Both *Place* and *MaterialEntity* inherit the *Id* attribute. In addition, *Feature* inherits everything from *Place* and *MaterialEntity*, which now includes the *Id* attribute for each of them. This means that *Feature* would seem to inherit the *Id* attribute twice, once through *Place* and once through *MaterialEntity*. This would not make sense, since we do not want to have entities with two identifiers; also, a class cannot have multiple attributes having the same name. This situation is often called the "diamond problem" in the conceptual modelling literature, since the four classes involved are usually arranged in a diamond shape.

ConML solves the diamond problem by asking you, the modeller, to decide which of the generalizations of *Feature* should dominate in case of conflict. We said in the previous section that a feature is both a place and a material entity, and hence the double generalization. But we did not specify any priority. Now we must think about this. Is a feature mainly a place, which also has something of a material entity? Or, to the contrary, is a feature mostly a material entity that also has a touch

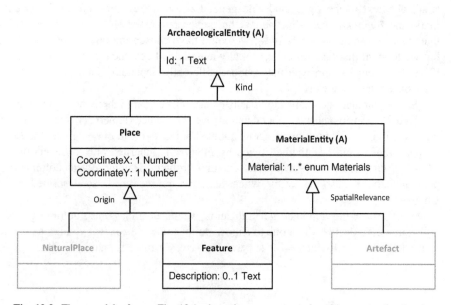

Fig. 12.3 The model from Fig. 12.1 has been augmented with a top-level class *ArchaeologicalEntity*. In this situation, *Feature* is subject to the "diamond problem"

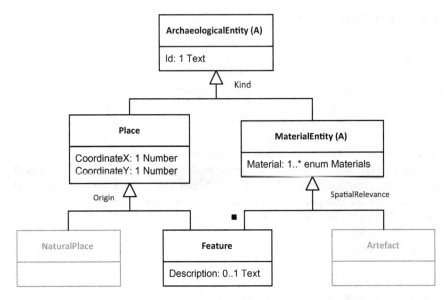

Fig. 12.4 The model from Fig. 12.3 has been completed by marking the dominant generalization for *Feature* with a selector dot

of place? Depending on the purpose of the model and our conceptualization of the involved categories, we must choose one or the other. Look at Fig. 12.4. Here, the small dot next to the right-hand side generalization line coming out of *Feature* marks the *dominant generalization*. We have chosen to make *MaterialEntity*, rather than *Place*, dominate over *Feature*; we could have chosen the other way around, but we thought that features are essentially material entities, their place component being secondary. Again, you may choose differently depending on your purpose and conceptual framework.

Once a dominant generalization has been established, any inheritance conflict is resolved by prioritising this generalization over any other (remember that a class may potentially have multiple generalizations, not just two). In our example, the *Id* attribute that would be inherited twice by *Feature* is inherited only once via the *MaterialEntity* path, thus solving the diamond problem. Having a clear dominant generalization is also necessary when features are redefined, as described in Chap. 17.

Always mark the dominant generalization whenever a class has multiple generalizations. To decide which one to choose, think about the concept you are trying to model, and select which of its superclasses gives it more semantic weight.

Other Inheritance Issues

In addition to the diamond problem, there are some situations where inheritance conflicts yield invalid models. Consider the situation depicted in Fig. 12.5.

Here, the *HeritageElement.Name* attribute is inherited by *Object* and *Agent* and then, in turn, by *Person*. However, *Person* declares a *Name* attribute of itself. This would cause two attributes with the same name to coexist in the same class, which is illegal. In general, if a feature inherited by a class results in a name clash with a feature owned by the class, the class is deemed illegal. Note that situations like these are unlikely to happen, because the fact that two features (such as the attributes in our example) share the same name indicates that they probably have very similar semantics. If this is the case, you should rethink your model and consolidate the two attributes into a single one, which would immediately solve the problem. Alternatively, you can find a better name for one of the involved features (or both) if they truly have different semantics.

A similar situation can occur when the conflict is between different features in different classes. Consider the example in Fig. 12.6. Here, the *Feature* class inherits two different attributes that happen to have the same name. Note that this is different from the diamond problem described in the previous section. In the diamond problem, one attribute is inherited twice via different paths; now, we have two different attributes with the same name. As long as these attributes are kept in their respective classes (*Structure* and *Place* in the example), there is no problem. But when a class is introduced that inherits from both, a clash ensues, producing an invalid model. If you find a problem like this, you should rename at least one of the attributes so that inheritance does not result in a name clash.

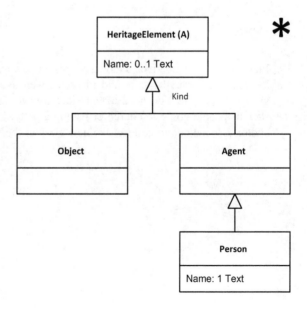

Fig. 12.5 The *Person* class inherits a *Name* attribute, which clashes with its own *Name* attribute. The asterisk indicates that this is an invalid model

Fig. 12.6 The *Feature* class
inherits two different
Description attributes via
different paths. The two
attributes clash once inherited.
The asterisk indicates that this
is an invalid model

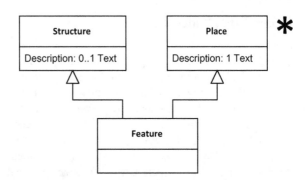

Summary

A class may not have multiple specializations, but it can have **multiple generalizations**.

When a class participates in multiple generalizations, it inherits via all of them simultaneously.

In a class with multiple generalizations, one of the must be marked as **dominant**, so that clashes due to features inherited through multiple paths can be resolved.

If a feature inherited by a class results in a name clash with a feature owned by the class, the class is deemed illegal.

If a feature inherited by a class from a given ancestor class results in a name clash with a different feature inherited by the class from a second ancestor class, the class is deemed illegal.

Exercises

19. Imagine that you are given a model having an *Event* class to describe things that happen in a particular time and place, as well as a *Group* class to describe groups of people. You need to introduce a new class to represent social acts such as people going to church or having a party. Use multiple generalization and/or associations to connect the new class to the existing ones.

Chapter 13
Model Architecture

Abstract In this chapter, we deal with the issue of organizing large and complex models so that they are easier to use and maintain. We introduce the notion of model *architecture*, which refers to the way in which we organize a model into a meaningful structure, so that classes and other elements are easy to locate and change. We explain how *packages* can be used to provide a model with a good architecture. Packages are groups of classes and enumerated types that share a common theme. For example, we can put all the classes related to interventions (such as *Excavation* or *Survey*) in a model about archaeology data management into an *Interventions* package.

The examples that we have been using so far to illustrate concepts and propose exercises involve very simple models of only a few classes. However, models created to solve real-world scenarios can grow much larger, sometimes in the hundreds or even thousands of classes. As you can imagine, managing a model that large can get complicated. Tasks such as adding a new class or altering the way in which two classes are associated can have unexpected effects on other areas of the model. To mitigate this and fight against complexity, the notion of model architecture must be introduced. *Model architecture* refers to the way in which we organize a model into a meaningful structure, so that classes and other elements are easy to locate and change according to some clear principles. Imagine a type model of a few hundred classes interconnected by dozens of associations. In the absence of architecture, the classes and association would make up a homogeneous mesh, in which everything is connected to everything in a more or less direct fashion. A good architecture would arrange these classes into meaningful groups, so that classes inside a group would be closely related, whereas classes of different groups, while still being related, would hold a much weaker connection.

In this manner, architecture gives "texture" to a model by creating "lumps" of classes and other elements. A model without an architecture is like a book with no chapters or paragraph breaks; finding or changing something is extremely difficult. Contrarily, a model with a well-designed architecture is similar to a book with a clear chapter structure and nicely separated paragraphs: finding information and

© Springer International Publishing AG 2018

C. Gonzalez-Perez, *Information Modelling for Archaeology and Anthropology*,

https://doi.org/10.1007/978-3-319-72652-6_13

changing it becomes much easier. Of course, architecture becomes more relevant as a model grows larger. Since you can never foresee how large your models will grow, it is good practice to consider architectural principles from the beginning, since retrofitting an architecture into a model that has grown large without one is often tedious and difficult.

Technical

The ability to provide structure through architecture is one of the biggest advantages of using conceptual modelling to represent the world at a high level of abstraction over the usage of data encoding techniques such as linked data by themselves. Using RDF [33], for example, data is viewed as a collection of subject–predicate–object triples, where any of the triple components may point to a resource or data type, and object components may additionally contain a literal. This allows for the construction of interlinked data "atoms" in more or less large meshes. However, there is no way to provide coarse-grained structure to these meshes. Conversely, conceptual modelling provides several levels of granularity and texture: for example, objects encapsulate atomic data values; whole/part associations create larger aggregates; and packages, as we discuss in this chapter, can organize related classes together. Other mechanisms such as patterns or clusters, which we describe in further chapters, also help in architecting a conceptual model.

Packages

In order to organize classes and other elements into meaningful groups in a type model, we use *packages*.

We define a package as follows:

Definition

A *package* is a group of related classes, enumerated types and possibly sub-packages.

As its name indicates, a package packs together classes and enumerated types that are related in some manner. For example, imagine that we want to create a model to describe archaeological intervention processes. We would need a few classes to represent the archaeological features and elements on which interventions occur; we would also need a few classes to represent the excavations, surveys and other relevant processes that operate on the former, and finally, we would need some classes to describe the places and other spatially related concepts to help us locate where everything takes place. As you can see, it is easy to come up with a rough idea of what class groups may exist in the model. Each of these groups would become a package.

A package has a *name* which briefly describes what the package is about. In our previous example, we could name our packages *ArchaeologicalRecord*, *Interventions* and *Places*, for example. A package may also have a *description* that declares the common theme of the elements grouped by it.

Note that packages group together related classes and enumerated types. Other model elements, such as generalizations, attributes and associations, are grouped indirectly, since they are tightly connected to classes. For example, if we put our *Excavation* class into the *Interventions* package, then all the attributes and semi-associations of this class will also be in the package, albeit indirectly. Classes and enumerated types that belong to a package are usually referred to by using the package name as a prefix of their own name and using a colon as separator. For example, we would refer to the *Excavation* class in the *Interventions* package as *Interventions:Excavation*. If this class had a *Date* attribute, for example, we would refer to it as *Interventions:Excavation.Date*.

Packages are not meant to be isolated from each other; in fact, type models are usually continuous, so that it is possible to travel from any class to any other by navigating associations. In this regard, associations between classes may cross package boundaries and thus provide the "glue" between packages. Consider the situation shown in Fig. 13.1. There are three classes in the *Interventions* package and another three in the *Places* package. Note that each class is placed in a package together with classes of a common theme. Although an association connects classes of different packages, most relationships occur within packages. In this manner, we keep dependencies between packages under control. Dependencies and model quality are a complex topic on which we elaborate in Chap. 31.

Also in Fig. 13.1, note that package names are shown explicitly as part of class names, as we described above. This is convenient when you want to show classes

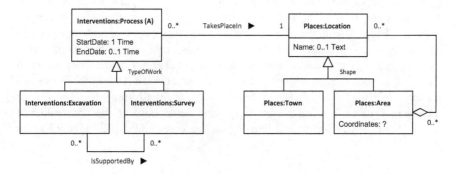

Fig. 13.1 A few classes in two different packages. Package names are used as prefixes to class names

package Interventions

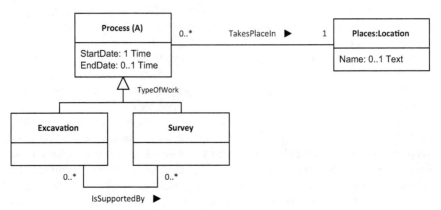

Fig. 13.2 Classes in the *Interventions* package plus an external class. Note the "package" declaration at the top left of the diagram

from different packages in a single diagram, but it can turn tedious when all the classes in your diagram belong to the same package. Imagine that you wanted to draw a diagram focusing on the *Interventions* package. You could do something like in Fig. 13.2. Here, an overall package declaration is made by writing the special word *package* followed by the package name that we are focussing on. Any class that is shown without an explicit package prefix to its name must be now interpreted as belonging to this declared package. You can still mix in some classes with explicit names, like *Places:Location* in the example.

In any case, bear in mind that packages are optional, that is, you can use packages to organize your models if you need to, or ignore them if not necessary. Most simple models with ten or twenty classes perhaps do not strictly need packages. Still, add them if you plan to grow your model or if there is a neat grouping of classes that you want to make.

Finally, packages can be nested. If you look again at the definition of package at the beginning of this section, you will see that it mentions subpackages. A "subpackage" is simply a package that is nested inside another package. You can use this to organize classes and enumerated types in very large models into hierarchical groups. For example, imagine that we develop our model from earlier in this section much further, adding a few dozen classes in the *ArchaeologicalRecord* package. We may want to add different subpackages to group together classes related to features, artefacts, stratigraphy and other areas of the archaeological record. Subpackages are named like regular packages and usually referred to by using the same prefix system described above for packaged elements. For example, our package about stratigraphy would be referred to as *ArchaeologicalRecord: Stratigraphy*, and the *Deposit* class inside it would be referred to as *ArchaeologicalRecord:Stratigraphy:Deposit.*

Summary

Providing a model with a clear and well-designed **architecture** is very important and absolutely crucial if the model is complex.

Packages are groups of classes and enumerated types that share a common theme.

Packages are optional and can be nested inside other packages.

Exercises

20. Take the model in Fig. 13.1 as a basis, and complete it by adding a *Team* class to represent the teams that carry out interventions, as well as a *Report* class to represent the documents generated by these teams. Put these classes in an existing package or create a new package if you think it is necessary.

Chapter 14
Vagueness

Abstract In this chapter, we deal with the fact that many aspects of the world are unclear, imprecise or not well defined, and when we try to represent them in a model, we are often confronted with the need to either remove or explicitly manage this vagueness. To this end, we introduce two kinds of vagueness: ontological and epistemic, the first dealing with entities that are naturally imprecise, and the second dealing with the fact that our knowledge about things is not always complete and accurate. To help in dealing with vagueness, we introduce null and unknown semantics. By using the *null* special keyword in a model, we can state that a fact does not exist; by using the *unknown* special keyword, we can state that a fact exists, but we are not aware of what it is. Then, we move on to describe some specific techniques to express ontological and epistemic vagueness in conceptual models. We focus on the use of abstract enumerated items (introduced in an earlier chapter), arbitrary time resolution, and the explicit modelling of vague situations through classes and features.

Conceptual modelling is a highly analytical technique through which we break reality down into small parts in order to represent it. Traditionally, and especially in engineering areas, conceptual modelling has excelled at capturing extremely well-detailed pictures of the world; however, it has struggled with vagueness. Despite our analytical efforts, many aspects of the world are unclear, imprecise or not well defined. When we try to represent them in a model, we are often confronted with the need to make arbitrary decisions in order to remove the vagueness. For example, think of something as simple as a hill that you are familiar with. This hill is probably a very clear entity to you, and you will probably even give it a name to individuate it from other entities. However, hills do not have clearly established boundaries. For example, is the slope part of the hill? How far do we need to walk to stop calling the place a hill? We may resort to administrative or legal boundaries to solve this, but these boundaries are themselves the result of an arbitrary decision made by someone according to some criteria. Depending on who you ask, what criteria you use and what your purpose is, your hill may encompass little or much territory.

© Springer International Publishing AG 2018

C. Gonzalez-Perez, *Information Modelling for Archaeology and Anthropology*,
https://doi.org/10.1007/978-3-319-72652-6_14

Vagueness has traditionally represented a problem for conceptual modelling, and the usual approach to dealing with it has been to ignore it or to simplify our conceptions of reality so that most vagueness is removed. Although this approach is useful in some scenarios, it should not be used all the time. ConML attempts to address vagueness through a few mechanisms that we introduce in this chapter.

Ontological and Epistemic Vagueness

The first thing we need to consider when discussing vagueness is that it comes in two flavours. On the one hand, there is ontological vagueness, also called *imprecision*, which refers to things in the world that are not clear-cut. A good example is that of natural places: if you are sitting at the top of our above-mentioned hill, you may certainly state that you are on the hill. If you are sitting at the bottom of the valley next to the hill, you can safely say that you are not on the hill anymore. Between these two extremes, there is a gradient of imprecision, so that if you start walking downhill from the top towards the valley, it is difficult, or even impossible, to determine when you stop being on the hill and start being outside it. In fact, "on the hill" and "outside the hill" are simplifications that do not make much sense when we are dealing with continuous phenomena. The sorites paradox [3, "Sorites Paradox"] is a well-known manifestation of this. This paradox says that if we take a grain of sand out of a big heap, the heap will still be a heap, because removing a single grain from a large heap does not make it stop being a heap. Using this logic and repeating the process, we can take a second grain, and the heap will still be a heap. The paradox becomes evident as we keep going until we have removed all the grains of sand in the heap and still claim that there is a heap where nothing is left. The error here is to assume that 'being a heap' is a clear-cut predicate, when it is not. Because of the nature of the 'heap' concept, whether something is a heap or not is imprecise. Similarly, the boundaries of a city or a hill are also imprecise. In summary, we define ontological vagueness as follows.

> **Definition**
> *A characteristic of a category is **ontologically vague**, or **imprecise**, if any statement about an entity of this category stays true even when the quality expressed for said characteristic varies.*

Think about the surface area of a city. According to our definition above, the *City.Area* attribute is imprecise, because we can make statement about a given city *c* such as *c.Area = 8512* and *c.Area = 8592* and, despite the variation, both of them are true.

On the other hand, there is epistemic vagueness, or *uncertainty*, which refers to situations where our knowledge about something is unclear or incomplete. For example, we can use radiocarbon techniques to date the age of an artefact, but the results will invariably contain an error margin, so that our knowledge about the artefact's age will be vague. Note that it is not the artefact age what is vague here; in fact, that particular artefact has a very precise age. On the contrary, it is our knowledge about it that is vague. Consider another example: we usually estimate population sizes of cities or villages through rough approximations such as in "Sydney has 5 million people"; however, there is a particular number of people, down to the very last digit, who are registered as Sydney dwellers at any moment. Since we do not know the exact number, and using it would be too cumbersome, we resort to a good enough approximation. This approximation contains uncertainty. In this manner, we define epistemic vagueness as follows.

Definition

*An object, value or reference is **epistemically vague**, or **uncertain**, if the belief that the statement represented by it is true is not complete.*

According to this, the value *s.Population* = *5.000.000*, where *s* stands for Sydney, is uncertain, because we are not completely sure that the statement is true.

There are a few differences between the two kinds of vagueness that we should consider. To start with, ontological vagueness affects some facts and phenomena, whereas epistemic vagueness affects *every* fact and phenomenon. There are characteristics, such as 'how many children Alexander the Great had', that contain no ontological vagueness: it was either zero, or one, or two, etc. However, any fact or phenomena are potentially known, unknown or partially unknown to us. This is why we say that epistemic vagueness is a cross-cutting concern that applies to anything, whereas ontological vagueness is an intrinsic property of some things only.

Note also that one good way to fight against epistemic vagueness is to use inaccuracy. For example, if we are not sure about the number of children of Alexander the Great, we can say that "he had between 2 and 5" and be pretty safe. Giving an interval is less accurate than giving a fixed number, and therefore more encompassing, so the chances that the true answer falls within the interval are larger. In other words, by decreasing accuracy we increase the chances that what we state is true, and this way we diminish uncertainty.

In addition, and in relation to the previous, ontological vagueness is universal, in the sense that, being intrinsic to the facts or phenomena, it will always be the same regardless of who observes or describes these facts or phenomena. Contrarily, epistemic vagueness is related to our knowledge about things, so that it will vary subjectively depending on who observes or describes something. In other words, you may know very well how many children Alexander the Great had, but I may ignore it or have doubts about it.

However, both ontological and epistemic vagueness admit degrees. That is to say, a fact can be more or less imprecise, and a value or object may be more or less uncertain. Vagueness is gradual rather than a black and white phenomenon.

Null and Unknown Semantics

To help deal with vagueness, ConML incorporates two special words that we can use to describe values and objects: *null* and *unknown*. We introduced *null* in Chap. 4 when discussing objects with non-existing values. We now complete this with additional scenarios and in opposition to *unknown*.

We can use *null* in a model to state that a value or an object does not exist. Existence pertains to the ontology of things. Consider the example in Fig. 14.1. Here, we write *Style = null* as part of object *b* to represent the fact that this building does not have a style. This does not mean that we do not know what style it is, but that it lacks a style altogether. Similarly, we write *Owner = unknown* as part of object *c* to indicate that this building does have an owner, but we do not know about them. As we explained in Chap. 6, a value may be null if its type attribute has a minimum cardinality of zero; this is the case for *Building.Style*. By deciding which attributes and semi-associations have zero minimum cardinalities when creating a type model, you are indicating which values and references may be null in any conforming instance model and thus capture a very rough form of ontological vagueness, that of simple absence. On the other hand, and as we said in the previous section, epistemic vagueness applies to everything, and so we can use *unknown* for any attribute or semi-association, regardless of its cardinality, in order to express epistemic vagueness. Fig. 14.1 uses compact notation for the *Owner* semi-association, but *unknown* can also be used with extended notation. See, for example, Fig. 14.2.

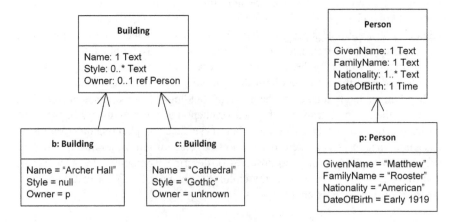

Fig. 14.1 Some objects showing *null* and *unknown* values and references

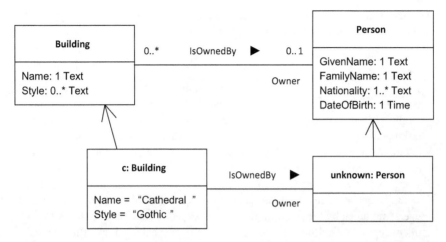

Fig. 14.2 The *Owner* semi-association in Fig. 14.1 is now depicted using extended notation. Note the *unknown* object on the bottom right

Here, the fact that building *c*'s owner is unknown is represented by an *IsOwnedBy* link from the *c* object to a person instance having *unknown* as identifier. Also, note that values for the *unknown* object are omitted. This object stands for *c*'s owner, which exists, but about which we know nothing.

Table 14.1 summarizes the meaning of *null* and *unknown*.

We also said in Chap. 4 that the concept of existence in conceptual modelling is rather informal. In fact, when we say that *null* means that a fact does not exist, and that *unknown* means that a fact does exist, we are talking about existence in the portion of the world that we are interested in. This may correspond to actual existence or not; for example, if we develop a model to describe British legends, we may include an object to represent the sword Excalibur. This sword exists as far as the model is concerned; that is, it is a part of the portion of reality that we are trying to model. Whether Excalibur is fictional or real does not matter in this context.

You must also bear in mind that values with some special contents may be easily confused with *null* or *unknown*, but they are different. For example, a value of zero for an attribute of type Number is a regular value and should not be confused with a *null* or *unknown* value. Similarly, a value of an empty text for an attribute of type Text is also a regular value, not related to *null* or *unknown*. In other words, *Description* = "" and *Description* = *null* are very different things: the former states

Table 14.1 Semantics of *null* and *unknown* as compared to non-vague information

Expression	Statement about fact	Statement about knowledge on fact	Example
null	Fact does not exist	n/a	Style = null
unknown	Fact exists	Fact is not known by us	Owner = unknown
(others)	Fact exists	Fact is known by us	Name = "Cathedral"

that there is a description, that we know about it, and that it is "" (an empty text); the latter states that there is no description.

> **Technical**
> If you are familiar with database development or computer programming, you may have come across situations where "magic" values such as zeros or empty strings are employed with special meanings, often used to indicate unknown or unavailable information. For example, a *Year* column in a database table holding excavation data may contain zeros to indicate that the excavation year is unknown. This is an implementation trick, which may work correctly if the necessary precautions (such as documenting it properly, writing special code to handle such cases or hiding them altogether from users) are taken by the programmer. However, you should not use these tricks in conceptual modelling because, conceptually, a special value is still a value. Instead, use *null* and *unknown* in your conceptual models as often as necessary and as described above.

Finally, we must remark that *null* and *unknown* are only very partial solutions to the problem of vagueness. In particular, *null* only allows us to state that something does not exist, but we cannot express degrees of imprecision, like in the case of the boundaries of a hill as exemplified above. Similarly, *unknown* is useful to declare that something is not known, but we cannot describe partial certainty or doubt. A comprehensive treatment of vagueness in conceptual modelling is not possible yet. We hope that additional research on this field will improve this situation over the next few years. The following sections, as well as Chap. 18 on metainformation, present additional techniques that can help us cope with vagueness in the meantime.

Using Abstract Enumerated Items

In Chap. 7, we introduced enumerated types and said that enumerated items can be organized in hierarchies. This is one of the examples we used:

```
WorldRegions:    Europe
                    France
                    Germany
                    Spain
                        Galicia
                            Lugo
                            Pontevedra
                        Andalusia
                 Asia
                    China
                    Japan
```

Hierarchical enumerated types, as we explained, may be used to represent subsumption or aggregation between items. In the example above, Galicia and

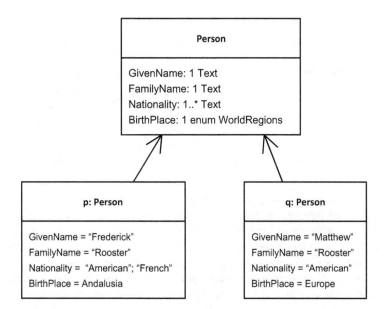

Fig. 14.3 Objects *p* and *q* use different levels of detail for the enumerated attribute *BirthPlace*

Andalusia are part of Spain, and Spain, together with France and Germany, is part of Europe. When we use an enumerated type like this to specify the location of something, we can choose what level of detail we want to use. Consider the situation in Fig. 14.3. Here, object *p* specifies the birthplace of the represented person by using a leaf enumerated item which, in this case, is at depth 2 in the hierarchy. Object *q*, however, uses an item at depth 0. As we said in Chap. 7, an item at depth 0 is much more abstract than an item at depth 2, and for this reason we can say that *p* is being more precise than *q* in the specification of its birthplace.

We can use varying depth of enumerated items to model different levels of vagueness, both ontological and epistemic. In the example above, we are using *Europe* as a value because we do not know exactly where Matthew Rooster (represented here by object *q*) was born. By stating *BirthPlace = Europe,* we are being purposefully inaccurate, and thus providing a representation of the world that is much less vague. Contrarily, we are sure that Frederick Rooster was born in Andalusia, so we can be much more accurate for object *p* and use a depth 2 enumerated item. This is a case of epistemic vagueness: the more details we have about something, the more accurate about it that we can be in the model and still be safe.

Hierarchical enumerated items can also be used to model ontological vagueness. Imagine, for example, that we want to express where the bell-beaker culture took place. We know that it happened in Western Europe, but its boundaries are naturally (ontologically) vague; for this reason, the best thing we can do is say *Europe* (or *WesternEurope* if this were an option in the enumerated type) instead of trying to be more specific. Note that, in this case, accuracy is not at play here, since we are dealing with an ontologically imprecise characteristic, rather than dealing with a relationship between a characteristic and our imperfect knowledge about it.

Sometimes, using abstract enumerated items can create ambiguous situations. For example, imagine that we are mapping language usage and, for a particular language, we state that *a.DistributionArea = Europe*. This may mean two things:

- The language is spoken in some uncertain area within Europe. We do not know where exactly, so we state *Europe* as an epistemically vague fact.
- The language is spoken throughout Europe. We are sure that it is spoken in the whole continent, so we state *Europe* as an epistemically certain fact.

The first interpretation entails epistemic vagueness, but the second does not. From the value statement *a.DistributionArea = Europe,* we cannot tell which one is the correct interpretation, and thus ambiguity ensues. Situations like these often appear when the enumerated type being used uses hierarchical items to represent aggregation, like in our world regions example. When the enumerated type represents subsumption, ambiguity rarely appears. In any case, be aware of the possibility of ambiguity and, if it exists, try to model your information in a different manner, as described at the end of this chapter.

Using Arbitrary Time Resolution

Another manner to express vagueness in a model is to use the arbitrary resolution of the Time data type. We described simple data types back in Chap. 6 and defined the Time type as one for which values are time points of any precision and not limited to the usual scheme of days, months, years, hours, minutes and seconds. Some example values could be *8 June 1917 at 17:30, May 2012* or *late twelfth century*. Since the Time type allows for a varying level of detail, we can choose to be more or less specific when stating a time "point". Consider the example in Fig. 14.4. Here, object *p* uses a quite detailed expression to describe Frederick Rooster's date of birth, since we have a high degree of confidence about it. However, object *q* uses a less detailed expression for Matthew Rooster's date of birth, because we are not as sure. We know he was born sometime in early 1919, so that is all we can state safely. Like in the case of hierarchical enumerated items, we are being purposefully inaccurate to gain in certainty and thus fight epistemic vagueness.

You can think of attributes of the Time type as being able to refer to any point in time, but this "point" can be as "thin" or "thick" as you need. However, note that, like in the case of abstract enumerated items, this may raise some ambiguities in certain situations. For example, imagine that we are trying to describe when a building was constructed, and that we express it as *b.ConstructionDate = late eighteenth century*. There are two potential interpretations for this:

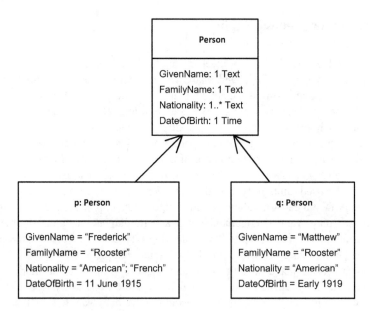

Fig. 14.4 Objects *p* and *q* use different levels of detail for the time-typed attribute *DateOfBirth*

- The building was constructed at some uncertain point within the late eighteenth century. Since we are not sure when, we state *late eighteenth century* as an epistemically vague fact.
- The building was constructed throughout the late eighteenth century. We are sure that construction was ongoing throughout the whole period, so we state *late eighteenth century* as an epistemically certain fact.

The first interpretation claims that construction took place at some point within the stated "thick" point of late eighteenth century, which we do not know for sure so that *late eighteenth century* is the best we can do. The second interpretation, on the contrary, claims that construction took place throughout the whole of the late eighteenth century; we do not state such a long period because we are not sure when construction actually happened, but because we are certain that it took that much time.

Other situations are not ambiguous like this, because our prior knowledge, as well as the definitions of the involved attributes, don't allow for it. For example, if we say that someone was born in the late eighteenth century, we can safely assume the first interpretation above rather than the second one. This is because we know that people are born at a very specific moment, so the second interpretation would not make sense. You should be aware of the possibility of ambiguity and, when detected, try to model your attributes in a different manner to avoid it, as we describe in the next section.

Modelling Vagueness Explicitly

So far, we have described a few mechanisms that are built into ConML to model some kinds of vagueness: *null* and *unknown*, abstract enumerated items and arbitrary time resolution. However, there are situations where none of these approaches works. Some of these situations are of an ontological nature and involve the description of imprecise qualities or quantities in scenarios where the approaches presented in previous sections are not appropriate. This may be due to the fact that the characteristic being described is not of a Time or enumerated type, so that the techniques discussed above cannot be used, or to the fact that, even if these techniques can be used, ambiguity would result. For example, we may want to document the surface area of a valley, which is inherently imprecise and of a numeric type, or we may want to document when a particular architectural style started being fashionable, which despite being of a Time type, using "thick" time points would be ambiguous as described in the previous section.

Other situations that also require an alternative approach to the modelling of vagueness are of an epistemic nature, and involve the need to express a variable degree of certainty about something. For example, we may want to state that we are not too sure that a particular book was written by someone, or that it is possible, but not very likely, that a building was destroyed in the late seventeenth century.

In situations like these, we must model vagueness explicitly in our model. This often entails adding attributes to the class involved to represent the degree of ontological or epistemic vagueness for a given characteristic. Consider the example in Fig. 14.5. Here, the *Settlement* class is used to represent archaeological settlements. In addition to the *Population* attribute, which is intended to describe how many people lived there, there is a *PopulationMargin* attribute, which is meant to

Fig. 14.5 The *Settlement* class explicitly represents epistemic vagueness through its *PopulationMargin* attribute

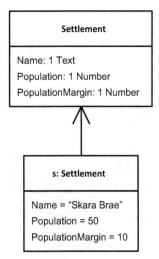

capture the error margin that we estimate for the population figure. As exemplified by the *s* object, Skara Brae is estimated to have housed about 50 people, and we estimate the error of this statement as plus/minus 10 people, which yields a range of 40–60 people in the settlement. Using an extra attribute to express an error margin is very common in many disciplines and is routinely used, for example, to convey radiocarbon dates.

Extra attributes can also be employed to represent our certainty about an epistemically vague characteristic, like in the example shown in Fig. 14.6. Here, the *Event* class is used to describe historical events. Note how the *Certainty* attribute is employed to capture what our certainty is about a particular event having happened as described. According to the example, we are sure that the fall of the Berlin Wall occurred in November 1989, and we consider it likely that Jesus of Nazareth was born in 4 BC.

The two examples above explicitly describe epistemic vagueness through additional attributes. Note that, however, this technique can also be employed to describe ontological vagueness. Consider the situation in Fig. 14.7. Here, the *Place* class uses a pair of attributes to represent the surface area of a place in square kilometres. By using *AreaMin* and *AreaMax* attributes, we can specify what the smallest and largest areas are that would be considered true for a place. Our definition of ontological vagueness states that a statement about an ontologically vague characteristic stays true even when the quality expressed for this characteristic varies, as explained at the beginning of the chapter. By using an attribute pair, we can express the valid range of variability and, in this manner, describe the inherent imprecision much better than with a single value.

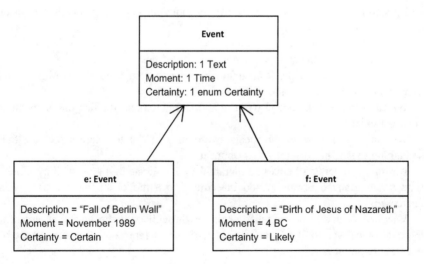

Fig. 14.6 The *Event* class represents our certainty about an event happening through its *Certainty* attribute

Fig. 14.7 The *Place* class
represents the ontological
vagueness of areas through a
pair of attributes

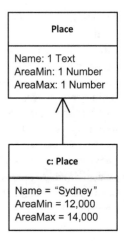

Of course, you can combine the different techniques described here to represent vagueness in your models. Complex situations are rarely solved through a single technique, so feel free to mix and match as necessary.

Summary

Ontological vagueness, or **imprecision**, is about entities in the world that have fuzzy characteristics.

Some characteristics are inherently imprecise, while others are not.

Epistemic vagueness, or **uncertainty**, is about our knowledge being unclear or incomplete about something.

Everything is subject to uncertainty.

Ontological and epistemic vagueness admit degrees.

We can be **purposefully inaccurate** in order to gain certainty. However, this may entail ambiguity in some situations.

We can use the *null* special word in a model to express the fact that something does not exist.

We can use the *unknown* special word in a model to express the fact that something exists, but do not know about it.

Abstract enumerated items in a hierarchical enumerated type, as well as "thick" time points, can be useful to add inaccuracy to a model so that uncertainty is decreased.

Vagueness can also be modelled explicitly through extra attributes that represent the ontological variability of the characteristic being represented, or our degree of uncertainty about it.

Exercises

21. Below you can find a list of characteristics. For each of them, state whether it admits ontological vagueness, epistemic vagueness, none or both.

    - A building's height.
    - A town's name.
    - The number of participants in an event.
    - The starting date of a war.
    - The entities affected by a social change process.

22. Create a type model to represent the fact that events happen at a particular place and time, and involve a number of people. Pay special attention to feature cardinalities, which will determine what features may take a *null* value. Then, create an instance model based on the former, to represent the event of the writing of the Voynich manuscript.

23. Modify the type model from the previous exercise with extra attributes to represent the ontological imprecision of the time when events occur.

Chapter 15
Temporality

Abstract In this chapter, we deal with the fact that the world is far from static, and changes constantly, making the models that we construct today invalid tomorrow if the things that they represent change in a significant way. We explain why simply updating values and links is not sufficient to mitigate this and introduce the aspect-oriented notion of *phase* as a solution. Phases are object "slices" that are valid for a particular moment or period of time. We explain how phase selectors can be used on values and links to create diachronic instance models. Then, we introduce the notion of temporal features so that time-aware type models can be constructed and adequately connected to conforming instance models. Similarly, the notion of temporal aspect is described as a central time-oriented class in a type model. Finally, the chapter ends with a discussion of explicit temporal modelling in absence of phases by using specific class features to describe temporal validity.

From the very beginning of this book, we have emphasized that models represent the world. However, the world is far from static and changes constantly. For this reason, a model that we construct today may become invalid tomorrow if the things that it represents change in a significant way. Although this applies to all kinds of models, instance models are much more sensitive to the passing of time than type models, because they represent specific entities that exist in the world rather than abstractions. For example, we can state today that *Height = 8* for a particular building, but this building may be extended, destroyed or otherwise altered in the future in a manner that changes its height, rendering our statement invalid. You may think that this is an easy problem to solve: it would be enough to keep the model up to date in accordance with whatever we observe. However, this solution has an important drawback: if we update *Height = 8* so that it becomes *Height = 12* when a new level is added to the building, we are losing the information that, at some stage, the building was 8 m high, which may be very valuable. In other words, an approach based on keeping the model up to date results in a freeze-frame picture of the world which, if we are lucky and diligent, will show a static picture of the last known state of things, with no historical information at all. Very often, however, we are interested in a diachronic view of the world, one that captures its history as well

© Springer International Publishing AG 2018
C. Gonzalez-Perez, *Information Modelling for Archaeology and Anthropology*,
https://doi.org/10.1007/978-3-319-72652-6_15

as the current state, so preserving information related to previous states of the world in the model becomes a crucial concern.

This problem also affects type models, but in a much weaker manner. Type models represent categories of things, which constitute abstractions that we develop in order to organize the world. Constructed abstractions usually take the shape and definition that we want to give them and are much less exposed to the usual changes in the concrete world than actual entities. For this reason, the risk that a type model becomes "out of sync" with the represented subjects is much lower than in the case of an instance model and often negligible for most practical purposes. In this chapter, we focus on the management of the temporality in instance models, using an approach based on the concept of *aspect*. An aspect is a cross-cutting concern that is modelled separately from the portion of the world being studied and then "woven" into the rest of the model through special mechanisms. Both temporality and subjectivity (described in the next chapter) are treated as aspects in ConML.

Technical

In the world of databases, the "bitemporal" approach to managing time is quite popular [34, 35]. According to this approach, anything that is stored in a database may be timestamped with two different pieces of data: its *validity time* and its *transaction time*. Validity time refers to when the information is considered to be true or applicable. For example, consider the fact of 'the construction of the Sphinx of Giza'. Its validity time would be 2500 BCE, meaning that this is when the sphinx was constructed. Transaction time, contrarily, refers to when a fact has been recorded. If we take the mainstream views on the Sphinx of Giza, we should say that it was in 1949 when the construction of the sphinx was determined as 2500 BCE, so this fact's transaction time would be 1949.

This approach, although practical in some scenarios, has been criticized [36, 37] because it confuses information and *metainformation*. Validity time is part of the information that we are dealing with and describes the associated entity in the world; in our example, saying that the construction of the Sphinx of Giza happened in 2500 BCE describes the sphinx. Contrarily, transaction time does not describe the entity: saying that it was in 1949 when the date of construction was estimated does not add information about the sphinx, but about the process of its description. In other words, and in relation to the entity being represented, validity time is information, whereas transaction time is metainformation. Mixing up the two hinders modularity and thus model quality, as described in Chap. 31.

For an extensive discussion on metainformation, please see Chap. 17.

Phases

Imagine that we are interested in recording the usage of a number of buildings. We may develop a model like that in Fig. 15.1. If we apply this model, we may end up with objects like those in Fig. 15.2. Here, the building represented by object *b* is used as a hospital, and the building represented by *c* is used as a temple. Note two things. First of all, there is no indication in the model as to when it is applicable. In other words, we do not know when building *b* was used at a hospital or when *c* was used as a temple. Often, we make the assumption that the model is valid now, that is, currently. But "currently" is a moving target, as we described above. Secondly, there is no way in which we can record the history of use changes that a building has gone through over time. That is to say, we cannot capture statements like "this building was used as a hospital during the sixteenth and seventeenth centuries, but today it is used for office space". We could create a very contrived model that used additional classes to represent this, but it would be tedious and unnecessary complex.

To address these problems, ConML introduces the notion of a *phase*. A phase is a version of an object that is applicable only at a certain point in time, and by "point in time", we mean anything from a very "thin" instant or a very "thick" period. When using phases, we can think of an object as a stack of "slices", each one being a phase, and all of them making up the whole object. Look at Fig. 15.3. This is an informal drawing of what we are after. Object *b* is pictured as a stack of versions, each one having a different value for *Use*, and corresponding to a particular period. The complete *b* object is the collection of versions that are stacked on top of each other. However, this is not the right way to depict object phases. Look at the diagram in Fig. 15.4.

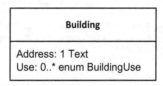

Fig. 15.1 The *Building* class with a *Use* attribute to record building usage

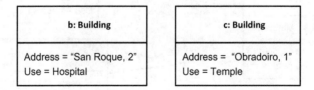

Fig. 15.2 Some instances of *Building* showing values for *Use* at some uncertain point in time

Fig. 15.3 Informal depiction
of the phases of building
b showing different values for
Use for different periods. The
asterisk indicates that this is
not a syntactically correct
model

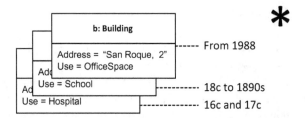

Here, three phases are shown for object *b*. The fact that the three rectangles in
the figure correspond to phases rather than complete objects is indicated by a *phase
selector*, that is, an expression written under the object identifier and class and
prefixed by an at sign @. Also, note that the three boxes show the same identifier, *b*;
this indicates that all of them refer to the same object. The @ sign can be read as
"at", so that the leftmost box in Fig. 15.4 can be read as "object *b* of type *Building*
at sixteenth and seventeenth centuries".

Also, note that in Fig. 15.4, none of the three boxes stands for the complete
b object. Actually, it would be difficult to draw the complete *b* object as a box by
employing the usual rules, since we would not know what to write for the *Use*
attribute, as it varies depending on time. In cases like this, we can use the ellipsis
notation to omit a particular value for attributes that are temporal, as in *Use* = ...

Phase selectors may be used on links as well. Consider the case in Fig. 15.5.

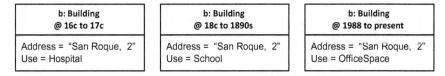

Fig. 15.4 Three object phases for object *b*, each with a different phase selector and a different
value for *Use*. You can imagine a time axis flowing from left to right

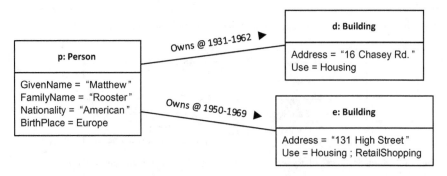

Fig. 15.5 Two links labelled with phase selectors, indicating their time validity

Here, two links of the same type are shown between the object for person p and two building objects. Note the phase selectors next to the semi-association names on the links. This model is stating that Matthew Rooster owned the house on 16 Chasey Rd. between 1931 and 1962, and the building at 131 High Street between 1950 and 1969. This indicates that two phases for object p exist: one for the first period of time, and holding a reference to building d, plus a second one for the second period of time and holding a reference to building e.

Either with values or links, there may be the case that the information to be represented is the same for two or more time periods. For example, look again at Fig. 15.5; we may need to say that Matthew Rooster owned the Chasey Rd. house between 1931 and 1962, but also between 1966 and 1968. Instead of drawing two links, each labelled with a different phase selector, we can draw a single link and label it with a combined selector, as in *Owns @ 1931–1962; 1966–1968*. A semicolon is used to separate different time periods.

Phases are optional. This means that we can create a new phase for an object when we alter a value or a reference, but we are not obliged to. For example, look again at Fig. 15.4. Imagine that we had written *Use = Commercial* instead of *Use = School* for the phase in the middle, which would be wrong. We can correct the mistake by rewriting the wrong value as *Use = School* as soon as we detect the issue, and we do not need to create a new phase for it, since the change does not involve a modification in the entity being described.

The time validity stated by a phase selector works by limiting the representational power of the corresponding model element to the time period mentioned. For example, the *16c to 17c* phase selector on the leftmost phase in Fig. 15.4 means that whatever is stated by that phase, namely that object b has *Address = "San Roque, 2"* and *Use = Hospital*, is only valid between the sixteenth and seventeenth centuries. The phase states nothing about the represented entity outside of this range. In Fig. 15.4, we can see two other phases that complement the first one, covering all the time line between the sixteenth century and the present, and thus giving us a fairly complete diachronic view of the building. However, this does not need to be the case: sometimes you will find a single phase making a statement that is only applicable for a given period of time; outside that time, we have no information whatsoever. The phase selectors on the links in Fig. 15.5 work in a similar way.

Finally, bear in mind that phases are useful to represent the ontological change of the world being modelled. That is, you should use phases when the portion of the world being modelled actually changes. You should not use phases to represent changes in our knowledge of the world or to fix mistakes. Use phases to represent actual changes to, for example, someone's name, or a building's height or materials, or the owners of a piece of land. Do not use phases to represent situations involving a change of mind about something, either because we obtain new information that allows us to come up with a better account or because we realize that we were wrong. For example, imagine that we describe a building b as having *b. ConstructionDate = 1715*, and later, we find new evidence that makes us realize that we were wrong, and the correct construction date is 1717. Do not use a phase to record this change, since it is our knowledge about the building what has changed, rather than the building itself.

In this regard, you must realize that, sometimes, we include classes in our models that are of an interpretive nature. For example, we may have an *Assessment* class in a model about heritage preservation. This class could have attributes such as *Description, Diagnosis, Date* and *Author*. This class is not representing entities in the physical world, but our subjective interpretation about a specific aspect of them. If you write a diagnosis about a building and later you change your mind, you can use a new phase to document the change in your interpretation, despite the fact that the building itself has not changed. This is because the *Assessment* class represents your ideas about the building, and these have actually changed.

Temporal Features

In the previous section, we explored how phases can help us represent specific values or links that are valid only for a specific period of time. In Fig. 15.4, for example, we used the *Building.Use* attribute as a time-varying characteristic that takes different values over time, while the *Building.Address* attribute stays unchanged. In fact, we can differentiate three kinds of features regarding its time variability:

- Those attributes or semi-associations that cannot change over time. These are called *constant*. For example, *Person.PlaceOfBirth*; once a person is born, there is no way in which their birth place can change.
- Those attributes or semi-associations that may change over time, but for which we are not interested in tracking their variations. These are called *variable*. For example, *Person.Age*, assuming that it is enough for us to know how old a person is today.
- Those attributes or semi-associations that may change over time and for which we want to track their variations. These are called *temporal*. For example, *Person.Name*, assuming that we are interested in keeping a historical record of the different names used by a person over their lifetime.

Note that this difference is barely ontological, but mostly arises from our modelling decisions. In other words, whether a feature is constant, variable or temporal is not a property of the underlying characteristic being modelled, but of the specific manner in which we choose to represent it. For example, a model to manage loans in a library will probably consider the *Person.Name* attribute to be variable, because knowing the currently valid name of library customers is enough. However, a model for a biographical study of a family would probably consider *Person.Name* as temporal, in order to maintain a historical trace of the different names used by each family members. Your model domain area and its purpose will determine whether a feature is constant, variable or temporal.

Fig. 15.6 In this diagram, the *Building.Use* attribute and the *Person.Owns* semi-association have been marked as temporal

Temporal features must be explicitly marked as such in a type model. Constant and variable features, contrarily, are not marked. Look at the example in Fig. 15.6.

Here, the *Building.Use* attribute has been marked as temporal by adding an upper case T in parentheses at the end of the line. This is called a temporal aspect marker. Similarly, the *Person.Owns* semi-association has also been marked as temporal. Other features in the model are not marked, meaning that they are either constant or variable.

Note that associations can be temporal in both ways or only one way; that is, one semi-association can be temporal while its inverse is not. The *Person.Owns* semi-association Fig. 15.6 is temporal, and although its inverse is not explicitly depicted in the diagram, it makes sense to assume that it would be temporal too, since a building can change its owner over time. But consider, for example, the association *Person.IsTheAuthorOf* pointing at *Book*. This would be temporal too, since a person can write additional books in the future, and thus, the collection of their authored books changes over time. However, the inverse semi-association *Book.WasWrittenBy* pointing at *Person* is not temporal but constant because, once a book is written, its author cannot change. You can explicitly show the names and temporal markers of both semi-associations in a diagram if you need to show that an association is temporal in both ways.

In addition, bear in mind that marking temporal features in a type model determines how phases will work in the associated instance models. When a variable (that is, not temporal) feature of a class is changed in an object, its value is simply overwritten. However, when a temporal feature is changed in an object, a new phase for the object may be created, so that the previous value of the feature is preserved in the older phase, and the new value is recorded in the new phase. This is illustrated in Fig. 15.7. In Fig. 15.7A, the value for *Address*, a non-temporal attribute, is changed. This results in the old value being lost and overwritten by the new one, so that, after the change, object *b* holds the new value. No phases are involved. In Fig. 15.7B, however, the value for *Use*, a temporal attribute, is changed. This results in a new phase being created so that the old *Use* value is preserved in the previous phase, and the new value is recorded in the new one.

In summary, if you want to keep track of the changes of a feature over time, mark it as temporal in your type model. Otherwise, leave it unmarked.

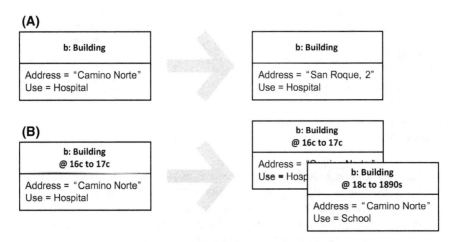

Fig. 15.7 Changes in an object when a feature is altered. In **A**, a non-temporal attribute is altered, so the old value is overwritten. In **B**, a temporal attribute is altered, so that a new phase is created. The large grey arrows represent the alteration event

Temporal Aspect

In the previous sections, we have described the concept of a phase selector, that is, an expression prefixed by an @ character that indicates when a phase applies. See, for example, Fig. 15.4. But, what are these expressions? How are they constructed?

We cannot write anything as a phase selector expression; whatever we use, it must follow a very specific rule: it must resolve to an object that represents a point in time. In other words, the expression in a phase selector is not a random description of a period or moment, but must be a reference to an object that represents a period or moment. For example, if we use @ *18c to 1890s* as a phase selector expression, as in Fig. 15.4, then this expression, *18c to 1890s*, must be a reference to an object that represents the period from the eighteenth century to the decade of the 1890s. We have said that objects represent entities in the world; objects used as phase selector expressions represent a very specific kind of entity: points in time, however "thick" or "thin". All the objects used in phase selectors in an instance model, furthermore, must be instances of a particular class. Which class it is and how it is named and characterized is up to us, but it must be a single class, in order to guarantee a homogeneous treatment of temporality in the model. Look at the example in Fig. 15.8. Here, two phases of an object are shown, together with their type class, *Building*. In addition, a *Moment* class is shown as part of the type model. Note that this class is marked with a temporal aspect marker, a T, in square brackets before its name. This means that this particular class, and no other, constitutes the *temporal aspect* of the model. The temporal aspect of a model is a class that represents temporal entities such as moments, instants, events, periods, stages or any other kind of time-related construct. Note that this class is not associated or

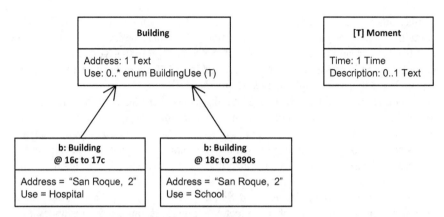

Fig. 15.8 Two phases of object *b*, which is an instance of the *Building* class. In addition, the temporal aspect *Moment* class is shown

explicitly related in any manner to the *Building* class; in fact, the aspect class does not need to (although it can) be connected to other classes in the model, because it is used in a very particular way: its instances are the objects referred to by phase selector expressions. The expressions *16c to 17c* and *18c to 1890s* in Fig. 15.8 are, in fact, references to instances of the *Moment* class. A more explicit representation of this is shown in Fig. 15.9. Here, the phase selector expressions for the *b* phases are now depicted as referring explicitly to the *m* and *n* objects, which are also shown as instances of the *Moment* class. This is equivalent to the model in Fig. 15.8, although more verbose: if you take the leftmost *b* phase, note that its phase selector points to *m*, which is an instance of the *Moment* class having *Time = 16c to 17c*. This is, in fact, equivalent to the previous diagram. In practice, we usually avoid the explicit depiction of temporal phase instances like in Fig. 15.9 in order to save paper or screen real estate and assume instead that the necessary objects exist and have the values described by the expressions in the phase selectors. However, you should feel free to depict these objects explicitly if you need to

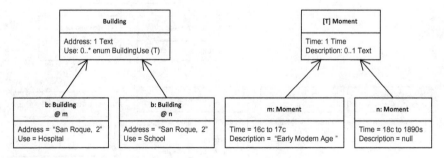

Fig. 15.9 The phase selector expressions from Fig. 15.8 are now shown as explicit references to object identifiers; the corresponding objects are shown as instances of *Moment*, the temporal aspect class

display other values or information about them. For example, object *m* in Fig. 15.9 contains a value for the *Description* attribute, which may be interesting to show in the diagram. In any case, remember that the only objects that you can refer to in phase selector expressions, either directly or indirectly, are those of the temporal aspect class, in our example above, *Moment*.

Of course, we can use inheritance and abstraction here (as described in Chap. 9) to obtain greater flexibility. For example, imagine that we want to use temporality in a model to track the changes in landscape forms. Sometimes, landscape elements stay stable for long periods of time, while some others they change as a response to processes of various kinds. Imagine also that we represent stable periods through a *StablePeriod* class and changing processes through a *Process* class. We would like to use instances of both *Process* and *StablePeriod* to mark phases of landscape elements, but we said that phase selector expressions must refer instances of a single class. We can solve this by acknowledging that both *Process* and *StablePeriod* are kinds of occurrences, and in this manner, we could introduce an abstract class *Occurrence* from which *Process* and *StablePeriod* would specialize. *Occurrence* would be our temporal aspect class, as shown in Fig. 15.10. This model states that the ridge #18 had a height of 23 m during the long stable period of wind action that started in the seventeenth century; then, the ridge had a height of 35 m during the mining stage period that local villagers caused between 1942 and 1965. Note how objects of both types *Process* and *StablePeriod* can be used in phase selector expressions, because, through abstraction, all of them can be seen as instances of *Occurrence*, which is the temporal aspect class. This allows you to represent different kinds of temporal entities in your model as long as all of them have the appropriate semantics as subclasses of the temporal aspect class.

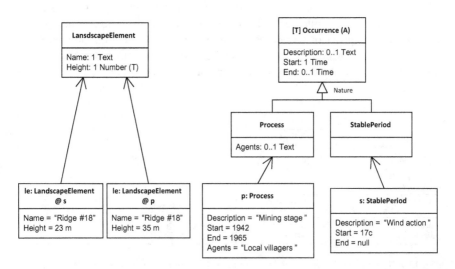

Fig. 15.10 An abstract temporal aspect class, *Occurrence*, is shown with two specialized classes, *Process* and *StablePeriod*. Instances of either subclass may be used in phase selector expressions

Of course, managing temporality as described so far is optional in a model. Use it only if you need to. If you do not, then you do not need a temporal aspect class, temporal marked features or phases.

Modelling Temporality Without Aspects

The approach described so far to represent the passing of time in conceptual models is based on treating time as a cross-cutting aspect. This means that a temporal aspect class is defined independently to the rest of the model in order to represent the necessary time-related entities and then the spots in the model (namely, features) where this class is to be applied are specified by using temporal aspect markers. However, this is not the only approach we can use, although is probably the most powerful and expressive in most cases. When appropriate, you can also use an explicit representation of time in the relevant classes. For example, consider the situation in Fig. 15.11. These two models are roughly equivalent. In Fig. 15.11A, the aspect-oriented technique described in previous sections is used: The *Use* attribute is marked as temporal, and we assume there is a temporal aspect class defined in the model. In Fig. 15.11B, on the contrary, time is explicitly represented: the time-dependent attribute *Use* has been factored out into a separate *BuildingStatus* class that contains, in addition, attributes to locate each particular building status in time. By using these classes, we could document a building as an instance of *Building*, and then attach to it as many instances of *BuildingStatus* as needed, adding more as the building's use changes over time. This class can be extended later with additional time-dependent attributes if necessary.

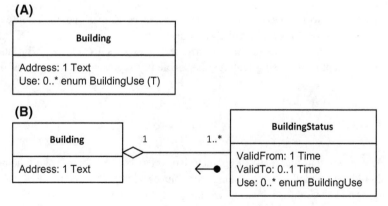

Fig. 15.11 Two equivalent models. In **A**, temporality is managed as an aspect, by using a temporal marker and a (not depicted) temporal aspect class. In **B**, temporality is managed explicitly through a separate class holding time-related attributes

Note the major differences between the two approaches. The model in Fig. 15.11A is much smaller and simpler to develop, maintain and understand. The model in Fig. 15.11B, on the contrary, shows time in a more explicit fashion. Note also that *BuildingStatus.Use* in Fig. 15.11B is not marked as temporal; this would be redundant, since changes in a building's use are already recorded through multiple instances of *BuildingStatus*. In general, we suggest that you use the aspect approach in Fig. 15.11A and only consider the explicit approach when you are developing a class that has strong temporal semantics. For example, classes that represent events, periods or processes, such as *BuildingStatus* in our example above, are good candidate for explicit temporal management Other classes should use the aspect-based approach described throughout this chapter.

Summary

Models are likely to get out of sync with the entities that they represent as they change over time.

You can use **phases** to represent specific moments or periods of an entity and provide values or links that apply only during this time.

In this manner, an object can be seen as a sequence of phases that describes how the represented entity has changed over time.

Each phase is characterized by a **phase selector**, which indicates when its values are valid. Similarly, phase selectors can also be added to links, so that they indicate when the link is valid.

Phases are useful to represent **ontological change** in the underlying entity, rather than epistemic change of our knowledge about it.

For a value or link to be labelled with a phase, the corresponding feature (an attribute or semi-association) must be **marked as temporal** in the associated type model.

The expressions in phase selectors refer to instances of a special class in the type model designated as the **temporal aspect** class.

Time can also be modelled in the absence of aspects for classes with strong temporal semantics, by using features that explicitly represent the passing of time.

Exercises

24. Below, you can find a list of characteristics. For each of them, state whether it should be modelled as constant, variable or temporal. Assume that we are trying to represent the internal workings of a museum.

    - The museum's name.
    - The museum's inauguration date.

- The items on display as part of the permanent collection.
- The number of visitors recorded each year.

25. Create a type model to represent archaeological sites and their occupation by different groups of people at different moments in time. Also, include in the model the ability to document the archaeological features found on the sites as they are excavated. Use aspect-based or explicit temporality as you see fit.

26. Using the model from Exercise 25 as a basis, create an instance model representing the following situation. The hillfort of Baroña was occupied between the first century BCE and the first century CE. It was excavated for the first time in 1933, and a large rampart was documented. Then, it was excavated again between 1980 and 1984 and two roundhouses described.

Chapter 16
Subjectivity

Abstract In this chapter, we deal with the fact that models are strongly shaped by the background, training, purpose and even cognitive preferences of the people constructing them and are therefore highly subjective. For this reason, two models having the same scope and purpose and created by different people will probably clash. In this context, we propose a theory of disagreement by which clashes in models can be ascribed to predication, classification or existence conflicts and introduce the aspect-oriented notion of *perspective* to address predication clashes. Like phases, perspectives are object "slices" that are valid from the viewpoint of some particular agent only. We explain how perspective selectors can be used on values and links to create multivocal instance models. Then, we introduce the notion of subjective features so that viewpoint-aware type models can be constructed and adequately connected to conforming instance models. Similarly, the notion of subjective aspect is described as a central agent-oriented class in a type model. Then, we discuss how explicit subjective modelling can be carried out in absence of perspectives, and by using specific class features to describe agent validity. The chapter ends with an explanation on how to combine subjective and temporal concerns in the same model.

As we described in the introductory chapters of this book, conceptual models are made of concepts in our minds. Being abstract things, they are strongly shaped by our background, training, purpose and even cognitive preferences. In other words, models are highly subjective. Two people constructing a model of the same things and having the same purpose would probably end up with very different results, very much like two people writing a description of something would probably write very different accounts. This means that a model that is useful for its creator, in the sense that it faithfully represents their perceived reality, may not be useful to other people, because the representations in the model are subjectively judged as flawed, awkward or incomplete. Like in the case of temporality, this applies to instance as well as type models, although instance models are much more sensitive to subjective disagreements than type models, because they represent specific entities that are perceived subjectively rather than shared abstractions. For example, I can state

© Springer International Publishing AG 2018
C. Gonzalez-Perez, *Information Modelling for Archaeology and Anthropology*,
https://doi.org/10.1007/978-3-319-72652-6_16

that *ConservationStatus = Good* for a particular building, but you may think that *ConservationStatus = Poor*, rendering my statement invalid to you. In the case of temporality, the linear advancement of time allows us to give more importance to some phases than others in some situations, such as considering the latest phase of an object to be the most useful, since it represents the most recent knowledge that we have about the entity. However, subjective views are not naturally ordered like phases are, so shortcuts like this cannot be taken. If we do not pay attention to subjectivity when constructing models, then we will end up with a representation of the world that is hegemonic and alienating to others. Instead, we should be interested in a multivocal view of the world, where different points of view are recorded or, at least, the only one that is recorded is clearly identified in terms of its authorship.

This problem also affects type models, but in a much weaker manner. Type models represent categories of things, which constitute abstractions that we develop in order to organize the world. Constructed abstractions are usually developed on top of shared consensus, and for this reason, they are much less prone to subjective disagreement. Consequently, the risk that a type model is disputed within the community that created it is much lower than in the case of instance models and often negligible for most practical purposes. As we did in the case of temporality, we focus in this chapter on managing the subjectivity of instance models, using also an approach based on the concept of aspects. Remember that an aspect is a cross-cutting concern that is modelled separately from the portion of the world being studied, and then "woven" into the rest of the model through special mechanisms.

Technical
As opposed to temporality, which has been studied in the database and information modelling literature, there are no works as far as we know that study the modelling of subjectivity. The tradition in the conceptual modelling community has a strong engineering bias which, being based on a classical view of science, usually rejects subjectivity as something to avoid and remove. This may be one of the major factors why subjectivity has not been studied so far in these fields.

Since little or no studies exist on subjectivity in conceptual modelling, we propose here a simple but useful theoretical framework.

Theoretical Framework

In our context, "subjectivity" refers to the fact that two or more agents may disagree about something. As a consequence, the conceptual models created by these agents will be different even if they share the same scope and purpose. We distinguish three kinds of disagreements, from the lightest to the strongest:

- A disagreement of the first kind, or *predication conflict*, occurs when two agents assign different values to a particular characteristic of a given entity. Consider an object *a* of type *T*, which has an attribute *P*; agent 1 would say *a.P* = *x*, while agent 2 would say *a.P* = *y*. In situations like this, both agents agree that there exists an object *a* and that it is of type *T*, but they disagree on the value of its attribute *P*. An example is the one in the previous section about the conservation status of a building.
- A disagreement of the second kind, or *classification conflict*, occurs when two agents classify a given entity in different manners. Consider an object *a*; agent 1 would say that *a* is of type *P*, while agent 2 would say that a is of type *Q*. Usually, different types mean different sets of features. In situations like these, both agents agree that there exists an object *a*, but they disagree on what kind of thing it is and, as a consequence, what properties it has. For example, one archaeologist may think that a particular find is a broken bone knife, whereas another may think it is part of a sculpted idol.
- A disagreement of the third kind, or *existence conflict*, occurs when two agents disagree on the existence of an entity, either because one believes it exists while the other believes it does not, or because the two agents discretize the world along different seams (see Chap. 2). Consider an object *a*; agent 1 would say that *a* exists, while agent 2 would say that *a* does not exist as such. For example, I know that the computer I am using to type this exists, whereas my grandmother, who watches me from her corner, lacks the idea of a computer and therefore conceptualizes the LCD display as a TV set; from her perspective, the computer as such does not exist.

ConML can successfully represent disagreements of the first kind, but not the second or third kinds. This is quite good, since most other modelling languages such as UML cannot represent disagreements at all. The following sections describe how predication conflicts can be represented in ConML through the use of perspectives.

Perspectives

Imagine that we are interested in recording the conservation status of a series of buildings. We may develop a model like in Fig. 16.1. If we apply this model, we may end up with objects like those in Fig. 16.2. Here, the building represented by object *b* is judged to be in a good state of conservation, whereas the building represented by *c* is judged to be in an acceptable state. Note two things. Firstly, there is no indication in the model as to who made these judgements. In other words, we do not know who thinks that building *b* is in a good state, or who thinks that *c* is in an acceptable state. We may make the assumption that status information about a building is an objective fact, but it is not. Secondly, there is no way in which we can capture the variable points of views of different people or groups with regard to a building's conservation status, that is, what we called a disagreement of

Fig. 16.1 The *Building* class
with a *Status* attribute to
record conservation status

Building
Address: 1 Text Status: 0..1 enum ConservationStatus

Fig. 16.2 Some instances of
Building showing values for
Status

b: Building
Address = "San Roque, 2" Status = Good

c: Building
Address = "Obradoiro, 1" Status = Acceptable

the first kind in the previous section. In other words, we cannot capture statements like "this building is OK according to the local town council, but in need of restoration according to the construction company".

To address these problems, ConML introduces the notion of a *perspective*. A perspective is a version of an object that corresponds to the judgment of a certain person or group. When using perspectives, we can think of an object as a stack of "slices", each one being a perspective, and all of them making up the whole object. This is very similar to what we did with phases in the previous chapter. Look at Fig. 16.3. This is an informal drawing of what we need. Object *b* is pictured as a stack of versions, each one having a different value for *Status*, and corresponding to a particular person or group. The complete *b* object is the collection of versions that are stacked on top of each other. However, this is not the right way to depict object perspectives. Look at the diagram in Fig. 16.4. Here, three perspectives are shown for object *b*. The fact that the three rectangles in the figure correspond to perspectives rather than complete objects is indicated by a *perspective selector*, that is, an expression written under the object identifier and class and prefixed by a dollar sign $. Also, note that the three boxes show the same identifier, *b*; this indicates that all of them refer to the same object. The $ sign can be read as "according to", so that the leftmost box in Fig. 16.4 can be read as "object *b* of type *Building* according to Alice".

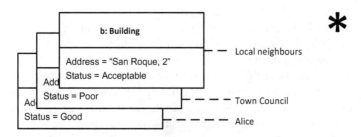

Fig. 16.3 Informal depiction of the perspectives on building *b* showing different values for *Status* for different people or groups. The asterisk indicates that this is not a syntactically correct model

b: Building \$ Alice	b: Building \$ Town Council	b: Building \$ Local neighbours
Address = "San Roque, 2" Status = Good	Address = "San Roque, 2" Status = Poor	Address = "San Roque, 2" Status = Acceptable

Fig. 16.4 Three object perspectives for object *b*, each with a different perspective selector and a different value for *Use*. You can imagine a time axis flowing from left to right

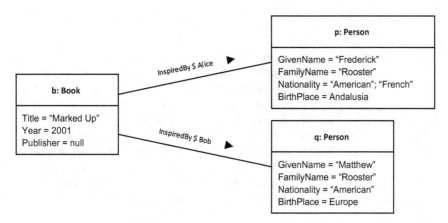

Fig. 16.5 Two links labelled with perspective selectors, indicating their time validity

Note that, in Fig. 16.4, none of the three boxes stands for the complete *b* object. Actually, it would be difficult to draw the complete *b* object as a box employing the usual rules, since we would not know what to write for the *Status* attribute as it varies depending on who we ask. In cases like this, we can use the ellipsis notation to omit a particular value for attributes that are subjective, as in *Status* = ...

Perspective selectors may be used on links as well. Consider the case depicted in Fig. 16.5. Here, two links of the same type are shown between the object for book *b* and two person objects. Note the perspective selectors next to the semi-association names on the links. This model is stating that the book "Marked Up" was inspired by the life of Frederick Rooster according to Alice, but Bob thinks that it was Matthew Rooster who actually inspired the book. This indicates that two perspectives for object *b* exist: one for Alice, and holding a reference to person *p*, plus a second one for Bob, and holding a reference to building *q*.

Either with values or links, there may be the case that the information to be represented is the same for two or more persons or groups. For example, look again at Fig. 16.5; we may need to say that both Alice and Bob agree that "Marked Up" was inspired by the life of Matthew Rooster. Instead of drawing two links, each labelled with a different perspective selector, we can draw a single link and label it with a combined selector, as in *InspiredBy \$ Alice; Bob*. A semicolon is used to separate different references to people or groups.

Like phases, perspectives are optional. This means that we can create a new perspective for an object when someone provides a value or a reference for it, but we are not obliged to. For example, look again at Fig. 16.4. Imagine that we had written *Status = Excellent* instead of *Status = Poor* for the perspective in the middle, which would be wrong. We can correct the mistake by rewriting the wrong value as *Status = Poor* as soon as we detect the issue, and we do not need to create a new perspective for it, since the change does not involve recording the judgment of a new person or group.

Like in the case of temporality, the subjective validity stated by a perspective selector works by limiting the representational power of the corresponding model element to the subjective views of the mentioned person or group. For example, the *Alice* perspective selector on the leftmost perspective in Fig. 16.4 means that whatever is stated by that perspective, namely that object *b* has *Address* = "*San Roque, 2*" and *Status = Good*, is only valid for Alice. The perspective states nothing about the represented entity as far as other people are concerned. In Fig. 16.4 we can see two other perspectives that complement the first one, covering the opinions of other relevant agents, and thus giving us a fairly complete multi-vocal view of the building. However, this does not need to be the case: sometimes you will find a single perspective making a statement that is only applicable to a single person or group, and we would have no information whatsoever about what others may think. The perspective selectors on the links in Fig. 16.5 work in a similar way.

Finally, and as opposed to temporality, bear in mind that perspectives are useful to represent the epistemic variations of people's views about the world being modelled, rather than actual changes in the world. That is, you should use per-spectives to capture different interpretive views on something that otherwise remains unchanged. You should not use perspectives to represent actual changes in the world. For example, use perspectives to represent views on a building's style or influences or on the value or importance of a heritage element. Also, do use per-spectives to represent situations when you change your mind about something, either because you obtain new information that allows you to come up with a better account or because you realize that you were wrong. For example, imagine that you describe an archaeological artefact *a* as having *a.EstimatedDating = 11c BCE*, and later you find new evidence that allows you to refine your estimate as 9 BCE. If you were interested in keeping track of your research process, you could use a per-spective to record this change in your views, since it is your knowledge about the artefact, rather than the artefact itself, what has changed.

Subjective Features

In the previous section, we explored how perspectives can help us represent specific values or links that are valid only according to someone. In Fig. 16.4, for example, we used the *Building.Status* attribute as an agent-varying characteristic that takes different values for different people or groups, while the *Building.Address* attribute stays unchanged. In fact, we can differentiate two kinds of features regarding its subjective variability:

- Those attributes or semi-associations that are fairly objective and therefore are not expected to vary regardless of who documents something. These are called *objective*. For example, *Building.Height*; anyone who can measure the height of a building will produce similar or identical results.
- Those attributes or semi-associations that are determined interpretively and for which we want to track their variations. These are called *subjective*. For example, *Building.Status*, assuming that we are interested in keeping a multivocal record of the different status judgments made by different people.

Like in the case of temporal features described in the previous chapter, this difference is barely ontological, but arises mostly from our modelling decisions. In other words, whether a feature is objective or subjective is not a property of the underlying characteristic being modelled, but of the specific manner in which we choose to represent it. For example, a model to manage the architecture heritage in a city will probably consider the *Buliding.ConstructionDate* attribute as constant, because the model users would be most interested in managing a shared and objectified view on what the construction date is for each building. However, a model to study the research process of a group of architects would probably consider *Building.ConstructionDate* as subjective, in order to document the multivocal variability of different researchers or even the same one over time. Your model domain area and its purpose will determine whether a feature is objective or subjective.

In this regard, we must clarify how subjective features can be used to track the changes of opinion of one individual over time. This would seem to be connected to temporality rather than (or in addition to) subjectivity, but it is not, because changing our mind about something does not entail an ontological change in the something being represented. When we change our mind, we can think of our points of view before the change and after the change as two different subjectivities. For example, imagine that I change my mind from thinking that a particular building is very representative of a style, to thinking that it isn't. Two subjectivities are involved: me before I changed my mind and me afterwards. In this manner, we would have two perspectives in the model, each corresponding to one of these subjectivities. In summary, do not assume that each subjective agent needs to be a different individual; it may also correspond to a single individual in different moments over time.

Fig. 16.6 In this diagram, the *Book.Genre* attribute and the *Book.InspiredBy* semi-association have been marked as subjective

Subjective features, like temporal features, must be explicitly marked as such in a type model. Objective features, contrarily, are not marked. Look at the example in Fig. 16.6. Here, the *Book.Genre* attribute has been marked as subjective by adding an upper case S in parentheses at the end of the line. This is called a subjective aspect marker. Similarly, the *Book.InspiredBy* semi-association has also been marked as subjective. Other features in the model are not marked, meaning that they are considered objective.

As opposed to the case of temporality, associations that are subjective in one way are almost certainly subjective in the inverse way too; that is, if one semi-association is subjective, then its inverse is subjective too. The *Book. InspiredBy* semi-association Fig. 16.6 is subjective, and although its inverse is not explicitly depicted in the diagram, it makes sense to assume that it would be subjective too. The reason for this is that subjectivity is about our interpretation of the world, rather than the world itself; since the two semi-associations that make up an association represent the same fact in the world, albeit expressed differently, it makes sense to think that we will have the same subjective views about them, because they are actually manifestations of a single fact.

In addition, and like in the case of temporality, bear in mind that marking subjective features in a type model determines how perspectives will work in the associated instance models. When an objective feature of a class is changed in an object, its value is simply overwritten. However, when a subjective feature is changed in an object, a new perspective for the object may be created, so that the existing value of the feature is preserved in one perspective, and the new value is recorded in the new perspective. This is illustrated in Fig. 16.7. In Fig. 16.7A, the value for *Address*, an objective attribute, is changed to fix a mistake. This results in the old value being lost and overwritten by the new one, so that, after the change, object *b* holds the new value. No perspectives are involved. In Fig. 16.7B, however, the value for *Status*, a subjective attribute, is changed. This results in a new perspective being created so that the old *Status* value is preserved in the previously existing perspective, and the new value is recorded in the new one.

In summary, if you want to keep track of the different views of people about a feature, mark it as subjective in your type model. Otherwise, leave it unmarked.

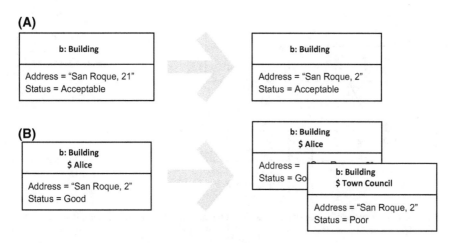

Fig. 16.7 Changes in an object when a feature is altered. In **A**, an objective attribute is altered, so the old value is overwritten. In **B**, a subjective attribute is altered, so that a new perspective is created. The large grey arrows represent the alteration event

Subjective Aspect

In previous sections, we have described the concept of a perspective selector, that is, an expression prefixed by a $ character that indicates the author of a perspective. See, for example, Fig. 16.4. These expressions are constructed in a manner that is very similar to that of phase selectors. We cannot write anything as a perspective selector expression; whatever we use, it must resolve to an object that represents an agent capable of issuing a judgment. In other words, the expression in a perspective selector is not a random description of a person or group, but must be a reference to an object that represents a person or group. For example, if we use *$ Alice* as a perspective selector expression, as in 81, then this expression, *Alice*, must be a reference to an object that represents this person named Alice. We have said that objects represent entities in the world; objects used as perspective selector expressions represent a very specific kind of entity: people or groups of people. All the objects used in perspective selectors in an instance model, furthermore, must be instances of a particular class. Which class it is and how it is named and characterized is up to us, but it must be a single class, in order to guarantee a homogeneous treatment of subjectivity in the model. Look at the example in Fig. 16.8. Here, two perspectives of an object are shown, together with their type class, *Building*. In addition, an *Agent* class is shown as part of the type model. Note that this class is marked with a subjective aspect marker, an S, in square brackets before its name. This means that this particular class, and no other, constitutes the *subjective aspect* of the model. The subjective aspect of a model is a class that represents subject entities such as people, communities, organizations, groups or any other kind of agent-related construct. Note that this class is not associated or

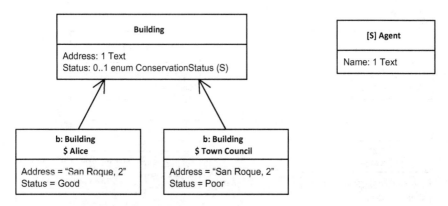

Fig. 16.8 Two perspectives of object *b*, which is an instance of the *Building* class. In addition, the subjective aspect *Agent* class is shown

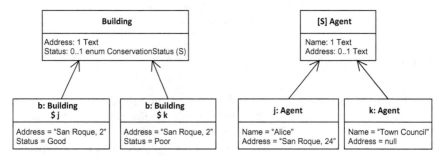

Fig. 16.9 The perspective selector expressions from Fig. 16.8 are now shown as explicit references to object identifiers; the corresponding objects are shown as instances of *Agent*, the subjective aspect class

explicitly related in any manner to the *Building* class; in fact, the aspect class does not need to (although it can) be connected to other classes in the model, because it is used in a very particular way: its instances are the objects referred to by perspective selector expressions. The expressions *Alice* and *Town Council* in Fig. 16.8 are, in fact, references to instances of the *Agent* class. A more explicit representation of this can be seen in Fig. 16.9. Here, the perspective selector expressions for the *b* perspectives are now depicted as referring explicitly to the *j* and *k* objects, which are also shown as instances of the *Agent* class. This is equivalent to the model in Fig. 16.8, although more verbose: if you take the leftmost *b* perspective, note that its perspective selector points to *j*, which is an instance of the *Agent* class having *Name* = "*Alice*". This is, in fact, equivalent to the previous diagram. In practice, we usually avoid the explicit depiction of subjective perspective instances like in Fig. 16.9 in order to save paper or screen real estate and assume instead that the necessary objects exist and have the values described by the expressions in the perspective selectors. However, you should feel free to depict these objects explicitly if you need to display other values or information about them. For example, object *j* in Fig. 16.9 contains a value for the *Address* attribute that shows that the person corresponding to this agent lives on the same street as the building being assessed, which may be interesting to consider. In any case, remember that the only objects that you can refer to in perspective selector expressions, either directly or indirectly, are those of the subjective aspect class; in our example above, *Agent*.

Of course, we can use inheritance and abstraction here (as described in Chap. 9) to obtain greater flexibility, as we explained in the previous chapter for the temporal aspect class. For example, imagine that we want to use subjectivity in a model to document feedback to a museum by its visitors. Some of these visitors are specialists in cultural heritage; some are groups of students that issue a shared comment, and some are individuals from the general public. Imagine also that we represent specialists and members of the general public through a *Person* class, and student groups through a *Group* class. We would like to use instances of both *Person* and *Group* to mark perspectives of comments, but we said that perspective selector expressions must refer instances of a single class. We can solve this by acknowledging that both *Person* and *Group* are kinds of agents, and in this manner, we could introduce an abstract class *Agent* from which *Person* and *Group* would specialize. *Agent* would be our subjective aspect class. Look at Fig. 16.10. This model states that the permanent collection of the museum is of excellent quality according to Claire Jones, but of a mere good quality according to a group of 27 people. Note how objects of both types *Person* and *Group* can be used in perspective selector expressions, because, through abstraction, all of them can be seen as instances of *Agent*, which is the subjective aspect class. This allows you to represent different kinds of subjective entities in your model as long as all of them have the appropriate semantics as subclasses of the subjective aspect class.

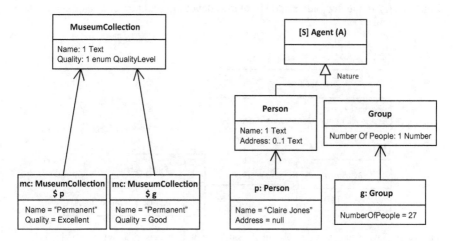

Fig. 16.10 An abstract subjective aspect class, *Agent*, is shown with two specialized classes, *Person* and *Group*. Instances of either subclass may be used in perspective selector expressions

Like in the case of temporality, managing subjectivity as described so far is optional in a model. Use it only if you need to. If you do not, then you do not need a subjective aspect class, subjective marked features or perspectives.

Modelling Subjectivity Without Aspects

The approach described so far to represent multivocality in conceptual models is based on treating subjectivity as a cross-cutting aspect, like we did for temporality. This means that a subjective aspect class is defined independently to the rest of the model in order to represent the necessary time-related entities, and then the spots in the model (namely, features) where this class is to be applied are specified by using subjective aspect markers. However, this is not the only approach we can use, although is probably the most powerful and expressive in most cases. When appropriate, you can also use an explicit representation of subjectivity in the relevant classes. For example, consider the situation in Fig. 16.11. These models are roughly equivalent. In Fig. 16.11A, the aspect-oriented technique described in previous sections is used: The *Status* attribute is marked as subjective, and we assume there is a subjective aspect class defined in the model. In Fig. 16.11B, on the contrary, subjectivity is explicitly represented: the subject-dependent attribute *Status* has been factored out into a separate *BuildingStatus* class that contains, in addition, an attribute to assign each particular building status to an agent. By using these classes, we could document a building as an instance of *Building*, and then attach to it as many instances of *BuildingStatus* as needed, adding more as the building is assessed by different people or groups. This class can be extended later with additional subject-dependent attributes if necessary.

Note the major differences between the two approaches. The model in Fig. 16.11A is much smaller and simpler to develop, maintain and understand. The

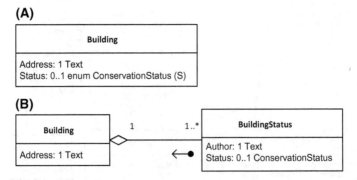

Fig. 16.11 Two equivalent models. In **A**, subjectivity is managed as an aspect, by using a subjective marker and a (not depicted) subjective aspect class. In **B**, subjectivity is managed explicitly through a separate class holding a subject-related attribute

model in Fig. 16.11B, on the contrary, shows subjectivity in a more explicit fashion. Note also that *BuildingStatus.Status* in Fig. 16.11B is not marked as subjective; this would be redundant, since perspectives on a building's status are already recorded through multiple instances of *BuildingStatus*. In general, we suggest that you use the aspect approach in Fig. 16.11A, and only consider the explicit approach when you are developing a class that has strong subjective semantics. For example, classes that represent points of view, assessments or interpretations, such as *BuildingStatus* in our example above, are good candidate for explicit subjective management Other classes should use the aspect-based approach described throughout this chapter.

Combining Temporality and Subjectivity

As we have explained throughout this chapter and the previous one, both temporality and subjectivity are often managed through an aspect-oriented approach. Although the semantics of these two aspects are very different, they are implemented in a very similar manner as far as ConML syntax is concerned. Sometimes you will need to combine both aspects; for example, you may find an attribute that is both temporal and subjective, such as *Monument.Status*. In this situation, you would be interested to manage temporality because monuments change over time, and keeping a historical record of how they changed may be relevant to your goals; at the same time, different people or groups may have different views on a monument's conservation status, so keeping track of multivocal information is also likely to be relevant.

In order to manage both temporality and subjectivity in your model, you only need to apply the techniques described in these two chapters at the same time. Specifically,

- In your type model, create in your model both a temporal aspect class and a subjective aspect class and mark them with the appropriate aspect markers. Usually, they will be different classes.
- Also in your type model, mark your temporal features with the temporal marker, your subjective features with the subjective marker and those features that are both temporal and subjective with both markers.
- In your instance model, use combined temporal and subjective selectors to depict phase-perspectives.

Consider the example in Fig. 16.12. Here, the two boxes at the bottom are combined phase-perspectives. That is, each box represents the views of a particular person or group at a particular moment in time. Note that phase and perspective selectors are both used to depict this. Correspondingly, the *Monument.Status* attribute is marked as both temporal and subjective by using a capital T and S separated by a comma and surrounded by parentheses.

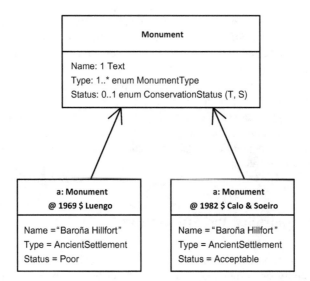

Fig. 16.12 Two phase-perspectives of object *a*, which is an instance of the *Monument* class. The temporal and subjective classes are not shown

Summary

Models are likely to appear invalid to some people unless we consider their subjective points of view.

You can use **perspectives** to represent specific points of view on an entity and provide values or links that apply only for the people holding these points of view.

In this manner, an object can be seen as a collection of perspectives that describes what different people think about the represented entity.

Each perspective is characterized by a **perspective selector**, which indicates to whom its values are valid. Similarly, perspective selectors can also be added to links, so that they indicate for whom the link is valid.

Perspectives are useful to represent **epistemic change** of our knowledge about the underlying entity, rather than ontological change of the entity itself.

For a value or link to be labelled with a perspective, the corresponding feature (an attribute or semi-association) must be **marked as subjective** in the associated type model.

The expressions in perspective selectors refer to instances of a special class in the type model designated as the **subjective aspect** class.

Subjectivity can also be modelled in the absence of aspects for classes with strong subjective semantics, by using features that explicitly represent the author of the point of view.

Subjectivity can be combined with temporality in order to obtain models that describe the world in a diachronic and multivocal manner at the same time.

Exercises

27. Below you can find a list of characteristics. For each of them, state whether it should be modelled as objective or subjective. Assume that we are trying to represent the internal workings of a museum.

    - The museum's inauguration date.
    - The quality of the lighting conditions in the exhibition halls.
    - The estimated dating of each item in the permanent collection.
    - The maximum allowed number of visitors that can be inside the museum at any given time.

28. Create a type model to represent the archaeological impact and correction work done a team during the construction of a pipeline. Pay special attention to the impact assessments and corrective measures that should be taken. Use aspect-based or explicit subjectivity as you see fit.

29. Using the model from Exercise 28 as a basis, create an instance model representing the following situation. A heavily deteriorated tumulus is found during the works, and the team decides that no correction measures should be taken given its poor status. This is in contrast with the views of the local council, who issues an assessment by which signalling and documentation is required. In addition, some unidentified features are discovered, which seem to be well enough preserved as to deserve a quick excavation documentation.

Chapter 17
Feature Redefinition

Abstract In this chapter, we describe the situation of inherited features not fitting the abstraction level or particular semantics of the recipient class. Since inherited features cannot be removed or ignored, we introduce a *redefinition* mechanism to alter some of their properties in a controlled manner. After describing the overall concept of feature redefinition, the chapter provides a comprehensive description of what redefinition rules exist to regulate how inherited features may be altered.

Previous chapters, especially Chaps. 9 and 12, have introduced and discussed generalization and inheritance. According to what we said, every feature in a class is either inherited from an ancestor or freshly declared by the class itself. In Fig. 9.10, for example, *Barn* inherits *Height* and *Material* from *Building* and, together with its own *Capacity*, propagates them down to *ProtectedBarn* and *NonProtectedBarn*. However, there are often cases where an inherited feature does not quite fit the abstraction level or particular semantics of the recipient class. This often happens in deep specialization hierarchies, where a feature that is declared at a very high abstraction level is passed down through inheritance to very specific classes, each with its own peculiar semantics. Of course, we cannot remove or ignore the feature; doing so would break the rule of inheritance. But we can alter some of its properties in a controlled way in order to adapt it to the recipient class. This is called *redefining* a feature.

Redefinition of Features

Imagine that we are interested in studying how different people employ material objects such as books during their daily lives. We may develop a model such as the one in Fig. 17.1. Here, we have decided that every element we are working with may have a name, and hence we have defined the *Element.Name* attribute. Also, we defined two subtypes of elements: material elements on the one hand, which have books as a particular subtype, and persons on the other hand. Note that we are

© Springer International Publishing AG 2018
C. Gonzalez-Perez, *Information Modelling for Archaeology and Anthropology*,
https://doi.org/10.1007/978-3-319-72652-6_17

Fig. 17.1 Classes *Book* and
Person inherit *Element.Name*,
which becomes redundant and
ill-adjusted

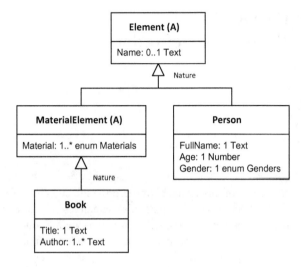

interested in documenting books' titles, as well as people's full names, among other characteristics.

Due to inheritance, every descendant of *Element* inherits the *Name* attribute, which is precisely what we wanted when we said that every element we work with may have a name. However, we are already documenting books' titles through the *Book.Title* attribute, which in practice work as their names; in fact, we often designate books by their title, and no other name is used. As a consequence, having both *Name* (inherited) as well as *Title* (owned) in the *Book* class is redundant. Something similar happens with the *Person.FullName* attribute: someone's full name usually works as that person's only name, and we don't need a separate *Name* attribute in this class.

You could argue that, in order to eliminate redundancy, we should remove the *Book.Title* and *Person.FullName* attributes, so that the inherited *Name* attribute is all we have to name things. However, this would have two unwanted consequences. First of all, using the words "title" and "full name" is much more specific than just "name". When we are describing things at the very abstract level of elements, "name" is all we can say; however, when we are discussing books, using the more specific "title" makes more sense and is more readable and intuitive to everyone. Similarly, using "full name" for a person provides more information than just "name". The second unwanted consequence is that elements may or may not have a name, as described by the 0..1 cardinality of the *Element.Name* attribute. However, books always have a name (their title), and people always have a name (their full name). In other words, what was optional at the very high level of abstraction of elements becomes mandatory at the much more specific level of people and books.

We can use feature redefinition to eliminate redundancy and keep a readable and useful model. By using redefinition, we don't add a new attribute to *Book* to

Fig. 17.2 Classes *Book* and *Person* redefine the inherited *Element.Name* attribute to match their specific semantics

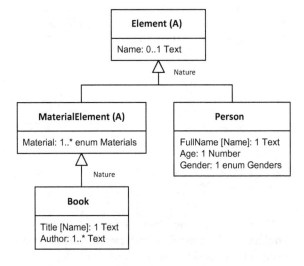

document books' titles, but redefine the inherited *Element.Name* as necessary. Similarly, we avoid the owned attribute *Person.FullName*; instead, we redefine the inherited *Element.Name* attribute so that it expresses people's full names. According to the discussion above, these redefinitions would involve changing the name of the inherited attribute and adjusting its cardinality. Look at Fig. 17.2. Here, the *Book.Title* attribute is a redefinition of the original *Element.Name*. This is indicated by the name of the original attribute in square brackets after the redefinition name, as in *Title [Name]*. This can be read as "title, redefining name". Also, note that the cardinality of *Title* is 1, while the cardinality of *Name* was 0..1. Similarly, the *Person.FullName* attribute is a redefinition of *Element.Name* too, and its cardinality has also been changed from the original 0..1 to 1.

Not only attributes can be redefined. Properties and semi-associations can be redefined too. Consider the situation in Fig. 17.3.

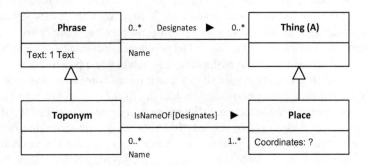

Fig. 17.3 Class *Toponym* redefines the *Designates* inherited semi-association, changing its name, cardinality and opposite class

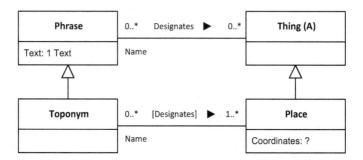

Fig. 17.4 Class *Toponym* redefines the *Designates* inherited semi-association, changing its cardinality and opposite class

Here, the *Toponym* class inherits the *Phrase.Designates* semi-association and redefines it to the name of "IsNameOf" and cardinality 1..* instead of 0..*. It also changes the opposite class, from *Thing* to *Place*. This model states that every phrase may designate a number of things, but every toponym, as a specific kind of phrase, is always the name of at least one place, which is a kind of thing. As you can see, redefinition is very useful to adjust the semantics of an inherited feature, such as *Phrase.Designates* in our example, to the more concrete semantics of the recipient class.

A few notes must be made about feature redefinition. First of all, if the redefinition does not change the name of the original feature, then you do not need to repeat it outside the square brackets. Look at the example in Fig. 17.4. Here, the *Toponym* class redefines *Phrase.Designates*, changing its cardinality and opposite class; however, it does not change its name, so that we just write the original name (which stays unchanged) in square brackets.

Secondly, and as illustrated by the previous examples, redefinition allows us to change the name of a feature. However, we should not change it in a way that breaks the semantics of the original feature. For example, it would not make sense to rename the *Phrase.Designates* semi-association in Fig. 17.4 to "IsLocatedIn", since being located in a place is something very different to designating a place. Remember the rule of inheritance from Chap. 9: anything that we may say about a class also applies to all its subclasses. This means that since *Phrase* has a *Designates* association to *Thing*, then all its subclasses, including *Toponym*, should have it too. Adjusting the name of the semi-association while preserving the overall semantics is fine; changing it radically so that it means something else is not.

Thirdly, redefining a semi-association, like in Fig. 17.4, does not automatically redefine the inverse semi-association. For example, we can assume that the inverse of *Phrase.Designates* would be named "IsDesignatedBy" or something like that. *Toponym* inherits *Phrase.Designates* and redefines it to have a different cardinality and opposite class. At the same time, *Place* inherits *Thing.IsDesignatedBy*, but this is not redefined, so it stays unchanged; this means that *Place* would have an inherited *IsDesignatedBy* semi-association pointing to *Phrase*, rather than

Toponym. If we wanted to redefine this inverse semi-association as well, we would need to explicitly indicate it in the diagram through a name in square brackets.

Finally, the examples above show how redefinition can change the name and cardinality of features, as well as the opposite class of semi-associations. However, we can change many other things by following a set of very specific rules, as described in the next section.

Redefinition Rules

You can redefine an inherited property, attribute or semi-association by following these rules.

All Feature Kinds

You can change a feature's name as long as the overall semantics is preserved. In particular, and to avoid breaking the rule of inheritance, you must ensure that the new name is a synonym, a quasi-synonym or a hyponym of the original one. To verify that your redefined name is good, use abstraction to imagine what an instance of the specialized class would look like if described in terms of the superclass. For example, look again at Fig. 17.3, and imagine what an instance of *Toponym* would look like if described in terms of *Phrase*: if we call this instance *t*, then the collection of places referred to through *t.IsNameOf* would now be referred to as *t. Designates* and would be considered abstract things instead of places. Saying that a toponym designates things, instead of saying that it is the name of places, still makes sense, despite being a bit too abstract, so the name change should be fine. If we had renamed the original semi-association to, say, "IsLocatedIn", then the result would be very different, because the collection of places referred to through *t. IsNameOf* would now be referred to as *t.IsLocatedIn* and would be considered abstract things instead of places. Since it does not make sense to say that a phrase is located in a number of places, the renaming is unacceptable.

Similarly, you can change a feature's definition as long as the overall semantics is preserved. The same rules as in the case of names apply: you must ensure that the new definition is nearly equivalent to the original one or subsumed by it.

The cardinality of a feature can be changed if the new cardinality is more restrictive than the original one, that is, if the new cardinality is a subset of the original one. For example, if the cardinality of the original feature is 1..*, the redefinition may specify 2..* or 1, but not 0..*.

The sorted semantics of a feature can be changed from non-sorted to sorted, that is, a non-sorted original feature can be redefined as sorted. However, the opposite change is not possible.

The temporal semantics of a feature can be changed from temporal to non-temporal and vice versa.

Similarly, the subjective semantics of a feature can be changed from subjective to non-subjective and vice versa.

Attributes

The data type of an attribute can be changed if the new data type can be "coerced" into that of the original attribute, as indicated in Table 17.1. For example, if the data type of the original attribute is Text, the redefinition attribute may specify Number, because Number can be coerced into Text, but not the other way around. As you can see, any type can be coerced into Data, and any type except for Data can be coerced into Text. This means that attributes of the Data and Text types are the most flexible, since they can be redefined into almost any other types.

Finally, an enumerated attribute can be coerced into a different enumerated type only if the new enumerated type is a descendant of the original one, as described in Chap. 10.

Semi-Associations

The role of a semi-association can be changed as long as the overall semantics is preserved, like in the case of names and definitions above. You must ensure that the new role is nearly equivalent to the original one or subsumed by it.

The strong semantics of a semi-association can be changed from non-strong to strong, that is, a non-strong original semi-association can be redefined as strong. However, the opposite change is not possible.

Finally, the opposite class of a semi-association can be changed if the opposite class of the new semi-association is a descendant of the opposite class of the original semi-association. This is what we did in Fig. 17.3: the opposite class of

Table 17.1 Data type coercion rules

		...be coerced into this type?					
		Boolean	Number	Time	Text	Data	Enumerated
Can a value of this type...	Boolean	n/a			Yes	Yes	
	Number		n/a		Yes	Yes	
	Time			n/a	Yes	Yes	
	Text				n/a	Yes	
	Data					n/a	
	Enumerated				Yes	Yes	(See caption)

Blank cells indicate "No"
An enumerated type can be coerced into another enumerated type if the source enumerated type is a descendant of the target enumerated type

Phrase.Designates, which is *Thing*, can be changed into *Place* when *Toponym* redefines the semi-association because *Place* is a descendant of *Thing*. We could not have changed it to a class that was not a descendant of *Thing*.

The whole/part semantics of a semi-association cannot be changed. That is, if a semi-association is whole/part, you cannot make it non-whole/part in a redefinition. Similarly, if a semi-association is not whole/part, you cannot make it whole/part in a redefinition.

Summary

It is possible to **redefine** an inherited feature in order to adjust it to the specific semantics of the recipient class.

All types of features can be redefined: properties, attributes and semi-associations.

Redefining a semi-association has no effect on the inverse semi-association.

A collection of redefinition rules determines what can be changed and how during redefinition.

In general, a redefined feature must preserve the semantics of the original one, in order to obey the rule of inheritance.

Exercises

30. Imagine that a study is to be carried out on how the people from a neigh-bourhood use some specific buildings over the day. The following model states that, for the purposes of the study, every person may be using a building at any point in time. Taking this model as a basis, add the necessary classes, attributes and associations to reflect the fact that there are two kinds of buildings to be considered in the study: houses, where people live, and factories, where people work. Use feature redefinition wherever necessary.

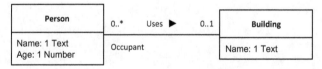

Chapter 18
Metainformation

Abstract In this chapter, we deal with the common but often misunderstood issue of "data about data", or metadata, also called metainformation. To begin with, we explain how the term "metadata" is often used in the digital humanities and other fields in a loose manner, producing ambiguity and confusion. We then carefully pinpoint proper usage. After that, we describe the fact that metainformation is also information, the "meta" prefix being a mere qualifier that does not indicate something of a radically different nature. In particular, we show that metainformation is information that, at some point, plays the role of informing us about other information but which, apart from this, constitutes regular information, so every technique and tool that we may use on information is also applicable to metainformation. Then, we examine some typical scenarios of metainformation usage, including the expression of uncertainty and a better implementation of "transaction time" than the one often offered by the well-known bitemporal approach.

If you are minimally aware of the digital humanities boom and the involved technologies, you have likely heard the word "metadata". Usually, metadata is defined as "data about data", or something similar. For example, imagine that an anthropologist is studying the social practices of teenagers in a large city. In this context, relevant data would probably include the description of the involved communities and groups, what social acts they carry out and how or why. Metadata, in turn, would include data about who documented the above-mentioned social acts or interviewed the relevant community members, when it was done and how reliable this data is. In fact, metadata describes data very much like data describes things in the world.

There are three issues with this conception. First, the prefix "meta" means "beyond" or "after" in Greek; "metadata" thus means "beyond the data". Furthermore, the "meta" prefix in "metadata" is qualifying the root word "data", so one would assume that metadata is one particular kind of data, like office chairs are a particular kind of chairs. However, most of the literature in the digital humanities conceptualizes and treats metadata as if it was something different and separate to

© Springer International Publishing AG 2018

C. Gonzalez-Perez, *Information Modelling for Archaeology and Anthropology*,

https://doi.org/10.1007/978-3-319-72652-6_18

regular data, as if metadata was essentially different to data. An example related to cultural heritage is that of Doerr's on metadata [23].

The second issue is that, by taking this approach, we are contradicting the fact that the "meta" prefix is relative; in other words, a piece of data may be "meta" in relation to another, but not "meta" in relation to a third one. For example, consider again the example that we described above about the social practices study in the city. We said that the data about who documented what and how constitutes what we call "metadata". Now, what would happen if someone, at the later stage, decided to study the research process that was used in that study? What we agreed that was metadata in the study would be primary data to them, and they would certainly generate metadata about it. So the same corpus of data is "meta" in one context but not in another.

Lastly, there is the issue that the word "metadata" is often used with a different sense to what we describe above. More and more, it is being employed to refer to the formal definition of the "shape" or structure of the data. For example, consider a database created by the researchers working on our example project. This database would contain data describing the social acts and the communities that are observed in the city. The structure of the database, including what tables and columns it has, of what data types and what relationships exist between them, would be called (by some) "metadata" or a "metadata schema". It is true that, in a sense, the structure of a database somehow describes the data that it holds; or, along the same lines, a type model somehow describes any instance model that conforms to it. However, this usage of "metadata" is confusing, because the structure of a database not only describes what data types and lengths each column has, but also determines what data is to be considered to start with. In other words, this kind of metadata not only describes the data, but also (and most importantly) specifies what the scope of the data is. This is extremely different to the situation described at the top of this chapter, where metadata truly describes the data without actually determining its scope. This is a good rule of thumb: metadata of the first kind documents other data and, as such, constitutes an additional layer of information that enhances our understanding of the data. If we strip some data of its metadata, we will lose some information, but the data will still be there. To the contrary, metadata of the second kind cannot possibly be removed from the data it describes, since it constitutes its very structure. For these reasons, we avoid the term "metadata" in the second sense and use it only to mean "data that describes other data", as in the first sense.

Furthermore, and as explained in Chap. 1, conceptual modelling works at the information or knowledge level, rather than at the data level, so in any case we should prefer "metainformation" rather than "metadata".

Technical
The software engineering literature has used the term "metamodel" for a long time. A *metamodel*, in this context, is a model that represents other models. A metamodel is a model like any other and is composed of the same "stuff" as other models. However, the entities that it happens to represent are models

and model elements, rather than, say, buildings or people. Metamodels in software engineering are used to specify languages, methodologies and other artefacts in a semi-formal fashion. Some examples are [38–40].

Metainformation as Information

Metainformation (rather than "metadata") can be very useful to describe or document different facets of model elements, such as who created or changed them, who owns them, what sources of information were used to derive them, when they were created or altered, what language they are expressed in, what quality, reliability or certainty applies to them, what usage rights exist in relation to them, etc.

We define metainformation as follows:

Definition

Metainformation is information that, in a given context, is relevant because it describes other information.

According to this, metainformation is such only in specific contexts, and only because it plays a certain role, namely, to describe other information. In our example above about the social practices study, the information about who recorded what and when is metainformation only in the context of the mentioned study, because it describes the information recorded by the anthropologists. It would not be metainformation, but regular information, in the context of the research process study that takes place afterwards.

Technical

You can find a comprehensive treatment of the metainformation approach taken here in [41].

Since metainformation is information, and it may be seen as plain information rather than metainformation, we should treat it very much like regular information and document it through regular instance models instead of through specifically designed languages or formalisms. Consider the example in Fig. 18.1. Here, *a* and *c* are objects that, in this context, play the role of metainformation. They are shown explicitly connected to the class that they document through a metainformation relationship. Note that this relationship is depicted as a line going from the metainformation object to the model element being described, in our case, the

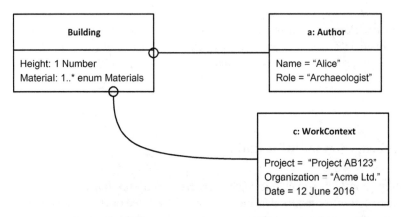

Fig. 18.1 Two metainformation objects *a* and *c*, explicitly connected to the class that they describe

Building class. This line has a hollow round end on the side of the documented model element, which can be read as "applies to". In this manner, and according to the figure, both author *a* (Alice, an archaeologist) and work context *c* (project AB123 of Acme Ltd. on 12 June 2016) apply to the *Building* class. Or, in other words, Alice, the archaeologist, is the author of class *Building*, which was created for the AB123 project of Acme Ltd. on 12 June 2016.

Note also that objects *a* and *c* in the example are of types *Author* and *WorkContext*, respectively, but these classes are not shown in the diagram. However, they must exist so that their instances *a* and *c* can exist in turn. Usually, metainformation classes are not shown in diagrams where metainformation objects are used, for the sake of simplicity. Also, the type model where metainformation classes are defined is very usually a different model to the one being documented. That is to say, the *Author* and *WorkContext* classes in our example are not part of the same model as *Building*. The reason behind this is that metainformation type models usually contain classes about the very specific kinds of things, such as authors, work contexts, information quality, provenance and related matters, regardless of what model we are trying to document. For example, the *Author* and *WorkContext* classes from our example may be used to document a model about cultural heritage but also a model about genomics or car manufacturing. For this reason, it is usual to find metainformation classes in models that are especially oriented to being independent of the particular domain being described. Having said this, nothing prevents us from using instances of classes in a model to document elements in that same model.

Also, and despite the fact that our example above shows metainformation for a class, bear in mind that metainformation can be applied to any kind of model element, both at the type and instance levels. For example, you can document classes, attributes, associations, generalizations, objects, values and links through metainformation. The example in Fig. 18.2 shows a few of these situations.

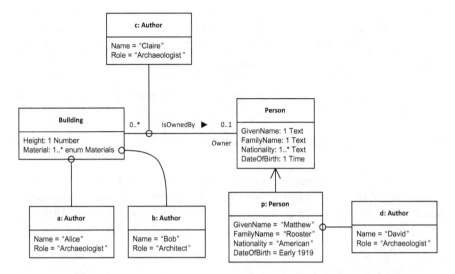

Fig. 18.2 The *Building* class, the *Building.Material* attribute, the *Building.IsOwnedBy* association and the *p* object are documented by metainformation

Here, different authors are shown for a class, an attribute, an association and an object. By convention, the round end of a metainformation relationship line documenting a class must intersect the class box perimeter, as shown for object *a*. Conversely, the round end of a metainformation relationship line documenting an attribute is usually placed in line with the attribute text without intersecting the class box line, to avoid confusion, as shown for object *b*. In any case, showing a lot of metainformation on a diagram can quickly become cumbersome, so unless you are trying to make a point or highlight something, metainformation is usually conveyed in a separate document using structured text descriptions. Still, and even when metainformation objects are not drawn as boxes in a diagram, metainformation is information expressed through objects, as we described at the beginning of this chapter.

And precisely because metainformation is information, we can document it too through metainformation, thus chaining metainformation relationships. This is not a very common thing to do, but it can be useful in some scenarios. See the example in Fig. 18.3. This model says that Alice, the archaeologist, created the *Building* class and that Bob, the architect, created the metainformation object *a*. Chained metainformation relationships like this can be useful in scenarios where quality control is paramount and we not only need to document our models, but also the documentation about the models itself.

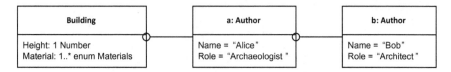

Fig. 18.3 Metainformation chaining. The *Building* class is documented by object *a* which, in turn, is documented by object *b*

Specific Uses of Metainformation

As we described in the previous section, metainformation is useful to document a wide range of facets about model elements, such as their authorship, provenance or quality. In this section, we describe a few specific metainformation-related scenarios that solve issues posed in previous chapters of the book.

Expressing Uncertainty

In Chap. 14, we discussed vagueness and, in particular, epistemic vagueness or uncertainty, which corresponds to those situations where our knowledge about something is unclear or incomplete. We also said that uncertainty affects every fact and phenomenon, since we can be more or less sure about anything. Metainformation can help us capture what degree of uncertainty exists for any particular model element, such as an object, a value or a link. Consider the example in Fig. 18.4.

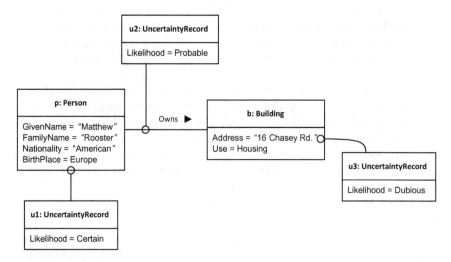

Fig. 18.4 Metainformation is used here, through various *UncertaintyRecord* objects, to document the uncertainty of various model elements

Here, several *UncertaintyRecord* objects are used to document the likelihood that various model elements are as described. Specifically, the diagram states that it is certain that person *p* was named Matthew Rooster, had American nationality and was born in Europe; it is probable that he owned the 16 Chasey Rd. house; and it is dubious that this was the actual address of the house. The example uses an *UncertaintyRecord* class with a single *Likelihood* attribute, but you can create your own classes to express uncertainty in any manner that is relevant to your model.

Implementing Transaction Time

In Chap. 15, we introduced temporality and briefly described the bitemporal approach that is common in the database literature. According to this approach, there are two time-related pieces of data that can be relevant for any piece of information: when it holds true and when it was recorded. We criticized this approach because these two concerns are very different and should not be managed together; the former relates to the information being dealt with and is implemented through the temporality techniques described in Chap. 15, whereas the latter relates to the metainformation about the information being dealt with. Consider the example in Fig. 18.5. Here, several *DocumentationRecord* objects are used to describe who documented various entities, when they did it and what method was employed to do it. Specifically, the diagram states that Alice created the *p* object on 6 February using an interactive session with the computer; then, Claire created the *b* object on 9 February through mass import of data; and finally, Alice created the link between *p* and *b* on 11 February through an interactive session again. You can see how the "transaction time", or time of recording, is documented in this scenario together with other relevant data such as the operator and the documentation method. Again, our metainformation approach gives you full liberty to define the metainformation classes that you need and apply them to any relevant model elements.

Summary

Most approaches to documenting information in the literature treat metadata as essentially different to regular data. Also, they focus on the data level instead of the information or knowledge levels.

Metainformation is defined as information that, in a given context, is relevant because it describes other information. As a consequence, metainformation is information too.

Metainformation is useful to document who created a model element, what sources of information were used to obtain it, when it was created, what quality or

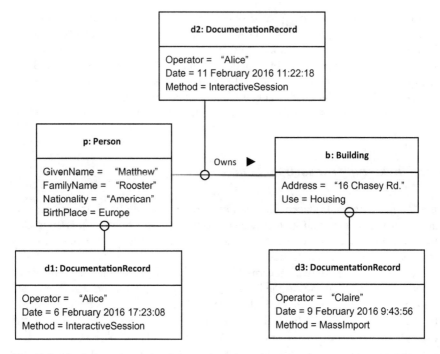

Fig. 18.5 Metainformation is used here, through various *DocumentationRecord* objects, to describe when various model elements were created, by whom and by which method

reliability applies to it, what usage rights exist in relation to it and many other things.

Metainformation can be expressed by attaching metainformation objects to the relevant model elements through a special **metainformation relationship**.

Every kind of model element can be documented in this manner, from classes and attributes to objects and links.

Metainformation is particularly useful to express **uncertainty** and implement the concept of **transaction time** described in the database literature.

Exercises

31. Below you can find a list of characteristics. For each of them, state whether it constitutes metainformation or regular information.

    - A book's author in a model describing a library.
    - The architect who designed a building in a monument management system.
    - The author of a photograph of a building in a monument management system.

- The author of a photograph in a historical documentation management system.
- The date when a ritual was first performed in a particular country.
- The date when a ritual was first documented in a particular country.

32. Create two type models, one for the following scenario and one for the necessary metainformation that would be necessary to collect. A study is to be carried out to analyse the feedback of visitors to a museum. For each visitor willing to participate in the study, a museum assistant will record their personal details, together with the date of the visit, the visitor's opinion about the quality of the exhibition and an optional comment by the visitor. It is necessary to document when each visit was recorded and who did it.

33. Using the models from the previous exercise as a basis, create an instance model plus the associated metainformation objects to describe the following situation. Alice, 54, visits the museum on 11 March 2016 and agrees to participate in the study. Bob is the assigned museum assistant who interviews her. Alice states that she found the collection to be of average quality and makes no further comments.

Part 3
Recap of Part III

This is the end of Part III. In this part, we have built on top of the basic conceptual modelling constructs presented in the previous one by adding more details and additional techniques to model specific situations. We have also introduced advanced modelling techniques in relation to the "soft" issues of vagueness, temporality and subjectivity, and discussed new topics including metainformation and feature redefinition. By now, you should be able to construct and interpret complex models of cultural heritage in a variety of settings.

This part concludes the description of ConML. Most of the contents of the ConML Technical Specification [32] have been covered in this book so far. If you need additional information on the background justification for ConML, see [42].

Part IV
A Model of Cultural Heritage

Up to this point, we have been studying the concepts and techniques of conceptual modelling. In this part, we change the angle and focus instead on presenting a comprehensive conceptualization (an "ontology") of cultural heritage based on CHARM (www.charminfo.org). Crucial conceptual areas of cultural heritage are discussed, including tangible entities, agents, performative entities, valorizations, representations, locations and occurrences. An example model involving a variety of related situations is developed over the chapters to illustrate how the different areas in CHARM fit together.

Once you complete this part, you will be able to construct and understand cultural heritage models based on CHARM and use CHARM as an infrastructure to express your own conceptualizations of cultural heritage phenomena.

Chapter 19
An Ontology for Cultural Heritage

Abstract In this chapter we introduce the foundations of CHARM, the Cultural Heritage Abstract Reference Model (www.charminfo.org). We describe the benefits of using CHARM to explore, document and communicate portions of archaeological and anthropological entities, among other things. We also consider some objections that are often posited against the use of CHARM or similar approaches, such as whether cultural heritage can be modelled at all, or whether having a common shared conceptual framework is possible or convenient. Then we discuss different approaches to the conceptualization of cultural heritage, exploring how in recent times we have seen a shift from an intrinsic value position to that of an extrinsic (or granted) value. We also deal with the issue of whether cultural heritage can or should be seen as a process rather than a collection of things. After that, we introduce some key concepts for an ontology of cultural heritage, offering clear and brief definitions for each of them. These concepts include culture, cultural product, cultural value, heritage value and cultural heritage. The chapter ends with a brief introduction to the three major concepts in CHARM: valuable entities, valorizations, and representations.

Cultural heritage is a complex reality with which people from multiple fields often interact. Cultural heritage specialists usually include anthropologists, archaeologists, architects, archivists, geographers, geoscientists, historians, palaeobiologists and sociologists, among others. Teams of experts working on cultural heritage are becoming larger and more heterogeneous, and are generating more and more information about their findings, observations, hypotheses and conclusions. In addition, non-specialists also play a crucial role in cultural heritage; the general public and the society at large are major actors in the construction and interpretation of cultural heritage.

In interacting with cultural heritage, different agents need to express what they find, observe, interpret and conclude. This need for expression comes from two sources and serves two purposes. First of all, it helps us understand the world in which we live; it supports our exploration, validation and reasoning about it. Secondly, it helps us to communicate with others; we can thus document our

© Springer International Publishing AG 2018
C. Gonzalez-Perez, *Information Modelling for Archaeology and Anthropology*,
https://doi.org/10.1007/978-3-319-72652-6_19

observations, hypotheses and conclusions about cultural heritage; we can convey them to others; and others can therefore reuse them later.

Helping us to explore, reason about, document and communicate the world is what conceptual models excel at, as we explained in Chap. 3. Conceptual models, in addition, often work as "ontologies" of the world, as described in Chap. 1. In other words, a conceptual model (a type model, more specifically) describes what categories of things are relevant to us, what characteristics they have and how they relate to each other. CHARM is a pre-defined (but flexible and extensible) model of cultural heritage; by providing this, we can help others to fulfil the above-mentioned goals of exploring, reasoning about, documenting and communicating cultural heritage, and in such a way that mutual understanding between collaborators is straightforward.

You may think that a pre-defined model of cultural heritage cannot possibly work. The next few sections explain why it does.

What Is CHARM?

CHARM stands for Cultural Heritage Abstract Reference Model. Firstly, CHARM is a model, that is, a purposeful representation of something relevant. Remember from Part I that every model necessarily entails a simplification, which removes some details from the represented entities and allows us to manage information that would be too complex to handle otherwise. Secondly, CHARM is a model of cultural heritage. By "cultural heritage" here we mean anything that may be the recipient of certain kind of value ascribed by an individual or group, plus the associated valorizations ascribed to said things, plus the representations of these things that may exist. In this way, CHARM not only represents the specific entities that might receive cultural heritage value, but also other entities which are necessary to describe and understand the former.

Thirdly, CHARM is a *reference* model. This means that CHARM is intended to be used by a wide and diverse range of organizations and individuals in order to achieve a common understanding. And, finally, CHARM is an *abstract* model. This means that, in order for CHARM to be used by a wide and diverse range of users, the model cannot be too specific about what it represents, since each organization, project and situation has different and unique needs, and even different and unique preferences and stances on what cultural heritage is about. CHARM provides an abstract view that can be, hopefully, shared by everyone, but it is up to each of us to define our own particularities by using extension mechanisms (see Chap. 33). This means that you do not use CHARM straight out of the box; rather, you need to extend it into a particular model that suits your specific needs.

Motivation and Benefits of CHARM

There is an ongoing tension in any modelling activity. On the one hand, we strive to express things in a manner that is as clear and understandable as possible, so that as many people as possible can benefit from it. This leads us to adopt conventions, standards, shared views of reality and agreed-upon approaches. But, on the other hand, we know that each project or task (such as an archaeological excavation or an ethnographic study) has its own peculiarities and specific needs, and so it needs a particular, unique way of expressing things. This leads us to employ special, unrepeatable ways of representing things to obtain the best possible fit for our purpose. Adopting conventions and employing unique solutions are, in fact, two contradictory strategies, each one having its pros and cons.

The overall adoption of standards, or widely shared conventions to conceptualize cultural heritage, has the obvious advantage of making interoperation and understandability much easier. However, it has a major drawback: everyone must adapt its way of working to what the standard dictates. Usually, this is not feasible or desirable, especially in research settings. A good example is ISO 21127 [21], also known as the CIDOC Conceptual Reference Model (CRM) [20], a museum-oriented standard that, while being well known in the cultural heritage community, is far from being mainstream in its adoption; despite the claim that CIDOC CRM can be extended and adjusted, this has not resulted in its wide adoption. The opposite strategy, that of totally avoiding standards and having each project or task to use its own particular conceptualization, has the benefit of providing an optimal fit for purpose; however, shared understanding and interoperation are very difficult in a setting like this.

CHARM adopts a new hybrid approach based on model extension, which has been employed by ISO for some ontology-related work [43, 44]. According to this approach, the shared standard must stipulate as few concepts as possible, and always at a very high level of abstraction, so that it is highly likely to be acceptable to a wide range of specialists. In addition, anyone wishing to use the standard must *extend* it; that is, add specific classes, attributes, associations and other model elements in order to provide the necessary details to adapt the standard to the specific needs of a given project or task. The result of carrying out an extension is called a *particular model* . The details of how particular models are constructed through extension are given in Chap. 33.

The extension approach employed by CHARM combines the advantages of the two previous strategies. On the one hand, it allows us to address the peculiarities of our projects by creating a particular model that is optimally fit to each of them. On the other hand, we are still using CHARM as a shared infrastructure, and therefore, interoperation and mutual understandability with other models created by other people also using CHARM is very easy.

CHARM contains over 160 classes and covers many areas in cultural heritage, including:

- Tangible entities such as places, buildings or books.
- Performative entities such as social acts, songs or trades.
- Occurrences such as processes, situations and changes.
- Abstract entities such as beliefs and category systems.
- Norms such as rights, obligations or conventions.
- Agents such as people or communities.
- Representations such as maps or photographs.
- Valorizations such as research works or community stances.
- Derived entities such as sites, landscapes or styles.
- Measures of length, area, mass and other quantities.
- Locations, including absolute and relative.

The following sections, and the remaining chapters of this part, describe CHARM in full detail. You will find a number of definitions and explanations of what cultural heritage is about according to CHARM. Often, you may feel that you do not agree with some of these definitions. When this happens, we suggest you keep reading until you obtain a comprehensive view of the full model and learn how everything falls into place.

Objections to CHARM

You may argue that cultural heritage cannot be described through a single model, since there might be multiple approaches to it, especially across cultures. Of course, we agree that different cultures have different views on what is valuable and what should be preserved and passed on to future generations. However, CHARM and the rest of this book assume a Western contemporary culture, which is that of the author and ascribes meaning to the term "cultural heritage" only in this context. In this sense, we adopt a humble position by acknowledging that we cannot possibly represent the conceptions of cultural heritage held by cultures that are different to our own, and therefore, we should stick to ours. This means that CHARM is likely to be impractical to represent cultural heritage *as seen by* cultures different to the Western contemporary one, although it can be used to describe other cultures' cultural heritage *as seen by us*. In summary, and for the sake of clarity, CHARM and the rest of this book assume that the concept of 'cultural heritage' occurs within the Western contemporary culture and makes no attempt to model other points of view.

Even so, you may think that cultural heritage cannot be modelled at all, or at least not through the approaches presented in this book. CHARM is a conceptual model based on the object-oriented paradigm inherent to ConML, which is highly linguistic as described in Part I. CHARM represents things in terms of classes, attributes and associations; this is what human language does through nouns, adjectives and verbs, and through mechanisms such as subsumption and classification, as described in Chap. 2. We cannot avoid modelling; the mere usage of language to share knowledge and communicate ideas implies a great deal of informal modelling and a shared understanding of reality. This is what CHARM does.

Still, you may argue that a common and shared understanding is not necessarily good, because tolerant conflict between incompatible discourses is what makes humanities and social sciences richer. We do not deny the value of conflict and debate for many purposes in the construction of intersubjective realities. However, there are pragmatic reasons that make a shared understanding a valuable resource. The exchange of information between individuals and organizations, especially if they do not share a similar background, is highly facilitated if a common and shared frame of reference is used. In fact, knowledge exchange is not possible unless some kind of shared frame of reference exists. Similarly, the existence of a well-known model helps us to reuse knowledge over time for new purposes and thus more easily create new knowledge based on the work of others. In addition, even when deep conceptual disagreements exist between theoretical positions, a minimum common frame of reference is necessary in order to discuss these disagreements. For example, some may think that history is just the simple listing of chronologically ordered events, while others would probably call this chronicle and insist that history is something else. For this discussion to take place, a shared notion of what "list", "event" and "chronology" mean must exist. Note that we are not saying that every party involved must use the same terms; we are saying that every party involved must know what others *mean* when using whatever terms. Precisely, CHARM aims to develop such a common frame of reference for the field of cultural heritage.

Nevertheless, you may think that you do not need a model as large or deep as CHARM for your particular field of interest. If this is so, you must bear in mind that CHARM is a descriptive, rather than prescriptive, model. That is, CHARM gives you some conceptual aids, but it does not tell you how you must conceptualize each thing in the world. In addition, you do not need to use everything in CHARM: you can pick only the elements that are useful to you, and extend them to match precisely the needs of your organization and project, and even your personal preferences, discarding the rest. By using CHARM, your information will be readily understandable by others with minimum effort and will benefit from a model that has been proven to work in a number of situations and conditions.

Approaches to Cultural Heritage

Co-authored with César Parcero-Oubiña, Incipit CSIC
Nowadays, cultural heritage is a contested concept, not only in practical terms (as in, should something be considered cultural heritage?), but also in theoretical terms. Although at a very general level, both legal and popular, a widespread consideration of cultural heritage exists as a cultural and identity legacy composed of objects, monuments and traditions, the last decades have witnessed the development of theoretical arguments challenging this vision. Reactions against these traditional views of cultural heritage have gained strong impetus in the specialized literature,

so that at first sight, there is currently no consensus on how cultural heritage should be defined or, more precisely, on what constitutes cultural heritage. In the words of Bendix [45], "Each grouping of practitioners and experts harbours its own conception of heritage; their expectations seldom harmonise with one another". We discuss some common approaches to cultural heritage in the rest of this section.

Cultural Heritage as a Process

Starting with the most recent and challenging approaches, triggered by the emergence of the now-contested concept of 'intangible heritage', voices began to be raised contesting the old and solid idea that cultural heritage was a matter of antiquity, authenticity and materiality [46]. A booming literature has developed in the last few decades that argues in favour of a different definition of cultural heritage.

Following this line, cultural heritage has been defined in different ways that always highlight the social processes that give meaning and significance to things. For instance, cultural heritage has been defined as "a mode of cultural production in the present that has recourse to the past" [47], "a mode of cultural production that gives the endangered or the outmoded a second life as an exhibition of itself" [48], "a form of communicative practice" [49], "a field of social/cultural action" [50] or "a social and cultural process that mediates a sense of cultural, social and political change" [51].

What lies behind these definitions is the idea that cultural heritage is not composed of passive and given things from the past, but of active social processes in the present. This reaction against a things-based view of cultural heritage has been expressed as provocatively as "there is no such thing as heritage" [52]. Cultural heritage would be in the processes through which people engage with what is around them. Cultural heritage would be a process of valorization, of giving different values and meanings to things, understanding "thing" here in its widest meaning, as any discrete manifestation that happens in the world. And by "things", we include here other things such as events [47].

Active processes by agents involving subjective perceptions and actions are therefore considered to be the main components of cultural heritage according to this view. We use the term "valorization" to refer to all such processes (as described in further sections and chapters). Even in its most extreme and radical forms, these definitions do not mean that valorizations are the only component involved in the construction of cultural heritage; by definition, something needs to exist in order to engage with it. As stated by [52], "Heritage becomes not so much the thing or place identified by the AHD [the Authorised Heritage Discourse, meaning the traditional practice, see below] as 'heritage', but instead the values and meanings that are constructed at and around them".

Consequently, and even if considered simply as pure raw matter, things (again, in the broadest sense of the word) also play a role in the creation of cultural heritage according to this view. Though passive and circumstantial, things are also part of the picture, since for a valorization to happen something must exist as the recipient or object of that valorization. Therefore, viewing heritage as a process means bringing actions to the forefront and pushing things into the background. This is precisely the opposite of the traditional views of cultural heritage, which apparently have considered it as being composed of things alone.

Cultural Heritage as Things

Long before the development of the trends referred to above, cultural heritage was viewed as consisting of things having special and usually inherent values. In fact, this is still what is agreed as the "common-sense definition", or the "natural way of thinking about it", as criticized by [52]. Cultural heritage is, from this widespread point of view, a collection of things (including here a wide range of sensorial elements, from objects to traditions) with an inherent, objective value. Processes of valorization, perception or reception play no apparent role in this view of cultural heritage. As argued in a recent paper [53], "This process [the changes in the concept of cultural heritage] is based on the substitution of an objective logic characterizing the historic monument with a subjective logic of heritage".

Surely enough, a significant change has come about in how cultural heritage is defined. However, it is not equally obvious that this change can be described in terms of the incorporation of a previously non-existent subjectivity. It is arguable that an objective logic behind the concept of monument has ever existed. Whether within the realm of cultural heritage norms and policies, or in the academic practice that simultaneously developed the very notion of cultural heritage, a process of valuation or valorization has always existed behind the consideration of some objects as part of cultural heritage. As a good example, not too far in time, the Venice Charter [54] states that "The concept of an historic monument (…) applies not only to great works of art but also to more modest works of the past *which have acquired cultural significance* with the passing of time" (our emphasis).

Even within the very concept of 'monument', an essential component of judgment has always existed. Why are some things culturally significant, and others are not? What exactly does "cultural significance" mean? Who assigns it, and how? In any case, it should be quite obvious that, seen from an analytical perspective, the condition or potential of anything as part of cultural heritage is not intrinsic to things, because *significance* is not an inherent property of things [55]. Although the loss of centrality of the concept of 'monument' has helped to eradicate this idea, the very concept of monument is not different to that respect: monumentality is not a property of things, but a value given by some common agreement [56].

As arguable as it is, the conception of cultural heritage behind formulations such as that from the Venice Charter is above all restrictive, but not concrete at all: no objective references are laid down to discern which entities do have a cultural significance and which do not. Traditional approaches of this kind, according to

[57], relied on the knowledge of experts who, based upon their disciplinary education in academic fields such as art history, history or archaeology, were implicitly assumed to be the only people capable to "identify the innate value and significance (…) often defined in terms of historical, scientific, educational or more generally 'cultural'" [51, 58, 59]. That is what Smith labels as an 'authorised heritage discourse' [51, Chap. 1], which is very clearly stated in such an influential document as the UNESCO World Heritage Convention of 1972 [60]: "For the purpose of this Convention, the following shall be considered as 'cultural heritage': monuments: architectural works, works of monumental sculpture and painting, elements or structures of an archaeological nature, inscriptions, cave dwellings and combinations of features, which are of outstanding universal value from the point of view of history, art or science".

A subjective, valorative process is always present here. No matter how much this judgment could be based on criteria that are shared by and agreed upon by all potential experts, so that the final diagnosis would always be the same, it still remains as a conventional adscription of something abstract (a value) to something concrete (an object) that does not hold the former inherently. This is accurately expressed by [61]: "Recognizing the fundamental contingency of heritage values does not preclude the possibility of some values that are universally held (or nearly so). These socially constructed values—think of the Great Pyramids, for instance—are seen as universal because they are so widely held, not because they are objective truths".

If the existence of such an objective truth were the case, and as pointed out by [62], this significance could be perceived by anyone, anywhere and at any time, in the same way that anyone can perceive specific colours or forms. This is not the case, even when a limited group of experts refer to a limited subset of cultural heritage: as pointed out by [63], expert approaches to such a concrete thing as 'heritage sites' have been largely characterized by "…an ad hoc approach (…) [implying that] the outcome is a number of small studies, none of which are easily comparable to each other. (…) As a result, much of the discourse surrounding heritage sites continues to be based upon an innate understanding of these places".

Thus, the main difference between the two approaches described above is not a change in the objective or subjective condition of cultural heritage. The assumption of the existence of an inherent value within things was (is) a false belief. The very concept of value implies a subjective and external judgment. The main difference lies in the context that is the origin of the valorizations that convert things into cultural heritage: who has the legitimacy to turn things into cultural heritage, from what standpoint it is done, and with what relationships to these things. The focus moved from the realm of the experts to the wider field of what is often rather vaguely labelled as "the community", "social groups" or simply "society". This does not mean that experts and their judgment play no role at all in the current practices of cultural heritage. What it does mean is that experts' judgment is no longer considered to be the one that decides which things should be considered as a part of cultural heritage.

Infrastructural Concepts

The previous section described various positions in relation to what cultural heritage is. In this section, we clarify what notions we adopt, and how they will be used throughout this book. Some of these terms and concepts have been explored and justified in [64].

> **Definition**
> A **culture** is *the collection of shared beliefs and norms that guide human action within a group.*

This definition has several consequences. Firstly, a culture occurs within a group and is local to it, so that it may not be applicable outside that group. This does not mean that we cannot observe, understand or reason about someone else's culture; we can, but it is *their* culture as opposed to *ours*, and therefore, it guides their actions rather than ours.

Secondly, culture guides human action. This means that cultural beliefs and norms do not fully determine what we do; rather, they influence and shape it without exerting a complete control. Other factors such as our biology, individual differences, or chance also play a part.

Finally, culture is composed of beliefs and norms, which implies that culture is abstract. Non-abstract entities such as books, films or songs are not part of the culture, but constitute cultural products.

This definition of "culture" does not capture the fact that a culture changes and evolves over time according to human action and other influencing factors. The reason for this is that it could not be otherwise, so this fact does not add to the definition. Still, it is an important characteristic of the culture concept.

> **Definition**
> A **cultural product** is *a thing generated within a group and that, as a consequence, reflects the culture of this group.*

This definition means that everything that we produce is a cultural product. Buildings, songs, social performances, dressing styles and many other things are cultural products. Things that are unintentionally produced by us, such as crop marks or pollution, are also cultural products. Things that are not produced by us, such as birds, mountains or the Moon, are not cultural products. You may argue that birds, mountains and the Moon are indeed cultural products as we hold subjective and culture-dependent conceptions about them. This is true; however, these conceptions constitute representations of birds, mountains and the Moon, rather than being identical to them. In this regard, distinguishing between a thing and its representations is of paramount importance, as it allows us to compare and reason about different perspectives on the same things.

Having said that, different cultural products involve different degrees of cultural influence. A landscape, for example, is a cultural product, but is strongly determined by the natural, non-cultural features of the terrain and environment, such as its geology or climate. However, the design of a company's logo is very strongly determined by our culture, bearing almost no non-cultural influences.

Regardless of whether they are cultural products or not, things may receive cultural value.

Definition

Cultural value is *the agreed-upon importance that a group grants to something as an acknowledgement that this thing incarnates values or rules representative of a culture that is relevant to them.*

This definition may look a bit complicated. Let us unpack it. First, cultural value is about the importance that we grant to something. Note that the definition requires that this importance has been agreed upon; in other words, cultural value is assigned by consensus, rather than on an individual basis. For example, I may consider a particular book in my collection to be extremely valuable, but since this importance is something that only concerns me, this would not constitute cultural value.

Also, note that cultural value is granted to something. In other words, cultural value is not intrinsic to the thing receiving it, but is something external to it, which is added by a group in specific circumstances. The thing receiving cultural value, in addition, does not need to be a cultural product. We can give cultural value to a building (which is a cultural product) but also to the Moon (which is not). Note here that things that are not cultural products, such as the Moon, may still incarnate values or rules of a culture, not by design but through other means such as social consensus, convention or even chance.

As discussed previously, you may argue here that the Moon (or birds, or the oceans) are indeed cultural products, since they are interpreted by groups within certain cultural settings, and they are conceptualized according to each group's culture. We agree that these phenomena occur, but this does not mean that the Moon or birds constitute cultural products, because they have not been generated through human action. In other words, they would still exist, and be very similar to what they actually are, had humans never appeared on Earth. Having said this, it is true that the *meaning* of birds or the Moon for a certain group is culturally constructed, but not the underlying physical entities on which this meaning occurs. Remember to always differentiate between a representation (especially, an interpretation) and what the representation refers to, as this is what allows us to consider multi-vocal scenarios.

In addition, we grant cultural value to something as a consequence of recognizing that this thing embodies or represents some of the values and rules of a

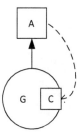

Fig. 19.1 A group G grants cultural value to a thing A because A embodies G's culture C. This diagram and others in this chapter do not use ConML notation. The solid arrow with a black head means 'grants value'; the dashed arrow with a simple head means 'embodies'

culture that is relevant to us. In other words, cultural value appears when we acknowledge that something is representative of a culture. This means that cultural value is never caused by situations not involving the embodiment of cultural values and rules; for example, the importance that we give something because it has a high economic value or because it is very rare would not constitute cultural value, but value of some other kind.

Finally, note that the values and rules that are embodied in something receiving cultural value do not need to pertain to our own culture. The definition only requires that this culture is relevant to the group granting cultural value, but this admits many variations. In the simplest scenario, we often give something cultural value because we agree that it embodies our own culture; for example, the novel *On the Road* by Jack Kerouac is often valued by contemporary American society as an insightful and powerful embodiment of some of their own cultural values. Situations like this are depicted by Fig. 19.1.

But we may also give something cultural value because we agree that it embodies a different culture that we want to study, admire or even censure, among other possibilities. An example would be *ikebana*, the Japanese art of flower arrangement, which is usually valued by Western societies because of its supposed embodiment of parts of the Japanese culture. This is shown in Fig. 19.2.

We may even give something cultural value because we agree that it represents what used to be our culture in the past or what we think will be our culture in the future. An example would be the novels written by Jane Austen, which often are culturally valued by the contemporary English society as good representatives of

Fig. 19.2 A group $G1$ grants cultural value to a thing A because A embodies another group $G2$'s culture $C2$, and $G1$ considers $C2$ to be relevant

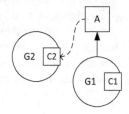

Fig. 19.3 A group G grants
cultural value to thing A in
moment 2 because
A embodies what used to be
G's culture C in a past
moment 1

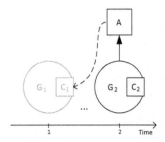

the values and norms of the English society of the late eighteenth and early nineteenth centuries. Figure 19.3 shows an example.

Cultural value is necessary to make something cultural heritage, but not enough. In this regard, note that something may receive cultural value and still not be part of cultural heritage. For example, the outdoors binge drinking parties that many teenagers go to in many Spanish towns definitely embody values from our culture. However, most of us would agree that they are not part of cultural heritage, as we do not consider them to be of cultural importance.

To make something part of cultural heritage, heritage value is necessary in addition to cultural value.

> **Definition**
> **Heritage value** is *the agreed-upon importance that a group grants to something as an acknowledgement that this thing may potentially benefit a relevant group in the future.*

Like in the case of cultural value, heritage value is granted to something by a group as the result of consensus. However, there is a substantial difference to the previous case. For heritage value, the reason why the value is granted does not reside in the embodiment of cultural values and rules, but in the shared belief that the thing being valued can produce certain benefits in the future. Like in the previous case, these benefits may be for our own group or some other group that is relevant to us. For example, most Italians value their Roman age monuments because of the potential economic benefits that these bring through tourism. This situation is illustrated by Fig. 19.4.

As in the previous case, the thing being valued does not need to be a cultural product, but can be anything. We can grant heritage value to cultural products such as a building, or to other things such as Antarctica or the oceans.

Also as in the previous case, the group receiving the benefit in a heritage valuation may be different to the one granting the value, as long as its culture is relevant; it can be a group that we want to study, admire or censure, among other possibilities. For example, most Western archaeologists probably agree in valuing the Uluru rock formation in Australia as potentially beneficial to the Aboriginal

Fig. 19.4 A group *G* grants heritage value to thing *A* because *A* may benefit *G* in the future. The solid line with a cross stroke at the end means 'may benefit'

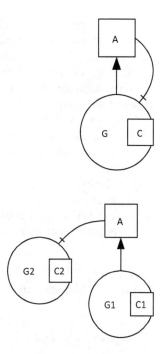

Fig. 19.5 A group *G*1 grants heritage value to thing *A* because *A* may benefit another group *G*2 in the future, and *G*1 considers *G*2's culture *C*2 to be relevant

communities of the area in relation to their identity, beliefs and even tourism-related revenue (despite the potential negative consequences of mass tourism). This is depicted in Fig. 19.5.

Note that the fact that a group agrees with or supports the value granting of another group does not mean that the first group also grants the same value. For example, city dwellers in Western societies often agree with, and support, the valuation that some farmers and country dwellers make of traditional ways of living as being likely beneficial in the future as income generators (through ecotourism, for example) and elements of social cohesion. This does not mean that city dwellers are granting this value themselves. This is illustrated in Fig. 19.6.

Heritage value falls within what in ethics is called *instrumental value* [3, "Instrumental Rationality"]. In other words, things don't receive heritage value as an end of itself, but are granted this value for a very particular purpose, namely,

Fig. 19.6 A group *G*1 grants heritage value to thing *A* because *A* may benefit *G*1 in the future. At the same time, another group *G*2 agrees with and supports *G*1's value granting. The solid arrow with a hollow head means 'agrees with and supports'

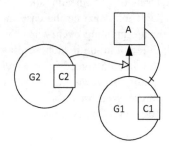

because we expect that a benefit will be obtained in the future from the valued things. Cultural value, contrarily, is not instrumental but *intrinsic* [3, "Intrinsic vs. Extrinsic Value"]; things with cultural value are not supposed to be "useful" or involved in any beneficial process; rather, we value them as an end of itself.

A consequence of our definition above is that anything that is consensually believed to have potential to benefit a group may be granted heritage value. This includes, for example, something of very high economic value such as an oil reserve; this constitutes economic heritage, also known as estate. Note that heritage value is necessary to make something cultural heritage, but not enough; for example, an oil reserve, despite having heritage value, would not be considered cultural heritage by most of us as it lacks the necessary cultural value.

To make something part of cultural heritage, cultural value is necessary in addition to heritage value. Both cultural and heritage values are so combined into the compound concept of 'cultural heritage value'.

> **Definition**
> **Cultural heritage value** is *the agreed-upon importance that a group grants to something as an acknowledgement that that this thing incarnates values or rules representative of a culture that is relevant to them, and that it may potentially benefit a relevant group in the future.*

Cultural heritage value combines the main notion of heritage value with the need for cultural value. This theory of cultural heritage, based on importance and potential future benefit, resonates with the overall view of heritage embodied in Resolution 11 of the World Archaeological Congress 30th Anniversary Plenary, also known as the Kyoto 2016 Statement on the Future Collaboration of International Archaeological Learned Communities [65] which, in point 1, commits to "protect vitally important traditions and heritages [...] for the well-being of diverse communities across the world". The future well-being mentioned in this statement corresponds to the potential future benefits in our theory.

Also, and as in previous cases, the group granting the value is often the same group that is potentially benefitted; for example, the French or the Italian usually value their food and food-related customs as representative of their respective cultures and believe that preserving these customs may benefit them in the future in terms of good health, social belonging and tourism. This is shown in Fig. 19.7.

It may also be the case that the expected benefit falls on the group doing the value granting even when the culture embodied by the valued thing is that of a different group if such a culture is considered to be relevant. An example would be the value assigned by researchers in anthropology or archaeology to the material culture of Maya art, due to the potential benefits that it may bring to present and future Western societies in terms of generation of new knowledge and understanding. This is shown in Fig. 19.8.

Fig. 19.7 A group G grants
cultural heritage value to
thing A because A, which
embodies G's culture C, may
benefit G in the future

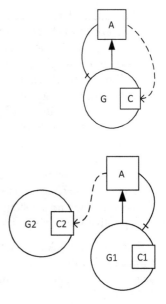

Fig. 19.8 A group $G1$ grants
cultural heritage value to
thing A because A, which
embodies $G2$'s culture $C2$,
may benefit $G1$ in the future,
and $G1$ considers $C2$ to be
relevant

Alternatively, it may be the case that the culture embodied by the thing being
valued is that of the same group doing the value granting, while the expected
benefits fall on a different group. This would be the case, for example, of the value
that used to be granted to Christian beliefs and norms by Christopher Columbus and
his supporters during his trips to America; while believing that Christianity was a
good representation of their own culture, they also thought that it would benefit
American natives. This is shown in Fig. 19.9.

So far, we have illustrated only a few typical situations, and many others are
possible. Also, we have extensively employed the notion of 'benefits' in our definitions. But, what kind of benefits can be expected from cultural heritage? At least,
the following:

- **Scientific-technical**. Something is valued because of its potentiality to generate
  new knowledge or goods within a group. For example, this includes situations
  where researchers learn new things about the world or engineers construct things
  that are needed or wanted.

Fig. 19.9 A group $G1$ grants
cultural heritage value to
thing A because A, which
embodies $G1$'s culture $C1$,
may benefit $G2$ in the future,
and $G1$ considers $C2$ to be
relevant

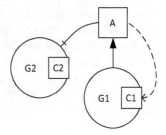

- **Administrative**. Something is valued because of its expected capacity to organize, provide cohesion to, and in general socially improve a group. For example, this includes situations where the managers develop policies in order to decrease the group's crime or poverty rates or increase the overall health or well-being of its members.
- **Community**. Something is valued because of its expected capacity to generate feelings of identity, belonging and continuity on the members of a group. For example, this includes situations where the people in a village or region maintain or reinforce their collective identity.
- **External**. Something is valued because of its expected capacity to induce feelings of admiration, fascination, and strangeness on the members of a group. For example, this includes situations where tourists or visitors are persuaded to admire something so far new and remarkable to them, and thus adopt a positive stance about it.

Cultural heritage value constitutes the basis for cultural heritage. Note that cultural heritage value may be given by anyone, as long as consensus is involved, rather than specialists only as in the traditional views described in previous sections. Through consensus, anyone may grant cultural heritage value to anything and of any of the types described above: scientific-technical, administrative, community or external.

> **Definition**
> **Cultural heritage** is *the set of things that are granted cultural heritage value by a group.*

In other words, something is part of the cultural heritage of a group if it receives cultural heritage value from this group. Note that cultural heritage, like all the previous concepts discussed in this chapter, is local to a group, because it is based on cultural heritage value, which is also local to a group. Something may be cultural heritage to a group but not to another. Note also that "group" here means any group, from a few individuals sharing some commonalities, to the whole world.

Also, note that cultural heritage is a *collection of things* . In this regard, anything may, at least in principle, be part of cultural heritage, depending on what value is granted to it. Interestingly, and as pointed out above, the things that compose cultural heritage do not need to be cultural products. For example, the biodiversity of the Amazon rainforest or the continent of Antarctica is often considered to be part of cultural heritage by many, but neither of them are cultural products in the sense we describe above. Figure 19.10 depicts cultural heritage plus other related concepts. Here, things inside C have received cultural value, such as binge drinking parties or Uluru. Things inside H have received heritage value, such as an oil reserve, Uluru or the oceans. Things inside the intersection CH, such as Uluru, receive both kinds of value and, therefore, are said to be cultural heritage. Things in

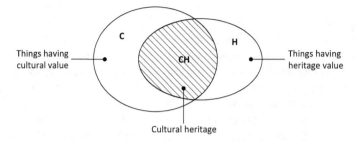

Fig. 19.10 Cultural heritage is the collection of things that have both cultural and heritage value

C but not in H are culturally valued, but lack the potentiality to provide benefits in the future. Things in H but not in C may produce benefits, but they do not embody a relevant culture.

As an additional consequence, this solves the sometimes muddled discussion about natural versus cultural heritage . In our usage of the term "cultural heritage", the word "cultural" points to the fact that whatever makes up cultural heritage does it because it embodies some relevant culture. It *does not* point to the fact that cultural value is granted within a culture; it would not make sense to point to this, as it is always the case and therefore it adds nothing to the definition. Since "cultural" in "cultural heritage" means that cultural heritage embodies a culture, then other kinds of heritage that are still heritage but do not embody a culture (H and not CH in Fig. 19.10) should not be called "cultural heritage". For example, Antarctica or the oceans may be termed "natural heritage"; an oil reserve may be classed as "economic heritage".

The definition above also implies that cultural heritage is not a process , as claimed by some authors and described in the previous section. A process is something that occurs in time and has a start and an end, so that sentences such as "before X", "after X" or "during X", where X is the process, make sense. For example, a war is a process, and so we can say things like "before the war" or "during the war"; however, it does not make sense to say "before cultural heritage" or "during cultural heritage". What definitely is a process, however, is the collection of practices or activities by which something is granted cultural heritage value; this has been called the *process of heritage formation* by some authors. But cultural heritage formation and cultural heritage are not the same thing, like a house and its construction are not the same thing. The authors who claim that cultural heritage is a process, such as Smith or Waterton [51, 52], have mixed up the process of heritage formation and heritage itself in their enthusiasm to highlight the valorization processes as opposed to the things being valorized. We agree that valorization processes are the key to cultural heritage formation, but this does not mean that the process and the thing undergoing the process are the same thing.

Technical

In this book, we commit to an ontological position often called the *substance paradigm*. This position maintains that things are the primary entities in the world, and changes to things, which also exist, are subsidiary to the former. The substance paradigm has been the mainstream position in Western philosophy for centuries, but is significantly opposed by the *process paradigm*. This approach argues that change and "becoming" are the primary kinds of entities that exist, and static physical things are just a secondary phenomenon. Although the process paradigm has its merits and the substance paradigm cannot explain everything, we have adopted the latter here for the sake of simplicity and intuitiveness, and the definitions and discussion in this chapter are especially based on it.

For more information on the process paradigm, see [3, "Process Philosophy"].

At this stage, we must clarify that the process of heritage formation is not necessarily linear. That is, situations where an entity receives heritage value and thus becomes cultural heritage may occur, but things are usually more complex. For example, heritage value is often constructed on top of previously existing values, and collections of entities may receive value as a set rather than one by one. Also, the very fact that an entity receives value and becomes cultural heritage may have a significant impact on the cultural setting where this occurs, thus closing a loop and producing feedback. The statement "entity plus value equals heritage" works as a definition, but should not be taken as a description of the heritage formation process.

Additionally, the definition given above shows that many of the usual subdivisions of cultural heritage that are commonly found, such as artistic heritage, intangible heritage, archaeological heritage, industrial heritage, are very ambiguous. Adjectives like these are usually applied to the word "heritage" to describe a collection of barely related aspects, including the nature of the underlying things that are considered heritage, or the academic discipline under which they have been studied. For example, intangible heritage is actually heritage composed by things which happen to be intangible or immaterial; in this case, the adjective "intangible" refers to a property of the things receiving cultural heritage value, but says nothing about how they are studied. Contrarily, archaeological heritage refers to things that have been studied by archaeology, regardless of their kind. Similarly, industrial heritage refers to things that have had (or still have) an industrial function, regardless of what disciplines study them and whether or not they are material. To avoid this confusion and overlapping designations, we adopt an approach here that avoids any qualifications of cultural heritage and instead categorizes only the things that receive cultural heritage value. In this manner, we can speak of immaterial entities or industrial entities, but not of immaterial or industrial heritage, for example.

You may have noticed that a key element is missing from the definitions above that is often cited as a crucial component of cultural heritage: the fact of preservation. Cultural heritage is to be preserved, and many authors consider this characteristic an essential and definitional trait of cultural heritage. We have not included it in the definitions above because we do not think it is a definitional characteristic, but a derived one. In this regard, the inherent potentiality of the things that constitute cultural heritage (as per the definition of "cultural heritage value") to provide benefits in the future usually entails a desire to preserve them over time. In other words, since, by definition, we believe that cultural heritage can be beneficial in the future, then we are usually impelled to preserve it. In this manner, our will to preserve cultural heritage is captured as a direct consequence of the provided definitions.

You may think that the definition of cultural heritage given above is too brief and simple, and that cultural heritage is too complex and intricate as to be defined by a single short sentence. However, bear in mind that the power of the definition rests on the other concepts that have been defined before, on which the definition stands. Chaining definitions like this is what allows us to develop a comprehensive and expressive conceptualization of very complex portions of reality.

Finally, you may think that other definitions of cultural heritage are possible, and that one should not be forced to accept the one provided here. We agree. The definitions given here work as a motivation for CHARM, but you can use CHARM even if you do not agree with these definitions. The only principles you need to agree with if you want to use CHARM are these:

- Cultural heritage is a collection of things, rather than a process.
- What makes a thing to be part of cultural heritage is some kind of value, externally assigned by agents.

In addition, and once we have agreed to the principles above, bear in mind that most definitions of cultural heritage that you may be able to think of are, in fact, special cases of the definition given here. For example, some argue that cultural heritage should be composed only of those that a relevant authority in the government of a state has recognized as such through legal or administrative procedures. Regardless of whether you agree or not with this definition, it is easy to see how it can be formulated as a special case of our definition that "cultural heritage is the set of things that are granted cultural heritage value by a group", by limiting this group to be composed of specialists from the corresponding authority, and the associated benefit (as referred to by "cultural heritage value is the agreed-upon importance that a group grants to something as an acknowledgement that this thing incarnates values or rules representative of a culture that is relevant to the group, and that it may potentially benefit a relevant group in the future") to be of an administrative kind. We would end up with definitions such as:

- Cultural heritage is the set of things that are granted cultural heritage value by a relevant state authority.
- Cultural heritage value, in turn, is the agreed-upon importance that said authority grants to something as an acknowledgement that this thing incarnates values or rules representative of and relevant to our culture, and that it may potentially benefit us in the future.

As you can see, this old-fashioned but plausible definition of cultural heritage can be obtained by replacing some terms in the provided definitions so that the groups and values involved are limited to specific scenarios. In general, we can argue that the definitions provided here are abstract enough as to encompass any sensible definition of cultural heritage that anybody may want to employ.

The Basic Concepts of CHARM

The conceptualization described in the previous section works as an infrastructure for the definition of CHARM. In this manner, CHARM is constructed around three basic pillars:

- **Valuable entities**. These are the things in the world that have received, currently receive, or may receive cultural heritage value. Almost anything can be a valuable entity, and CHARM does not impose any restrictions in this regard.
- **Valorizations**. These are the cultural heritage values that are granted to things, and are shaped by the four kinds of benefits outlined in the previous section.
- **Representations**. These are accounts or portrayals of other things, including valuable entities and valorizations, which are used as intermediaries when we interact with cultural heritage.

As you can see from this organization, CHARM starts from the basis that valuable entities and valorizations are different and separate things, although valorizations are always applied to valuable entities. In other words, things do not have an intrinsic cultural heritage value; there needs to be a valorization for this to happen.

The remaining chapters in this part describe CHARM in its entirety, according to the conceptual principles that we have established here. If you would rather have a quick overview of the contents of CHARM, rather than a comprehensive explanation, see the CHARM White Paper [66].

Summary

CHARM is a very abstract conceptual model of cultural heritage, intended to be used by different individuals and organizations as a common and shared reference.

CHARM cannot be used as is; you need to **extend** it first by adding the necessary details for your specific situations and thus obtaining a **particular model**.

CHARM covers most areas related to cultural heritage, including tangible, performative, abstract and derived entities, as well as occurrences, agents, representations, valorizations and locations.

CHARM is based on the precept that things do not possess intrinsic cultural heritage value; there needs to be a group who grants something **value** for it to become cultural heritage.

Cultural value may be granted to something if it embodies or represents the culture of a relevant group.

Heritage value may be granted to something if it is likely to produce benefits to a relevant group.

Cultural heritage value is a combination of the two former; it is granted to things that embody the culture of a relevant group and are likely to produce benefits to a relevant group.

Cultural heritage is the collection of things that are granted cultural heritage value, regardless of whether they are cultural products or not.

Based on these ideas, CHARM is organized around the concepts of **valuable entities**, **valorizations** and **representations**.

Chapter 20
Overview of CHARM

Abstract In this chapter, we provide a comprehensive overview of the complete CHARM, using the major concepts introduced in the previous chapter. We explain the major notions of primary and derived entities, tangible entities, agents, manifestations, performative entities, occurrences, abstract entities, valorizations and virtual entities. We also describe how these major concepts are organized in the model and how they relate to each other.

We closed the previous chapter saying that CHARM is organized around three major ideas: valuable entities, valorizations and representations. In this chapter, we describe the specific classes and related model elements that implement these notions. In general, we will describe the classes in CHARM from the most abstract to the most concrete.

A full reference of CHARM is available online at http://www.charminfo.org/Reference, including a complete description of each class, attribute, semi-association and enumerated type, as well as comprehensive diagrams and a full-text search feature. The version of CHARM described in this book is 0.9.4.2, the latest at the time of writing. However, it is possible that the online reference shows a newer version if you visit the Website long after the publication of this book.

Top View of CHARM

Look at the diagram in Fig. 20.1. This shows the classes at the "top" of CHARM, that is, its most abstract classes. Most of the other 160-plus classes in the model are descendants of these. At the top, you can see *ValuableEntity*, which represents *an entity that has received, currently receives or may receive cultural heritage value*. As introduced in the previous chapter, almost anything can be a valuable entity, which agrees with the notion of value-based cultural heritage. Each valuable entity may have a number of names; this allows us to refer to them as necessary.

© Springer International Publishing AG 2018

C. Gonzalez-Perez, *Information Modelling for Archaeology and Anthropology*,
https://doi.org/10.1007/978-3-319-72652-6_20

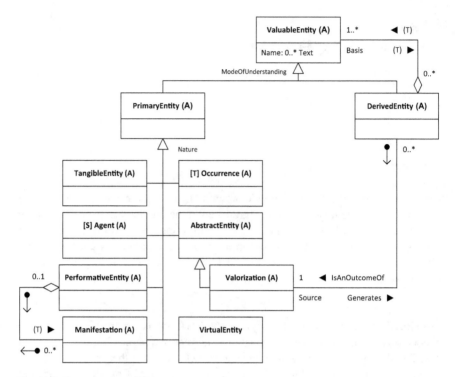

Fig. 20.1 Topmost view of CHARM

There are two kinds of valuable entities, implemented by the classes *PrimaryEntity* and *DerivedEntity*. A primary entity is *a valuable entity which, when perceived, is understood without the need of explicit interpretive processes*. This does not mean that primary entities are completely objective or that everyone understands them in the same manner. Different people usually understand primary entities in different ways since their perception is mediated by different and implicit subjectivities that shape the primary entity distinctly. What it does mean is that anyone who perceives a primary entity will understand it as such, be able to distinguish it from other entities in the world and be able to categorize it, without the aid of external or additional information. You may recall the two premises of conceptual modelling that we introduced in Chap. 2. First, we said that reality can be discretized into separate things; then, we added that things can be categorized in a meaningful way. Primary entities, precisely, are defined as those things that can be discretized and categorized immediately and by anyone, whatever the form or manner, without additional information. Examples of primary entities include a mountain, a house, a book or a song; anyone who sees a mountain or a house, or holds a book in their hands, or hears a song, is capable of separating these entities from the rest of the world as something specific and will assign them to a category that feels appropriate to them.

A derived entity, on the contrary, is *a valuable entity that is not understood in an immediate and implicit manner when perceived but requires an explicit reception process*. In other words, derived entities cannot be immediately discretized and categorized by anyone when perceived, in the absence of an external explanation. An example of derived entity would be that of an archaeological site; an archaeologist more or less familiar with a site may recognize it when they see it; however, someone who is not familiar with the site or, more especially, someone who has no archaeological training may not be able to separate the site from its surrounding environment or assign it to a category. Archaeological sites are the product of complex interpretations based on material evidences, background knowledge and context, and it may be very difficult for someone unfamiliar with it to recognize a site as such in the absence of an explicit description of these interpretive aspects.

Each derived entity has a number of valuable entities as a basis. This means that derived entities are always grounded on at least another valuable entity. For example, an archaeological site is defined around a place; the place acts as the basis for the site. Derived entities are explored in depth in Chap. 29; the remainder of this chapter focuses on primary entities.

There are multiple subtypes of primary entities, depending on the main mode of understanding. First of all, the class *TangibleEntity* represents *a primary entity that is fundamentally perceived in a direct fashion and through its materiality*. As the class name indicates, tangible entities are composed of matter and can be touched. Examples of tangible entities include a place, a house, a book, a hole in the ground or a painting. Chapter 22 describes tangible entities in detail.

Second, the class *Agent* represents *a primary entity corresponding to a person or group of people*. Basically, agents are people but they can be described in terms of the role that they play in their community or in a heritage-related study. Also, agents include groups, such as the neighbours of a village, a business organization or a family.

The *Agent* class constitutes CHARM's subjective aspect. This means that perspectives of objects for any subjective feature that may appear in CHARM are multi-vocally situated in terms of agents. Chapter 23 describes agents in depth and explains how they can be used to construct perspectives and manage subjectivity in CHARM.

Third, the class *Manifestation* represents *a primary entity corresponding to a human expression at a given time and place, and which is fundamentally perceived in a direct fashion and through performative aspects*. Manifestations constitute performances carried out by people at a particular time and place, such as Mike Oldfield playing *Crises* at Wembley on 22 July 1983, or Martin Luther King, Jr. and others during the rally in Memphis on 29 March 1968. When Mike Oldfield played *Crises* again in 1995 at a different venue, that constituted a different manifestation.

Fourth, the class *PerformativeEntity* represents *a primary entity that abstracts similar manifestations and is fundamentally perceived in an indirect fashion through them*. Performative entities are interpretive constructs that are built from the perception and interpretation of similar manifestations. As such, their ontology is much more subjective than that of tangible entities (the materiality of which gives them certain objectivity) or even manifestations (the phenomenology of which plays a similar role to materiality in the previous case). For example, after observing Mike Oldfield play at different venues over time, we may construct the abstraction 'Mike Oldfield concert', which can be described and studied as such and as a separate thing from each of the associated manifestations, namely, each individual concert. The 'Mike Oldfield concert' construct is a performative entity. Similarly, constructions such as the Burning Man of Black Rock City or attending mass on Sunday are performative entities. We perceive them through the specific manifestations they may have, such as particular editions of Burning Man or particular groups of people attending mass at specific times and places.

Note the whole/part association between *PerformativeEntity* and *Manifestation*. It states that each performative entity is composed of a number of manifestations, which may vary over time. Also, it states that each manifestation may be part of a performative entity. In fact, many manifestations are never aggregated into a performative entity, such as one-off performances that do not present a clear pattern. Note that the performative entity, to which a manifestation belongs, if any, is not temporal; that is, a manifestation is unchangeably connected to a particular performative entity, or to none at all. Chapter 24 describes manifestations and performative entities in detail.

Fifth, the class *Occurrence* represents *a primary entity corresponding to an event or situation that happens in relation to one or more valuable entities.* In other words, an occurrence is something that occurs in relation to other primary entities and cannot be described or understood in the absence of them. An example of occurrence is the construction of a building; the building is a tangible entity, but its construction, as such, is an occurrence. Similarly, a war, the erosion of a rock by the wind, the burning of wood in a hut to cook food or the high crime rates in a city are all occurrences.

It is important to note that the *Occurrence* class constitutes CHARM's temporal aspect. This means that phases of objects for any temporal feature that may appear in CHARM are situated in time in terms of occurrences. Chapter 25 describes occurrences in depth and explains how they can be used to construct phases and manage temporality in CHARM.

Sixth, the class *Abstract-Entity* represents *a primary entity that is socially constructed and comprised of abstractions or ideas only, with no concrete realization whatsoever.* Abstract entities pertain to the realm of ideas, and they do not manifest materially. This does not mean that other entities that represent abstract entities cannot exist; on the contrary, abstract entities are often embodied and communicated through representations. However, and as opposed to performative entities, abstract entities are seldom realized in their entirety when represented by other entities in this manner. Examples of abstract entities include languages such as English or Aymaran, beliefs such as Christianity or Marxism, norms and conventions, or valorizations. Chapter 26 explores abstract entities in detail.

Valorizations, comprising the second basic notion in CHARM, are represented by the *Valorization* class, which is a subclass of *AbstractEntity*. A valorization is *an abstract entity of a discursive nature that adds cultural heritage value to other valuable entities through interpretive processes that have been agreed upon within a group or discipline.* Valorizations are constructed interpretively, rather than by observation or description. However, not every interpretation is a valorization; a valorization must have been relatively agreed upon within a given group or discipline. Each valorization is built on one or more valuable entities, and each valorization may use other valorizations as base. Examples of valorizations include a research essay about an archaeological site, the impact assessment of a motorway on a nearby monument, or the identity and belonging feelings of the members of a community about their local church.

Note the association between *Valorization* and *DerivedEntity*. It means that every valorization may generate a number of derived entities or, in other words, every derived entity is always an outcome of a particular source valorization. In this manner, the model captures the fact that derived entities are constructed interpretively through specific valorizations. Chapter 28 describes valorizations in greater detail.

Finally, the class *VirtualEntity* represents *a primary entity that can be perceived only by intermediation of an artificial device.* Virtual entities often correspond to highly technological information records such as encoded recordings or computer files, which cannot be perceived without the necessary mechanical, electrical or electronic devices. Examples of virtual entities include a digital photograph stored as a computer file or an audio recording on magnetic tape. The *VirtualEntity* class is not abstract and has no subclasses.

Summary

The things that may receive cultural heritage value are called **valuable entities** in CHARM.

There are two kinds of valuable entities: **primary entities**, which can be immediately discretized and categorized when perceived in the absence of additional information, and **derived entities**, which cannot.

Derived entities are always grounded on some basis valuable entities.

There are multiple kinds of primary entities depending on their nature.

Tangible entities are composed of matter and perceived mostly through their materiality.

Manifestations are performances that involve specific people at a given time and place.

Performative entities are abstractions constructed to stand for similar manifestations.

Occurrences are events or situations that happen in relation to other valuable entities.

Abstract entities are socially constructed abstractions with no concrete realization.

Valorizations are a subtype of abstract entities and correspond to agreed-upon interpretive discourses that add cultural heritage value to other valuable entities.

Valorizations may generate derived entities as a result.

Agents are people and groups of people.

Virtual entities are things that can only be perceived through intermediary devices.

Exercises

34. Below you can find a list of entities. For each of them, state what CHARM class of those described in this chapter would be more suitable to model it.

    - The oldest member of a family.
    - A period of abandonment of a settlement.
    - A voodoo ritual performed in Limbé, Haiti, on 22 June 1972.
    - A leaf in a book.
    - Feminism.
    - A rocky outcrop.
    - The Klondike gold rush of the late nineteenth century.
    - The obligation to pilgrimage to Mecca in some Islamic societies.
    - The Rolling Stones.
    - A recording in a vinyl LP.
    - The Chinese New Year festival celebrated all over the world.

Chapter 21
CHARM General Concepts

Abstract In this chapter, we describe the elements in CHARM that can be used in a model to provide context or auxiliary information. First, notions related to measures are described, including named measures. Then, the concept of location is introduced, and a distinction is made between absolute and relative locations. Different kinds of locations are explored and defined, from absolute points and lines to relative locations given by reference to other entities.

Before we continue to discuss each area of CHARM in detail, we need to describe some classes that work to provide context for other entities in the model. Specifically, CHARM contains classes representing quantitative measures, which can be used to describe tangible entities, as well as classes representing locations, which can be used to situate valuable entities in space. Measures and locations describe characteristics of other classes and are always used in combination with valuable entities of some kind, so they have no autonomous existence of their own. For this reason, measures and locations are not considered to be valuable entities in CHARM.

Measures

Fig. 21.1 depicts measures in CHARM. Here, measures are represented by two classes: *NamedMeasure* and *Measure*. A named measure is *a measure qualified by a specific name*, and it always describes one particular tangible entity through the associated measure. A measure, in turn, is *the amount or degree that something has in relation to a given quantity*. A measure always has a value, which expresses the actual measurement being done; a margin, which optionally describes the tolerance or error variance that can be expected in the measurement; and a certainty, which subjectively expresses how sure we are that the measure is as documented, expressed through the *Certainty* enumerated type. The *Margin* and *Certainty*

© Springer International Publishing AG 2018

C. Gonzalez-Perez, *Information Modelling for Archaeology and Anthropology*,
https://doi.org/10.1007/978-3-319-72652-6_21

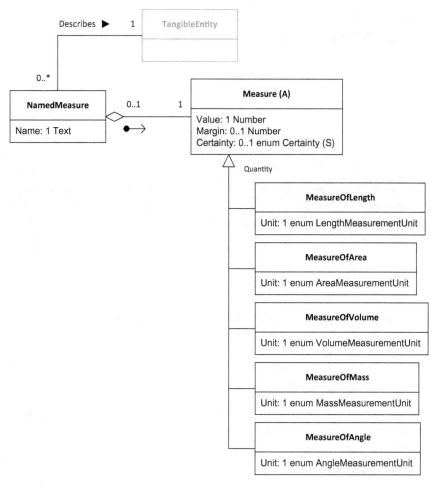

Fig. 21.1 Measures in CHARM

attributes constitute an explicit implementation of vagueness as described in Chap. 14.

There are various subclasses of *Measure* depending on the quantity being measured: *MeasureOfLength* to quantify lengths, width, depths, diameters and similar things; *MeasureOfArea* to document areas and surfaces; *MeasureOfVolume* to measure capacities and volumes; *MeasureOfMass* to quantify weights; and *MeasureOfAngle* to document angles. Each of these subclasses contains a *Unit* attribute to document what units are employed to express the measurement, expressed through the respective enumerated types *LengthMeasurementUnit*, *AreaMeasurementUnit*, *VolumeMeasurementUnit*, *MassMeasurementUnit* and *AngleMeasurementUnit*.

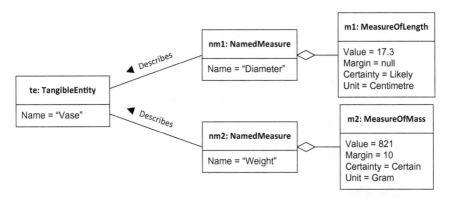

Fig. 21.2 Objects representing a vase weighing 821 ± 10 g and likely to be 17.3 cm in diameter

The *NamedMeasure* and *Measure* classes often work together. For example, imagine that we want to describe the diameter and weight of a vase. The vase would be the tangible entity being described. We would define two instances of named measure linked to the vase: one having *Name* = *"Weight"*, linked to a measure of mass, and another one having *Name* = *"Diameter"*, linked to a measure of length. Then, we would document the value, margin, certainty and units employed for each of the two measures. This is illustrated in Fig. 21.2. Notice how the measure objects describe the actual measures of the vase, and the associated named measure objects describe what those measures are measuring. By using named measures and measures together like this, we can describe a wide range of quantitative aspects of any tangible entity.

Locations

Fig. 21.3 shows location-related classes in CHARM. As you can see, every valuable entity in CHARM may be located at a number of locations, which may vary over time. The *Location* class is a very abstract way of expressing a location, and corresponds to *a specification of the spatial situation of a valuable entity*, which can be accomplished in a number of ways as established by its many descendant classes.

To start with, *Location* is specialized into *AbsoluteLocation* and *RelativeLocation*. An absolute location is *a location of a direct kind, based on a spatial reference system and which is independent of the spatial situation of any other entity*. In other words, absolute locations allow us to state where something is without referring to any other valuable entity, by specifying a set of coordinates in a particular reference system. The reference system of an absolute location is represented by the *ReferenceSystem* attribute, which is expressed in terms of the associated enumerated type *SpatialReferenceSystem*. This enumerated type takes its

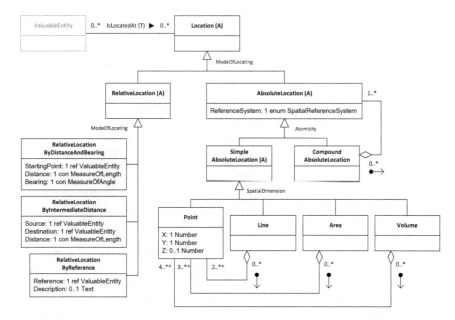

Fig. 21.3 Locations in CHARM

items from the EPSG Geodetic Parameter Dataset of the International Association
of Oil and Gas Producers (OGP); see http://www.epsg.org/ for a comprehensive list.
There are two kinds of absolute locations, represented by *SimpleAbsoluteLocation*
and *CompoundAbsoluteLocation*. A simple absolute location is *an absolute location of an atomic kind, representing a simple spatial position,* such as a point or a
polygon. A compound absolute location, in turn, is *an absolute location that is
composed of other absolute locations.* For example, some things such as an
aggregation of buildings are located through a collection of points or areas rather
than a single point or area.

Also, there are several specific classes for simple absolute locations depending
on the spatial dimension being used, namely *Point, Line, Area* and *Volume*. A point
is a simple absolute location corresponding to a simple set of X and Y coordinates;
a line is a simple absolute location corresponding to a sequence of points that
compose a line; an area is a simple absolute location corresponding to a sequence of
points that enclose an area; and a volume is a simple absolute location corresponding to a sequence of points that bound a volume. Note also that lines, areas
and volumes are always expressed in terms of sequences of points; also, each point
has X and Y coordinates plus an optional Z coordinate. In this manner, it is possible
to locate any valuable entity in zero, one, two or three dimensions. For example, we
could locate a road by using a multi-point line in 2D or 3D or an ashlar block in a
wall by using a volume with 3D information.

A relative location, as opposed to an absolute location, is *a location of an
indirect kind, based on the reference to other valuable entities.* Instead of using a

spatial reference system and a set of coordinates, relative locations work by expressing where something is in relation to other things. There are three kinds of relative locations. The *RelativeLocationByReference* class corresponds to *a relative location that uses a reference valuable entity plus an optional description in order to locate something*. Using this kind of location, we could say, for example, that a village is located close to a road or that a celebration is often held in a particular town square. The valuable entities being used as reference (the road and the town square in our examples) are represented by the *Reference* semi-association, and the *Description* attribute can document any relevant information that may aid to find the located thing.

The second type of relative location is given by the *RelativeLocationByIntermediateDistance* class, which corresponds to *a relative location that uses two reference valuable entities plus a distance between them in order to locate something*. Using this kind of location, we can say, for example, that a battle happened 8 km from Brussels in direction to Antwerp. The valuable entities being used as "from" and "to" reference places (Brussels and Antwerp in our example) are represented by the *Source* and *Destination* semi-associations, and the location distance (8 km in our example) is represented by the *Distance* semi-association. Note that *Distance* is not a Number-typed attribute but a semi-association to *MeasureOfLength*, so that different units, certainty degrees and error margins can be used.

Finally, the third type of relative location is given by the *RelativeLocationByDistanceAndBearing* class, which corresponds to *a relative location that uses a reference valuable entity, a bearing and a distance in order to locate something*. Using this kind of location, we can say, for example, that a church is 850 m south-west of a particular house. The valuable entity being used for reference (the house in our example) is represented by the *StartingPoint* semi-association. The distance from this point where the located thing can be found is represented by the *Distance* semi-association, which points, like in the previous case, to *MeasureOfLength*. And the direction in which this distance should be measured is represented by the *Bearing* semi-association, which points to *MeasureOfAngle*, thus allowing for multiple combinations of linear and angular units and measures.

Figure 21.4 shows an example of location classes being used in different manners. This example states the following situation. A celebration (object *ve1*) was located next to a church (object *ve2*) between 1932 and 1965. This church, in turn, was documented as being located 16 km (object *m1*) north-east (object *m2*) from a village (object *ve3*) as of June 2007. This village, in turn, has been located since the eighteenth century around an area given by three points (objects *p1*, *p2* and *p3*) forming a triangle. Here, you can see how relative locations work by locating something in relation to something else, and how absolute locations are expressed in terms of coordinates and a spatial reference system. Also, you can see how locations can be "chained" in order to construct complex geographical networks.

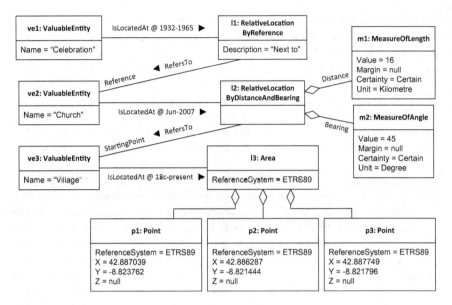

Fig. 21.4 Objects representing various valuable entities and their locations. Note how relative locations use other valuable entities as reference

Summary

There are some classes in CHARM that are designed to provide context for other classes: measures and locations.

Measure classes allow you to express named measures of tangible entities by indicating a value, an error margin, a certainty level and the units being used.

There are different types of measures, depending on what quantity is being measured: length, area, volume, mass and angle.

Location classes allow you to express where valuable entities are in space, either in absolute or relative terms.

Absolute location classes work by specifying a coordinate set in a given reference system and can use zero, one, two or three dimensions.

Relative locations work by using other valuable entities as reference, and providing distances, bearings or textual descriptions to aid in the location.

Exercises

35. Create a CHARM-compliant instance model to describe the following situation. In 1979, a ceremonial pool measuring 2.5 m by an estimated 1.8 m was found inside a crypt, which is built between 0.6 and 1.1 m below the ground surface. This crypt is located in the outskirts of the town of Scheden in Germany.

Chapter 22
Tangible Entities

Abstract In this chapter, we introduce CHARM tangible entities, that is, those which are fundamentally perceived in a direct fashion and through their materiality. We explore the different types of tangible entities in CHARM, including places (such as a valley), structures (such as a wall or a building), objects (such as a coin or a pebble), stratigraphies and samples. Other more uncommon kinds of entities are also discussed, such as material aspects (such as graffiti on a wall).

Tangible entities are perhaps the most intuitive and straightforward ones to think about when we discuss cultural heritage. As described in the previous chapters, the class *TangibleEntity* represents *a primary entity that is fundamentally perceived in a direct fashion and through its materiality*. Tangible entities are composed of matter and can be touched. Examples include a place, a house, a book, a hole in the ground or a painting.

This chapter discusses how tangible entities are conceptualized in CHARM and what subtypes there are. Figure 22.1 shows an overview of tangible entities. As you can see, there are four major kinds of tangible entities depending on their nature: places, material entities, stratigraphic entities and samples. Stratigraphic entities and samples are methodological tangible entities, because they are strongly determined by the methodology being used. These classes are discussed in the remainder of this chapter.

Places

The class *Place* corresponds to *a tangible entity that is defined by a region in physical space*. The identity of a place is given by its location in space plus other properties (size, shape, orientation) of the corresponding region, rather than its materiality, which is secondary and does not determine the identity of the place. In other words, a place is what it is because it is in a particular region of space. We can change its materiality, for example by constructing a building or digging a hole, and

© Springer International Publishing AG 2018

C. Gonzalez-Perez, *Information Modelling for Archaeology and Anthropology*,
https://doi.org/10.1007/978-3-319-72652-6_22

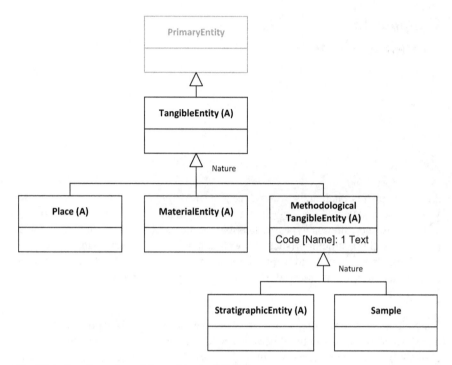

Fig. 22.1 Overview of tangibles entities in CHARM

the place is likely to stay the same place. However, we cannot move a place to a different spot and still consider it the same place. Figure 22.2 shows more details about places. As you can see, places may be subdivided into subplaces, that is, smaller places that are spatially contained inside them; conversely, places may be aggregated into frame places, or places containing them. For example, a region may contain multiple areas, and multiple regions, in turn, may belong to a continent.

Also following the diagram, *Place* is specialized into two subclasses, *NonMaterial Place* and *StructureEntity*, depending on the materiality of the place boundaries. A non-material place is *a place having boundaries with material characteristics that do not distinguish it from its surroundings*. In other words, a non-material place is a place which, despite being recognized as such, has fuzzy, imprecise or materially unclear boundaries, since there is no materiality that clearly establishes where the place begins and where its surroundings end. This kind of boundary corresponds to what have been called "fiat boundaries" by Smith and Varzi [67], and they are often subject to imprecision as described in Chap. 14. Examples of non-material places include a mountain or a forest.

Land divisions are a particular kind of non-material places. The *LandDivision* class corresponds to *a non-material place that has been defined with a land management purpose*. Since they are management-oriented, land divisions always

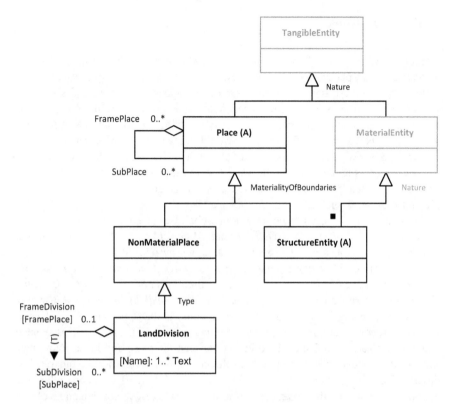

Fig. 22.2 Places in CHARM

have (at least) one name. Note that the whole/part self-association that
LandDivision inherits from *Place* is redefined in order to cater for the specific
cardinalities of land divisions. Examples of land divisions are countries, states,
provinces or municipalities.

In opposition to *NonMaterialPlace*, the class *StructureEntity* represents places
having boundaries with material characteristics that distinguish them from their
surroundings. In fact, *StructureEntity* could be also named "MaterialPlace", since it
stands for those places that do have clear material boundaries around them. Note in
Fig. 22.2 that *StructureEntity* specializes not only from *Place*, but also from
MaterialEntity and that, in fact, this latter specialization is the dominant one. This
means that structure entities are places but, more strongly, are material entities too.
For this reason, we discuss them in the following section together with other
material entities.

Note that a place's location is not intrinsically determined in CHARM. This
allows you to describe and study places regardless of where they are, or even
describe hypothetical or imaginary places that cannot be located in the physical
world. If you want to document where a place is, you need to use the location
classes described in Chap. 21.

Material Entities

The class *MaterialEntity* corresponds to *a tangible entity that is defined by its materiality*. As opposed to places, the identity of a material entity is given by its materiality and the properties of this (such as composition, texture and size). The spatial location of a material entity is secondary and does not determine its identity. In principle, we could move a material entity to a different spot and, as long as we do not alter its material configuration, it would likely stay the same material entity. Figure 22.3 shows details about material entities. The matter that defines each material entity is represented by the *Material* attribute, which is expressed in terms of the associated *Material* enumerated type. This enumerated type includes a hierarchy of items such as *Ceramic*, *Bone* or *Wood*.

MaterialEntity is specialized into four subclasses according to their nature: *StructureEntity*, *ObjectEntity*, *Deposit* and *MaterialAspect*. The first subclass, *StructureEntity*, is also a subclass of *Place*, as we introduced in the previous section. A structure entity corresponds to *a place having boundaries with material characteristics that distinguish it from its surroundings and, also, a material entity that shapes the space where it is located, influencing visibility and/or mobility over it*. A structure entity is a place and a material entity at the same time. As a place, it has very specific and materially well-defined boundaries, since the associated materiality clearly establishes the division between the place and its surroundings. This kind of boundaries corresponds to the concept of "bona fide boundaries" as described by Smith and Varzi [67]. As a material entity, its existence alters the visibility and/or mobility over the surrounding area, as a consequence of the materiality involved. Due to this materiality, structure entities often have well-defined and quite precise boundaries, unlike the non-material places discussed in the previous section. The concept of structure entity roughly corresponds to what in some fields is often referred to as "non-movable elements". Usage of this term,

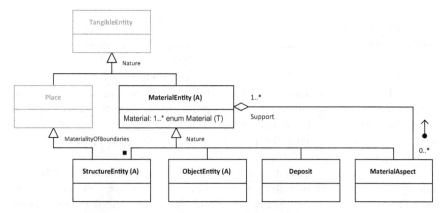

Fig. 22.3 Material entities in CHARM

however, has been discarded because it is difficult to define and because it is based on a characteristic (the movability of things) that is circumstantial and prone to exceptions. Structure entities include, for example, buildings, enclosures, ditches and caves.

Another kind of material entity is given by the *ObjectEntity* class. An object entity, in contrast to structure entities, is *a material entity that does not shape the space where it is located, not influencing visibility or mobility over it*. An object entity does not alter the visibility and/or mobility over the surrounding area, as opposed to the case with structure entities. This is usually because object entities are smaller, more mobile and less dependent on their spatial context than structure entities. The concept of object entity roughly corresponds to what is often referred to as "movable element" in some fields. Like in the previous case, however, usage of this term has been discarded because it is difficult to define and because it is based on a characteristic (the movability of things) that is circumstantial and prone to exceptions. Object entities include, for example, books, vases and pebbles.

A third kind of material entity is described by the *Deposit* class. A deposit is *a material entity corresponding to matter that has deposited gradually through accumulative processes*. As such, deposits are usually tightly integrated in their environment, and sometimes are difficult to discern. Also, they are often underground. As we describe in the next section, deposits constitute the "raw matter" of which many stratigraphies are made.

Finally, the fourth kind of material entity is given by the *MaterialAspect* class. A material aspect is *a material entity that is inextricably embedded into another material entity, called its support, and which has been added to it after the creation of the latter*. A material aspect always constitutes an integral part of its support, even though it has been added to it once it existed. Examples of material aspects include graffiti on a wall, the painting on a canvas or a rock carving. Note that the support of a material aspect can be any kind of material entity, although most material aspects are supported by either structure entities or object entities.

The following sections describe structure entities and object entities in greater detail.

Structure Entities

StructureEntity is an abstract class and has a hierarchy of descendants that allows us to model structures in quite precise ways. See Fig. 22.4. *StructureEntity* has a temporal whole/part association to *MaterialEntity*, which allows us to document what things are contained in a structure, such as a house being inside an enclosure. *StructureEntity* is specialized into two subclasses: *CompleteStructure* and *StructureFragment*. A completestructure is *a structure entity having an unaltered material integrity*. This means that the entity we are describing has not been fragmented after its creation in any significant manner. Sometimes this is difficult to determine, especially for things that are specifically created to be broken. Note that

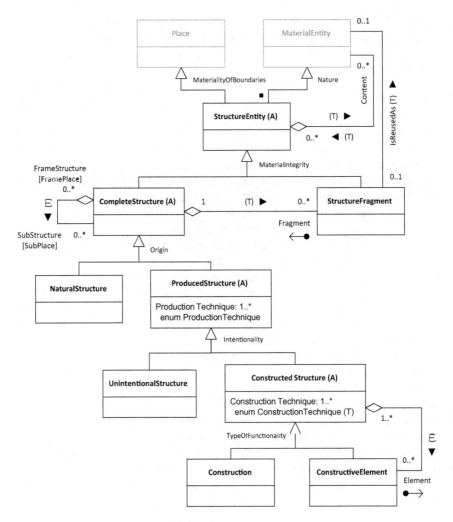

Fig. 22.4 Structure entities in CHARM

complete structures can be contained in larger frame structures and also be decomposed into smaller substructures. For example, a farm belonging to a village can be decomposed into a main building and various outbuildings. Complete structures include, for example, a house, a trench or a cave.

In opposition to complete structures, a structure fragment is *a structure entity corresponding to a separate portion of a complete structure having an altered material integrity*. In other words, structure fragments are what remains after a complete structure is broken down. This is captured in the model by the whole/part association between *CompleteStructure* and *StructureFragment*. A structure fragment, in addition, may be reused over time as a different thing. For example, an ashlar block from a wall can be used later as part of a road paving.

CompleteStructure, in turn, is specialized into *NaturalStructure* and *ProducedStructure* depending on origin. A natural structure is *a complete structure in the genesis of which no direct human intervention was involved*. Examples of natural structures include a grotto or a rocky outcrop. A produced structure, on the contrary, is *a complete structure in the genesis of which direct human intervention was involved*. Since humans are involved in the creation of produced structures, the *ProducedStructure* class has a *ProductionTechnique* attribute that represents the technique by which the structure was created, expressed in terms of the associated enumerated type *ProductionTechnique*, which contains the items *Industrial* and *Manual*.

ProducedStructure is further specialized into *UnintentionalStructure* and *ConstructedStructure* according to intentionality. An unintentional structure is *a produced structure in the genesis of which involves a direct human intervention having a purpose different to that of creating said structure*. In other words, unintentional structures are created by accident or as a by-product of an action intended to do something else. Examples of unintentional structures include fossilized plough marks or a path created by repeatedly treading on grass. In opposition, a constructed structure, which may also be called an intentional structure, is *a produced structure created by the intentional modification and/or bounding of physical space through the addition and/or removal of materials, and which, by virtue of the structural arrangement of its parts, or that of its own within a bigger whole, performs a given function*. This means that constructed structures are intentionally produced for a particular purpose that is dependent on its material organization. Since constructed structures are intentional, the *ConstructedStructure* class has a *ConstructionTechnique* attribute that represents the general approach to the use of materials to compose the structure, including their nature, treatment and disposition; this is expressed in terms of the associated enumerated type *ConstructionTechnique*, which contains a hierarchy of items such as *Mortar*, *Textile* or *Stonework*.

ConstructedStructure is finally specialized into two classes, *Construction* and *ConstructiveElement*, depending on the type of functionality involved. A construction is *a constructed entity that provides direct functionality to its users*. Constructions, being intentionally materialized places, are defined by the structuration of space. Also, constructions possess direct functionality for their users; this means that a construction's structure provides it with functionality that people using it can harness directly. Examples of constructions include a church, a megalithic tomb, a livestock pen, a monastery or a pit. In opposition, a constructive element is *a constructed entity which, despite not providing direct functionality to its users, constitutes a material part of a larger constructed entity, to which it contributes structure and/or function*. A constructive element is always a part of a larger constructed structure, as defined by the whole/part association between *ConstructedStructure* and *ConstructiveElement* in Fig. 22.4. A constructive element does not possess direct functionality for people, but for the constructed entity to which it belongs. For example, the columns of a house serve the house as a whole; the house, in turn, serves its users. Examples of constructive elements include a pillar of a bridge, the roof of a building or the access system of a livestock pen.

Object Entities

ObjectEntity is an abstract class and has a hierarchy of descendants that allows us to model objects by using a similar organization to that of structures and *StructureEntity*. See Fig. 22.5. *ObjectEntity* has a temporal whole/part self-association, which allows us to document what objects are located inside

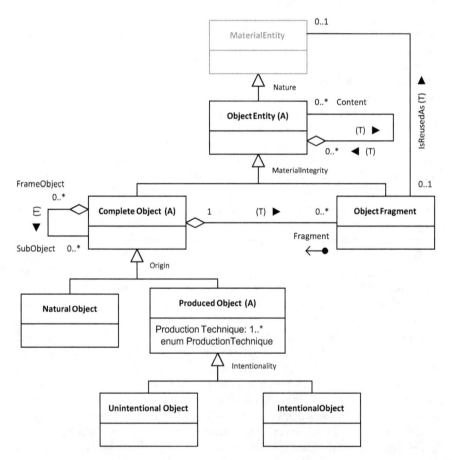

Fig. 22.5 Object entities in CHARM

another object, such as a basket containing tools. *ObjectEntity* is specialized into two subclasses: *CompleteObject* and *ObjectFragment*, following the same pattern as in the case of structures. A complete object is *an object entity having an unaltered material integrity*. This means that the object we are describing has not been fragmented after its creation in any significant manner. Like in the case of structures, this can be difficult to determine in some cases, especially for objects that are specifically created to be broken. Note that complete objects can be contained in larger frame objects and also be decomposed into smaller subobjects. For example, a buckle belonging to a belt can be decomposed into a frame, a prong and other parts. Example of complete objects includes a belt, a hammer or a pebble. There are material things that may be difficult to categorize as either structures or objects, such as a car or a pole planted in the ground. CHARM is not prescriptive in this regard: you can model them as either objects or structures, depending on what makes the more sense to your modelling purpose.

In opposition to complete objects, an object fragment is *an object entity corresponding to a separate portion of a complete object having an altered material integrity*. In other words, object fragments are what remains after a complete object is broken down. This is captured in the model by the whole/part association between *CompleteObject* and *ObjectFragment*. An object fragment, in addition, may be reused over time as a different thing. For example, a shard from a broken clay beaker can be reused later as a loom weight.

CompleteObject, in turn, is specialized into *NaturalObject* and *ProducedObject* depending on origin. A natural object is *a complete object in the genesis of which no direct human intervention was involved*. Examples of natural objects include a pebble or a clamshell. A produced object, on the contrary, is *a complete object in the genesis of which direct human intervention was involved*. Since humans are involved in the creation of produced objects, the *ProducedObject* class has a *ProductionTechnique* attribute identical to that of *ProducedStructure*, which represents the technique by which the object was created, expressed in terms of the associated enumerated type *ProductionTechnique*, which contains the items *Industrial* and *Manual*.

Finally, *ProducedObject* is further specialized into *UnintentionalObject* and *IntentionalObject* according to intentionality. An unintentional object is *a produced object in the genesis of which involves a direct human intervention having a purpose different to that of creating said object*. In other words, unintentional objects are created by accident or as a by-product of an action intended to do something else. Examples of unintentional objects include a coprolite or knapping flakes. In opposition, an intentional object is *a produced object in the genesis of which involves a deliberate human intervention having the purpose of creating said object*. This means that intentional objects are intentionally produced for a particular purpose. Examples of intentional objects include a book or a necklace.

Stratigraphic Entities

The class *StratigraphicEntity* corresponds to *a methodological tangible entity that corresponds to one or more stratigraphic units*. Stratigraphic entities are methodologically created and their definition is highly influenced by the methodology being used. The identity of a stratigraphic entity is given by its materiality, dating and relationships to other stratigraphic entities. Figure 22.6 shows details about stratigraphic entities. Note that *StratigraphicEntity* is a subclass of *MethodologicalTangibleEntity*; as a consequence, it inherits the *Code* attribute that we can use to document the unique code assigned to each stratigraphic entity.

StratigraphicEntity is specialized into *StratigraphicSequence* and *Stratigraphic Unit* according to atomicity. A stratigraphic sequence is *a stratigraphic entity composed of a collection of stratigraphic units that are physically interrelated*. Stratigraphic sequences allow us to group and manage the stratigraphic units of a particular place as a cohesive whole. This is supported by the whole/part association from *Place* to *StratigraphicSequence*. Note that, because stratigraphic sequences are assigned to places, we can equally describe the underground stratigraphy of a site or the above-ground stratigraphy of a structure such as a building.

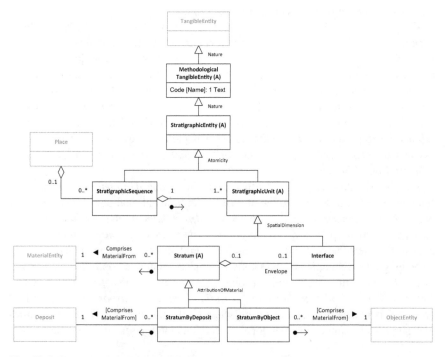

Fig. 22.6 Stratigraphic entities in CHARM

A stratigraphic unit, in turn, is *a stratigraphic entity made of matter or the trace of removed matter, arranged as a layer with regard to others, and reflecting a specific order of deposition, construction or destruction*. Every stratigraphic unit belongs to a stratigraphic sequence as described by the whole/part association between these two classes.

There are two kinds of stratigraphic units depending on spatial dimension. On the one hand, *Stratum* represents *a stratigraphic unit consisting of a material volume*. The material that makes up a stratum is always taken from a particular material entity, as specified by the *ComprisesMaterialFrom* semi-association. On the other hand, *Interface* represents *a stratigraphic unit consisting of a material surface*. Strata and interfaces can be connected by an envelope relationship, so that an interface is the envelope of a particular stratum, although we can also have interfaces that are not enveloping any stratum or strata without a documented envelope.

Finally, *Stratum* is specialized into *StratumByDeposit* and *StratumByObject* depending on the attribution of material. A stratum by deposit is *a stratum comprising matter from a deposit*, while a stratum by object is *a stratum comprising matter from an object entity*. Strata by deposit correspond to sections of deposits, or whole deposits, that are methodologically created; this is the most typical case of strata in archaeological settings. Similarly, strata by object correspond to objects or object fragments that appear embedded in a stratigraphic sequence and, therefore, are considered to be a stratum like any other. This is often the case when describing stratigraphies of constructed entities or when recording objects embedded in deposits in archaeological contexts. As you can see in Fig. 22.6, the two classes redefine the *ComprisesMaterialFrom* semi-association of *Stratum* to point to the specific classes *Deposit* and *ObjectEntity*.

The separate conceptualization that CHARM makes of the matter that makes up things (through *MaterialEntity* and its subclasses), and its stratigraphic study (through *StratigraphicEntity* and its subclasses) means that you can easily describe and interpret each of them separately or in an interconnected manner. The advantages of this approach have been described in depth and illustrated in [15].

In addition to the stratigraphic entities depicted in Fig. 22.6, CHARM includes some classes to describe stratigraphic relationships. See Fig. 22.7. Here, the *StratigraphicRelationship* class represents any relationship between two stratigraphic units, and as a consequence has two associations towards *StratigraphicUnit* with roles *Source* and *Destination*, which stand for the two stratigraphic units being connected through a relationship. Depending on the contiguity of the units, *StratigraphicRelationship* is specialized into *PhysicalStratigraphicRelationship* and *NonPhysicalStratigraphicRelationship*. A physical stratigraphic relationship is *a stratigraphic relationship between two adjacent stratigraphic units, which provides information about the temporal order between them*. This means that the units being connected through a relationship of this kind must physically touch, and the way they touch may provide information about their temporal sequence. To document this, *PhysicalStratigraphicRelationship* has an attribute *TemporalOrder*, which is

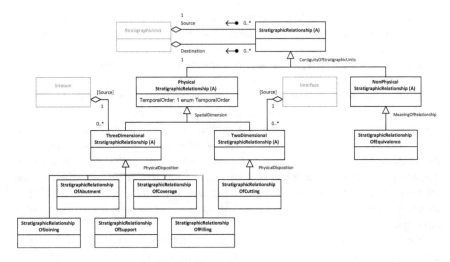

Fig. 22.7 Stratigraphic relationships in CHARM

expressed in terms of the *TemporalOrder* enumerated type, which contains items *Prior*, *Contemporary* and *Posterior*.

Unlike the physical, a non-physical stratigraphic relationship is *a stratigraphic relationship between two non-adjacent stratigraphic units*. This means that the units connected by a relationship of this kind do not physically touch. *NonPhysicalStratigraphicRelationship* only has one subclass, *Stratigraphic-RelationshipOfEquivalence*, which represents *a non-physical stratigraphic relationship that indicates the material and interpretative equivalence of the involved stratigraphic units*. Equivalence, in this context, means that the two stratigraphic units connected by this relationship pertain to the same material entity (either a deposit or an object). This stratigraphic relationship is symmetric; that is, if we state in a model that a unit A is equivalent to another unit B, this implies that B is also equivalent to A.

PhysicalStratigraphicRelationship, in turn, is specialized into *ThreeDimensionalStratigraphicRelationship* and *TwoDimensionalStratigraphicRelationship*, depending on its spatial dimension. A three-dimensional stratigraphic relationship is *a physical stratigraphic relationship having a three-dimensional source stratigraphic unit; that is, a stratum*. This is shown in the model by the fact that this class redefines the *Source* semi-association to point to *Stratum* rather than *StratigraphicUnit*. There are multiple types of three-dimensional stratigraphic relationships, depending on the physical disposition of the stratigraphic units involved. *StratigraphicRelationshipOfJoining* represents *a three-dimensional stratigraphic relationship consisting of a source stratum that horizontally touches the destination stratigraphic unit without fusing with it*. This stratigraphic relationship is symmetric; that is, if we state in a model that unit A joins unit B, this implies that B also joins A. This stratigraphic relationship allows all temporal orders: the source stratum may be prior, contemporary or posterior to the destination stratigraphic unit. An example of this relationship would be two walls that come together at a corner. *StratigraphicRelationshipOfAbutment* represents *a three-dimensional stratigraphic relationship consisting of a source stratum that horizontally fuses with the destination stratigraphic unit*. Like the previous, this stratigraphic relationship is symmetric; that is, if we state in a model that unit A abuts unit B, this implies that B also abuts A. Also like the previous, this stratigraphic relationship allows all temporal orders: the source stratum may be prior, contemporary or posterior to the destination stratigraphic unit. An example of this relationship would be a wall that, after being erected, is extended along the same plane using a different kind of masonry.

StratigraphicRelationshipOfSupport represents *a three-dimensional stratigraphic relationship consisting of a source stratum that touches the destination stratigraphic unit vertically and from above, resting on it*. This stratigraphic relationship is anti-symmetric; that is, if we state in a model that unit A is supported by unit B, this implies that B cannot be supported by A. This stratigraphic relationship allows all temporal orders: the source stratum may be prior, contemporary or posterior to the destination stratigraphic unit. However, the most frequent situation is that the source stratum is posterior to the destination stratigraphic unit. An example of this relationship would be a deposit that accumulated on top of another. *StratigraphicRelationshipOfCoverage* represents *a three-dimensional stratigraphic relationship consisting of a source stratum that attaches tightly to the surface of the destination stratigraphic unit, covering it*. Like the previous, this stratigraphic relationship is anti-symmetric; that is, if we state in a model that unit A covers unit B, this implies that B cannot cover A. This stratigraphic relationship allows one temporal order only: the source stratum is always posterior to the destination stratigraphic unit. An example of this relationship would be a paint or rendering layer applied to a wall or other structure. Finally, *StratigraphicRelationshipOfFilling* represents *a three-dimensional stratigraphic relationship consisting of a source stratum that fills a concavity of the destination stratigraphic unit*. Again, this stratigraphic relationship is anti-symmetric; that is, if we state in a model that unit A fills unit B, this implies that B cannot fill A. This stratigraphic relationship allows one temporal order only: the source stratum is always posterior to the destination stratigraphic unit. An example of this relationship would be a deposit of gravel or dirt filling out a pit.

The other subclass of *PhysicalStratigraphicRelationship* is *TwoDimensionalStratigraphicRelationship*, which represents *a physical stratigraphic relationship having a two-dimensional source stratigraphic unit, that is, an interface*. This is shown in Fig. 22.7 by the fact that this class redefines the *Source* semi-association to point to *Interface* rather than *StratigraphicUnit*. There is only one subclass of *TwoDimensionalStratigraphicRelationship*, namely *StratigraphicRelationshipOfCutting*, which represents *a two-dimensional stratigraphic relationship consisting of a source interface pertaining to a trace of removal of matter from the destination stratigraphic unit*. This stratigraphic relationship is anti-symmetric; that is, if we state in a model that unit A cuts unit B, this implies that B cannot cut A. Obviously, this stratigraphic relationship allows one temporal order only: the source interface is always posterior to the destination stratigraphic unit. An example of this relationship would be a hole dug in the ground.

You may think that having so many types of stratigraphic relationships is overkill and that one or two would suffice for the accurate documentation of stratigraphic sequences. However, bear in mind that the conceptualization of stratigraphy in CHARM must cater for both underground sequences as well as constructed sequences such as those of walls and other structures. Also, different methodologies and approaches to stratigraphy employ relationships that are slightly different. In any case, you do not need to use all the relationships that are described in CHARM; if only a couple of them are enough for your model, you can safely ignore the rest.

Samples

The *Sample* class is the last one in the *TangibleEntity* specialization hierarchy. A sample is *a methodological tangible entity corresponding to a fragment of another tangible entity the properties of which it aims to represent*. Like in the case of stratigraphic entities, the definition of samples is highly influenced by the methodology being used. Examples of samples include a sample of water from a stream or each "slice" in a stratigraphic sample column. Figure 22.8 shows details about samples. Being methodologically defined, *Sample* inherits the *Code* attribute from *MethodologicalTangibleEntity*. *Sample* also has an association to *TangibleEntity* that allows us to document what thing a sample is aiming to represent.

Fig. 22.8 Samples in CHARM

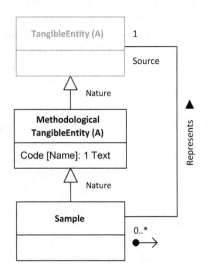

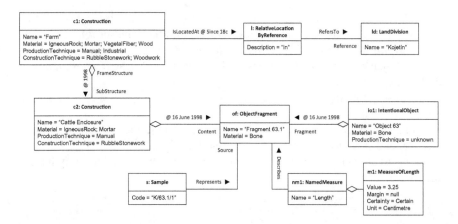

Fig. 22.9 Example model involving a number of tangible entities, locations and measures

Example Model

Let's imagine that we want to document a bone fragment that appeared inside a cattle enclosure during an archaeological survey in Kojetín, Czech Republic on 16 June 1998. The cattle enclosure is part of a farm dating back from the eighteenth century and is built of rubble and mortar. The bone fragment is 3.25 cm long and clearly belongs to a larger unknown object, but no other fragments have appeared. A sample is taken from the bone fragment for later analysis. You can see a model for this situation in Fig. 22.9. This model uses many of the classes that we have described in this chapter, including *Construction*, *LandDivision*, *ObjectFragment*, *IntentionalObject* and *Sample*. Also, it integrates measures and locations from the previous chapter. In further chapters, we add extra information to this model as we learn about new classes in CHARM.

Summary

Tangible entities are composed of matter and are perceived directly through their materiality.

Places are tangible entities that are defined by where they are, rather than what they are made of.

Material entities are tangible entities that are defined by their matter.

Structure entities are places with a material boundary, and also material entities that influence the visibility and/or mobility over the space where they are located.

Object entities, on the contrary, are material entities that do not influence the space where they are located.

Both structure and object entities can be classified into wholes and **fragments**, and wholes can be in turn classified as **natural, unintentional** or **intentional**.

Stratigraphic entities are tangible entities corresponding to matter or traces of removed matter, arranged in layers and reflecting deposition, construction or destruction processes.

Stratigraphic units include **strata** that take their material from deposits or objects, as well as **interfaces**.

Stratigraphic units can be related one to another through various kinds of physical and non-physical **stratigraphic relationships**.

Samples are tangible entities that aim to represent other tangible entity through their materiality.

Exercises

36. Below you can find a list of entities. For each of them, state what CHARM class of those described in this chapter would be more suitable to model it.

    - A cave.
    - The paintings in the cave.
    - A sacred tree.
    - A clay pot.
    - The lid of the clay pot.
    - A millstone that is being reused as part of a paving.
    - The materials of a collapsed wall as found during excavation.
    - A set of Galician bagpipes.
    - A river.
    - A gate in a cattle pen.

37. Create a CHARM-compliant instance model to describe the following situation. The Dombate dolmen in Galicia, Spain, consists of a polygonal chamber formed by seven vertical granite slabs, covered by a single capstone and protected by a tumulus made of rocky fragments and compacted dirt. All the vertical slabs have been decorated with geometric paintings. A small idol was found inside the dolmen.

Chapter 23
Agents

Abstract In this chapter, we introduce the major concepts to describe CHARM agents, that is, those entities corresponding to a person or a group of people. We explore different kinds of agents and introduce the distinction between identity agents (which provide identity) and roles (which do not). We also explain that agents work in CHARM as the subjective aspect class, so that instance models can be constructed such that subjective information is recorded depending on which agent states their views.

Agents represent people in CHARM. As we said in Chap. 19, people are a crucial component in cultural heritage processes, since it is people who give value to things so that they become cultural heritage. Also as introduced in previous chapters, the *Agent* class represents *a primary entity corresponding to a person or group of people*. This means that people, in CHARM, can be treated individually or as members of a group. Examples of agents include a particular individual, the mayor of Paris, the Amish community in Pennsylvania or an organization such as the International Monetary Fund. Agents are also the major way in which we can express subjective information in CHARM. In fact, *Agent* is the subjective aspect class in CHARM, as shown in Fig. 23.1. As shown in the diagram, agents may make use of other valuable entities, as captured by the intermediate *Use* class. A use is *a description of a situation of usage of some valuable entities by some particular agents*. The type of use that an agent makes of something is characterized by the *Type* attribute in terms of the *UseType* enumerated type, which defines items such as *Recreational*, *Symbolic* or *Transformative*. This allows us to document, for example, that a particular community uses a forest for extractive purposes or that a person employs an object with symbolic goals.

There are two kinds of agents, represented by the classes *SpecificAgent* and *MethodologicalRoleOfAgent*. A methodological role of agent is *an agent described*

© Springer International Publishing AG 2018

C. Gonzalez-Perez, *Information Modelling for Archaeology and Anthropology*,
https://doi.org/10.1007/978-3-319-72652-6_23

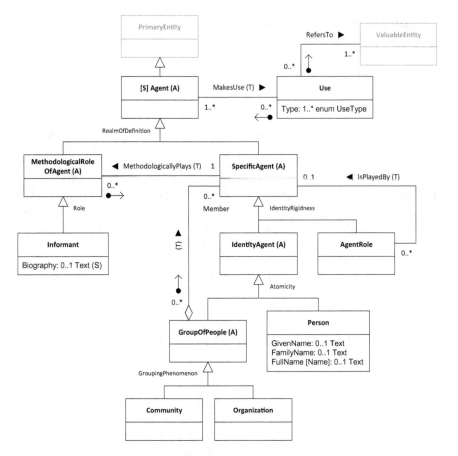

Fig. 23.1 Overview of agents in CHARM

in terms of the role it plays within the context of the usage of a particular methodology, whereas a specific agent is *an agent described in terms of its specific characteristics, regardless of the methodological role that it may play*. This allows us to consider agents *per se*, regardless of our involvement with them (in the latter case), or within the context of a particular project or task (in the former case). Also, it allows us to keep track of who plays what methodological roles by using the *MethodologicallyPlays* association.

There may be potentially many different methodological roles that agents may play; however, CHARM only incorporates the very common *Informant* class, which corresponds to *a methodological role of agent that occurs when the associated agent provides information that is modelled in the context of an ethnographic methodology*.

Regarding specific agents, there are two subclasses according to identity rigidness: *IdentityAgent* and *AgentRole*. An identity agent is *a specific agent possessing social identity, which is reflexively expressed*. In other words, identity agents self-recognize themselves as what they are. There are two kinds of identity agents according to atomicity, modelled by the *Person* and *GroupOfPeople* classes. A person is, evidently, *an identity agent corresponding to a single individual* and, as such, is characterized by *FamilyName*, *GivenName* and *FullName* attributes. A group of people, in turn, is an identity agent corresponding to multiple individuals. The *GroupOfPeople* class, consequently, has a whole/part association towards *SpecificAgent* so that we can document who is a member of which groups.

There are two kinds of groups of people, depending on the groping phenomenon, as described by classes *Community* and *Organization*. A community is *a group of people who share a common culture and identify themselves as belonging to said group*. Examples include the people in a village or the French-speaking cultural elites in Quebec. An organization, on the other hand, is *a group of people who share a common corporate identity and act together towards a common goal*. Examples include a commercial company such as Microsoft or a local gardening club in a town.

Finally, an agent role is *a specific agent not possessing a social identity, but defined through a set of responsibilities that another agent must take in a given context*. Agent roles are "labels" or "positions" that get defined within a group and may be fulfilled by other agents over time, such as 'the mayor of the town' or 'the eldest member in the family'. This is expressed through the *IsPlayedBy* association from *AgentRole* to *SpecificAgent*.

Expressing Points of View with Agents

As we said at the beginning of this chapter, *Agent* is the subjective aspect class in CHARM. This means that every subjective attribute or semi-association that is instantiated must refer to an agent as the mechanism to assign it a point of view. In other words, we use agents in CHARM to express who says what. We can use any of the descendant classes from *Agent* for this purpose. For example, we could document the description and degree of certainty of a reported event by specifying different values for *Occurrence.Description* and *Occurrence.Certainty* (see Chap. 25) according to who informs us about it. We can use individual people, groups or even roles as sources of information for this purpose. Figure 23.2 shows an example. In the figure, a person *p*, named Alice Doe, is playing the methodological role of informant. The data collected as part of her informant record (object *i*) is self-reported, and therefore is qualified by a perspective selector pointing to herself. In addition, the fire of 1971, which supposedly destroyed the town hall building, is documented by object *dch*, which is also shown as Alice's perspective and consequently qualified with the appropriate perspective selector. In summary, this model can be read as "Alice Doe is an informant in this project, and she reports her details to be...; also, she believes that a fire destroyed the town hall in 1971".

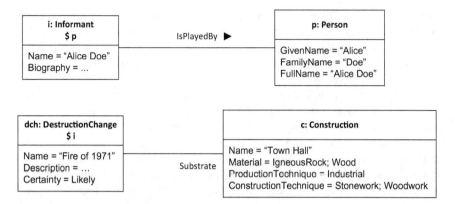

Fig. 23.2 Example model involving subjective facts

Example Model

Please look again at the *Example Model* section in the previous chapter. Now we extend the previous situation with additional information. The town people in Kojetín use the fields next to the cattle enclosure where the bone fragment was found to celebrate an annual summer festival. You can see the augmented model in Fig. 23.3. Here, the model has been completed with an instance of *Community* to represent the town people, as well as an instance of *Use* linked to an instance of *NonMaterialPlace* so that the use that people make of the adjacent fields for the summer festival is captured. In further chapters, we show how to represent the summer festival itself.

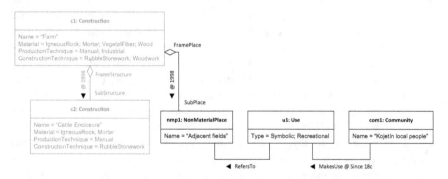

Fig. 23.3 Augmented example model involving agents

Summary

An **agent** is a person or group of people.

Agents can be used to qualify subjective information, since *Agent* is the **subjective aspect** class in CHARM.

Informants constitute a particular kind of methodological role that agents may take.

A **community** is a group of people with a common culture and self-identification as such.

An **organization** is a group of people who pursue a common goal.

An **agent role** is a "position" that exists within a group and which may be fulfilled by other agents over time.

Exercises

38. Below you can find a list of entities. For each of them, state what CHARM class of those described in this chapter would be more suitable to model it.

    - The winner of a yearly sporting competition.
    - The members of a Quaker meeting for worship.
    - A person who reports relevant information about their community.
    - The Russian people.

39. Create a CHARM-compliant instance model to describe the following situation. A family belonging to a large group has a representative in a government council. In April 1911, this person dies, and a new individual is chosen as a representative.

Chapter 24
Manifestations and Performative Entities

Abstract In this chapter, we introduce the closely related notions of manifestation and performative entity in CHARM. Manifestations are human expressions at a given time and place, which are fundamentally perceived in a direct fashion and through performative aspects. Performative entities, in turn, abstract similar manifestations and are fundamentally perceived in an indirect fashion through them. For both manifestations and performative entities, differences are made to distinguish social acts, understandings and expressive designs. In relation to the latter, different kinds are discussed, such as sound, gestural or language expressive designs, which include proper names and other linguistic constructs.

Manifestations and performative entities are closely related, and very often they are confused with each other. As we described in Chap. 20, the class *Manifestation* represents *a primary entity corresponding to a human expression at a given time and place, which is fundamentally perceived in a direct fashion and through performative aspects*. Manifestations take place when someone manifests something somewhere and sometime and are observable only if you happen to be there and then; examples include a live concert, a Catholic mass, the inauguration of a new house by a family, someone singing a tune to themselves or a baker preparing halva.

Sometimes, we observe manifestations that are similar in content (that is, in what people do) and which tend to occur at the same or similar places and perhaps regularly over time. When this happens, we are able to study the overall recurring phenomenon as well as its individual incarnations. For example, after repeatedly observing that thousands of people usually get together every year at the end of summer in Black Rock City, USA, to burn a large wooden human figure and carry out other experimental art activities, we end up giving that pattern a name ("Burning Man") and describing the phenomenon in general terms, by focusing on what usually happens rather than what actually happened one or another time. Such an abstract construction is called a performative entity. As we described in Chap. 20, the class *PerformativeEntity* represents *a primary entity that abstracts similar manifestations and is fundamentally perceived in an indirect fashion*

© Springer International Publishing AG 2018

C. Gonzalez-Perez, *Information Modelling for Archaeology and Anthropology*,
https://doi.org/10.1007/978-3-319-72652-6_24

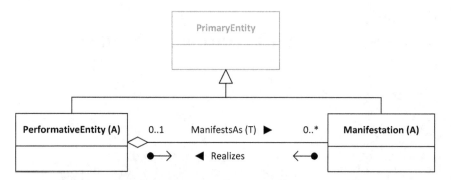

Fig. 24.1 The relationship between manifestations and performative entities in CHARM

through them. Performative entities do not actually happen; what happens is the associated manifestations. Examples of performative entities include the Burning Man festival, the *Otello* opera, the Catholic mass liturgy or the preparation of halva.

This chapter discusses how manifestations and performative entities are conceptualized in CHARM, what subtypes of each there are, and how they relate to each other, as depicted in Fig. 24.1. As you can see here, each performative entity may manifest a number of manifestations over time; at the same time, each manifestation may realize a particular performative entity whenever it occurs. The descendant hierarchies of *Manifestation* and *PerformativeEntity* are extremely similar, almost a mirror image of one another, and the *ManifestsAs* association depicted in Fig. 24.1 is accordingly redefined by each pair of descendant classes. In the remainder of this chapter, performative entities are discussed first, then followed by manifestations.

Performative Entities

The class *PerformativeEntity* corresponds to *a primary entity that abstracts similar manifestations and is fundamentally perceived in an indirect fashion through them.* Performative entities are interpretive constructs that are built from the perception and interpretation of specific manifestations. As such, their ontology is much more subjective than that of tangible entities (the materiality of which gives them certain objectivity) or even manifestations (the phenomenology of which plays a similar role to materiality in the previous case). As opposed to abstract entities (see Chap. 26), performative entities constitute abstractions constructed from specific manifestations, which incarnate them in full. This means that performative entities are secondary and dependent on the associated manifestations, whereas abstract entities do not depend on anything for their definition. Figure 24.2 shows details about performative entities.

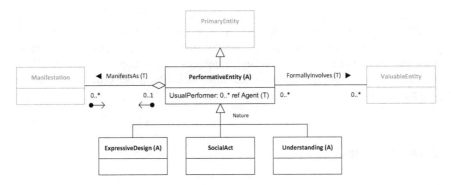

Fig. 24.2 Performative entities in CHARM

The agents that usually participate in each performative entity are represented by the *UsualPerformer* association. In addition, any other valuable entities that may be involved in each particular performative entity are represented by the *FormallyInvolves* association; the name of this association alludes to the fact that the involvement of these valuable entities is expected in any manifestation of the performative entity being described, but the specific valuable entities that are actually involved in each of them are documented separately. Finally, the *ManifestsAs* association captures the fact that each performative entity necessarily manifests as a number of manifestations over time.

PerformativeEntity is specialized into three subclasses according to their nature: *ExpressiveDesign*, *SocialAct* and *Understanding*. An expressive design corresponds to *a performative entity that has the main function of conveying a message between people*. Expressive designs may be intentionally created or emerge more or less unintentionally. In either case, they are based on universal expression phenomena, that is, basic expressive modes that appear in every culture and every time: natural language, sound, gestures and forms. This classification is only related to the expression vehicle being used and does not consider the specific manner in which the expressive design is rendered on a material medium; for example, a language design could be just oral, be written down or be preserved as an audio recording. These specific rendering modes of an expressive design on a medium constitute representations, which are dealt with in Chap. 27. Expressive designs include, for example, folk tales, melodies, hand gestures and computer icons.

Another kind of performative entity is given by the *SocialAct* class. A social act is *a performative entity that captures specific practices shared by a group*. Social acts may be manifested individually or collectively; for example, one may pray alone or in a group. In either case, praying is the social act and, as such, constitutes a practice that expresses values shared by a group, even when it is performed by a single person. Social acts include, for example, mass celebrations, binge drinking parties or town fairs.

Finally, the third kind of performative entity is given by the *Understanding* class. An understanding is *a performative entity that captures human experiences, insights or traditions as maintained and transmitted by individuals.* An understanding is always held by some people, practiced by them, and transmitted to others, who carry out performing in a similar manner. Understandings include, for example, particular cooking or fishing techniques or traditional trades.

The following sections describe the different kinds of performative entities in greater detail.

Expressive Designs

ExpressiveDesign is an abstract class and has a hierarchy of descendants that allows us to model expressive designs in quite precise ways. Look at the diagram in Fig. 24.3. *ExpressiveDesign* shows a *Contents* attribute, which represents the "substance" matter of the associated message being conveyed. Note that a Data type is employed, since the contents of a message can be of any type, and not necessarily textual. In addition, the association *FormallyDesignates* connects expressive designs to those valuable entities that are designated, or referred to, by the expressive design. *ExpressiveDesign* is specialized into a number of subclasses, depending on the universal expression phenomenon involved: *LanguageExpressiveDesign, SoundExpressiveDesign, GesturalExpressiveDesign, FormalExpressiveDesign* and *CombinedExpressiveDesign*. A language expressive design is *an expressive design based on human language as vehicle of expression.* This is probably the most intuitive kind of expressive design, since natural language constitutes the most immediate communication manner between us. In fact, *LanguageExpressiveDesign* is associated to the *Language* class (to be described in Chap. 26) so that a particular language expressive design is always expressed in a particular language. Also, the *Contents* attribute is redefined as of type Text, because linguistic messages are easily represented as such.

LanguageExpressiveDesign is specialized into two subclasses: *Discourse* and *ProperName*. A discourse is *a language expressive design of a narrative nature.* Discourses usually correspond to complete sentences or groups of them. Discourse includes, for example, the text of a speech or a poem. A proper name, in turn, is *a language expressive design having the purpose of designating entities.* Proper names are usually short phrases or single words with which people refer to things. *ProperName* redefines the *Name* attribute (inherited from *ValuableEntity*) so that it can only hold one value, namely, the proper name being described. Also, proper names are special in the sense that their contents coincide with their name; for example, the contents of the proper name with name "Sydney" are also "Sydney". This is not the case for discourses; for example, the contents of the discourse with name "The Catcher in the Rye" constitute the complete text of the novel.

In turn, *ProperName* is specialized into two subclasses: *Toponym* and *Anthroponym*. A toponym is *a proper name having the purpose of designating places.* In this regard, *Toponym* redefines the *FormallyDesignates* association so

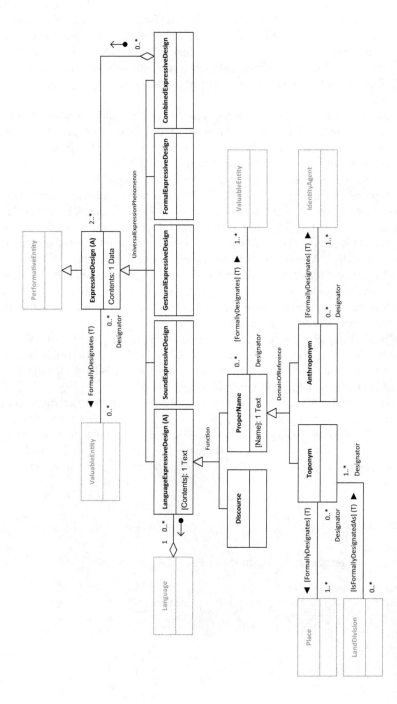

Fig. 24.3 Expressive designs in CHARM

that it points to *Place* (Chap. 22) rather than the more abstract *ValuableEntity*. In addition, there is the requirement that every land division is named through at least one toponym, as a consequence of the fact that land divisions are created for management purposes, as described in Chap. 22. To reflect this, the class *LandDivision* redefines the inherited association to *Toponym* so that the cardinality is 1..*. Examples of toponym include city or mount names such as "Sydney" or "Everest".

An anthroponym, similarly, is *a proper name having the purpose of designating people*. Like in the previous case, *Anthroponym* redefines the *FormallyDesignates* association so that it points to *IdentityAgent* rather than *ValuableEntity*. Anthroponyms may be individual proper name such as "Alice" or "Bob" but can also be group names such as "Hitorangi", "the French people" or "Microsoft".

As opposed to language expressive designs, a sound expressive design is *an expressive design based on sound as vehicle of expression*. Despite the fact that language communication implies sound when in spoken form, communication through sound is possible beyond language. Examples of sound expressive designs include a melody, tutting or whistling to express joy or displeasure.

Similarly, a gestural expressive design is *an expressive design based on the position and movement of the human body, optionally augmented by accessories, as a vehicle of expression*. Examples of gestural expressive designs include a dance or non-verbal communication through facial expressions.

A formal expressive design, in turn, is *an expressive design based on the formal properties of its parts, as well as on the relationships between them, as a vehicle of expression*. Examples of formal expressive designs include a logotype, a three-dimensional model of a building or a Harris matrix.

Finally, a combined expressive design is *an expressive design that aggregates other expressive designs, potentially of different types and therefore using different vehicles of expression*. Examples of combined expressive designs include a song (which includes the lyrics, which are a language design, plus the music, which is a sound design) or an opera (which includes the former plus a gestural design).

Social Acts

SocialAct is a concrete class, as shown in Fig. 24.4.

Fig. 24.4 Social acts in CHARM

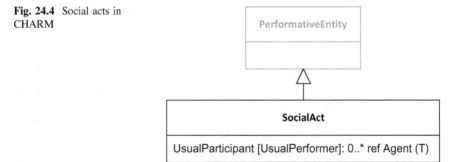

SocialAct redefines the inherited *UsualPerformer* association as *UsualParticipant*, to reflect the fact that people participate in social acts.

Understandings

Understanding is an abstract class and has a hierarchy of descendants that allows us to model understandings with more detail. Look at the diagram in Fig. 24.5. In a similar way as with social acts, *Understanding* redefines the *UsualPerformer* association as *UsualOwner*, to reflect the fact that understandings are always "owned" by people. Furthermore, the *Supports* self-association captures the fact that some understandings support some others. For example, some special angling techniques are necessary in order to perform some fisherman trade styles. Finally, *Understanding* is specialized into three subclasses, depending on what the application mode is: *Knowledge*, *Trade* and *Technique*. A knowledge is *an understanding related to people's memory, ability to perceive or ability to use information*. In other words, knowledges represent what people know and are able to apply for practical purposes. Examples of knowledges include fishing or administering herbal medicine.

A trade, in turn, is *an understanding related to people's habitual occupation, which may require specific knowledges or techniques that have been acquired.* Trades describe what people do for a living and are often supported by other kinds of understandings through the above-mentioned *Supports* association. Examples of trades include fisherman or cobbler.

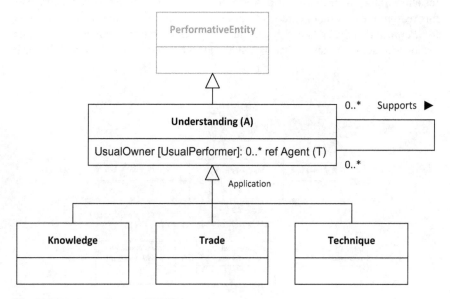

Fig. 24.5 Understandings in CHARM

A technique, finally, is *an understanding related to a particular way of doing which, usually supported by knowledge, includes both the process that is followed as well as the products that are used and produced.* Techniques correspond to the manner in which people do things and often involve following a particular process and employing or creating particular artefacts. Examples of techniques include trawling fishing or oil painting on canvas.

Manifestations

As we described above, a manifestation is *a primary entity corresponding to a human expression at a given time and place, which is fundamentally perceived in a direct fashion and through performative aspects.* Looking at it from the other way around, performative entities are abstractions that we construct after detecting patterns in a series of manifestations. As a consequence, manifestations are organized in CHARM in a manner that closely resembles that of performative entities, and the class hierarchy under *Manifestation* is extremely similar to that of *PerformativeEntity.* The classes in both parallel hierarchies are connected in pairs through redefinitions of the association shown in Fig. 24.1, connecting *Trade* to *ManifestationOfTrade, SocialAct* to *ManifestationOfSocialAct* and so on. Since each pair of classes redefines the association in a similar way, we do not show it in the diagrams for the sake of simplicity. Figure 24.6 shows details about manifestations. The agents that participate in each manifestation are represented by the *Performer* association. Note that this represents the actual performers of a manifestation, rather than the usual performers that *PerformativeEntity* described. For this reason, the minimum cardinality of the association is 1 rather than 0 as it was for *PerformativeEntity,* since by definition a manifestation requires at least one person. In addition, any other valuable entities that become involved in each

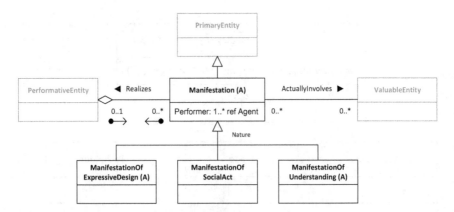

Fig. 24.6 Manifestations in CHARM

particular manifestation are represented by the *ActuallyInvolves* association; the name of this association alludes to the fact that the involvement of these valuable entities is actual, as opposed to the formal or expected involvement that we described for *PerformativeEntity*. Finally, the *Realizes* association, inverse to *ManifestsAs* previously described, captures the fact that each manifestation may realize a particular performative entity. Note that a manifestation does not need *necessarily* to realize a performative entity and hence the 0..1 cardinality; in fact, manifestations that do not fall in a known pattern such as those of an improvised nature cannot be linked to a meaningful performative entity.

Like *PerformativeEntity* above, *Manifestation* is specialized into three subclasses according to their nature: *ManifestationOfExpressiveDesign*, *ManifestationOfSocialAct* and *ManifestationOfUnderstanding*. A manifestation of expressive design corresponds to *a manifestation that realizes a given expressive design*. In other words, if expressive designs are specific ways to communicate, manifestations of expressive designs constitute particular usages of the former. For example, Mike Oldfield's *Crises* (a song) constitutes an expressive design; each time *Crises* is played, this constitutes a manifestation of an expressive design.

Another kind of manifestation is given by the *ManifestationOfSocialAct* class, which corresponds to *a manifestation that realizes a given social act*. These manifestations correspond to the actual performances of the associated social act by specific people in specific places and at specific times. For example, 'rock concert' is a social act; every time a rock concert happens, this constitutes a manifestation of the 'rock concert' social act.

Finally, the third kind of performative entity is given by the *ManifestationOfUnderstanding* class, which corresponds to *a manifestation that realizes a given understanding*. These manifestations describe actual performances of trades, techniques or knowledges. For example, 'trawl fishing' is an understanding; every time someone uses trawl fishing somewhere, this constitutes a manifestation of the former understanding.

The following sections describe the different kinds of manifestations in greater detail.

Manifestations of Expressive Designs

ManifestationOfExpressiveDesign is an abstract class and has a hierarchy of descendants that allows us to model these manifestations in quite precise ways. Look at the diagram in Fig. 24.7. *ManifestationOfExpressiveDesign*, like its performative counterpart, shows a *Contents* attribute that represents the "substance" matter of the associated message being conveyed. In the previous case, this referred to the usual message that is expected; in this case, it refers to the actual conveyed message. In addition, the association *ActuallyDesignates*, analogous to *Formally Designates* of the performative classes, connects manifestations of expressive designs to those valuable entities that are actually designated, or referred to, by the

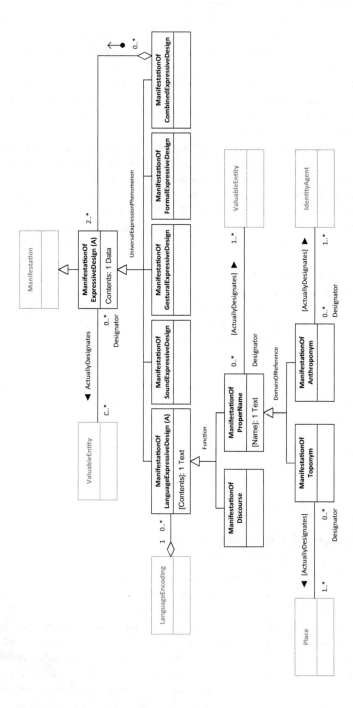

Fig. 24.7 Manifestations of expressive designs in CHARM

manifestations. Like its counterpart, *ManifestationOfExpressiveDesign* is specialized into a number of subclasses, depending on the universal expression phenomenon involved: *ManifestationOfLanguageExpressiveDesign*, *ManifestationOf
SoundExpressiveDesign*, *ManifestationOfGesturalExpressiveDesign*, *Manifestation
OfFormalExpressiveDesign* and *ManifestationOfCombinedExpressiveDesign*. As
you can imagine, a manifestation of language expressive design is *a manifestation
that realizes a given language expressive design*. These manifestations correspond
to the utterance of specific instances of the linguistic contents of the associated
expressive design by specific people in specific places and at specific times. As
such, *ManifestationOfLanguageExpressiveDesign* is associated to the *Language
Encoding* class (to be described in Chap. 26) so that a particular manifestation of
language expressive design is always conveyed by using a particular encoding.
Also, the *Contents* attribute is redefined as of type Text, because linguistic messages are easily represented as such.

ManifestationOfLanguageExpressiveDesign is specialized into two subclasses:
ManifestationOfDiscourse and *ManifestationOfProperName*. A manifestation of
discourse is *a manifestation that realizes a given discourse*. Similarly, a manifestation of proper name is *a manifestation that realizes a given proper name*.

In turn, *ManifestationOfProperName* is specialized into two subclasses:
ManifestationOfToponym and *ManifestationOfAnthroponym*. A manifestation of
toponym is *a manifestation that realizes a given toponym*. Like its performative
counterpart, *ManifestationOfToponym* redefines the *ActuallyDesignates* association
so that it points to *Place* (Chap. 22) rather than the more abstract *ValuableEntity*.

A manifestation of anthroponym, in turn, is *a manifestation that realizes a given
anthroponym*. Again like in the previous case, *ManifestationOfAnthroponym*
redefines the *ActuallyDesignates* association so that it points to *IdentityAgent* rather
than *ValuableEntity*.

As opposed to manifestations of language expressive designs, a manifestation of
sound expressive design is *a manifestation that realizes a given sound expressive
design*. Examples include someone humming a melody or tutting or someone
whistling to express joy or displeasure.

Similarly, a manifestation of gestural expressive design is *a manifestation that
realizes a given gestural expressive design*. Examples include a dance being performed or someone giving the Nazi salute.

A manifestation of formal expressive design, in turn, is *a manifestation that
realizes a given formal expressive design*. Examples include a particular copy of a
logotype, a sketch being drawn or a particular rendering of a three-dimensional
model of a building.

Finally, a manifestation of combined expressive design is *a manifestation that
realizes a given combined expressive design*. Examples include a song being sung
(which includes the lyrics being uttered, which are a manifestation of language
design, plus the music being sung, which is a manifestation of sound design) or an

Fig. 24.8 Manifestations of
social acts in CHARM

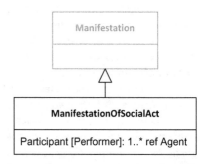

opera performance (which includes the former plus a manifestation of gestural
design).

Manifestations of Social Acts

ManifestationOfSocialAct is a concrete class, as shown in Fig. 24.8.
ManifestationOfSocialAct redefines the inherited *Performer* association as
Participant, to reflect the fact that people participate in social acts.

Manifestations of Understandings

ManifestationOfUnderstanding is an abstract class, having a hierarchy of descendants that allows us to model understandings with more detail. Look at the diagram
in Fig. 24.9. Like with manifestations of social acts, *ManifestationOfUnderstanding*
redefines the *Performer* association as *Owner*, to reflect the fact that understandings
are always "owned" by people, as we said above. Furthermore, the *Supports*
self-association captures the fact that some manifestations of understandings support
some others. Finally, *ManifestationOf Understanding* is specialized into three
subclasses, depending on what the application mode is: *ManifestationOfKnowledge*,
ManifestationOfTrade and *ManifestationOfTechnique*. A manifestation of knowledge is *a manifestation that realizes a given knowledge*. In other words, these
manifestations correspond to the possession and usage of instances of the associated
knowledge by specific people in specific places and at specific times. Examples
include someone providing herbal medicine at some specific point or someone in the
act of fishing.

A manifestation of trade, in turn, is *a manifestation that realizes a given trade*.
These correspond to the carrying out of instances of the associated trade by specific
people in specific places and at specific times. Examples include a fisherman or a
cobbler carrying out their trades.

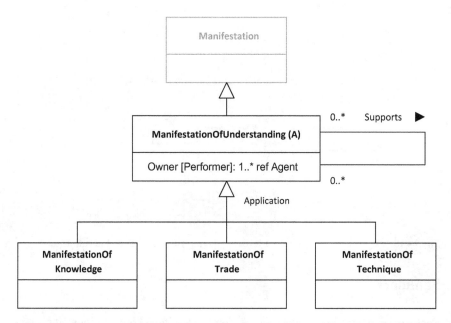

Fig. 24.9 Manifestations of understandings in CHARM

Finally, a manifestation of technique is *a manifestation that realizes a given technique*. These correspond to the execution of instances of the associated technique by specific people in specific places and at specific times. Examples include someone trawl fishing or painting with oil on canvas.

Example Model

Look again at the *Example Model* sections in previous chapters and consider the following additions. The fields next to the cattle enclosure where the bone fragment was found are used by the local townsfolk as part of old grounds where summer harvest festivities are celebrated every year. A written account of the 1836 celebration is found in a historical document kept in a local library, which also quotes the words of a song that used to be sung at the festival. You see a model for this situation in Fig. 24.10. This model augments the previous ones with instances of some of the classes that we have described in this chapter, including *SocialAct*, *ManifestationOfSocialAct* and *Discourse*. Most of the objects from the previous chapter are omitted for simplicity, but you can easily see how the model is a single continuous mesh, thus potentially connecting the bone fragment described in previous chapters to the summer festival described here and the agents that participate in it. In further chapters, we will keep adding extra information to this model as we learn about new classes in CHARM.

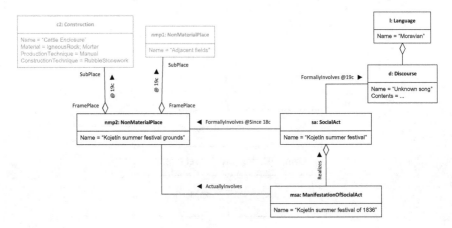

Fig. 24.10 Augmented example model involving performative entities and manifestations

Summary

Performative entities should not be confused with **Manifestations**; the latter constitute performances carried out by someone at some place and some time, whereas the former are abstract constructs that we manage in order to describe the latter.

Each particular kind of performative entity is repeatedly realized by manifestations of that kind.

Expressive designs are meant to convey a message between people through language, sound, gestures, forms or a combination of these.

Social acts embody specific practices shared by a group.

Understandings capture human experiences, insights or traditions as maintained and transmitted by individuals.

Exercises

40. Below you can find a list of entities. For each of them, state what CHARM class of those described in this chapter would be more suitable to model it.

    - An opera performance.
    - The lyrics of *Wuthering Heights* by Kate Bush.
    - The name "Uluru" as spoken by a tourist.
    - The well-known thumbs-up hand sign.

- The way in which craftsmen construct Galician bagpipes.
- Flamenco.
- A jazz jam session.

41. Create a CHARM-compliant instance model to describe the following situation. In 1991, the relics of Russian monk, St. Seraphim of Sarov, were rediscovered after being hidden in a museum for a long time. This was received with awe in post-Soviet Russia, so a procession was formed to take the relics from Moscow to the St. Seraphim-Diveyevo convent in the town of Sarov.

Chapter 25
Occurrences

Abstract In this chapter, we introduce CHARM occurrences, which correspond to events or situations that happen in relation to other valuable entities. We distinguish between absolute and relative occurrences and, within the latter, between circumstances (such as the building of a house), situations (such as a high unemployment rate) and activities (such as an archaeological excavation). We also explain that occurrences work in CHARM as the temporal aspect class, so that instance models can be constructed such that temporal information is recorded diachronically in terms of the associated occurrences.

As introduced in previous chapters, an occurrence is *a primary entity corresponding to an event or situation that happens in relation to one or more valuable entities*. Occurrences are things that happen in time and in a more or less close relationship to other valuable entities. The construction of a building, a war or the drifting of the coastline due to erosion constitute occurrences.

Occurrences play an important role in CHARM, since they are the major way in which we can express time-related concerns. In fact, *Occurrence* is the temporal aspect class in CHARM, as shown in Fig. 25.1. The *Occurrence* class, in addition to inheriting the *Name* attribute from *ValuableEntity*, declares two additional attributes: *Description* and *Certainty*. The *Description* attribute represents what happened during the occurrence, especially in relation to the associated valuable entities. The *Certainty* attribute, in turn, is useful to represent the degree of certainty that exists with regard to the occurrence having happened as described. Certainty degrees are expressed through the associated *Certainty* enumerated type, which allows values *Possible*, *Likely* and *Certain*. Note that both *Description* and *Certainty* are marked as subjective. This allows us to document occurrences as interpreted by specific individuals or groups.

Occurrences may happen within specific cultural classification contexts; for example, the construction of a building may be documented as belonging to the Late Middle Ages. This is captured through the *OccursInTheContextOf* association towards the *CulturalClassification* class (see Chap. 29). Furthermore, occurrences

© Springer International Publishing AG 2018
C. Gonzalez-Perez, *Information Modelling for Archaeology and Anthropology*,
https://doi.org/10.1007/978-3-319-72652-6_25

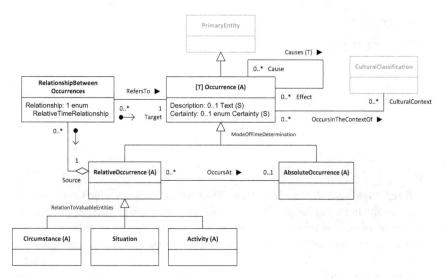

Fig. 25.1 Overview of occurrences in CHARM

can be connected to other occurrences through the *Causes* association so that cause/effect networks can be modelled.

There are two kinds of occurrences: relative and absolute. Relative occurrences are always located in time in relation to other occurrences, whereas absolute occurrences are located in time through dates or similar data. A relative occurrence can be located in time through the *OccursAt* association to a related absolute occurrence; for example, we could say that the construction of a building (a relative occurrence) happened between the late sixteenth century and 1612 (an absolute occurrence).

In addition, relative occurrences can be related to other occurrences (of whichever kind) through the intermediate *RelationshipBetweenOccurrences* class. This class carries a *Relationship* attribute expressed in terms of the *RelativeTimeRelationship* enumerated type, which allows values such as *OccursBefore*, *StartsDuring* or *EndsAtTheSameTimeAs*. This allows us, for example, to state that a mass migration started before the end of a war or that the collapse of a building happened during a particular year.

Finally, relative occurrences are further specialized as circumstances, situations and activities, depending on their relationship to other valuable entities. The remaining of this chapter describes the different kinds of occurrences in greater detail.

Absolute Occurrences

The class *AbsoluteOccurrence* corresponds to *an occurrence that is directly situated in time, usually through an explicit time reference*. Like absolute locations in Chap. 21, which were defined as not depending on anything else but an absolute frame of reference, absolute occurrences behave in a similar way, being usually characterized by specific dates and/or times. Figure 25.2 shows details about absolute occurrences. *AbsoluteOccurrence* is specialized into three classes according to nature: *PointInTime*, *TimeSpan* and *CompoundAbsoluteOccurrence*. A point in time is *an absolute occurrence of a simple nature that happens in a relatively short time*. As such, points in time are characterized by a *Moment* attribute of type Time. As we described in Chap. 6, the Time data type does not imply a conventional date/time as given through day, month, year, hour, minute and second; to the contrary, it can describe any point, as "thick" or "thin" as needed. For this reason, points in time can be documented as taking as much or as little time as necessary. Examples of points in time include the year 1931 or the eleventh century.

A timespan, in turn, corresponds to *an absolute occurrence that spans from one point in time to another*. This fact is captured by the two whole/part associations with *Start* and *End* roles towards *PointInTime*. An example time span could be the period between 8 and 16 June 2001.

Finally, a compound absolute occurrence is *an absolute occurrence of a complex nature as determined by a collection of other absolute occurrences*. In other words, compound absolute occurrences are collections of points in time or time spans (or other compound absolute occurrences), so they frequently represent discontinuous portions of time. Example compound absolute occurrences include the years in which a manned spatial flight took place, or the "ice age" periods on Earth.

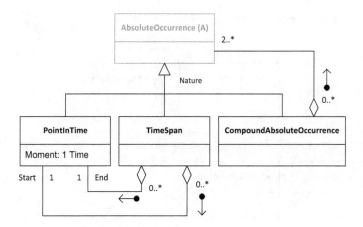

Fig. 25.2 Absolute occurrences in CHARM

Circumstances

The class *Circumstance* corresponds to *a relative occurrence that happens inherently to one or more valuable entities*. Like absolute locations in Chap. 21, which were defined as not depending on anything else but an absolute frame of reference, absolute occurrences behave in a similar way, being usually characterized by a date or time span. Figure 25.3 shows details about circumstances. *Circumstance* has an *IsInherentTo* association towards *ValuableEntity*. This captures the fact that circumstances are inherent to valuable entities and cannot occur by themselves. For example, the construction of a building inheres the building and cannot be explained in its absence. Furthermore, *Circumstance* is specialized into *Phase* and *Change* according to nature. A phase is *a circumstance that corresponds to a stable period of the associated entities*. Phases are useful to document periods of stability

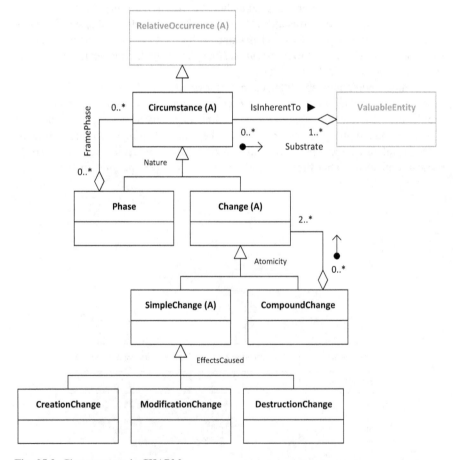

Fig. 25.3 Circumstances in CHARM

of things in relation to whatever variable and are often relatively long in time. Examples of phases include 'in construction' or 'first occupation' (regarding a building), or 'abandoned' (with regard to a site).

A change, contrarily, is *a circumstance that corresponds to an instable moment of the associated entities*. Changes entail some alteration to the associated valuable entities and are often shorter in time than phases, although some changes are very slow and definitely longer than many phases.

The specific nature of a change is captured by subclasses; *Change* is specialized into *SimpleChange* and *CompoundChange*. A simple change is *a change of an atomic nature*, whereas a compound change is *a change of a complex nature, which corresponds to the occurrence of a number of different but related changes*. Compound changes, in fact, are defined through an aggregation of two or more changes, thus allowing us to document changes in things that involve multiple aspects or variables at the same time, such as a situation where an object is destroyed in order to create another.

SimpleChange is specialized into *CreationChange*, *ModificationChange* and *DestructionChange*, depending on the effects caused on the associated valuable entities. A creation change is *a simple change that describes the creation of the associated entities*. It is safe to assume that the entities associated to a creation change do not exist before the change happens. Creation changes include, for example, the construction of a building or the starting of a fire.

A modification change, in turn, is *a simple change that describes the modification of the associated entities*. Modification changes necessary alter the associated valuable entities, but they do not need to modify all of their properties. Modification changes include, for example, the refurbishment of a building or the variation of a few words in a song.

Finally, a destruction change is *a simple change that describes the destruction of the associated entities*. It is safe to assume that the entities associated to a destruction change do not exist after the change happens. Destruction changes include, for example, the extinction of a species or the collapse of a settlement.

Situations

The class *Situation* corresponds to *a relative occurrence that happens as configured by other valuable entities*. Situations constitute "the state of things", and while they are not inherent to those things, they are strongly affected by them. Figure 25.4 shows details about situations. *Situation* has a temporal *IsConfiguredBy* association towards *ValuableEntity*. This captures the fact that situations are configured by other valuable entities over time and cannot be understood without them. For example, the situation of gender discrimination in the workplace is configured by a set of values, norms and processes that strongly influence it. There is a single subclass of *Circumstance,* namely *Phenomenon*. A phenomenon is *a situation perceived and conceptualized by some particular agents*. In other words, a

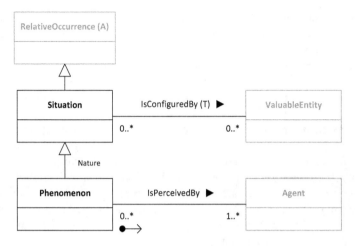

Fig. 25.4 Situations in CHARM

phenomenon is a situation as seen from the viewpoint of someone. This is modelled through the *IsPerceivedBy* association. Examples of phenomena include gender discrimination as experienced by a particular individual, or the global financial crisis as experienced by a particular bank.

Activities

The class *Activity* corresponds to *a relative occurrence that happens separately from other valuable entities*. Activities are the least dependent on valuable entities of all occurrences. Still, they can be mediated by them. Figure 25.5 shows details about activities. *Activity* has a temporal *IsMediatedBy* association towards *ValuableEntity*. This captures the fact that activities, despite happening quite independently from other valuable entities, can still be mediated or modulated by them over time. For example, the action of wind erosion over a wall is affected by the materials of the wall and its orientation. There are two subclasses of *Activity*: *Process* and *Action*. A process is *an activity of a complex nature, usually affecting multiple valuable entities*. In other words, a process is usually composed of other activities, such as subprocesses or individual actions; also, a process often affects, or is affected by, a number of valuable entities. Processes also tend to take a long time to happen as compared to other activities. Examples of processes include a war, a mass migration or the construction of a settlement.

Process has one subclass, *Project*, which corresponds to *a process mediated by agents and purposefully managed*. This means that a project is a special kind of project that is organized and managed by some agents in order to achieve a goal. This is captured by the redefined *IsMediatedBy* association towards *Agent*.

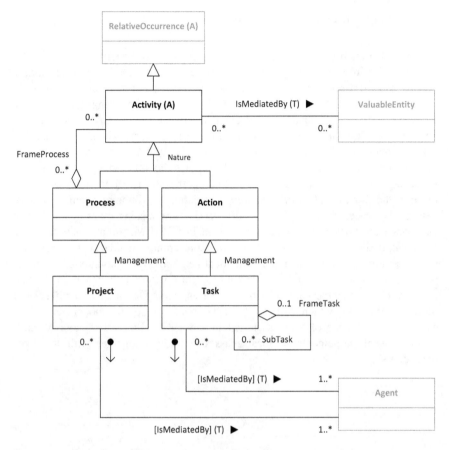

Fig. 25.5 Activities in CHARM

Examples of projects include carrying out a survey campaign, the planned development of a city or waging a war.

In contrast, an action is *an activity of a simple nature, usually affecting a few valuable entities*. This means that actions are rarely decomposed into other activities, and they affect, or are affected by, a very small number of valuable entities. Actions also tend to take a much shorter time to happen as compared to processes. Examples of actions include the erosion of a rock by the wind, the burning of wood in a hut to cook food or the visit to a museum.

Like in the case of *Process*, *Action* also has a management-oriented subclass, *Task*, which corresponds to *an action mediated by agents and purposefully managed*. In other words, tasks are actions that are organized and managed in order to achieve a goal. Like in the previous case, this is captured by the redefined *IsMediatedBy* association towards *Agent*. Examples of tasks include planning a survey campaign, building a roof or interviewing a group of people.

Expressing Time with Occurrences

As we said at the beginning of this chapter, *Occurrence* is the temporal aspect class in CHARM. This means that every temporal attribute or semi-association that is instantiated must refer to an occurrence as the mechanism to locate it in time. In other words, we use occurrences in CHARM to express when things happen. Since *Occurrence* has a wide range of descendant classes, we can use any of them for this purpose. For example, we could document the different materials that were used in a tower over time by specifying different values for *MaterialEntity.Material* in different phases of the tower. Or we could document how the usual participants in a social act have changed over time by linking the social act to different agents through the *SocialAct.UsualParticipant* association as different changes or processes take place. Phases, changes and processes are specific types of occurrence and hence the power of temporal expression in CHARM. Figure 25.6 shows an example. In the figure, the social act *sa*, representing attendance to mass in a particular town, is shown as having the local neighbours (community *c1*) as usual participants. Also, the tourists (community *c2*) are shown as being usual participants in relation to a particular situation, *s*, corresponding to the intense affluence of tourists to the town, which started in the 1960s. In summary, the model can be read as "Intense affluence of tourists started in the 1960s. Since then, tourists have become usual participants in local mass celebrations together with the local neighbours".

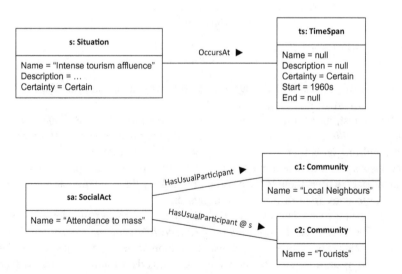

Fig. 25.6 Example model involving temporal facts

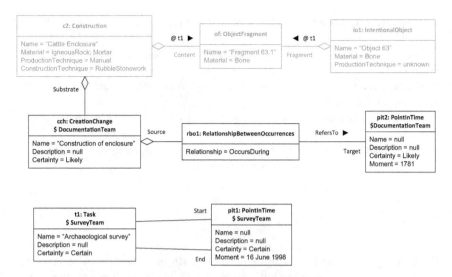

Fig. 25.7 Augmented example model involving various occurrences

Example Model

Refer to the *Example Model* section in previous chapters, and consider the following additional information. A documentation team finds out that the cattle enclosure was probably built in 1781. We can use occurrences to explicitly describe the temporal aspects of the model, including the new information about the enclosure as well as the fact that the bone fragment was found during a particular survey. You can see a model for this situation in Fig. 25.7. This model augments the ones in previous chapters by showing instances of some *Occurrence* subtypes, including a *CreationChange*, *Task* and *PointInTime*. Some of the objects from previous chapters are omitted for simplicity. Note that a task to represent the archaeological survey has been added, and its identifier *t1* used as in the aspect markers for associations involving the bone fragment. Also, the construction of the enclosure is explicitly modelled through a creation change associated to the year 1781.

Summary

Occurrences are useful to document events or situations that are related to other valuable entities.

Occurrences can be used to qualify temporal information, since *Occurrence* is the **temporal aspect** class in CHARM.

Absolute occurrences are characterized by time values indicating when they occurred.

Relative occurrences are characterized by their relationships to other occurrences.

Circumstances represent things that happen to other valuable entities and therefore are inherent in them.

Situations represent the "state of things" and are configured by other valuable entities.

Activities represent relatively independent occurrences, although they can also be mediated or affected by other valuable entities.

Exercises

42. Below you can find a list of entities. For each of them, state what CHARM class of those described in this chapter would be more suitable to model it.

    - The time span between 8 June 2001 and 19 January 2002.
    - The period of time that a concentration camp survivor spent there.
    - The refurbishment of an old house.
    - The fourteenth century.
    - The interwar period of 1918–1939 in Europe.
    - The sinking of the Titanic.
    - The construction of the Great Pyramid of Giza.

43. Create a CHARM-compliant instance model to describe the following situation. An archaeological excavation takes place between June and September 2013. As a consequence of it, an old wall is exposed and heavily altered by wind erosion over the following months.

Chapter 26
Abstract Entities

Abstract In this chapter, we introduce abstract entities in CHARM, which are those that are socially constructed and comprised of abstractions or ideas only, with no concrete realization whatsoever. We explore some kinds of abstract entities, including category systems, languages and, very importantly, culturally shared concepts such as beliefs, values and norms. Norms are further explored, and a distinction is made between conventions, rights, obligations and prohibitions.

So far we have described tangible entities, which are mainly perceived through their materiality; performative entities, which are perceived through the performance of the associated manifestations and occurrences, which are things that happen in time. We now look at abstract entities, which correspond to *a primary entity that is socially constructed and comprised of abstractions or ideas only, with no concrete realization whatsoever.* As opposed to tangible entities, abstract entities lack materiality. As opposed to performative entities, they do not manifest or are performed by agents. However, abstract entities can still be communicated through representations, as described in Chap. 27. Figure 26.1 shows an overview of abstract entities. As you can see, abstract entities include very different things. In fact, *AbstractEntity* is specialized into *CategorySystem*, *Language*, *LanguageEncoding*, *SharedConcept*, *Culture* and *Valorization*, depending on their nature. A category system is *an abstract entity corresponding to a collection of categories that work together for a well-known purpose.* We can use category systems to organize reality in any meaningful way. For example, prehistoric periods such as Neolithic or Bronze Age make up a category system. Similarly, tree families or species such as Oak or Pine also make up a category system. A category system is composed of individual categories, although this is not visible in Fig. 26.1 since categories are dealt with in Chap. 29.

A language is *an abstract entity corresponding to a human language.* This is usually a natural spoken language such as French or Mandarin, but it can also be a constructed language such as Láadan or a non-spoken language such as the American Sign Language.

© Springer International Publishing AG 2018   277
C. Gonzalez-Perez, *Information Modelling for Archaeology and Anthropology*,
https://doi.org/10.1007/978-3-319-72652-6_26

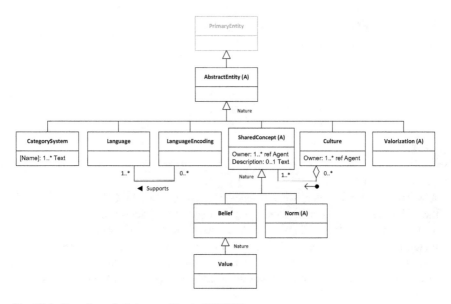

Fig. 26.1 Overview of abstract entities in CHARM

A language encoding, in turn, is *an abstract entity corresponding to an alphabet, syllabary or logography.* Language encodings can always express at least one language, which is captured by the *Supports* association. Many language encodings are writing systems, but some are not, such as oral or gestural encodings. Examples of language encodings include the Cyrillic script, Egyptian hieroglyphs, Braille, *Silbo Gomero* or Katakana.

A shared concept is *an abstract entity corresponding to a mental state that is shared by many individuals.* Shared concepts are ideas that exist in the "collective mind" of a society or group, which is captured by the association to *Agent* with role *Owner.* Also, shared concepts are usually described with regard to their conceptual content, through the *Description* attribute. *SharedConcept* has two subclasses: *Belief* and *Norm.* A belief is *a shared concept corresponding to the assumption that a given set of statements are correct.* According to the classical conceptualization of knowledge, introduced in Chap. 1, beliefs that are true and can be justified are the basis of knowledge. Examples of beliefs include religions (such as Islam or Catholicism), worldviews (such as atheism or humanism) or ideologies (such as Marxism or feminism).

A particular kind of belief, modelled by the *Value* class, corresponds to a belief about the degree of importance of something. A norm, on the other hand, is *a shared concept corresponding to a law, rule or piece of guidance applying to one or more agents, possibly in relation to some valuable entities.* Norms are a complex matter and are discussed in a separate section below.

A culture, in turn, is *an abstract entity corresponding to the collection of shared beliefs and norms that guide human action within a group.* Note that this definition matches the one we gave in Chap. 19 and is captured by the strong whole/part association from *Culture* towards *SharedConcept*. Also, the link between a culture and the associated group is captured by the association to *Agent* with role *Owner*.

Finally, a valorization is *an abstract entity of a discursive nature that adds cultural heritage value to other valuable entities through interpretive processes that have been agreed upon within a group or discipline.* As we said in Chap. 20, valorizations are interpretive constructs built on one or more valuable entities. Valorizations constitute a very important part of CHARM and are described in detail in Chap. 28.

Norms

A norm, as introduced above, is *a shared concept corresponding to a law, rule or piece of guidance applying to one or more agents, possibly in relation to some valuable entities.* Figure 26.2 shows details about norms. Some norms may imply other norms, as captured by the *Implies* self-association. For example, the right of ownership over a house usually implies a right to use the house as well as the obligation to keep it in good condition. Also, norms always apply to some agents, as described by the *IsNormativeSubjectOf* association. Furthermore, norms may refer to other valuable entities as captured by the *RefersTo* association. For example, the house ownership norm mentioned above applies to the house owner and refers to the house. In this regard, norms connect agents to other valuable entities, establishing what is expected from the former over the latter. Notice also that norms do not necessarily need to be written and formal; in fact, many norms are tacit and informal.

There are two kinds of norms depending on their atomicity, described by *CompoundNorm* and *SimpleNorm*. A compound norm is *a norm of a complex nature, corresponding to the aggregation of other norms.* For example, the constitution of a country or the Ten Commandments in the Bible constitute compound norms.

A simple norm, to the contrary, is *a norm of an atomic nature.* There are four different subclasses of *SimpleNorm*: *Convention*, *Right*, *Obligation* and *Prohibition*. A convention is *a simple norm that impels its subjects to behave in a particular manner.* In other words, conventions drive people to behave in certain ways, usually through tradition or custom. Examples of a convention include the custom to shake hands when being introduced to someone in the Western world, or the unspoken "pecking order" that is observed when sharing food in some groups.

A right is *a simple norm that grants its subjects specific liberties, guarantees or benefits.* Through rights, people are allowed to behave in certain ways that are considered acceptable within their group. There are different kinds of rights depending on the nature of what is being granted: *RightToDo*, *RightOfUse*, *RightOfOwnership* and *RightOfCustody*. A right to do is *a right that grants its subjects the benefit to carry out the associated valuable entities.* For example, the

Fig. 26.2 Norms in CHARM

right to demonstrate in public spaces allows citizens to carry out a particular social act. A right of use, in turn, is *a right that grants its subjects the benefit of being able to use the associated valuable entities.* For example, the right to live in a rented house grants the subjects permission to use the house according to the agreed conditions. A right of ownership is *a right that grants its subjects the benefit of owning the associated valuable entities.* For example, buying a house and becoming its owner grants the involved people certain rights over it. Finally, a right of custody is *a right that grants its subjects the benefit of keeping the associated valuable entities in their possession.* For example, a museum often has the right to keep a collection of objects even when they are owned by someone else.

An obligation, on the other hand, is *a simple norm that that imposes specific duties or responsibilities to its subjects.* Obligations strongly drive people to behave in certain ways and often impose penalties when the expected behaviour is not fulfilled. As with rights, there are different kinds of obligations depending on the nature of the imposed duty: *ObligationToDo*, *ObligationToConserve* and *ObligationToAllowUse*. An obligation to do is *an obligation that requires its subjects to carry out the associated valuable entities*. Examples include the obligation to go through conscripted military service in some countries or the requirement to pay out a debt. Note that obligations to do refer to the occurrence that is expected to take place. For example, an obligation to pay a debt would be linked to the action of paying, rather than the debt itself. An obligation to conserve, in turn, is *an obligation that requires its subjects to keep the associated valuable entities in good condition*. An example would be the requirement that the owner of a heritage-listed building maintains it according to certain standards. Finally, an obligation to allow use is *an obligation that requires its subjects to allow the use of the associated valuable entities to certain third parties*. The involved third parties are modelled by the *ThirdParty* association to *Agent*. Examples of obligations to allow use include a museum, who may keep a right of custody to some objects, but also an obligation to let citizens visit them; or the above-mentioned owner of a heritage-listed building, who despite keeping a right of ownership over the building, also has the obligation to allow others to enjoy it according to some guidelines.

Lastly, a prohibition is *a simple norm that forbids its subjects from doing something*. If conventions guide you, rights allow you and obligations compel you, then prohibitions disallow you. As with the previous cases, there are different kinds of prohibition depending on the ban being imposed: *ProhibitionToDo* and *ProhibitionToUse*. A prohibition to do is *a prohibition that forbids its subjects from carrying out the associated valuable entities*. For example, in some countries people cannot demonstrate publicly or drink alcohol. Like in the case of obligations to do, a prohibition to do refers to the occurrence that is not expected to take place. For example, a prohibition to drink alcohol in a particular place would be linked to the activity of drinking alcohol, rather than the drink itself or the associated place. A prohibition to use, in turn, is *a prohibition that forbids its subjects from using the associated valuable entities*. Examples include the ban on black citizens to employ certain kinds of public transport in the USA during the mid-twentieth century, or the prohibition for Jews to fly the Reich flag during the rule of the Nuremberg Laws in Nazi Germany.

Norms constitute a complex aspect of the culture and, consequently, are central to cultural heritage. Some other aspects related to normativity, such as privacy and trust, are not currently considered by CHARM, but a proposal has been put forward in [16].

Example Model

Refer to the *Example Model* section in previous chapters, and consider the following additional information. One of the activities that is traditionally carried out during the summer festival is the making of bone tools, and only men are allowed to do it. You can see a model for this situation in Fig. 26.3.

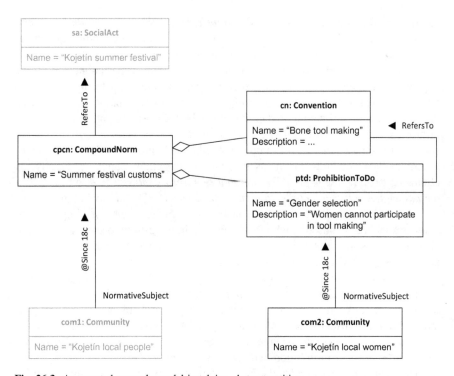

Fig. 26.3 Augmented example model involving abstract entities

This model augments the ones in previous chapters by showing instances of some *AbstractEntity* subtypes, namely *CompoundNorm*, *Convention* and *ProhibitionToDo*. As usual, some of the objects from previous chapters are omitted for simplicity. Note how the set of rules that govern the summer festival have been modelled as a compound convention, and two of these rules, the custom to make bone tools and the prohibition for women to participate, have been modelled as parts.

Summary

Abstract entities are composed of ideas, and they are not performed by people like performative entities do.

Shared concepts are inter-subjective ideas within a group.

A **culture** is a collection of shared concepts that belongs to a group.

Norms, a specific type of shared concept, connect agents to other valuable entities in relation to socially accepted behaviour.

Conventions are norms that guide people.

Rights are norms that grant people liberties or benefits.

Obligations are norms that impose requirements on people.
Prohibitions are norms that forbid people from doing something.

Exercises

44. Below you can find a list of entities. For each of them, state what CHARM class of those described in this chapter would be more suitable to model it.

    - The custom to exchange business cards when meeting someone.
    - The heraldry conventions of canting arms.
    - Marxism.
    - The preference for male rather than female children in some cultures.
    - The entitlement to keep what one has inherited.
    - The set of race and ethnicity labels used by the US Census.

Chapter 27
Representations

Abstract In this chapter, we introduce the notion of representation in CHARM, which corresponds to the fact that certain contents are persistently captured on an embodiment, reflecting the forms and characteristics of the former. Other representation-oriented relationships are also discussed, such as those related to reference and copying.

The previous few chapters have described most of CHARM's classes under *ValuableEntity*, with only valorizations and derived entities to be described in forthcoming chapters. In addition to valuable entities and valorizations, Chap. 19 mentioned representations as the third major component of CHARM. In this chapter, we deal with them.

Representations play a crucial role in the world of cultural heritage. It is through representations that we reason about, feel, learn and study the world where we live. For example, an excavation report describing the work that was done on site is a representation of that site. Also, the tombs that we use to bury the deceased are constructed, placed and kept according to our culture, and hence, we can say that they represent it, or aspects of it. As a third example, conceptual modelling itself is a representational activity, as explained in Chap. 1, so every time that we create a model of some aspect of cultural heritage we are also representing it.

The word "representation" is ambiguous and can have two meanings. On the one hand, representation means the process of re-presenting something, that is, the process of creating something else that, in one way or another, looks like the original thing. But representation also means the resulting product of this process. For example, we can say that a photograph of the cathedral in Burgos is a representation of the building. However, we can also say that the process of choosing the framing, time and technique in order to take the picture constitutes the process of representation. This ambiguity is difficult to avoid, and we will try to be as clear as possible throughout this chapter. Most of the times that we use the word "representation" we will be referring the products, not the process.

© Springer International Publishing AG 2018
C. Gonzalez-Perez, *Information Modelling for Archaeology and Anthropology*,
https://doi.org/10.1007/978-3-319-72652-6_27

Representations, Contents and Embodiment

We conceptualize a representation (the product, not the process) as an entity that captures the properties of something else, so that we can obtain information about the latter by looking at the former. For example, the photograph of the cathedral is a representation because we can learn about the cathedral by looking at the photograph. This brings up the issue of whether representations are always intentionally constructed or not. Some authors argue that an entity that captures the properties of something else is a representation, regardless of how, when and why it was created. In this regard, the photograph is a representation of the cathedral, but then, the cathedral is also a representation of the photograph. Taking this even further, there are things that fortuitously look like something else without any human intervention; for example, the Ursa Major constellation looks like a bear to many, so it would be a representation of bears according to this stance. However, stretching the concept of representation so much makes it almost useless, because we would be putting intentional designs and random coincidences of nature under the same term. For this reason, and especially within the field of cultural heritage, we prefer to save the term "representation" for those things that have been constructed by people and, as a result, look like something else. Notice that we do not include intentionality in this notion: a representation may or may not have been deliberately designed to look like whatever it represents. The only requirement is that it has been built by humans and, as a consequence, it re-presents something that the humans know about. The photograph of the cathedral would be an example of an intentional representation. The tombs that we use to bury our dead may be representing values and norms in our culture in a non-deliberate way.

In CHARM, the class *Representation* corresponds to *the fact that certain contents are persistently captured on an embodiment, reflecting the forms and characteristics of the former*. In other words, a representation connects together contents and embodiment. Figure 27.1 shows an overview of representations. As shown in the diagram, *Representation* has a *Describes* association towards *ValuableEntity*. This allows us to document the contents that are captured by a representation. In our example with the photograph of the cathedral, the cathedral would be the contents. In addition, *Representation* has an *IsEmbodiedIn* association towards *PrimaryEntity*. This allows us to document the entities that embody the contents. In our photograph example, the piece of paper where the photograph is printed in the case of an old film photograph, or the computer file where it is stored in the case of a digital photograph, constitutes the embodiment.

Several points must be clarified. First of all, it may be tricky to distinguish between a representation and its embodiment. Distinguishing representation and contents is easy: nobody would mistake the photograph of the cathedral for the cathedral itself. However, it is easier to mix up a representation and its embodiment, because we usually and informally refer to the embodiment as a "representation". For example, think of an old photograph of the cathedral that is printed on paper. The piece of paper with an image of the cathedral that you can hold with your hands

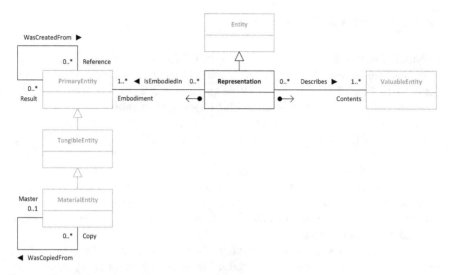

Fig. 27.1 Overview of representations in CHARM

is not the representation; it is a physical object and, as such, would be described in CHARM as an intentional object. The representation is the *fact* that this piece of paper displays a photographic image of the cathedral. In other words, a representation is a fact, rather than an object.

Secondly, and in relation to the former, notice in Fig. 27.1 that *Representation* does not descend from *ValuableEntity*. Representations are not considered to be valuable entities in CHARM because what gets valued is the entity holding the representation, that is, the primary entity that we call the embodiment, or the contents. In our previous example, cultural heritage value may be ascribed to the piece of paper showing the cathedral, as well as the cathedral itself, but not to the fact that the cathedral is represented in that particular piece of paper.

Finally, you can see that the *Representation* class in CHARM has no subclasses. This does not mean that there cannot be different kinds of representations. In fact, photographs, maps, sheet music, sketches or class diagrams constitute well-known kinds of representations. The *Representation* class could be subtyped according to the form of representation, that is, the collection of techniques and conventions that are employed in order to embody some contents. However, CHARM does not include classes like these because there can be very many, and it would be impractical to list all of them. If you want to add your own representation subtypes, see Chap. 33 where the topic of model extension is introduced.

In summary, representations are facts involving the capture of properties of some contents on a particular embodiment, where both the contents and the embodiment are (relatively) independent entities. Examples of representations include a map of a place (the contents) drawn on paper (the embodiment), or a fairy tale (the embodiment) that alludes to Christian elements (the contents).

Other Relational Connections

In addition to the *Representation* class itself, CHARM incorporates two associations that can be useful to document relational connections between entities, as depicted in Fig. 27.1. First of all, *PrimaryEntity* has a *WasCreatedFrom* self-association. This is useful to describe situations where an entity (called the result) has been created by taking other entities (called the reference) as a starting point. For example, the acanthus leaves in a Corinthian capital are sculpted by looking (directly or indirectly) to a real leaf of a plant in the *Acanthus* genus. Therefore, we can say that a Corinthian capital was created from a plant leaf. The *WasCreatedFrom* association is useful to document situations where result and reference bear some similarity of any kind, even when the materiality, purpose or overall configuration do not coincide. For example, some old flying machines were inspired by bird or bat wings.

Secondly, and in addition to the previous, *MaterialEntity* has a *WasCopiedFrom* self-association. This is useful to describe situations where an entity (called the copy) has been created by imitating most or all the properties of another (called the master). For example, the Nashville Parthenon is a full-scale replica of the original, so we would say that the former was copied from the latter. The *WasCopiedFrom* association is "stronger" than *WasCreatedFrom*, since it requires a much higher degree of resemblance between the two entities involved. Also, most cases of copying entail an implicit *WasCreatedFrom* relationship as well.

Example Model

Refer to the *Example Model* section in previous chapters, and consider the following additional information. By using the bone fragment as a starting point, a speculative reconstruction of the original tool of which the fragment is supposed to be a part is crafted in plastic and displayed in a local museum. A map showing the location of the original find is also displayed. You can see a model for this situation in Fig. 27.2. This model augments the ones in previous chapters by showing instances of *Representation*, as well as a *WasCreatedFrom* link. Note how the reconstruction (object *io3*) was created from the bone fragment, but represents the complete bone tool (object *io1*).

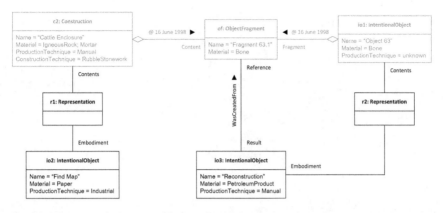

Fig. 27.2 Augmented example model involving representations and relational connections

Summary

Representations are facts about some properties of an entity being reproduced on another.

In this manner, representations connect an entity, called the **contents**, to another, called the **embodiment**.

In addition to representations, reference and copy situations between entities can be documented.

Exercises

45. Create a CHARM-compliant instance model to describe the following situation. A historical map of north-east Hokkaido is to be exhibited at a museum. In order to protect the map, a replica is made and exhibited instead of the original.

Chapter 28
Valorizations

Abstract In this chapter, we introduce the key idea of valorization in CHARM, as a particular case of abstract entity (explored in an earlier chapter). Valorizations are defined as abstract entities of a discursive nature that add cultural heritage value to other valuable entities through interpretive processes that have been agreed upon within a group or discipline. Different kinds of valorizations are discussed, including scientific-technical, administrative, community and external ones.

Together with valuable entities and representations, valorizations constitute one of the major building blocks of CHARM. As we described in Chap. 19, things become part of cultural heritage because someone gives them value. Cultural heritage value is captured in CHARM in the form of valorizations.

The *Valorization* class corresponds to *an abstract entity of a discursive nature that adds cultural heritage value to other valuable entities through interpretive processes that have been agreed upon within a group or discipline*. Note that valorizations are abstract entities, which were described in Chap. 26. This means that everything we said there about abstract entities in general also applies to valorizations. For example, valorizations do not manifest or are performed by agents, as opposed to performative entities; however, they can still be communicated through representations. In addition, valorizations, being abstract entities, are also valuable entities. This means that valorizations can add value not only to tangible or performative entities but also to other valorizations. This allows us to describe chained valorizations to represent the complex interpretive networks that occur within cultural heritage.

Also, remember that valorizations are constructed interpretively, rather than by observation or description. However, not every interpretation is a valorization; a valorization must have been relatively agreed upon within a group or discipline. Each valorization is built on one or more valuable entities and may use other valorizations as a base. Figure 28.1 shows an overview of valorizations in CHARM. The *Valorization* class declares a *Contents* attribute, which represents the interpretive discourse inherent to the valorization. In addition, *Valorization* has three associations. First of all, valorizations can be linked to the agents that issue

C. Gonzalez-Perez, *Information Modelling for Archaeology and Anthropology*,
https://doi.org/10.1007/978-3-319-72652-6_28

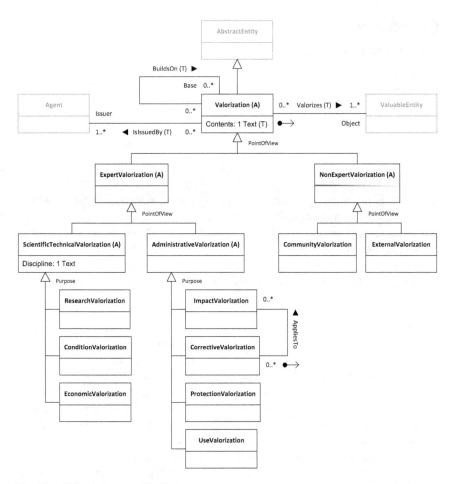

Fig. 28.1 Valorizations in CHARM

them through *IsIssuedBy*, thus allowing us to document who gave what value. Secondly, valorizations can be linked to the things that get valued through *Valorizes*, so that we can document what is being valued by whom. Finally, valorizations can take into account other pre-existing valorizations when being constructed; this is captured in CHARM by the self-association *BuildsOn*, so that we can express what other valorizations are being taken into account when a new one is issued. Note that all the features in *Valorization*, including the *Contents* attribute and the three associations, are marked temporal, so that we can keep track of how a valorization changes over time.

Since valorizations encapsulate the cultural heritage value that people give to things, they are organized in CHARM according to the types of cultural heritage value that we described at the end of Chap. 19: scientific-technical, administrative, community and external. However, this is done in two specialization steps. As shown above, *Valorization* has two subclasses: *ExpertValorization* and *NonExpertValorization*. An expert valorization is *a valorization produced by consensus within a group of experts, and issued in a formal manner*. In opposition, a non-expert valorization is *a valorization produced by a community from a non-expert and non-scientific perspective, and issued in an informal manner*. Note that a valorization is expert or non-expert depending on the point of view taken by the issuers, and not who the issuers are or what their background is. For example, a government-employed heritage manager would be issuing expert valorizations when carrying out their job, but a non-expert valorization when visiting a nearby monument and filling out an opinion survey at the exit. Similarly, a member of a local community would be issuing a non-expert valorization when judging the importance of the local chapel for their daily life, but an expert valorization when joining other citizens in a local association to issue a press release about the effects of tourism on the village.

The major differences between expert and non-expert valorizations include the following. Expert valorizations are always issued formally and explicitly, very often in writing, and following a well-known methodology. Usually, the issuers are aware that they are issuing a valorization. Also, expert valorizations are usually communicated to others by the same people who issue them. Examples of expert valorizations include a research paper about an archaeological site or the decision to establish a curtilage around a monument to protect it from various threats. Non-expert valorizations, on the contrary, are always issued informally, rarely in writing, and never follow a specific methodology. Often, the issuers are not aware that they are issuing a valorization. Also, non-expert valorizations are rarely communicated and, when they are, it is usually people other than the issuers who do it. An example of non-expert valorization is the feeling of identity and belonging experienced by a local member of a community about their village.

The following sections describe the different kinds of expert and non-expert valorizations in detail.

Expert Valorizations

An expert valorization, as introduced above, is *a valorization produced by consensus within a group of experts, and issued in a formal manner* (see Fig. 28.1). There are two kinds of expert valorizations depending on the point of view, represented by the classes *ScientificTechnicalValorization* and *AdministrativeValorization*. A scientific-technical valorization is *an expert valorization produced from the perspective of a specific discipline*. Usually, scientific-technical valorizations are produced by researchers or technical staff, but this does not need to be the case.

Depending on the purpose, there are three kinds of scientific-technical valorizations, given by the classes *ResearchValorization*, *ConditionValorization* and *EconomicValorization*. A research valorization is *a scientific-technical valorization produced with the purpose of generating new knowledge about the valorized object.* A typical example of research valorization is a scientific article in a journal. A condition valorization, in turn, is *a scientific-technical valorization produced with the purpose of determining the condition or status of the valorized object.* An example of condition valorization is a technical report on the state of the structure of a historical building and the necessary maintenance actions. Finally, an economic valorization is *a scientific-technical valorization produced with the purpose of ascribing an economic value to the valorized object.* An example of economic valorization is the valuation of a work of art.

As opposed to scientific-technical valorizations, an administrative valorization is *an expert valorization produced from the perspective of heritage management.* The word "administrative" in the name of this class refers to the administration or management of cultural heritage, rather than public administration. Having said this, administrative valorizations are usually produced within a competent authority for cultural heritage management.

Depending on purpose, there are four kinds of administrative valorizations, given by the classes *ImpactValorization, CorrectiveValorization, ProtectionValorization* and *UseValorization*. An impact valorization is *an administrative valorization produced with the purpose of determining the impact that one or more external factors have caused, are causing or will cause on the valorized object.* An example of an impact valorization is an archaeological impact assessment due to the planned construction of a road next to a megalithic necropolis. Complementarily, a corrective valorization is *an administrative valorization produced from one or more impact valorizations, with the purpose of mitigating or removing said impact on the valorized object.* Note that, to implement this, *CorrectiveValorization* has an *AppliesTo* association towards *ImpactValorization*. An example of corrective valorization is a list of precautions to implement during the construction of a road next to a megalithic necropolis, plus the directions for an excavation intended to gather minimal information about the archaeological structures that are unearthed during the works. A protection valorization is *an administrative valorization produced with the purpose of protecting the valorized object from destruction or alteration, either by legal, physical or other means.* An example of a protection valorization is the declaration of a historical town as a UNESCO World Heritage Site. Finally, a use valorization is *an administrative valorization produced with the purpose of regulating the modes of utilization of the valorized object.* An example of use valorization is an urban development plan that establishes specific zoning classes for different areas in a city.

Non-expert Valorizations

A non-expert valorization, as introduced at the beginning of this chapter, is *a valorization produced by a community from a non-expert and non-scientific perspective, and issued in an informal manner* (see Fig. 28.1). There are two kinds of non-expert valorizations depending on the point of view, represented by the classes

CommunityValorization and *ExternalValorization*. A community valorization is *a non-expert valorization expressed in terms of identity, continuity and/or closeness.* An example of community valorization is the sense of belonging and attachment that neighbours of a village feel towards their local chapel and associated social practices. Contrarily, an external valorization is *a non-expert valorization expressed in terms of wonder and distant appreciation.* An example of external valorization is the sense of awe and respect that pilgrims or tourists experience when entering a large Gothic cathedral for the first time.

Example Model

Look again at the *Example Model* section in previous chapters, and consider the following additional information. In 2005, a group of people in Kojetín starts promoting the preservation of the old summer festival. One year later, they are successful as the regional Heritage Department lists the festival as a protected immaterial heritage element. You can see a model for this situation in Fig. 28.2. This model adds two valorization objects to the ones in previous chapters. On the one hand, the appreciation by the local people of the summer festival (as well as the festival grounds) is represented by object *cv*. On the other hand, the recognition of

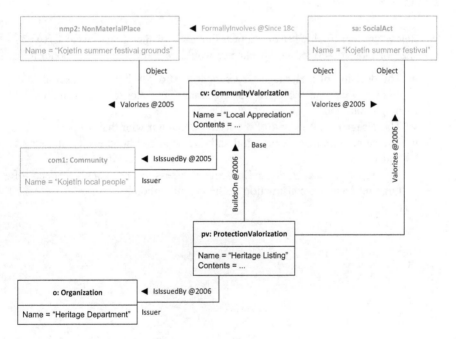

Fig. 28.2 Augmented example model involving valorizations

the heritage value by the Heritage Department is represented by object *pv*. Note how the protection valorization *pv* builds on top of the existing community valorization *cv*.

Summary

Valorizations constitute the interpretive cultural heritage value that is given to some valuable entities by some agents.

There are different kinds of valorizations depending on the **point of view** taken by the issuers, regardless of who they are or what their background is.

Expert valorizations are formally and explicitly produced, usually in writing, and are often communicated to others by the same issuers.

Expert valorizations can be **scientific-technical** or **administrative**.

Non-expert valorizations are informally and implicitly produced, rarely in writing, and are seldom communicated to others; when they are, it is usually people other than the issuers who do it.

Non-expert valorizations can be **community** or **external**.

Exercises

46. Below you can find a list of entities. For each of them, state what CHARM class of those described in this chapter would be more suitable to model it.

    - The decision of a Heritage Department to strongly limit the materials and colours that can be used to construct new houses in a traditional neighbourhood.
    - The disagreement of part of the local population with that decision.
    - The admiration that the beautiful and tidy neighbourhood evokes in tourists and visitors.
    - The report of the Heritage Department assessing the negative effects of ongoing unkempt construction in the neighbourhood.

Chapter 29
Derived Entities

Abstract In this chapter, we explore CHARM derived entities in depth, empha-sizing the fact that they cannot be understood in an immediate and implicit manner when perceived, but require an explicit reception process. We show how val-orizations constitute the "glue" that connects derived entities to the valuable entities that constitute their basis. Also, we explore some common kinds of derived entities, including cultural landscapes, sites, styles and cultural resources.

Derived entities constitute the counterpart to primary entities. As we explained in Chap. 20, primary entities (including tangible, performative and abstract entities, as well as agents, manifestations and occurrences) are understood by any observer without the need of explicit reception processes. In other words, there is no inter-pretive process that needs to be explained in order for someone to understand the entity. To the contrary, derived entities need a reception process in order to be understood as such. By "understood", we mean two things: being able to separate the entity from its surrounding environment and assigning it to a category. These two cognitive tasks correspond to the premises of conceptual modelling that we described in Chap. 2 and constitute the basic mechanisms through which we understand the world. We used the example of an archaeological site as a derived entity. An archaeologist who is more or less familiar with the site should recognize it when they see it; however, someone who is not familiar with the site or, more specifically, someone who has no archaeological training may not be able to sep-arate the site from its surrounding environment or assign it to a meaningful category such as 'site'. Archaeological sites and other derived entities are the product of more or less complex interpretations based on material evidences, background knowledge, and context, and it may be very difficult for someone unfamiliar with these aspects to recognize them as such in the absence of an explicit description of these interpretive elements.

A derived entity, therefore, is *a valuable entity that is not understood in an immediate and implicit manner when perceived but requires an explicit reception process*. This reception process entails describing and/or explaining the interpretive processes that took place in order to define the derived entity. In our previous

© Springer International Publishing AG 2018 297
C. Gonzalez-Perez, *Information Modelling for Archaeology and Anthropology*,
https://doi.org/10.1007/978-3-319-72652-6_29

example, a visitor with no archaeological background may be able to finally "see" the site once an explanation is given of the material evidences that were found, how they relate to previous knowledge of the area and the associated culture, and what assumptions or conclusions were involved in the archaeological work.

Figure 29.1 shows an overview of valorizations in CHARM. Derived entities are called "derived" because each of them has a number of other valuable entities as a basis, from which they derive. This is implemented in CHARM by the *Basis* semi-association role. For example, an archaeological site is usually defined around a place; this place acts as the basis for the site. Or, in other words, the site has been derived from the place. In this regard, we can say that derived entities are a result of deriving more or less tentative conclusions from a collection of primary entities through interpretation. The interpretation that produces the derived entity is captured in CHARM through the *Source* semi-association role. For example, the site mentioned above is a site because someone, possibly an archaeologist, issued a valorization stating so. In this manner, derived entities are always linked to the valorization that created them, as well as the underlying valuable entities on which this valorization rests. In addition, a derived entity, being an interpretive construct, is often situated within a particular cultural context. This is captured by the *IsAscribedTo* association in CHARM.

As you can see in Fig. 29.1, derived entities are specialized along the same lines as valorizations. This makes sense, given the connection between the two. As shown above, *Derived Entity* has two subclasses: *ExpertDerivedEntity* and *NonExpertDerivedEntity*, depending on the type of the source valorization. An expert derived entity is *a derived entity that results from an expert valorization*. In opposition, a non-expert derived entity is *a derived entity that results from a non-expert valorization*. Remember from the previous chapter that a valorization is expert or non-expert depending on the point of view taken by the issuers, and not

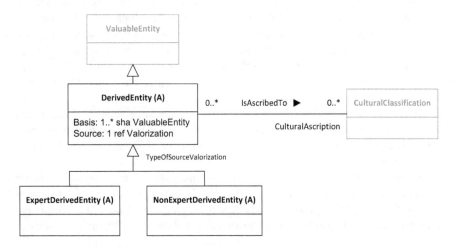

Fig. 29.1 Overview of derived entities in CHARM

who the issuers are or what their background is. As a consequence, a derived entity would be called "expert" or "non-expert" depending on this point of view rather than other characteristics of the issuer agent.

The following sections describe the different kinds of expert and non-expert derived entities in detail.

Expert Derived Entities

An expert derived entity, as introduced above, is *a derived entity that results from an expert valorization*. Figure 29.2 shows expert derived entities in detail. As shown in the diagram, *ExpertDerivedEntity* redefines the inherited *Source* valorization to be of type *ExpertValorization*. From now on you will see that each derived entity class redefines this to match the necessary valorization type. To start with, the *ScientificTechnicalDerivedEntity* class corresponds to *an expert derived entity that results from a scientific-technical valorization*. As such, it redefines

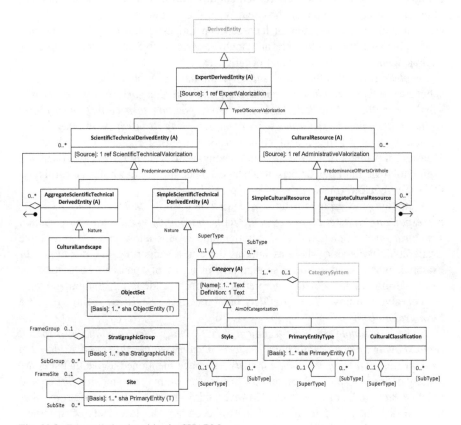

Fig. 29.2 Expert derived entities in CHARM

Source as being of type *ScientificTechnicalValorization*. There are two kinds of scientific-technical derived entities, depending on the predominance of parts or whole, represented by the classes *SimpleScientificTechnicalDerivedEntity* and *AggregateScientificTechnicalDerivedEntity*. A simple scientific-technical derived entity is a *scientific-technical derived entity in which the cohesion of the whole dominates over the diversity and variety of its parts.* In other words, these are entities that appear to us as a cohesive whole rather than a collection of things, despite the fact that they may be decomposable into parts. Contrarily, an aggregate scientific-technical derived entity is a *scientific-technical derived entity in which, being composed of other scientific-technical derived entities, the diversity and variety of the parts dominate over the cohesion of the whole.* In other words, these are entities that appear to us as a collection of things rather than a single monolithic one. A good example is provided by the only subclass of *AggregateScientificTechnicalDerivedEntity*, namely *CulturalLandscape*, which corresponds to *an aggregate scientific-technical derived entity corresponding to a system of places plus optionally other spatially nearby valuable entities that are interpreted as being culturally related.* This means that cultural landscapes are defined as collections of loosely related entities within a particular area. Examples of cultural places may include the Great Wall of China or the ancient Lower Egypt area. In both cases, the cultural landscape encompasses not only the associated geographic area but also the relevant tangible, performative and abstract entities as well as agents, manifestations and occurrences.

SimpleScientificTechnicalDerivedEntity, on the other hand, has a number of subclasses: *ObjectSet*, *StratigraphicGroup*, *Site* and *Category*. An object set is *a simple scientific-technical derived entity corresponding to a collection of object entities that cannot be separated without the set losing its integrity.* In other words, an object set is a collection of objects having a strong connection, such as the Treasure of Villena or all the artefacts belonging to a household. Object sets are useful to treat multiple objects that share something as a whole. Accordingly, *ObjectSet* redefines *Basis* as being of type *ObjectEntity*.

A stratigraphic group, in turn, is *a simple scientific-technical derived entity corresponding to a set of stratigraphic units that jointly work towards a common structural and/or functional goal.* Stratigraphic groups allow us to treat multiple stratigraphic units as a whole as long as there is a supporting interpretation. For example, when we describe a stratigraphy in terms of "phases", "activities" or similar terms, we are actually interpreting sets of the underlying stratigraphic units as cohesive groups. *StratigraphicGroup* redefines *Basis* as being of type *StratigraphicUnit*.

A site is *a simple scientific-technical derived entity corresponding to a spatial region having an abnormally high density of primary entities that are considered to be the result of a focussed human activity.* We have mentioned above that sites are usually defined around a place, and for this reason we may assume that *Site* should redefine *Basis* to be of type *Place*. However, this is not the case because some sites may be difficult to locate in space due to secondary displacements of materials. Accordingly, *Site* redefines *Basis* to be of type *PrimaryEntity*, thus leaving the possibility open to define a site around a place or other kinds of primary entities such as structures, objects or even performative entities.

Finally, a category is *a simple scientific-technical derived entity corresponding to a type or kind of valuable entities that share some common properties.* Categories are usually organized into category systems, such as the organization of prehistoric or historic stages of a certain area into a periodization system or the organization of species and genera of living beings into a taxonomy. There are three kinds of categories in CHARM depending on the aim of categorization, corresponding to the classes *Style*, *PrimaryEntityType* and *CulturalClassification*. A style is *a category aimed at the definition of a specific, multi-dimensional and recognizable kind in terms of representative characteristics.* This means that styles allow us to refer to a wide range of things by specifying what characteristics are expected for something to be a member of the category. Examples of styles include 'cubism', 'Penha' or 'Moche'.

A primary entity type, in turn, is *a category aimed at defining a grouping of similar primary entities.* This definition is quite wide and allows us to use primary entity types to organize primary entities in any way we want. Accordingly, this class redefines *Basis* as being of type *PrimaryEntity* We should make an important point here. Primary entities, as any other, are expected to be organized in CHARM through specific subclasses, such as *ObjectFragment* or *SocialAct*. This class, however, is provided as an additional mechanism to represent categories in a model, which may be useful in those cases where using a class for each category would be too cumbersome or inadequate. Examples of types of primary entities include 'megalithic tomb', 'oak tree' or 'Christmas carol'. We could add a *Megalithic Tomb* class to CHARM in order to characterize something as such. However, if there are too many categories to model, or we do not need to document different things depending on what category something belongs to, then we may as well avoid introducing any classes and using instances of *PrimaryEntityType*, probably collected into a cohesive category system.

Finally, a cultural classification is *a category aimed at defining a specific cultural context.* Examples of cultural classifications include 'Early Roman', 'Olmec' or 'post-soviet'.

So far, we have described scientific-technical derived entities. As a counterpart, the *Cultural Resource* class corresponds to *an expert derived entity that results from an administrative valorization.* As such, it redefines *Source* as being of type *AdministrativeValorization*. Note that cultural resources may have been called "administrative derived entities" for better symmetry with the rest of the model. However, we chose to name them "cultural resources" given the fact that there is a well-known term in the cultural heritage field. Like in the previous case, there are two kinds of cultural resources, depending on the predominance of parts or whole, represented by the classes *SimpleCulturalResource* and *AggregateCultural Resource*. A simple cultural resource is a *cultural resource in which the cohesion of the whole dominates over the diversity and variety of its parts.* Again as before, these are entities that appear to us as a cohesive whole rather than a collection of things, despite the fact that they can often be decomposed into parts. Examples of simple cultural resources include a cathedral, a painting or a traditional celebration, understood as interpreted realities. Note that the cathedral *per se* could be probably modelled in CHARM as a construction. However, once an administrative valorization claims its relevance as an element of cultural heritage, the cathedral plus the valorization become a cultural resource. Similar things can be said about the painting or the traditional celebration.

In opposition, an aggregate cultural resource is a *cultural resource in which, being composed of other cultural resources, the diversity and variety of the parts dominate over the cohesion of the whole.* In other words, these are entities that appear to us as a collection of things rather than a single monolithic one. Examples of aggregate cultural resources include a series of interpreted archaeological sites in a region or a city's historical set of neighbourhoods.

Non-expert Derived Entities

A non-expert derived entity, as introduced above, is *a derived entity that results from a non-expert valorization.* Figure 29.3 shows expert derived entities in detail. As shown above, *NonExpertDerivedEntity* redefines the inherited *Source* valorization to be of type *NonExpertValorization*, along the lines of previous derived entity classes. There are two subclasses: *CommunityDerivedEntity* and *ExternalDerivedEntity*. A community derived entity corresponds to *a non-expert derived entity that results from a community valorization.* As such, it redefines *Source* as being of type *CommunityValorization*. Examples of community derived

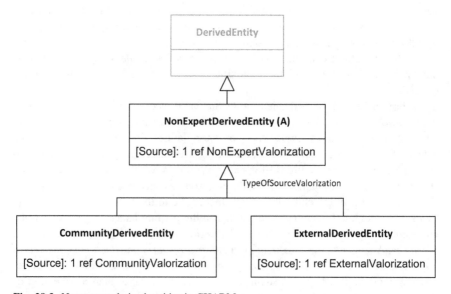

Fig. 29.3 Non-expert derived entities in CHARM

entities include the land that is felt as one's own by a local community or the areas considered to be "manso" (tame) and "bravo" (wild) by the neighbours of a village.

In contrast, an external derived entity corresponds to *a non-expert derived entity that results from an external valorization*. As such, it redefines *Source* as being of type *ExternalValorization*. An example of external derived entity is the constructed image and reputation of a community as viewed by a different group, based perhaps on prejudice and stereotyping.

Example Model

Look again at the *Example Model* section in the previous chapters and consider the following additional information. Right after the summer festival is heritage listed in 2006 by the regional Heritage Department, the complete festival grounds plus the associated farm and festival practices are delimited as a whole and added to a larger "traditional Bečva" cultural landscape. You can see a model for this situation in Fig. 29.4. This model adds two derived entities to the ones in previous chapters. On the one hand, the delimitation of the festival grounds plus other elements (such as the festival practice itself) as a meaningful whole is represented by object *s*, a site. Then, a valorization *uv* is shown to document the decision by the Heritage Department to include site *s* into the pre-existing "traditional Bečva" cultural landscape *cl*. Finally, the fact that the site is now part of the cultural landscape is captured by a phase of object *cl* for 2006 showing the newly created site *s* as well as the valorization *uv* as elements of its basis.

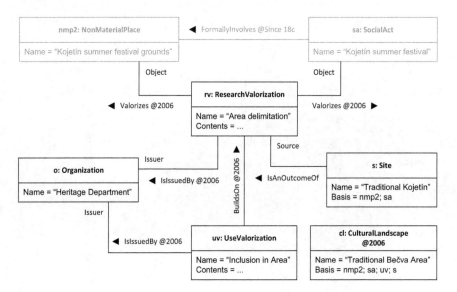

Fig. 29.4 Augmented example model involving derived entities

Summary

Derived entities are valuable entities that are not understood immediately unless assisted by an explicit reception process.

Derived entities are created **as a result** of valorizations.

The reception process that is needed for people to understand a derived entity entails an explanation of the associated valorization.

Derived entities are **based on** other valuable entities, which support the associated valorization.

Derived entities are organized like valorizations, into expert and non-expert types, and then into scientific-technical, administrative, community and external subtypes.

Exercises

47. Below you can find a list of entities. For each of them, state what CHARM class of those described in this chapter would be more suitable to model it.

    - The Early Neolithic period in Europe.
    - The "Extraterrestrial Highway" in Nevada, USA.
    - Machu Picchu in Peru.
    - The sacred kondō in a Buddhist temple.
    - The romantic literature of the eighteenth–nineteenth centuries.
    - A collection of Yoruba masks in a museum.

Part 4
Recap of Part IV

This is the end of Part IV. In this part, we have explored the Cultural Heritage Abstract Reference Model (CHARM) in depth. We started by proposing an ontology for cultural heritage on which CHARM is supported. This ontology sees cultural heritage as a collection of things that have received cultural heritage value, which is granted by people on the grounds of cultural representativeness and potential benefits. Taking this ontology as a basis, we described the three major aspects of CHARM: valuable entities, valorizations and representations. Then, we gave definitions, descriptions and examples for most of the classes in the model.

Although the three major aspects of CHARM make sense from a philosophical point of view, we must emphasize that valorizations and derived entities are also valuable entities and, in fact, almost every class in CHARM is a descendant of *ValuableEntity*. This allows us to describe recursive situations where a valorization is developed on top of previous valorizations or derived entities are constructed taking other derived entities as a basis.

We must also emphasize that CHARM is an abstract reference model. As such, it is not intended to be used by itself as a finished product. In fact, this would be quite difficult, since it does not contain classes that are specific enough as to be directly useful. Before you can use CHARM, you need to extend it in order to construct a particular model. Chapter 33 explains how to do this.

Part V
Applying Conceptual Modelling

In this part, we discuss various techniques and concerns that you can or should use when doing conceptual modelling for cultural heritage, such as modelling patterns or quality factors. Also, we introduce additional issues that need conceptual modelling as a basis, including model extension and the development of database systems to record and manage information.

After completing this part, you will have a comprehensive view of conceptual modelling and its potentialities for cultural heritage. You should be able to use conceptual modelling for your cultural heritage work in a practical and straightforward manner.

Chapter 30
Modelling Patterns

Abstract In this chapter, we deal with the issue that many common situations that repeatedly arise when doing conceptual modelling can be codified as patterns and applied when necessary. We introduce the notion of *modelling pattern*, which is taken from the architecture and software engineering worlds, and involves a known problem, an application context, and a suggested solution. Then, we explore various kinds of patterns and document the most common ones. We start with hierarchical patterns for aggregation and subsumption, and then, we move to cover composite and state patterns.

Developing conceptual models is a highly creative task. As with other tasks where creation and problem-solving are involved (such as designing bridges or formulating social policies), you will need a good dose of originality and background knowledge. However, you will also find situations where you find yourself making the same choices and repeating the same steps that you have previously done, perhaps for a different model or even in a totally different area. In fact, there are common situations that come up again and again, and which have been repeatedly modelled over time by many people. We have accumulated a lot of knowledge about common situations, and we know how to model them fairly well. Instead of tackling them as if they were new, it is wise to draw on the experience of others when looking at a recurring problem, very much like a doctor does when finding very common symptoms or a civil engineer when confronted with very usual topographic and traffic conditions. Well-known solutions to common situations are called *design patterns* or simply *patterns*.

A pattern is often defined as a proven solution to a well-known problem in a specific context. In this manner, a pattern always involves a solution that relies on a clear and explicitly formulated problem to solve, and a particular context. In our case, the problems to solve are situations to be modelled; the context is often given by other parts of the model, as well as the model purpose; and the solution is provided in terms of model elements to create. For example, a very simplistic pattern is illustrated in Table 30.1.

© Springer International Publishing AG 2018
C. Gonzalez-Perez, *Information Modelling for Archaeology and Anthropology*,
https://doi.org/10.1007/978-3-319-72652-6_30

Table 30.1 Sample pattern

Problem	You have a category of things that are composed of entities of another category
Context	You need to describe entities of both categories with detail
Solution	Model each category as a class, and link them through a whole/part association

In the text above, the problem to solve is given by the first line, the context is provided by the second line, and the solution is suggested by the third. Of course, using a whole/part association when we have two categories related by aggregation semantics is quite trivial, so this pattern is barely worthwhile. However, some more complex situations that appear very often benefit enormously from having clear patterns that can be applied to them.

Patterns, however, will not give you all the details to construct your model. In the example above, the pattern does not suggest a name for the classes or tell you whether the classes make sense or not in your model. What it says is that you may want to add two classes plus a whole/part association if some well-known situation and context are given. Always treat patterns as a recommendation, guidance or advice rather than a strict law to be obeyed.

Patterns originated with the work of architect Christopher Alexander in the 1970s. Alexander proposed a system of proven solutions to well-known and recurring situations that often appear when designing buildings or urban landscapes. His work became a source of inspiration for a wide community in software engineering, who have since applied the pattern concept to the design and construction of information-related artefacts.

Technical

Christopher Alexander, together with some collaborators, wrote a famous trilogy where patterns are explained. In *The Oregon Experiment* [68], Alexander describes an experimental approach to the planning of a university campus that would later serve as a basis to develop the theory of design patterns. In *A Pattern Language* [69], a large number of specific patterns are described and documented so that they can be reused by others. In *The Timeless Way of Building* [70], finally, he proposes a comprehensive theory of architecture based on the notion of design patterns.

The work of Alexander has been tremendously influential in software engineering as well as architecture. A classic text on design patterns applied to the construction of software is [71].

The remainder of this chapter explores some patterns that you can apply to the conceptual modelling of cultural heritage.

Hierarchical Aggregation Patterns

Hierarchies are everywhere. From the arrangement of divisions and departments in corporations to land divisions in the territory, to the way we manage files on our computers, we employ hierarchies as a fundamental approach to organize the world. A hierarchy is a structure composed of elements that may be 'above', 'below' or 'at the same level as' each other. For example, countries such as France or Italy are 'at the same level' because all of them are countries. Also, all European countries are 'above' regions such as Brittany or Lazio, and 'below' the Europe continent. We use quotes around 'above', 'below' and 'at the same level' because these terms are used metaphorically, and the exact semantics of the relationships vary from one hierarchy to the next. In any case, any hierarchy will always show relationships of the three kinds.

The particular level at which an element is positioned within a hierarchy is called the element's *rank*. In the example above, we could say that Europe has a rank of 1, France and Italy (as well as any other European countries) would have a rank of 2, and regions such as Brittany or Lazio would be at rank 3.

Some hierarchies are defined by the way in which elements make up others or, seen from the opposite point of view, how elements can be decomposed into others. In cases like this, the 'above' and 'below' relationships have the actual semantics of 'composed of' and 'part of', respectively. This corresponds to the concept of aggregation. A common example is that of land divisions, as mentioned above. We can say that France *is composed of* (i.e. aggregates) regions such as Brittany, Normandy and Corsica, and that France, together with Italy and other countries, *is part of* Europe. We could go on by saying that Europe, together with other continents such as the Americas and Asia, makes up the world. And that Brittany itself, for example, is divided into departments such as Morbihan and Côtes-d'Armor.

In this example, each rank in the hierarchy can be referred to by a well-known name, such as "continent", "country", "region" or "department". Furthermore, there are clear rules that establish how ranks are related to each other: countries make up a continent, departments make up a region, etc. It would not make sense to have a department as part of a continent without an intermediate country and region. In other words, the hierarchy has a fixed, named and well-differentiated set of ranks that relate to each other in a fixed sequence. Hierarchies like this are sometimes called *taxonomies*. In contrast, other hierarchies have a number of ranks that is not fixed, each rank lacking a distinct name or definition that may differentiate it from the rest. Hierarchies like this are called *recursive hierarchies*. For example, think of the way in which folders are nested within each other in your computer's file system. The number of depth levels (i.e. ranks) at which a folder may exist is not fixed, and each level of folders does not have a particular name or definition; all are equally folders, which happen to be at one level or another.

A word of caution is worth putting here. The human mind tends to name things in order to organize the world. As a consequence, sometimes we would find ourselves naming the different ranks of a recursive hierarchy for the sake of clarity, especially if we are too fond of tidiness and structure. For example, we could say things like "this is a second-level folder" or "this is a subfolder". However, folders, subfolders and second-level folders in your computer are entities of exactly the same kind: they do not exhibit different characteristics or can be defined in different ways. They only receive those names because they happen to be at one particular place in the hierarchy. In fact, you can move a second-level folder so that it becomes third-level, without any changes to the folder's characteristics or appellation. For this reason, if a hierarchy looks recursive to you, then it is probably so. However, if a hierarchy looks like a taxonomy, think twice before modelling it as such. Try to come up with names or definitions for elements at different ranks; if you cannot, then the hierarchy is probably recursive despite the fact that we may sometimes assign names to ranks for practical purposes. This difference is important because taxonomies and recursive hierarchies are modelled in very different ways.

In addition, when modelling an aggregation hierarchy, we need to decide whether we need to *describe* the involved entities with detail or, on the contrary, we only need to *refer* to them and use them as labels. An example of a descriptive hierarchy would be a model of land divisions where we need to document the name, population and coordinates of each country, region and department. On the contrary, an example of a reference hierarchy would be a model of a list of historical periods such as Roman Age, Middle Ages (Early, High and Late), and Renaissance where we only use them to categorize or classify other things, such as buildings or works of art, but we do not need to describe any characteristics of each period.

The next sections describe how to model descriptive and reference aggregation hierarchies, taking into account whether they are taxonomic or recursive.

Descriptive Aggregation

A descriptive aggregation hierarchy is an aggregation hierarchy that allows us to describe each entity in the hierarchy with detail, considering its type and the potential peculiarities that it may exhibit in terms of attributes and associations.

If the hierarchy is a taxonomy, then we may apply the Taxonomical Decomposition pattern. This involves using a separate class for each rank in the hierarchy and a separate whole/part association for each connection between ranks. See Fig. 30.1 for an example.

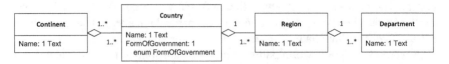

Fig. 30.1 Type model using the Taxonomical Decomposition pattern. Each rank is represented by a class, and each relationship is represented by a whole/part association

In the figure, note that some classes and associations have different features; for example, *Country* has a *FormOfGovernment* attribute, and the whole/part association between it and *Continent* has a 1..* cardinality on the whole side. This is because each rank in the taxonomy constitutes a different concept and, as such, has a different name and may have a different definition that manifests as different attributes and cardinalities in the model.

Taxonomical decompositions are very useful when the associated conceptualization of the world in terms of ranks and relationships is very clear. However, they can be too rigid for situations that exhibit irregularities. For example, the model in Fig. 30.1 may work well for France or Italy, but there are countries which are not divided into regions and departments. Some countries may use a two-level division like this but with different names, such as Spain, which uses autonomous regions and provinces; some others may use a totally different taxonomy with fewer or more ranks, or even different ranking systems within each subdivision.

Table 30.2 shows a concise description of the Taxonomical Decomposition pattern.

If the aggregation hierarchy to be modelled is recursive rather than a taxonomy, then we may apply the Recursive Decomposition pattern. This involves using a single class to represent any entity involved in the hierarchy, no matter what its rank, plus a whole/part self-association to represent connections between entities. See Fig. 30.2 for an example about historical periods. In the figure, historical periods such as the Roman Age or the Late Middle Ages are represented by the *Period* class. This is so regardless of each period's rank. Aggregation connections between periods are captured by the whole/part self-association, so that any period may have zero, one or more subperiods, and optionally be part of one frame period. A single class is sufficient because the hierarchy being modelled does not involve

Table 30.2 Taxonomical Decomposition pattern

Problem	You have an aggregation taxonomy
Context	You need to describe entities at each rank with detail
Solution	Model each category as a separate class, and link them through a set of whole/part associations

Fig. 30.2 Type model using the Recursive Decomposition pattern. A single class and whole/part self-association are used to represent the complete hierarchy

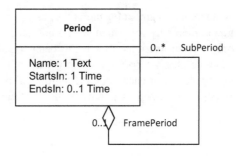

Table 30.3 Recursive Decomposition pattern

Problem	You have an aggregation recursive hierarchy
Context	You need to describe the involved entities with detail
Solution	Model all the categories in the hierarchy through a single class plus a whole/part self-association with clear role names

different concepts; all periods are just periods, no matter where they are in the hierarchy. Note also that role names are used in the model to clarify how periods relate to each other: either as subperiods or frame periods.

If different names and definitions were to be introduced at each rank, as for example with geological aeons, eras, periods and epochs, then we would be transforming this recursive hierarchy into a taxonomy, and the Taxonomical Decomposition pattern described above, rather than the Recursive Decomposition pattern described here, would be applicable.

Recursive decompositions are very useful when the number of ranks in the hierarchy is undefined, so that an arbitrary number of nesting levels may occur. Cardinalities of the whole/part self-association must be chosen carefully, and a minimum of zero is almost always needed. Otherwise, the hierarchy would be infinite. For example, if the model depicted in Fig. 30.2 had a 1..* cardinality on the *SubPeriod* end, then every period would need to have at least one subperiod; and each of these, at least one sub-sub-period, and so on and so forth. As introduced in Chap. 8, infinite regress is uncommon in the physical world and rarely useful because it tends to produce information that is very difficult to manage.

Table 30.3 shows a concise description of the Recursive Decomposition pattern.

Finally, bear in mind that the whole/part associations involved in the modelling of descriptive aggregations can be easily transformed into plain associations (i.e. without whole/part semantics) if the categories involved so require. Although aggregation is a phenomenon that is usually best modelled through whole/part semantics, there may be cases where regular associations are preferred. Use your own judgment to decide.

Reference Aggregation

A reference aggregation hierarchy, as opposed to a descriptive one, is an aggregation hierarchy for which we do not need to document the involved entities, but only refer to them as a means to categorize or classify other things. Imagine, for example, that we do not need to gather information about the form of government or population of each country, region and department, but only use a list of these places to document where different buildings are located.

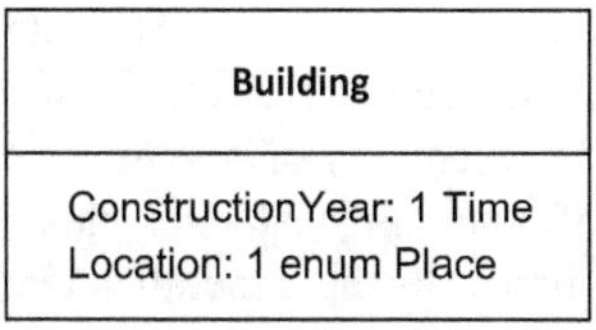

```
                    Building

          ConstructionYear: 1 Time
          Location: 1 enum Place
```

Fig. 30.3 Type model using the Reference Decomposition pattern. The whole hierarchy is represented as an enumerated type (not shown in the diagram) and referenced by the *Building. Location* attribute

Table 30.4 Reference Decomposition pattern

Problem	You have an aggregation hierarchy of any kind
Context	You need to use entities in the hierarchy as labels to categorize or classify other entities
Solution	Model instances for the whole hierarchy as an enumerated type, and then refer to it through attributes in the relevant classes

In cases like this, and regardless of whether the hierarchy is a taxonomy or not, we may apply the Reference Decomposition pattern. This involves the modelling of instances for the whole hierarchy as an enumerated type, and then referring to this type through attributes in the relevant classes. For example, we could define the following enumerated type in our model.

```
Place:          Europe
                  France
                    Brittany
                      CotesDArmor
                      Morbihan
                    Corsica
                    Normandy
                  Italy
                    Lazio
                      Rome
                      Viterbo
                    Tuscany
                      Lucca
                      Prato
```

Then, we would use the enumerated type as illustrated in Fig. 30.3.

Table 30.4 shows a concise description of the Reference Decomposition pattern.

Hierarchical Subsumption Patterns

The previous section described some patterns to model situations involving aggregation hierarchies. Now, we focus on a different kind of hierarchies, namely those based on subsumption rather than aggregation. Aggregation hierarchies, as described above, capture the way in which entities are 'above' or 'below' other entities over different ranks; in subsumption hierarchies, however, the elements that are 'above' or 'below' others are not entities but categories. In this regard, subsumption hierarchies organize categories, rather than entities, in a hierarchical manner. In line with this, the elements of a subsumption hierarchy are not composed of others or are part of others. Instead, elements are hypernyms or hyponyms of one another. This corresponds to the generalization/specialization relationships that we have been studying throughout the book, and especially in Chap. 9. Note that, in a subsumption hierarchy, the elements 'below' one element are not its parts, but subtypes of it. Similarly, an element that is 'above' others is not an aggregate but a supertype. Figure 22.1 constitutes a good example; in fact, the whole of CHARM is organized around a central generalization/specialization hierarchy that starts at the abstract-most *Entity* class and goes all the way down to very concrete classes such as *Construction* or *Person*. Many models exhibit a central generalization/specialization hierarchy like this, and, in fact, the most common way to introduce a new class into a model is to place it into an existing generalization/specialization hierarchy.

Subsumption hierarchies, like aggregation ones, can also be taxonomic or recursive. An example of a taxonomic subsumption hierarchy is the usual classification of living beings in kingdoms, phyla, classes, orders, families, etc. Each of these words ("phylum", "class", "order", etc.) refers to a particular rank in the hierarchy and has its own definition. However, rank names do not need to be explicitly included in a model of a subsumption hierarchy, because it is the relationships between the categories, rather than their ranks, what matters. Also, taxonomic subsumption hierarchies are not very common, though, and most subsumption hierarchies that you will find as generalization/specialization trees are of a recursive nature. All the generalization/specialization hierarchies in CHARM, for example, are of a recursive nature, since there is no particular name or definition for the classes at each level in the hierarchy.

When modelling a subsumption hierarchy, and like in the case of aggregation hierarchies, we need to decide whether we need to document instances of each category in the hierarchy or, to the contrary, just list the involved categories so that they can be used as labels to characterize other entities. Whether the hierarchy is a taxonomy or not does not matter in this case, since both are modelled in the same manner. The next sections describe how to model descriptive and reference subsumption hierarchies.

Descriptive Subsumption

A descriptive subsumption hierarchy is a subsumption hierarchy that allows us to document instances of the categories involved in the hierarchy, considering its particular type and the potential peculiarities that it may exhibit in terms of attributes and associations. The pattern to apply is called Descriptive Subtyping and involves using separate classes for each category involved in the hierarchy, plus

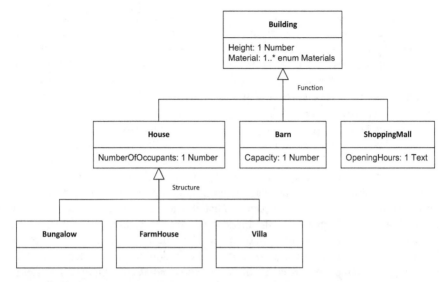

Fig. 30.4 Type model using the Descriptive Subtyping pattern. Each category involved in the hierarchy is represented by a class, and these are connected together by generalization/specialization relationships to organize the relevant ranks

generalization/specialization relationships to link them in the appropriate rank levels. See Fig. 30.4 for an example. The figure shows a subsumption hierarchy with three ranks. At the top, the *Building* class is specialized into *House*, *Barn* and *ShoppingMall*, and *House* is in turn specialized into three additional classes. Ranks are clearly visible as they are defined by generalization/specialization relationships.

Note that, as we introduced above, whether this is a taxonomic or recursive hierarchy does not matter much as long as the model is concerned. You may argue that the classes at the top rank (*Building*) are 'structure types', the classes at rank 2 (*House*, *Barn* and *ShoppingMall*) are 'building types', and the classes at the bottom rank (*Bungalow*, *FarmHouse* and *Villa*) are 'house types'. This would constitute a taxonomy. However, there is no meaningful way in which we could capture these terms and their possible definitions in the model.

Table 30.5 shows a concise description of the Descriptive Subtyping pattern.

Table 30.5 Descriptive Subtyping pattern

Problem	You have a subsumption hierarchy
Context	You need to describe instances of the categories in the hierarchy with detail
Solution	Model each category as a separate class, and organize them in ranks by linking them through generalization/specialization relationships

A few issues may appear when applying this pattern. First of all, you must be careful to respect the rule of inheritance that we described in Chap. 9: anything that we may say about a class also applies to all its subclasses. This means that definitions and features of any class in the hierarchy must be applicable to every downstream class. If it is not, then the hierarchy is incorrect. For example, the definition of the *House* class in Fig. 30.4 must be such that it also applies to *Bungalow*, *FarmHouse* and *Villa*.

Secondly, and in relation to the previous one, you must strive to place features at the right level of abstraction. For example, the *NumberOfOccupants* attribute in Fig. 30.4 has been placed in the *House* class, because it was determined that every house has a number of occupants (whatever it is), regardless of whether it is a bungalow, a farmhouse, a villa or any other kind of house that we might add later. However, barns do not have occupants, so that it would not make sense to place this attribute in a class higher up in the hierarchy so that *Barn* would inherit it.

Lastly, sometimes you may find the need to develop parallel subsumption hierarchies to represent structures of varying abstraction that are connected at each rank. A good example of this is that of *Valorization* and *DerivedEntity* in CHARM. As described in Chap. 29, *DerivedEntity* is specialized along the same lines as *Valorization*, and the *Source* association between both is refined for each pair classes. In this manner, *Valorization* is associated to *DerivedEntity*, *ExpertValorization* is associated to *ExpertDerivedEntity*, *CommunityValorization* is associated to *CommunityDerivedEntity*, etc. We say that the two subsumption hierarchies are parallel because they have the same structure and the same number of ranks, and a class from each is connected into a pair at each point in the hierarchy. Although not extremely common, this scenario is not rare, and you will find it every now and then once you have spent some time developing models.

Reference Subsumption

A reference subsumption hierarchy, as opposed to a descriptive one, is a subsumption hierarchy for which we do not need to document instances of the involved categories, but only refer to these categories as a means to label or classify other things. Imagine, for example, that we do not need to gather information about the number of occupants of houses or the capacity of barns, but only express what kinds of buildings (houses, barns, etc.) are shown in each photograph of a historical collection.

In cases like this, and regardless of whether the hierarchy is a taxonomy or not, we may apply the Reference Subtyping pattern. This involves the modelling of the categories in the hierarchy as an enumerated type, and then referring to this type through attributes in the relevant classes. For example, we could define the following enumerated type in our model.

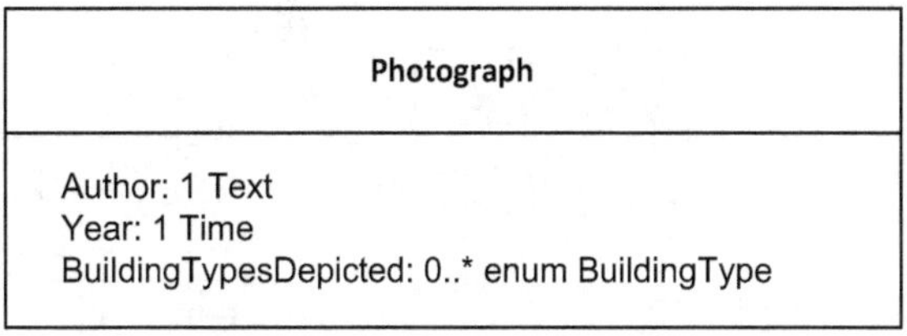

Photograph
Author: 1 Text Year: 1 Time BuildingTypesDepicted: 0..* enum BuildingType

Fig. 30.5 Type model using the Reference Subtyping pattern. The whole hierarchy is represented as an enumerated type (not shown in the diagram) and referenced by the *Photograph. BuildingTypesDepicted* attribute

Table 30.6 Reference Subtyping pattern

Problem	You have a subsumption hierarchy of any kind
Context	You need to use categories in the hierarchy as labels to classify other entities
Solution	Model categories in the hierarchy as an enumerated type, and then refer to it through attributes in the relevant classes

```
BuildingType:    Building
                 House
                   Bungalow
                   FarmHouse
                   Villa
                 Barn
                 ShoppingMall
```

Then, we would use the enumerated type as illustrated in Fig. 30.5.

Table 30.6 shows a concise description of the Reference Subtyping pattern.

Composite Patterns

So far, we have described aggregation and subsumption hierarchies as different kinds of structures. This is usually so, and the patterns described above can be very useful when dealing with them. However, sometimes we will find that hierarchies may present a combined nature where both aggregation and subsumption play a central role. Imagine again how files are organized in your computer. There is a hierarchical file system where folders can contain other folders as well as files. Also, files and folders are different kinds of things, but present many common characteristics: they always reside inside a folder, they have a name and a size, and they can be renamed, deleted or moved around. From a conceptual modelling point of view, two observations can be easily made. First, there is aggregation at work here, since a folder contains other folders as well as files. Second, there is subsumption as well, since both files and folders are special cases of a more abstract construct that we may call a file system item. As we described in Chap. 9, a direct consequence of subsumption is abstraction, the phenomenon by which we can

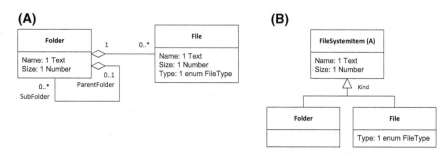

Fig. 30.6 Both aggregation and subsumption play a part in structuring a computer file system. In **A**, folders are composed of files as well as other folders. In **B**, folders and files are both subtypes of file system items

discard details and focus only on what is essential. When carrying out operations such as renaming, moving or deleting, we do not need to know whether something is a file or a folder, since these operations are the same for both kinds of things: we can abstract and consider them equivalent. Figure 30.6 shows a summary of these ideas. In Fig. 30.6A, we state the fact that folders may contain files as well as other folders. In Fig. 30.6B, we represent the fact that both folders and files are subtypes of an abstract construct called *FileSystemItem*. By using abstraction, we have factored out every characteristic that is common to *Folder* and *File* and moved them up to *FileSystemItem*. In order to provide a complete model of your computer's file system, these two situations must be reconciled in a single model. To do this, we need to realize that *Folder* and *File* in Fig. 30.6A share a common characteristic that has not been abstracted out into *FileSystemItem* in Fig. 30.6B: namely the fact that both classes are located on the part end of a whole/part association with *Folder*. On the one hand, *File* is evidently related to *Folder* through a whole/part association in which *File* acts as the part and *Folder* as the whole. Perhaps not as evidently, *Folder* is also related to *Folder* through a whole/part association in which *Folder* acts as the part through the *SubFolder* role; in this case, *Folder* also works as the whole through the *ParentFolder* role, since this is a whole/part self-association. Since both *File* and *Folder* share the characteristic of being parts of *Folder*, then this should be abstracted out into *FileSystemInfo* together with the *Name* and *Size* attributes. Figure 30.7 shows the result. Here, the situations depicted in Fig. 30.6A and B have been consolidated into a single model, showing that there are two kinds of file system items, folders and files, both having a name and a size. Furthermore, both may be contained in a folder. The structure in Fig. 30.7 corresponds to a Composite pattern.

This pattern is very common. Think, for example, of the way in which norms are modelled in CHARM, as described in Chap. 26. An excerpt of Fig. 26.2 is shown here as Fig. 30.8. Here, we state that there are two kinds of norms depending on their atomicity: simple norms and compound norms, and that compound norms, in turn, are composed of either simple norms or other compound norms. Of course,

Fig. 30.7 The A and B
situations from Fig. 30.6 have
been reconciled into a single
model

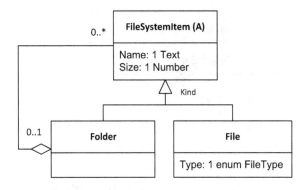

Fig. 30.8 Norms in CHARM
are modelled by using a
Composite pattern. See
Fig. 26.2 for a complete
diagram

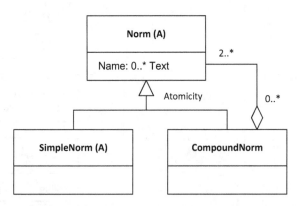

this occurs within a much larger context that involves other classes and associations
(see Fig. 26.2 for a larger view), but the fact that these three classes are organized in
a Composite pattern is still true.

In a Composite pattern, there are always three elements:

- An atomic category, the instances of which may be parts of instances of an
  aggregate category.
- An aggregate category, the instances of which are composed of instances of the
  same category or the atomic category.
- An abstract category, which generalizes the two previous ones by capturing all
  their common characteristics, most importantly the fact that their instances may
  be parts of instances of the aggregate category.

In our previous examples, the atomic categories were *File* and *SimpleNorm*; the
aggregate categories were *Folder* and *CompoundNorm*; and the abstract categories
were *FileSystemItem* and *Norm*.

Composite patterns are useful to generate heterogeneous hierarchies where
instances of the atomic category always appear in leaf position, and instances of the
aggregate category appear as either leaf or non-leaf positions. Figure 30.9 shows an
example.

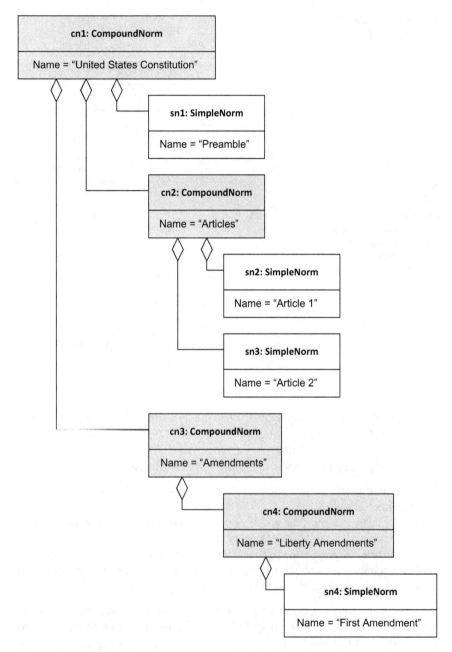

Fig. 30.9 Fragment of an instance model conforming to the type model in Fig. 30.8. Compound norms have been shaded grey, and simple norms have been left unshaded

Table 30.7 Composite pattern

Problem	You have a situation involving an aggregate category whose instances may be composed of instances of the same aggregate category as well as an atomic category
Context	You need to document entities of both the aggregate and atomic categories, as well as the hierarchical relationships between them
Solution	Model the aggregate and atomic categories as classes, and introduce an abstract class that generalizes both. Use a whole/part association from the aggregate class to the abstract class

Figure 30.9 represents a small part of the United States Constitution. Compound norms such as the constitution itself as well as the articles block or the liberty amendments block are shaded in grey. Simple norms, such as the preamble or the individual articles or amendments, are shown in white. Note that instances of *SimpleNorm*, the atomic category, appear always in leaf positions, that is, do not have anything 'below' them, whereas instances of *CompoundNorm*, the aggregate category, appear elsewhere in the hierarchy. Any application of the Composite pattern will show this behaviour.

Table 30.7 shows a concise description of the Composite pattern.

Sometimes you will see cases of the Composite pattern that seem to be "upside down". Look, for example, at how constructed structures are modelled in CHARM, as per Chap. 22. Constructed structures were roughly defined as structures created by the intentional modification and/or bounding of physical space through the addition and/or removal of materials, and which, by virtue of the structural arrangement of its parts, or that of its own within a bigger whole, perform a given function. There are two kinds of constructed structures. Firstly, constructions provide direct functionality to their users and include buildings, pits or cattle enclosures. Secondly, constructive elements which, despite not providing direct functionality to their users, constitute a material part of larger constructed entities, to which they contribute structure and/or function, and include the columns of a house or the access system of a cattle enclosure. Figure 30.10 shows the corresponding class diagram. Here, as opposed to what the Composite pattern says, the whole/part association goes from the abstract class to one of the concrete classes rather than the other way around. Let us examine what the semantics of this are. Like in the case of a genuine Composite pattern, there is both aggregation and subsumption at work here. Aggregation plays a role in stating that constructed structures may be composed of constructive elements. Subsumption, in turn, is important to express that constructive elements and constructions are subtypes of constructed structures. Note that, here, both concrete classes (*Construction* and *ConstructiveElement* in our example) inherit the fact that they may be composed of something. In this sense, both are aggregates, and there is no atomic category. One of the aggregates (*ConstructiveElement* in the example) is composable, in the sense that it can be part of the aggregates, whereas the other (*Construction*) is not composable, because it cannot.

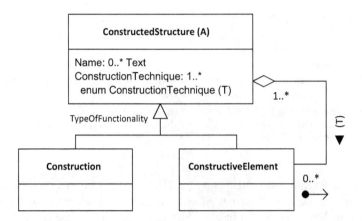

Fig. 30.10 Constructed structures in CHARM are modelled by using an apparently "upside down" Composite pattern. See Fig. 22.4 for a complete diagram

As opposed to a true Composite pattern, this situation cannot generate a hierarchy with instances of the atomic category always appearing in leaf positions, since there is no atomic category. Rather, "upside down" situations like this generate heterogeneous hierarchies where instances of the composable class anywhere in the hierarchy, either as leaf or non-leaf, and instances of the non-composable class appearing only in a root position. Figure 30.11 shows an example. In Fig. 30.11, note that there is only one instance of *Construction* at the root of the hierarchy, since *Construction* is the non-composable class; it does not participate in the whole/part association as depicted in Fig. 30.10.

Situations like this where an "upside down" Composite pattern seems to be involved correspond to the Inverted Composite pattern. In an Inverted Composite pattern, there are always three elements:

- A composable category, the instances of which may be parts of instances of other categories as well as be composed of instances of the same category.
- A non-composable category, the instances of which cannot be part of any other things, but which can be composed of instances of the composable category.
- An abstract category, which generalizes the two previous ones by capturing all their common characteristics, most importantly the fact that their instances may be composed of instances of the composable category.

In our previous example, the composable category was *ConstructiveElement*; the non-composable category was *Construction*; and the abstract category was *ConstructedStructure*.

Table 30.8 shows a concise description of the Inverted Composite pattern.

There is one final remark to make. When applying the Composite or Inverted Composite patterns, bear in mind that minimum cardinalities for every whole/part semi-association must almost certainly be zero. As we said when discussing

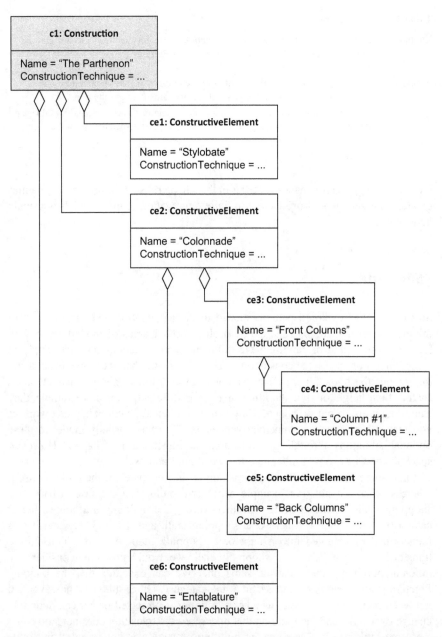

Fig. 30.11 Fragment of an instance model conforming to the type model in Fig. 30.10. Constructions have been shaded grey, and constructive elements have been left unshaded

Table 30.8 Inverted Composite pattern

Problem	You have a situation involving a composable category whose instances may be parts of instances of the same composable category as well as a non-composable category
Context	You need to document entities of both the composable and non-composable categories, as well as the hierarchical relationships between them
Solution	Model the composable and non-composable categories as classes, and introduce an abstract class that generalizes both. Use a whole/part association from the abstract class to the composable class

hierarchical aggregation patterns earlier in this chapter, using minimum cardinalities greater than zero would produce an infinite aggregation regress, which is usually undesirable.

State Patterns

So far, we have explored patterns related to the aggregation and subsumption of things. However, patterns can also be useful in other areas of modelling. A very relevant case is that of capturing the different states or modes that may apply to something. For example, consider the *Building* class that we have been using throughout the book for multiple examples. In addition to having characteristics such as their height or style, buildings may be in different states. For example, they can be new, used, old or ruined. They can be protected or not. They can work as housing, public spaces, commercial venues, etc. We have usually modelled these optional situations through specialization, as illustrated in Chap. 9. However, specialization has some limitations that we should address.

First, some subtypes of buildings pertain to the "essence" of the building itself, whereas others do not. For example, whether a building is a house, a barn or a shopping mall is quite essential; in other words, if a building is a house, then it cannot (usually) be also a barn or a shopping mall, and it is unlikely that it gets transformed or changed into a barn or a shopping mall. And, if a house were transformed into a barn or a shopping mall, we would probably consider it a different building rather than the same one. We can conclude that the building function is an *essential* characteristic of the category. Other subtypes, however, are not as essential. For example, whether a building is protected or not can definitely change over time, and the building that undergoes the transition does not stop being the same building. In this case, the building protection is not essential but quite *accidental* to the building category. Essential distinctions can be adequately modelled through generalization/specialization hierarchies, and the rigidity imposed by these hierarchies is rarely an obstacle since things seldom change their essential characteristics. Accidental distinctions, however, may also be modelled through

Fig. 30.12 Buildings'
protection status modelled as
a specialization hierarchy

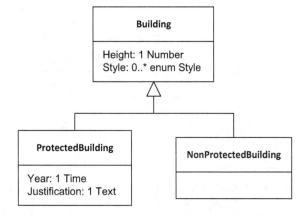

specialization, but this usually results in models that are too rigid. See Fig. 30.12. Now imagine that we have an unprotected building that we want to document. We would add an object of type *NonProtectedBuilding*. Imagine that, later, this building gets protected. We should "move" the object to *ProtectedBuilding* instead. However, and as we explained back in Chap. 5, an object can only have one class as its type, and this class can never vary. Indeed, the model in Fig. 30.12 is probably quite poor for any possible purpose, since the distinction between protected and non-protected buildings is accidental rather than essential, so we should not use specialization to construct categories like these. Rather, we should realize that being protected or not are possible states of buildings, rather than kinds of buildings.

A second limitation of generalization/specialization relationships is that subtypes of a class are exclusive, meaning that an object can only be an instance of one of them. This is again due to the fact that objects have one and only one class as their type. In Fig. 30.12, it is quite evident that a building cannot be protected and not protected at the same time, so this would not be a problem here. However, consider a situation involving the modelling of how people interact with an ethnographic study about tourism. Some people will be researchers, some will be informants, some will be members of the local community, and some will be tourists. This is shown in Fig. 30.13. Now imagine that we need to record the details about an informant. According to the figure, we would add an object having *Informant* as its type. However, this person may also be a tourist or a community member, or even a researcher. Indeed, any combination of roles is possible. We cannot have multiple type classes for an object, so this would be a problem. Again, we should realize that the roles that someone plays in relation to something are not an essential part of that person, but some accidental characteristic; for this reason, using specialization to capture this is not a good idea.

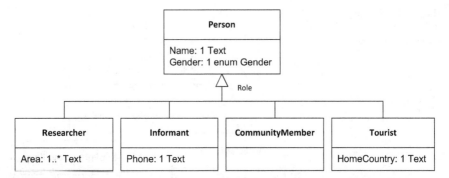

Fig. 30.13 Roles of people modelled as a specialization hierarchy

When trying to model states of things, you should use the State pattern. To use this pattern, you need to consider three aspects:

- The category that can be in a number of states. In our previous example, this would correspond to the *Person* class.
- The discriminant that captures what the possible states are about. In our previous example, this was represented by the *Role* discriminant.
- The list of possible states that the above category can go through depending on the above discriminant. In our previous example, this corresponds to the subclasses of *Person*.

Instead of using a generalization/specialization rooted in the category class, we use a different strategy. See Fig. 30.14. Here, a new *PersonRole* abstract class has been introduced to capture the discriminant, and the specialization hierarchy is rooted in this new class instead of *Person*. Also, *Person* and *PersonRole* are connected through a whole/part association with strong semantics on the *PersonRole* side, meaning that a person role does not make sense without an accompanying person. The class that captures the discriminant, *PersonRole* in our example, is called the *state class*.

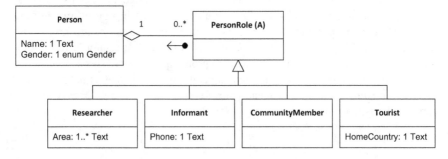

Fig. 30.14 Possible roles of people modelled by using a state pattern

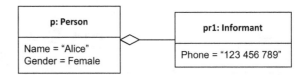

Fig. 30.15 A person playing the role of informant, documented by using the model in Fig. 30.14

Note a few things about the model in Fig. 30.14. First, we still have a specialization hierarchy capturing the necessary categories to document the different roles of people in relation to the project. However, these are not subtypes of *Person*, but subtypes of *PersonRole*. Applying specialization semantics, this means that researchers, informants, community members and tourists are not kinds of people but kinds of roles that people may play. This is exactly what we wanted to express.

Secondly, note that the *Person* and *PersonRole* classes are tightly coupled. *Person* has a whole/part association towards *PersonRole*, which, in turn, is defined in terms of *Person*. This expressed the fact that person roles are not independent entities but, to the contrary, they are inherent to persons. As an example, Fig. 30.15 shows how a particular person playing the role of informant would be documented through this model. Note that the fact that *p* is an informant is not shown through instantiation, but through the fact that *p* aggregates an object of the *Informant* type. Finally, and most importantly, note that this model can be easily used and extended to cater for the needs that we outlined at the beginning of this section. For example, we can easily express that a person plays multiple roles simultaneously, as shown in Fig. 30.16.

Also, we can capture the temporality of the roles that a person plays by simply making the whole/part association temporal. This would allow us to document not only what roles a person plays, but also when they played each. Figure 30.17 shows an example.

State patterns are not as common as Composite or hierarchical patterns; however, they are extremely useful when you need them. The *MethodologicalRoleOfAgent* class in CHARM, for example, is a state class of *SpecificAgent*, as described in Chap. 23.

Table 30.9 shows a concise description of the State pattern.

The State pattern can be easily extended to cater for multiple concurrent state discriminants. For example, we could add another state class to the model in

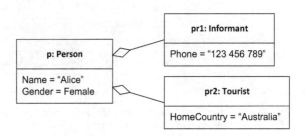

Fig. 30.16 A person playing the simultaneous roles of informant and tourist, documented by using the model in Fig. 30.14

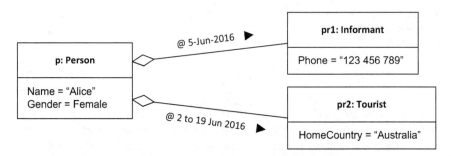

Fig. 30.17 A person playing the roles of informant and tourist at different times, documented by using a variant of the model in Fig. 30.14 with a temporal whole/part association

Table 30.9 State pattern

Problem	You want to document the different states or modes that entities of a category may be in
Context	You need to describe each state with detail, and perhaps combine them and add temporal information
Solution	Model the category undergoing states as a class, and the state discriminant as a new abstract class. Connect both by using a whole/part association from the former to the latter, and use strong semantics in the opposite direction. Add as many subclasses of the state class as necessary to represent each of the relevant states

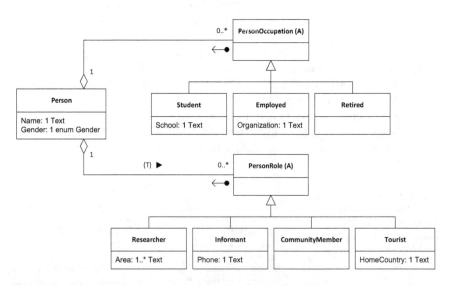

Fig. 30.18 A new state class has been added to the model in Fig. 30.14 to capture the occupation of people in addition to their relationship to the project

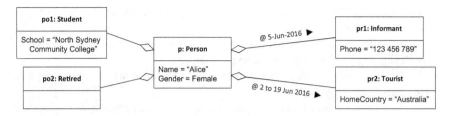

Fig. 30.19 A person playing multiple roles from two different discriminants, documented by using the model in Fig. 30.18

Table 30.10 Multi-State pattern

Problem	You want to document multiple sets of different states or modes that entities of a category may be in
Context	You need to describe each state with detail, and perhaps combine them and add temporal information, within or across state sets
Solution	Model the category undergoing states as a class, and each of the state discriminants as a new abstract class. Connect the category class to each state class by using a whole/part association from the former to the latter, and use strong semantics in the opposite direction. Add as many subclasses of each state class as necessary to represent each of the relevant states

Fig. 30.14 in order to describe a different range of states that people can go through, and combine them at will. For example, imagine that, in addition to knowing the roles that people play in relation to our project, we also want to document whether they study, work or are retired (or a combination). Figure 30.18 shows the result.

By using this model, we can capture complex situations such as "Alice, a retired community college student from Australia, visited us as a tourist between 2 and 19 June 2016, and was also an informant of the project on 5 June 2016". Figure 30.19 shows this. Using the State pattern multiple times on a single category, like this, is called the Multi-State pattern. Table 30.10 shows a concise description of this pattern.

Summary

A **design pattern** (or just **pattern** for short) is a well-known solution to a recurring problem in a particular context.

Patterns provide **guidance and advice**, but they are not laws that must be obeyed no matter what.

To document entities involved in an aggregation hierarchy with detail, apply a **Taxonomical Decomposition** pattern if the hierarchy is a taxonomy, or a **Recursive Decomposition** pattern if the hierarchy is recursive.

To list and use the entities involved in an aggregation hierarchy as labels, apply a **Reference Decomposition** pattern.

To document instances of the categories involved in a subsumption hierarchy with detail, apply a **Descriptive Subtyping** pattern.

To list and use the categories in a subsumption hierarchy as labels, apply a **Reference Subtyping** pattern.

To document entities of an atomic and an aggregate category, where instances of the aggregate may be composed of instances of either the aggregate or atomic categories, apply a **Composite** pattern.

To document entities of a composable and a non-composable category, where instances of the composable category may be parts of instances of either the composable or non-composable categories, apply an **Inverted Composite** pattern.

To document the states that an entity may be in, optionally using temporal semantics, apply a **State** pattern. Multiple state patterns can be combined into a **Multi-State** pattern.

Exercises

48. Below you can find a list of modelling situations. For each of them, state what pattern you would apply, if any.

    - A family tree including only parent–child relationships.
    - The fact that archaeological sites may be excavated or not, and when.
    - A study of urban landscapes where cities are considered to be composed of neighbourhoods, neighbourhoods are composed of areas, and areas are composed of streets.
    - The description of author's marks on artworks, which may be placed on the artwork itself or on a previous mark.
    - The composition of a thesaurus of traditional trades to tag a collection of literary works that may mention them.

Chapter 31
Constructing Quality Models

Abstract In this chapter, we introduce the concept of quality as related to conceptual models and provide two non-exclusive approaches through which a model's quality may be assessed: how well the model allows us to achieve our purpose and how well the model can be understood or modified. Each of these is fleshed out into various quality factors, including functional ones such as correctness and robustness as well as non-functional ones, such as usability or readability. Then, we introduce the notion of *modularity* as a way to achieve better quality in conceptual models, using Bertrand Meyer's influential work in software languages. We define a module as a portion of a model that exhibits high internal cohesion and low external coupling and explore five quality criteria that can help us produce more modular models: decomposability, composability, understandability, proportion and protection. Finally, the chapter closes with a discussion on the cost of quality and the need to achieve a balance between quality, time and resources.

We have said throughout this book that models are created for a purpose. As any other goal-oriented human creation, models can be of a varying degree of quality; that is, some models are of good quality whereas others are not so good. What do we mean by *quality*? Roughly speaking, the quality of a goal-oriented artefact is related to its capacity to help us achieve its goal. In the case of models, this means that a good model is one that represents the modelling scope in an appropriate manner so that we can successfully do whatever we thought about when constructing the model. As described in Chap. 3, the major goal areas of models include exploration, documentation, communication, design and interoperability. A model that allows us to successfully explore, document, communicate, design and/or interoperate, therefore, would be a good model.

We must also consider other factors when thinking about model quality. For example, a model may allow us to carry out the intended purpose very nicely, but what if it is extremely difficult to change when the scope changes? What if it is difficult to understand by others or even ourselves? What if it contains redundant or

© Springer International Publishing AG 2018
C. Gonzalez-Perez, *Information Modelling for Archaeology and Anthropology*,
https://doi.org/10.1007/978-3-319-72652-6_31

irrelevant classes or attributes? Factors like these are also important despite not being directly related to the model's purpose. This chapter explores model quality in general and gives some advice on how to construct high-quality models.

Quality Factors

We said above that model quality is related to two major concerns:

- How well the model allows us to achieve our purpose.
- How well the model can be understood or modified.

The first is often expressed in terms of correctness, robustness and related quality factors, whereas the second is usually expressed in terms of "-ilities" such as maintainability, usability, readability. Quality factors can be expressed in terms of degree rather than as a binary yes/no. In other words, they are not black or white properties of models, but properties that can be possessed in a variable amount. Whether they can be easily measured or not, however, is another question. For example, giving figures for how correct or usable a model is can be very difficult.

Also, you must bear in mind that it is impossible to maximize all quality factors for any given model. Ideally, we would like our models to score very high for everything. However, quality factors overlap with each other and are often inter-related in complex manners, so that increasing quality for some factors entails a decrease for some others. For example, making a model more robust usually implies making it less readable. Quality is a matter of priorities and trade-offs. For example, you may decide that your particular modelling purpose suggests that robustness is not that important (perhaps because the model will be used in a very well-known setting), but readability is crucial since the model is going to be used by beginners. In this case, you would place readability above robustness in your scale of priorities and trade off robustness for readability every time (or most times) that a modelling decision must be made that involves both.

The following sections explore the main model quality factors.

Functional Quality Factors

Functional quality factors are those that are directly related to the ability of a model to achieve the purpose for which it was created.

Correctness

A model is *correct* if it represents its scope according to the intended purpose in a complete, precise and accurate way.

- A model is more or less *complete* depending on how much of the scope it represents. A model that captures the whole scope is fully complete; a model that leaves relevant things out is incomplete to some degree.
- A model is more or less *precise* depending on how much detail is incorporated about the entities that are represented. A model that incorporates the right amount of detail is very precise; a model that is vague or lacks necessary detail is imprecise.
- A model is more or less *accurate* depending on how well its scope is represented. A model that uses elements that faithfully represent its scope is highly accurate; a model that does not match its scope, even if it is highly precise, is inaccurate.

Correction constitutes the essential quality factor; if a model ranks high in other quality factors such as robustness or usability, but lacks in correctness, then it is a poor model. Consequently, correction must be always at the top of the scale of priorities when creating a model.

A correct model allows us to carry out our purpose, and an incorrect model does not. Furthermore, we can rely on a correct model as a convenient representation of reality, whereas an incorrect model is unreliable. You may think that this clashes with what we said back in Chap. 1, regarding George Box's aphorism, that "all models are wrong; some models are useful". It does not. What Box means by "wrong" is that all models leave things out when simplifying their scope in order to represent it. In this sense, models are "wrong" or, rather, incomplete. However, good models must still be correct in the sense described here of being complete, having the necessary precision, and being as accurate as possible.

Note also that precision and accuracy are independent of each other. Precision is about the level of detail in the model, regardless of how well this detail matches the scope being represented. Accuracy, on the other hand, is about having a good match, regardless of how much detail the model employs. A model can be highly precise and very inaccurate at the same time, such as a model using many classes with many attributes to express something that does not match, or even contradicts, the observed reality. A model can also be very imprecise but highly accurate, such as one using very few elements and making a very shallow description of its scope, but matching it very well.

Robustness

A model is *robust* if it allows us to achieve our purpose even in unexpected conditions. In other words, robustness is about going beyond correctness and reaching out for more. Figure 31.1 shows an example.

In Fig. 31.1A, a model is provided for a project aiming to study how utensils found in traditional houses are employed by their owners. It covers the whole scope by including the *House* and *Utensil* classes, it does it with adequate precision, and it is quite accurate. Overall, model A is acceptably correct. The model in Fig. 31.1B, however, adds an intermediate level of abstraction to the specialization hierarchy by adding the *Structure* and *Object* abstract classes. These classes are not strictly necessary for the above-mentioned study, and in fact, they contribute no attributes or new associations. However, imagine that, midway through the project, the need to include other objects in addition to utensils, such as pieces of furniture, comes up. If we were using model A, we would need to add a new *PieceOfFurniture* class, make it specialize from *MaterialElement* and connect it to *House* with an association to capture the fact that pieces of furniture are located in houses. This association would be very similar to the one coming out of *Utensil*, and thus redundant. We would end up with a model that is overly complex and harder to understand. Instead, if we were using model B from the beginning, we could easily add *PieceOfFurniture* under *Object*, and that would be all. In model B, the *Structure* and *Object* classes are there to cater for future extension needs despite the fact that they are not strictly needed to start with.

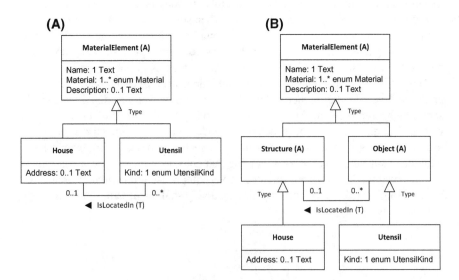

Fig. 31.1 Model **A** is correct, but model **B** is much more robust. See the text for a complete explanation

Sometimes, robustness is said to be about underpromising and overdelivering. Both models A and B in Fig. 31.1 "promise" to help us document utensils in houses; however, model B "overdelivers" by allowing us to document other kinds of objects (and other kinds of structures, too) with very little effort.

Non-functional Quality Factors

Non-functional quality factors are those that are not directly related to the ability of a model to achieve the purpose for which it was created. Rather, they describe how well the model can be used or changed.

Usability

A model is more or less *usable* depending on how easy it is to apply. As opposed to correctness, which is described in terms of the model's properties in relation to its scope and purpose, usability is empirically defined in terms of how useful the model is for its users. Of course, incorrect models are usually highly unusable, but models that are correct may still be not too usable. For example, a model may be complete, precise and accurate (i.e. correct), but use awkward terminology for class and feature names, or be too hard to understand. Aspects such as elegance, aesthetics, balance and presentation also play an important role regarding usability. Even the manner in which the model is introduced to its potential users can have an impact. For example, is the model attractive? Is it easy to grasp for its users? Is it expressed in their own terminology?

Efficiency

A model is more or less *efficient* depending on how many elements it needs to describe its scope. A model that employs many classes, features and other elements to describe a simple scope is an inefficient model, since it requires a lot of cognitive effort from its users. However, a model that employs few classes and features to describe a complex scope would be highly efficient. In this regard, models work as text: use as few words as possible (but not fewer) to express what you need to say.

Efficiency has a positive impact on usability. The more efficient a model is, the easier it is to use.

Maintainability

A model is more or less *maintainable* depending on how easy or difficult it is to change it. "Maintaining" a model means keeping it up to date when its scope or purpose changes. This usually entails making small alternations. A model that was "designed for change", therefore, would be more maintainable than one created with only short-term goals in mind.

Readability

A model is more or less *readable* depending on how easy or difficult it is for users to understand what it is supposed to express. A very readable model is one that users "see through" into the represented scope; an unreadable model, on the contrary, stands between the user and its scope, hindering comprehension.

Readability is crucial for maintainability and usability. If you cannot read a model, you will not be able to use it or change it.

Modularity

The previous section described quality factors. So far, we have learnt what a good model should be like. However, how do we get there? The answer is modularity.

If you look at a modern car, or any other piece of engineering, you will notice that they are highly *modular*. This means that they are made of small parts that can be easily exchanged when they wear out or stop working. For example, you can replace your car's spark plugs when they get too old. This ability needs to be designed into the car from its inception; that is, car engineers must foresee the fact that spark plugs eventually will become old, and a replacement will be needed. In consequence, they design cars in a modular fashion so that old spark plugs can be easily removed and new ones inserted.

Modularity is the property of a system (such as a car or a model) by which this system, rather than being a large monolithic unit, can be understood in terms of component modules. A *module*, in turn, is a portion of a system that exhibits two complementary properties:

- High internal cohesion
- Low external coupling.

By internal cohesion, we mean that a module cannot be split in parts easily, because everything inside it is intimately interrelated. Think of our car example again: you can certainly disassemble a spark plug, but its parts are so intimately connected to work as a whole, that it is more practical to consider the spark plug as a cohesive thing rather than an assembly of parts when looking at the car as a system. When we say that modules exhibit high internal cohesion, we mean that a module may be made of parts, but these parts work together as a whole and are difficult or inconvenient to separate.

Of course, a spark plug can be disassembled, and if you think from the perspective of a spark plug manufacturer, they will probably have a very clear vision of spark plugs as assemblies of smaller parts. However, this does not contradict what we said above; when looking at a car as a system, then spark plugs are better seen as units; when focussing on a spark plug as a system, then we can decompose it into elements. But spark plug manufacturers do not worry too much about the details of other components in the car. This is to say, we can shift our abstraction level from the car as a system to the spark plug as a system, each time seeing the immediate constituent parts as modules.

The second property of modules is related to external coupling. This means that a module is connected to other modules in a weaker manner than the parts of the module to one another. In other words, a module does have connections to other modules in the system; however, these connections are not as strong as the connections that exist within a module. In our car example, spark plugs are designed to work together with other engine parts; however, they can be easily removed and replaced, and they are manufactured separately, which shows that their connection to the rest of the engine is not as strong.

If you think of a car engine as a mesh of small parts, where each part is related to many others, modules make up the "lumps" in this mesh. See Fig. 31.2 for an illustration. Note how, in Fig. 31.2B, parts within modules are strongly connected to other parts within the module, whereas very few connections exist between modules. This is precisely what we mean by high internal cohesion and low external coupling.

You may recall the concept of package that we discussed in Chap. 13. A package is a group of related classes, enumerated types and possibly subpackages. Packages comprise one of the major mechanisms by which we can organize models in a modular fashion. The classes and enumerated types within any given package are supposed to be closely related to each other and work together as a comprehensive whole. At the same time, associations or generalization/ specialization relationships to classes in other packages are supposed to be fewer and weaker. We can use packages to clearly establish modules in a model, although this is not compulsory. We can also establish modules by designing classes and relationships between them in a manner such that high cohesion and low coupling are attained.

The modules in a system can be made to correspond to any well-defined concern. For example, when describing how a car works, we often talk about the electrical subsystem, the fuel subsystem or the steering elements. Electrical, fuel and steering are valid modules, because they correspond to parts of the car with high internal cohesion and low external coupling. In this case, we have modularized the car according to the function of the different parts. But we might have used a different criterion. Think, for example, of CHARM, as described throughout

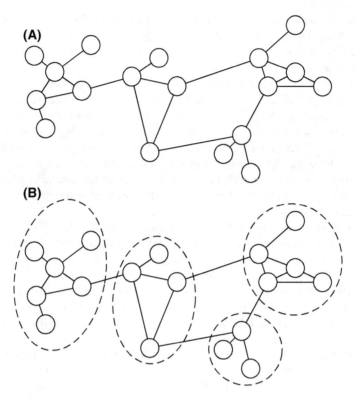

Fig. 31.2 Informal depiction of a system made of small parts. In **A**, some parts are closely connected to other parts, forming "lumps" that are loosely linked to other "lumps". In **B**, "lumps" are highlighted

Part IV. CHARM is modularized in terms of types of things, and thus we have tangible entities, agents, manifestations, performative entities, occurrences, etc. Classes within each of these modules work together as a whole to describe a portion of the cultural heritage world and are connected to classes in other modules through fewer and weaker relationships.

At this point, you may be wondering how modularity is related to quality. In brief, *the more modular a model is, the higher its quality*. The reasons behind this are explained in the next section.

Meyer's Five Criteria

In his 1997 book "Object-Oriented Software Construction" [72, Chap. 3], Bertrand Meyer describes five criteria that must be satisfied by a system in order to be called highly modular. Meyer is discussing software systems, but his arguments can be adapted for conceptual models as well. Based on Meyer's work, the five modularity criteria for conceptual modelling are:

- Decomposability
- Composability
- Understandability
- Proportion (called "Continuity" by Meyer)
- Protection.

Each criterion is described throughout the next sections.

Decomposability

A model exhibits modular *decomposability* if it can be easily decomposed into modules. Large modules, similarly, should be decomposable into submodules, and perhaps repeat this a few times until you obtain modules of a manageable size.

Decomposability is the key strategy to tackle complexity. By applying a "divide-and-conquer" approach, a model can be seen as a collection of interrelated modules, and work in each module can be carried out in a more or less independent fashion once their relationships are clear.

For example, CHARM can be easily seen as a collection of modules such as tangible entities, performative entities, agents, abstract entities. Performative entities, in turn, can be seen as a collection of modules such as expressive designs and understandings.

Composability

Related to the previous, modular *composability* in a model means that modules in the model, and even the model as a whole, can be easily composed into larger systems. This means that each module, in addition to comprising a relatively self-contained unit, can be connected to other modules. And the whole model itself can be connected to other models.

For example, the performative entities and agents modules in CHARM can be composed into a larger element by using the *PerformativeEntity.UsualPerformer* association that links both modules.

Together, composability and decomposability make up the basis for modularity. The remaining three criteria provide further insights into why high modularity leads to high quality.

Understandability

A model exhibits modular *understandability* if each module can be understood by a human without looking at other modules. This is based on modular decomposition, since we need to be able to decompose something into modules in order to understand each module.

Modular understandability is a crucial criterion for quality, because understanding a whole non-trivial model is usually a daunting task for anyone. Modular understandability has a positive impact on usability and readability. For example, look again at Fig. 24.3. By looking at this figure, which depicts the expressive designs module in CHARM, you can easily learn what subtypes of expressive designs exist in CHARM, see that every expressive design may formally designate a number of valuable entities, and that some specific kinds of expressive design, such as toponyms and anthroponyms, are related to places and agents, respectively. You can understand all this by looking at this figure only, because CHARM is constructed in a manner such that good modular understandability is achieved. In other words, you do not need to look at the rest of CHARM to understand how expressive designs work.

A model with low modular understandability would be very difficult to grasp, and therefore to use or maintain, because you would need to look at most of its elements in order to understand even a small part.

Proportion

A model exhibits modular *proportion* if making a small change requires a small effort, and making a large change requires a large effort. In other words, the amount of work needed to carry out a change in the model must be proportionate to the magnitude of the change.

Modular proportion is also a crucial criterion for quality, and it has a clear positive impact on maintainability. A model with low modular proportion would require a large effort even to make small changes, which would make it difficult to maintain or adapt. Your modelling scope or purpose will likely change over the lifetime of the model, and you will need to adjust the model as needed. A model that becomes too difficult to change, even for small alterations, is a poor model.

Imagine that we wanted to incorporate a new way of locating things into CHARM. Because everything related to locations is placed in a locations module, as shown in Fig. 21.3, we would only need to modify a few classes in this module, at most, to incorporate the change. Thanks to the modular organization of the model, any other class such as those in the tangible entities or agents modules would be immediately able to use this new location class without further adaptation.

Imagine, to the contrary, that every class related to tangible entities in CHARM had an embedded *Location* attribute or something like this. If we wanted to add a new way of locating things, we would need to change every class in the tangible entities modules, which would be a lot of work. By keeping location-related classes in a separate module, we achieve a good degree of modular proportion.

Protection

A model exhibits modular *protection* if defects or issues in one module are kept isolated from affecting neighbouring modules. In other words, a model has good modular protection if we hide as much as we can inside modules and allow neighbouring modules to "know" as little as possible about other module's details. Modular protection has a positive impact on robustness.

For example, consider the fact that the derived entities module in CHARM is organized around the same specialization discriminants as the valorizations module, yielding a parallel hierarchy, as depicted in Fig. 29.1 and following. For this reason, we can say that the derived entities module "knows" the structure of the valorizations module and follows it. If the way in which valorizations is ever found to be incorrect, this would make the derived entities module also incorrect. In this regard, CHARM's quality is not perfect, and better modular protection would be valuable here. However, quality comes to a cost.

The Cost of Quality

Quality comes to a cost. As we introduced at the beginning of this chapter when we described the car and spark plugs example, modularity must be engineered into a system from its inception. And this means extra work, time and cost. As in any other development process, you must often find a balance between what is acceptable quality and what takes too long or costs too much. Perfect quality is never feasible, but low quality is undesirable. Depending on how much time and resources you have to develop your model and how familiar you are with the modelling scope, you should trade quality for time or cost as appropriate.

Summary

Quality is a measure of how well a model allows us to carry out its intended purpose.

Quality is also related to how well the model can be used or changed to satisfy a changing purpose.

Maximizing every quality factor is not possible. You must make trade-offs depending on your priorities and available resources.

A model must be **correct** in terms of completeness, precision and accuracy.

A model may go beyond correction and strive for **robustness**, so that it works even under unexpected conditions.

A model should be **usable**, that is, easy to apply for the intended users.

A model should also be **efficient**, that is, it should use as few elements as possible to express what it needs to express.

A model should be **maintainable**, that is, easy to alter when its scope or purpose changes.

A model should be **readable**, that is, easy to understand by a potential user.

The more **modular** a model is, the higher its quality.

A **module** is a collection of model elements that exhibit high internal cohesion and low external coupling.

A good model must be **decomposable** into modules, and a large module must also be decomposable into smaller ones.

A good module must be **composable** (together with others) to make up larger modules or a complete model.

A good module is **understandable** without the need to look at other modules.

A good module shows **proportion** regarding changes and effort, being easy to alter for small changes and harder to alter for larger changes.

A good module is **protected** from defects or issues in other modules through the hiding of details.

Quality comes to a **cost**. Do not aim for perfection; make realistic trade-offs.

Exercises

49. Below you can find a list of modelling situations. For each of them, describe the three quality factors that you consider the most important, and in what order.

    - A model for a short research project involving only one person.
    - A shared model to be implemented as a database in a large company for a wide range of projects.
    - A government-sponsored large model intended as a reference for anyone in a given country doing archaeological fieldwork.

50. Look at the diagram below. What changes would you make in order to improve the model's quality in relation to the different quality factors?

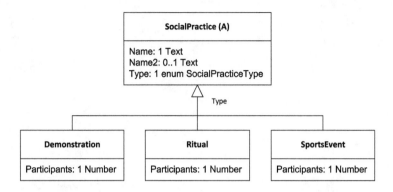

51. Consider a model containing the classes listed below. Describe how you would group these classes into modules, and explain why.

- *Barn*
- *Farm*
- *FarmAnimal*
- *FarmingActivity*
- *FishingActivity*
- *Forest*
- *House*
- *HuntingActivity*
- *Orchard*
- *Stream*
- *TraditionalSettlement*
- *Well*

Chapter 32
The Modelling Process

Abstract In this chapter, we explain how a model is constructed, using a process-oriented approach. We distinguish two major kinds of scenarios when doing conceptual modelling: constructing a model from scratch and altering an existing model to adapt, enhance or improve it. We link back to the philosophical underpinnings of modelling that were discussed in Chap. 2 to establish a basic modelling processes consisting of four different tasks: perceive what is to be modelled, conceptualize the relevant entities into ideas, formalize these ideas by using a modelling language and depicting the resulting model for exploration, communication or whatever other purpose. We emphasize that these activities should be tackled in an iterative and incremental manner, rather than linearly. Then, we focus on the specific scenario of altering an existing model and introduce the notion of *refactoring* as a way to improve the quality of a model by changing it, but while maintaining the purpose and scope untouched. After this, we provide some specific techniques that can be used when creating or modifying a model, such as word highlighting, using refactoring cues and finding model symmetry and coverage. The chapter finishes with a discussion on the issue of model *implementation*, which involves adding detail to the model in order to obtain a useful product such as a database or a surveying form. In this context, we explore the concept of "implementation noise" and separation of concerns, especially in relation to linked data technologies.

The previous parts in the book have described a modelling language, ConML, and presented a model, CHARM, constructed with it. Using a chess analogy, you now know what the different pieces look like and how they move on the board, and you have seen the outcomes of a game played by proficient players. However, you are still relatively far from being able to play chess well. Or, in other words, you still need to understand how the *process* of modelling works. Going from a fuzzy understanding to a well-engineered model is not trivial in most cases, and the quality of the resulting model will be better or worse depending on what process is followed and what practices are applied. In this chapter, we focus on the modelling process.

© Springer International Publishing AG 2018
C. Gonzalez-Perez, *Information Modelling for Archaeology and Anthropology*,
https://doi.org/10.1007/978-3-319-72652-6_32

There are two major kinds of scenarios when you are doing conceptual modelling. Sometimes you need to create a model from scratch, and the only "input" that you have is a set of vague ideas or fuzzy understanding of what is to be modelled. Some other times you want to alter an existing model to adapt, enhance or improve it; in this case, you start with a model and you also have some vague ideas or fuzzy understanding of how it must be altered. The outcome of the process in either case is a model. Since both cases involve vague ideas as a start and a model as an outcome, we will focus on this situation as the general case and add the necessary remarks when needed to cater for other more specific situations. In addition, altering a model may involve interoperability requirements that are described in Chap. 33.

Creating a Model from Scratch

The best approach to modelling is an iterative and incremental one. By iterative we mean that the process that you follow is repeated in multiple "passes", rather than being carried out just once. By incremental we mean that the products that you generate (and, specifically, the final model) are constructed in increments or small changes, rather than going from zero to complete in a single go. Usually, every time that you cycle through the process you add something to the resulting model, thus uniting the iterative and incremental properties of the approach. However, the first time you carry out the process the model does not exist yet. Consequently, the first iteration requires some special work in order to create the first version of your model.

Figure 32.1 reproduces a figure from Chap. 2. As you can see in the figure, the conceptual modelling process involves four basic tasks:

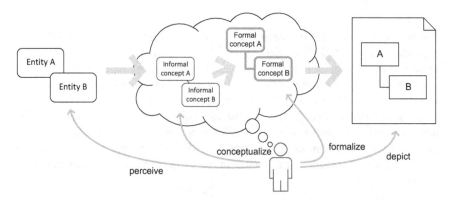

Fig. 32.1 Overview of the modelling process. This is identical to Fig. 2.1

1. **Perceive** what is to be modelled. This includes identifying what the scope is and what its boundaries are, determining what entities are inside (and which are left outside), and making sure that we can discretize these entities in relation to each other. Remember that the ability to discretize or "cut" reality into separate things was the first premise that we assumed for conceptual modelling in Chap. 2.
2. **Conceptualize** the relevant entities into ideas. This includes assigning a category to each entity to be modelled and deciding what details are kept and which are discarded. Remember that the ability to classify entities into categories was the second premise that we assumed for conceptual modelling in Chap. 2. Also, remember that the decision on what to keep and what to drop must be strongly guided by the modelling purpose.
3. **Formalize** these ideas by using a modelling language. This includes using the best language constructs to represent each thing being modelled. For example, and assuming that we are using ConML, we must decide at this stage if something is to be modelled as an attribute or an association. The result of this task is a model in our head.
4. **Depict** the resulting model for exploration, communication or whatever other application. This includes the graphical representation of the model on paper or screen by using diagrams or similar artefacts. Remember that the major kinds of applications that we described in Chap. 3 included exploration, documentation, communication, design and interoperability.

These tasks are usually carried out in sequence. That is, we cannot depict a model that we have not created before. And we cannot model something in our head that we have not previously conceptualized or perceived. However, and as introduced above, we perform these tasks iteratively; this means that we repeat them again and again until the resulting model remains stable, as shown in Fig. 32.2. In the figure, the four tasks (*perceive, conceptualize, formalize* and *depict*) are performed in sequence. The *perceive* task looks at the entities around us; the *conceptualize* task helps us assimilate them in our mind; the *formalize* task produces the model, and the *depict* task puts it on paper or screen. The first time around the *formalize* and *depict* tasks will create the model and diagrams; on further iterations, they will modify the existing ones. Now look at the decision diamond at

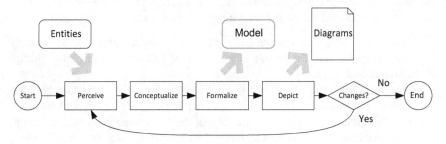

Fig. 32.2 Iterative and incremental modelling process

the end of the sequence: if the results (model and diagrams) have not changed from the previous time around, then we are done, and we can consider our model (and diagrams) final. However, if the results have changed, even so slightly, we need to go back to the *perceive* task and start a new iteration taking into account the interim model that we got. This new iteration will possibly alter the model and diagrams, and so on.

For example, imagine that we want to construct a model to represent the conflicting views of local communities and tourists about the Berlin Wall. The following may happen:

1. We examine what we know about the Berlin Wall in order to *perceive* it, focus on the materiality of the wall as a first step and realize that the Berlin Wall should not be seen, for our purpose, as a monolithic whole, but as a collection of elements such as the remaining sections of the wall, the checkpoints and other associated structures.
2. We *conceptualize* these elements and categorize them as structure fragments and constructive elements, all of them located in a common place. We also decide to document materials, visibility and relationships to additional structures and landmarks that may exist.
3. We *formalize* the above by creating a model having classes such as *WallSection*, *Checkpoint*, *AssociatedStructure* and *ExternalStructure*.
4. We *depict* a diagram containing the above classes as well as some tentative relationships among them.
5. We have a new model (plus diagram), so we start a new iteration.
6. We go again to *perceiving,* by focussing this time on the communities that we want to contemplate. We find that we at least need to differentiate between Jews and non-Jews and nationals versus visitors or tourists.
7. We *conceptualize* these as different communities, which may have potentially different relationships to each Berlin Wall element.
8. We *formalize* the above by introducing a new *Community* class. Since we need to associate this class to *WallSection*, *Checkpoint* and *AssociatedStructure*, we decide to generalize these three into an abstract *WallElement* class and add two associations between it and *Community* to represent positive and negative relationships, respectively.
9. We *depict* the changes by rearranging our diagram into a new one.
10. We have changed the model (and diagram), so we start a new iteration.

We will stop here our fictional description. You can imagine that the process continues in cycles until we find ourselves unable to find anything to add or change in the model and diagrams, and we stop.

There are a few things that must be emphasized. First, the distinction between perceiving, conceptualizing, formalizing and depicting is helpful but a bit artificial. It may help you to focus selectively on each of the tasks when you start modelling, but once you gain some experience, you will find yourself "just modelling", which will certainly involve all the previous four aspects in a fuzzy continuum. In fact, you will find many occasions when jumping from one task to another feels adequate. For example, you may be depicting your altered diagram and realize that a class is better conceptualized in a different way, so you just jump back and reconceptualize the class before coming back to depicting. Jumps like this are fine, and you will find yourself skipping forward or jumping back very often. However, try to adhere to the ideal sequence the first few times so that you learn how to focus on each kind of task.

Second, and as indicated above, do not attempt to create a model in a single go. This is possible only for very simple situations and to very experienced modellers, and even in these cases, you are likely to make serious mistakes. Iterate over the process until the model stabilizes and you are happy with it.

Third, be aware that the model will be in a state of flux while you work on it. In other words, the model will provide only a very partial representation of its scope while you are still iterating. During this work, you can use properties (see Chap. 5) to capture modelling concerns that are still not very clear. As you come back to them during subsequent iterations, you will be able to refine properties into either attributes or associations to other classes.

Finally, beware of "analysis paralysis". That is, don't forget that eventually you must stop iterating. The fact that we propose an iterative approach does not mean that the model is never done or it is always fluid. This is not so. Avoid perfectionism and gold plating your work, and stop iterating once you are confident that no further changes are needed in the model.

Modifying an Existing Model

To modify an existing model, use the same approach as to create a new one, but consider the existing model from iteration one. Given the iterative and incremental approach that we have described above, creating a model from scratch actually consists of creating an initial model during the first iteration, and then making changes to it during the following iterations until complete. For this reason, modifying an existing model is very much like creating one from scratch, but without the first iteration.

The only significant difference between the two scenarios may be the fact that, when modifying a model, the starting point already involves a model that is finished and therefore solid and stable, rather than a work in progress. For this reason, any changes that we make should be aligned with the overall spirit of the model and its underlying philosophy. For example, imagine that the starting model contains a specialization hierarchy where different kinds of buildings are described through a single *Building* class having a *Kind* attribute of an enumerated type. If you need to add a few extra building types, try to avoid adding specific classes to do it; rather, add new enumerated items for the necessary building kinds. Change the modelling decisions embedded in the starting model only if you have very compelling reasons to do so. For example, if you wanted to document different things depending on the kind of building in the previous example, then you would need to remove the enumerated type attribute and instead create a specialization hierarchy rooted on *Building*.

When making changes to a model, sometimes we find the need to alter a part of it in order to enhance its quality, rather than change what is expressed in the model. In other words, we may find the need to change how the model says what it says, without changing what it says. Making a change of this kind is called *refactoring* the model. Refactoring involves changes that preserve what the model expresses, but hopefully improve the way in which it does so. Consider Fig. 32.3. In the figure, the original model contains a *Painting* class describing the painting's title, year and technique, as well as its author name and nationality. The *AuthorName* and *AuthorNationality* attributes are blatantly calling to be extracted, given the noun adjunct "author" in their names. The refactored model shows that a new *Author* class has been created, and the necessary attributes moved over to it. Note that the original and refactored models both express the same: the fact that paintings are painted by an author having a name and a nationality. No information has been added or removed to the model. However, the refactored model has better quality as it is more modular and easier to understand and extend.

The topic of model refactoring has received a significant amount of attention in the software engineering literature, often in the context of the Unified Modeling Language (UML).

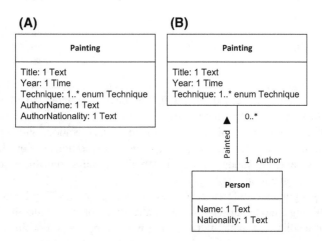

Fig. 32.3 Refactoring a model. In **A**, an original model is shown. In **B**, a refactored model is shown after extracting two attributes as a new class from **A**

Specific Techniques

In the previous sections, we have described what we should do in order to create or modify a model. However, we did not say much about how to do it. Now we present some techniques that can help us to perceive, conceptualize, formalize and depict our models.

Word Highlighting

This technique can help us identify and conceptualize classes, attributes and associations, so it is especially useful during the perceive and conceptualize tasks. The technique assumes that you have some sort of written description of the situation that you are trying to model. If you do not, do it yourself and write it down. A short text describing what is supposed to be in the model should suffice.

Once you have this text, highlight all the nouns, adjectives and verbs using different colours for each. You can do this on the computer or on paper. Then make an alphabetical list with all the nouns, another with the adjectives and another one with the verbs. Remove any duplicates, and bear in mind that some nouns, adjectives or verbs may encompass multiple words, such as "common room", "very small" or "carry out".

The nouns list will contain mostly candidate classes and attributes. The countable nouns will suggest categories that may eventually become a class in your model, such as "house", "folk song" or "place". Perhaps, many of the nouns in the list do not make sense as classes; reject them straight away. It is always better to have to reject half of the nouns than to forget an essential class. Also, be aware that lists of nouns in the text (such as "…public, private and commons land plots") may suggest subtypes of some abstract concept, and that some countable names will be better modelled as enumerated items rather than classes. Finally, some countable nouns (such as "child" or "residence") may point at role names in associations rather than classes. In cases like this, try to find the corresponding association by looking up the associated verb, as described below.

On the other hand, most uncountable nouns (such as "size" or "importance") will suggest attributes which, again, may or may not make sense. Like in the previous case, you will need to select and discard those that are not adequate, and transform the others if needed. For example, a noun such as "size" may be relevant to your model, but adding a *Size* attribute may not be appropriate, since it is too complex to describe and does not have a clear data type; instead, you may want to decompose "size" into separate attributes for *Width* and *Height*.

The adjectives list, in turn, will contain samples of values that should be permissible in the model. For example, if you find an adjective such as "circular" referring to a particular noun, this would be an indication that the class associated to this noun will need a *Shape* or similar attribute that can take values such as "circular".

The verbs list, finally, will contain potential associations. Transitive verbs, which are associated to a subject and an object, are especially relevant. Again, discard those that do not make sense, and check which nouns in the text are related by verbs which do. Remember that associations can usually be expressed from two different points of view, so you may find that there are two different verbs hinting at the same association.

Also, when converting a noun, adjective or verb from your lists into a model element, always remember to modify the words as necessary so that you adhere to good naming conventions as described in Part I. For example, class names should be countable nouns in singular.

Figure 32.4 shows an example involving the modelling of megalithic tumuli. In the example, nouns are highlighted with light grey rectangles, adjectives are underlined and verbs are highlighted with darker grey rounded rectangles. Duplicates have been removed for simplicity. The lists of nouns, once sorted and put in singular, are as follows.

- Burial
- Chamber tomb
- Cist
- Dolmen
- Enclosure
- House
- Long barrow
- Method of inhumation
- Passage grave
- Round barrow
- Shape
- Tumulus

Some nouns look like very good class candidates, such as "tumulus" or "burial". Others, like "method of inhumation", look like candidates for enumerated types, since it seems to encompass other nouns in the list such as "cist", "dolmen" and

Tumuli are often categorized according to their external apparent shape. In this respect, a long barrow is a long tumulus, usually constructed on top of several burials, such as passage graves. A round barrow is a round tumulus, also commonly constructed on top of burials.

The method of inhumation may involve a dolmen, a cist, a mortuary enclosure, a mortuary house, or a chamber tomb. Examples of barrows include Duggleby Howe and Maeshowe.

Fig. 32.4 An example of a text where word highlighting is being used to help identify and conceptualize classes, attributes and associations. Text taken from "Tumulus", *Wikipedia, The Free Encyclopedia*, https://en.wikipedia.org/w/index.php?title=Tumulus&oldid=739167972 (accessed 28 September 2016)

Tumulus	IsConstructedOnTopOf ▶	Burial
Shape: 1 enum TumulusShape	0..1 1..*	Method: 1 enum MethodOfInhumation

Fig. 32.5 Tentative model constructed from the text and lists above. See the text for enumerated types

"chamber tomb". Finally, some other nouns such as "shape" look like good attribute candidates. Note that the fact that we have highlighted the adjectives "long" and "round" in relation to "tumulus" reinforces the idea that "shape" should become an attribute of this class.

The list of verbs is as follows. Associated subject and object nouns are shown in parenthesis.

- Constructed on top of (tumulus, burial).
- Involve (method of inhumation, dolmen/cist/enclosure/house/chamber tomb).

The first item, "constructed on top of", looks like a very good candidate for an association, since it links a subject ("tumulus") and an object ("burial") that we also found interesting as class candidates in the nouns list. In turn, the second item, "involve", looks more like "grammatical noise" used to enumerate a list of possible inhumation method types, rather than a real association. This is also very interesting, because it gives us a clue that a specialization hierarchy or an enumerated type should be involved.

A tentative model constructed from the above text and lists is shown in Fig. 32.5. The *TumulusShape* enumerated type would contain items such as *LongBarrow* and *RoundBarrow*. The *MethodOfInhumation* enumerated type would contain items such as *Dolmen*, *Cist* or *ChamberTomb*, possibly arranged in a hierarchy.

The word highlighting technique can be extremely useful to identify what should be in the model, but it does not help much with formalizing it as specific model elements. We need other techniques for this.

Refactoring Cues

While you develop your model, keep an eye on signs that some refactoring may be needed. For example, look for classes that have no attributes and no generalization/specialization relationships to other classes. These "empty" classes may make sense in your model, but often they are superfluous and can be removed. If you remove an "empty" class, make sure that you incorporate its semantics into other elements of the model.

Also, look for "islands" in the model, that is, classes or collections of classes that are disconnected from the rest. In a good model, you can always navigate from any class to any other by traversing associations and generalization/specialization relationships. If you cannot find a route between two classes in the model, then you have an "island" that you must resolve. The most obvious way to do it is by adding an association, but don't do it before making sure that the new association makes sense. Alternatively, you can resolve an "island" by adding a generalization/specialization relationship or incorporating a class to an already existing generalization/specialization relationship. Finally, there might be the case that you are attempting to model a situation having a very wide scope or that is too vague; in this case, perhaps you need to split your model in two or discard one of the "islands" altogether.

In addition, look inside the classes for hints about the need to refactor. For example, and as we discussed above, noun adjuncts (that is, nouns working as qualifiers such as "author" in *AuthorName*) in attribute names often suggest that a new class should be extracted from an existing one, especially if multiple attributes share the same noun adjunct (*AuthorName*, *AuthorAddress*, etc.). Figure 32.3 shows a good example.

Also, look for hints that your model may benefit from the application of patterns. A specialization hierarchy sometimes is better expressed as a State pattern, and whole/part associations linking a class to its superclass may be calling for a Composite pattern. Sometimes, patterns emerge by themselves, and you will realize that you have created a Composite or State pattern without thinking about it; this is very good. Some other times you will need to stop and refactor your model to "shape" it in the proper way. Modelling patterns were discussed in Chap. 30.

Finally, be aware of model quality issues. Always try to keep a good degree of modularity, and observe the five principles of modular quality that we discussed in Chap. 31.

Striving for Symmetry and Coverage

Another valuable idea to bear in mind when modelling is that of *symmetry*. By this we refer to the fact that the overall structure of the classes and other model elements should be clearly organized and balanced in relation to well-defined axes. If you look at CHARM, for example, you will see that both structures (Fig. 22.4) and objects (Fig. 22.5) are modelled by using a similar scheme around fragmentation, origin and intentionality of the material entities. Although the models for structures and objects are different, they are "symmetric" in the sense that they are organized using common criteria, which helps with readability and usability.

Similarly, valorizations (Fig. 28.1) and derived entities (Fig. 29.1 and following) in CHARM are organized according to the perspective of the associated agent, which yields two parallel hierarchies exhibiting very strong symmetry. In this case, however, and as we introduced in the previous chapter, this also entails a certain degree of redundancy and hinders modular protection. Once again, quality is a matter of trade-offs, and in this case the extra symmetry gained by having two parallel hierarchies was considered to be more valuable than the lost modular protection.

In addition to symmetry, you should strive for *coverage* in your models. By this we mean that you should make sure that your model covers the target scope without leaving anything out. Using again CHARM as an example, the model is supposed to cover all the possible manifestations of cultural heritage. Similarly, and at a lower level of abstraction, tangible entities, for example, are also supposed to cover all possible kinds of tangible things that may be of interest in relation to cultural heritage. If we found something in the world that was interesting to cultural heritage and could not be ascribed to any class in CHARM, we would have found a coverage issue, and the model should be amended.

Coverage issues are especially significant when developing specialization hierarchies. Whenever you specialize a class into subclasses, make sure that every possible case is considered, that is, that the subclasses represent all possible kinds in relation to the associated discriminant. For example, look at Fig. 24.3 about expressive designs. The specialization under *ExpressiveDesign* must guarantee that every expressive design that we can think of is easily accommodated as one of the five subclasses. If we could think of an expressive design that is not a language, sound, gestural, formal or compound expressive design, then we should augment the model by adding a new subclass or expanding an existing subclass to cater for the "outlying" entity.

Implementing Models

We have said throughout this book that modelling always involves a purpose. Sometimes, however, you may need to go beyond the model in order to achieve your purpose. For example, imagine that you create a model with the purpose of documenting some monuments in a city. The model is necessary, but you will not be able to actually document the monuments unless you construct a database or some other tool that allows you to gather and store the necessary information. Or, for example, you may need to develop a mobile phone app so that tourists can find monuments in your city and provide feedback about them. In either case, the database and the mobile phone app would be constructed by using your model as a starting point and would be shaped and organized as dictated by the model. In this regard, the model acts as a blueprint or specification. In fact, an *implementation* of a model is an artefact that is constructed by using the model as a specification of its structure and/or functionality. Implementations are usually computer-oriented artefacts such as databases or other software and/or hardware systems. Implementing a model is a very complex topic, and a multitude of technologies and approaches may be involved. Chapter 34 provides specific advice on the development of database systems, but many other types of implementations are possible. The remainder of this section discusses some general aspects of model implementation.

First of all, you must bear in mind that implementation entails *adding detail to the model*. For example, a type model composed of a few classes, attributes and associations gives you the overall structure of a very small part of the world; if you want to implement a database that conforms to this model, you will need to make a number of decisions such as what database tables you will create, which columns you will have in each table and of which data types. The specific kinds of details that you add to a model during implementation are strongly determined by the type of implementation artefact being constructed, as well as the selected technologies. For example, you do not add the same kind of details when creating a database or a mobile phone app; and, at an even lower level of abstraction, you do not add the same kind of details when creating an app for Android phones or an app for iOS phones.

Abstraction, in fact, plays a crucial role during implementation. We said back in Chap. 1 that a model is a simplification of the world and, as such, modelling entails removing details from the represented scope. Implementing a model, interestingly, entails adding details to the model. The kind of details that you add during implementation, however, is totally different to those that you removed during modelling. Similarly, the model's purpose is your guide to deciding what details to remove while modelling. During implementation, the kind of artefact being constructed and the chosen technologies work as guides to what kinds of details should be incorporated.

In any case, a model is the most abstract artefact between two much more concrete things: the scope that it represents and the implementations constructed from it. It is not possible, or extremely difficult and error-prone, to construct implementations by directly looking at the scope without modelling. That is why architects create plans when they need to build a house: the plans are supposed to capture the needs of the house owners, the conditions of the environment and other relevant concerns. Then, the actual house is constructed by using the plans as a guide. It would be extremely difficult to construct a good house without plans, only by looking at the terrain and talking to the future owners. Similarly, models are needed to bridge the gap between the scope and the implementation through the use of abstraction.

However, you may find multiple occasions where models are skipped altogether in information systems development. For example, it is not uncommon to see projects where linked data RDF or OWL representations of knowledge are developed from scratch by looking at the entities to be represented. This is analogous to someone attempting to construct a house by going straight into lying bricks without having developed any blueprints, and evidently not a good practice. RDF or OWL representations are intended to be used by computers, whereas conceptual models are targeted at humans. For this reason, RDF or OWL representations constitute implementations, very much like databases or mobile phone apps. You need to develop them by using conceptual models as guidance.

There is an additional consequence of model implementation that must be highlighted. Sometimes we create a model while knowing that this model will be eventually implemented, perhaps even knowing what kind of implementation technology will be used. For example, we may be creating a model that we know will be implemented as a relational database on Microsoft SQL Server once it is finished. In cases like this, it is extremely easy to incorporate implementation concerns into the modelling process, which is, again, not a good practice. For example, in the previous example, we might be tempted to incorporate "id" or "key" attributes to the classes in the model because we know that database tables will need primary key columns once the model is implemented. However, entities in the world rarely have ids or keys; we assign these only to take stock or store information about them into a computer system. Since ids or keys are not properties of the entities themselves, they should not be in the model. Rather, we should wait until the model is implemented and then, and only then, add these details.

Projects using linked data technologies are especially at risk here, since these technologies, by their own nature, make us incorporate, from the very beginning, issues that are completely disconnected from the things being modelled but pertain to the computing domain. For example, you need to decide on URIs and namespaces and other computer-related artefacts when creating a class in OWL. This goes against the good practice of keeping conceptual models free of "implementation noise". If you use linked data technologies to implement your models, make sure that you do not bring the implementation concerns that are inherent to these technologies into your models.

There is a simple way to determine whether something should be in a conceptual model or not, which works most of the time. When in doubt, ask yourself "does this characteristic apply to the entity in the absence of a model?". If the answer is affirmative, then you should put it in the model; if negative, the characteristic is likely to be "implementation noise". For example, would the ISBN of a book apply to the book in the absence of a model? Clearly, yes: books have ISBNs regardless of whether we model them or not; for this reason, book ISBNs can be part of a model. Would the scanned image of the book cover be part of the book in the absence of a model? Clearly, no: books do not have a scanned image attached to them; we attach a scanned cover image for the purpose of implementing a model. Consequently, scanned cover images should not be part of a model.

In summary, do your models first, and make sure they are free from implementation issues. Once you are happy with them, implement them as computer-oriented artefacts.

Summary

Modelling is **iterative** and **incremental**; you iterate over a process to gradually construct a result.

You may want to **refactor** your model in order to enhance its quality while keeping the scope and purpose.

Word highlighting is a good starting point for modelling.

Watch for refactoring cues while you are modelling.

Strive for symmetry and coverage in your model.

Model before you **implement**.

Avoid **implementation noise** in your models.

Exercises

52. Construct a type model from the text below, using the word highlighting technique.

    Tourist guides must always accompany a group during the tours. Each tour may visit one or more areas of the mansion, including halls, gardens and the cellar. Tours must be booked in advance with the guide by a contact person, specifying when the visit is to occur, which areas are to be visited and how many people will be in the group.

53. Below you can find a list of concerns that are likely to come up during the modelling of a museum collection. For each of them, state whether it is a genuine conceptual concern that should be captured in a model or, to the contrary, it is an implementation issue that should be left out of the model and tackled only during implementation.

    - The name given to each artefact in the collection, such as "Lithic arrow head".
    - The number of decimals to use when stating artefact dimensions.
    - The id assigned to each artefact sample by museum technicians.
    - The sections of the museum Website where each artefact is to be shown.

Chapter 33
Extending Models

Abstract In this chapter, we continue with the discussion on model modification from the previous one, but now focusing on the specifics of *model extension* and *particular models*. We explain that, as opposed to refactoring or other kinds of changes, extension entails making changes to a model while guaranteeing that the resulting particular model is Liskov-compatible with the original one, so that interoperability becomes possible. We define what Liskov compatibility means, and then, we consider different kinds of needs for model extension, including adding extra elements, and modifying or removing existing elements. Then, we provide a comprehensive list of model extension mechanisms and associated reinterpretation rules. Extension mechanisms regulate what kinds of changes we can carry out on a model while keeping it Liskov-compatible with the original one, whereas reinterpretation rules specify how the resulting model must be reinterpreted for the sake of interoperability. Finally, we provide a worked example that illustrates the creation of a particular model using CHARM as a base, its use and its reinterpretation for interoperability.

In the previous chapter, we learnt how to create or modify models. We assumed that a model is created by someone and then used by that same person or delivered to someone else. These model users receive the model and are supposed to use it for some particular purpose, perhaps involving specific implementations. Sometimes, however, a model cannot be used straightaway and must be adjusted or tuned for the desired usage scenario. This may be so for a number of reasons, most of them involving the addition of extra detail to the model, or organizing the model elements in a particular manner that is better suited to the task at hand.

In fact, models are rarely "frozen" untouchable once they are created. Contrarily, they must remain open to adjustments and tweaking for whatever purpose they are employed. However, it is necessary to regulate how this tweaking may take place; otherwise, we run the risk of altering the model so much that it loses any resemblance to its original form. Imagine the following situation. A company specialized in archaeological monitoring of public works develops a conceptual model for the management of their excavations. The model is intended to work as the basis for the

© Springer International Publishing AG 2018

C. Gonzalez-Perez, *Information Modelling for Archaeology and Anthropology*,

https://doi.org/10.1007/978-3-319-72652-6_33

implementation of a central database system, a tablet app for fieldwork data collection and a fieldwork guide on recording best practices. Each of these applications will likely need to add specific details to the model in order to adapt it to the technologies and organizational setting where it is to be deployed. However, indiscriminately adding classes and features to the model, or modifying existing ones, may well result in a model that bears little resemblance to the original. In order to control and manage the ways in which models may be altered, we must differentiate between plain changes, which may alter the model in any direction, and model *extension*. Plain changes are what you make while constructing the model, in any way you judge appropriate. While changing a model, you are free to add, modify or delete as much as you want. However, extending a model means adding new elements or changing existing ones *while guaranteeing that the resulting model is fully compatible with the original one*. In this context, the result of extending a model is called a *particular model*, and the model it is based on is called the *base model*. Similarly, model elements (such as classes, attributes or enumerated items) added to a model during the extension process are called extended model elements or, in short, *extended elements*, whereas the elements that pre-exist in the base model are called *reused elements*.

Extension makes sense when you want to provide the freedom to alter or tweak the model, but within limits so that the resulting model will always be compatible with the original one. In practice, this means that the scope and goal of the original model will be honoured, and only slightly changed if at all. This chapter describes what extension mechanisms exist and how they can be applied to create useful particular models.

Reasons for Extension

Extending a model may be necessary for a number of reasons. Most often, the need is related to the addition of extra detail, the modification or tuning of existing model elements, including their removal in very specific circumstances, or the arrangement of model elements in specific ways. In this section, we explore what these scenarios entail.

Adding Extra Model Elements

Adding classes, features and other model elements is the most common reason to extend a model. For example, in Chap. 19, we explained that CHARM is an abstract reference model and, as such, is not expected to be used as is, but extended into particular models. When constructing a particular model from CHARM, you will very likely want to add new classes that specialize from the classes in CHARM to represent the specific categories that you need to describe your scope.

For example, imagine that you are extending CHARM to describe the towns and urban areas where specific trading processes take place. In this situation, you would probably add classes such as *City*, *Square* or *TradingActivity* as specializations of *LandDivision*, *Construction* and *Process*, respectively. The resulting particular model would be identical to CHARM, plus these new three classes. Of course, you may as well add attributes to the new classes and connect them to others through new associations. You may also add attributes and associations to classes that already exist in CHARM. In any case, the resulting particular model would be a superset of CHARM.

Modifying Existing Model Elements

Sometimes, adjusting the base model to your needs cannot be fully accomplished by adding elements alone, and you need to modify the contents of the base model themselves. A simple case of this corresponds to the renaming a class or feature to adjust it to your preferred terminology. Imagine that you are extending CHARM as described in the previous section. The CHARM class *ExpressiveDesign* (and its subclasses) may be very useful to represent how people communicate during trading activities; however, you prefer to talk about "communication acts" rather than "expressive designs", and therefore you rename the class. Similarly, you may rename an attribute or association name to best fit your usual terminology.

Model elements can be modified in more profound ways, though. For example, you may need to adjust the cardinality of an attribute or semi-association, or make an attribute subjective or temporal. In situations like these, we need to be very careful with what we alter, since some changes may make the resulting particular model not compatible with the base model.

Removing Existing Model Elements

As an extreme case of modification, you may want to fully remove some classes or features from the base model, because you do not need them or they do not make sense in your project or situation. Going back to our CHARM example above about trading activities, you may remove all the CHARM classes relating to stratigraphy, because they are not relevant to your scope. You can also remove specific attributes or associations; for example, you may be interested in using the *Occurrence* class in CHARM, but you are not interested in documenting the certainty of each instance, so you remove the *Certainty* attribute from the class.

As in the previous situation, the particular model that results from removing elements may or may not be compatible with the base model.

The remaining sections in this chapter describe how to ensure that compatibility is maintained when extending a model.

Liskov Compatibility

In the previous section, we said that extending a model may involve adding new elements or changing or deleting existing ones while guaranteeing that the resulting model is fully compatible with the original one. But, what do we exactly mean by "compatible"?

To answer this question, we build on the work by Barbara Liskov on type substitutability [28]. We briefly touched on this in Chap. 9 when discussing generalization/specialization relationships. Basically, Liskov's substitution principle states that if class S is a subtype (i.e. a descendant) of class T, then objects of type T can be safely replaced with objects of type S. We exemplified this by stating that if you ask me for a fruit and I give you an apple, you cannot complain that I have not fulfilled your request. In this example, *Apple* is a subtype of *Fruit*.

Liskov's substitution principle regulates what it means to say that a class is a subtype of another class from a practical point of view. We can extend this principle to regulate how models work together, in the following manner.

> **Liskov Compatibility**
>
> A type model P is Liskov-compatible with another type model B if any existing or potential instance model K that conforms to P also conforms to B.

First of all, note that Liskov compatibility occurs between type models. In this regard, we can say that a type model is (or is not) Liskov-compatible with another type model. Instance models do not contain classes, so it does not make sense to discuss whether or not they are Liskov-compatible with anything.

Secondly, and despite what we said in the previous paragraph, note that Liskov compatibility is defined through instance models. In other words, we need to examine all the instance models of a type model in order to determine whether this type model is or is not Liskov-compatible with another one.

However, it would be impractical to examine every instance model of a given type model, because there may be too many of them and, most importantly, because we cannot possibly examine all *potential* instance models. In practice, we never look at each individual instance model to determine whether two type models are Liskov-compatible or not. Rather, we apply some criteria that, if held, guarantee that any possible instance model of a type model will also conform to a second type model.

Liskov compatibility is relevant to model extension because a particular model must be Liskov-compatible with its base model for the sake of interoperability. In other words, a model that is not Liskov-compatible with another cannot be said to be its particular model. Let us use an example. Consider the three type models in Fig. 33.1.

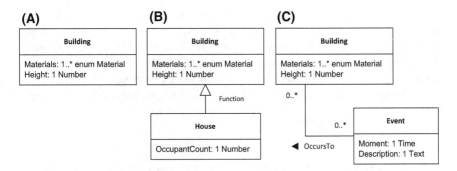

Fig. 33.1 In **A**, a simple type model. In **B**, a type model that extends **A** by adding a subclass. In **C**, a type model that extends **A** by adding a class and an association

Now, let us try to answer the questions of whether B or C in Fig. 33.1 is Liskov-compatible with a. First, let us observe that type model A is extremely simple, and so any instance models that conform to it will be exclusively composed of instances of *Building*.

With regard to particular model B, it extends the base model *A* by simply adding a *House* subclass to *Building*. This means that any instance model that conforms to B will potentially contain instances of *House* as well as *Building*. Since *House* is a subtype of *Building*, we can apply abstraction (see Chap. 9) and treat any instance of *House* as if it were a direct instance of *Building*. In this manner, we can pretend that *House* is not there (as required by the base model A) and still make sense of any instance of *House*, since they are understandable (through abstraction) as instances of *Building*. We do not need to examine every possible instance model conforming to B; we know that they will always conform to A as well. This means that B is Liskov-compatible with A and, therefore, we can say that B is a particular model based on A.

With regard to C, it extends the base model A by simply adding an *Event* class and connecting it to *Building* through an association. This model is not much more complex than B. However, let us consider what instance models of C would look like. Any instance model that conforms to C will potentially contain instances of both *Building* and *Event*, as well as links between them. The instances of *Building* present no problem, since this class also exists in A. However, what are we supposed to do with instances of *Event*? Type model A does not have any class that can work as type for them, and therefore, we cannot guarantee that instance models of C will also conform to A. This means that C, as it stands, is not Liskov-compatible with A and, therefore, we cannot say that C is a particular model based on A.

In Chap. 3, we discussed interoperability as one of the motivations to carry out conceptual modelling. We said there that conceptual modelling can help us to compare and relate information sets that obey to different conceptualizations, and, in this manner, facilitate the mutual understanding between different people, groups or communities. We also discussed interoperability in the context of model quality (Chap. 31) and the modelling process (Chap. 32). In a nutshell, two models are interoperable if they can work together. Liskov compatibility is the basis on which models (and their implementations) can interoperate. For example, a database constructed as an implementation of type model B can easily interoperate with a survey form constructed according to type model A in Fig. 33.1. However, none of them could easily interoperate with an information system constructed as an implementation of type model C, since this is not Liskov-compatible with either of them.

Extension Mechanisms and Reinterpretation Rules

If you take a type model and make some changes, it is likely that the model will cease being Liskov-compatible with the original one and, therefore, cannot be called a particular model. This would mean that the resulting model is not compatible with the original, which in turn means that interoperation between both becomes difficult. So, what kinds of changes may we exert on a type model and still guarantee that the resulting model stays Liskov-compatible with it?

Some approaches to model extension are very conservative in what kinds of changes they allow. This is convenient because it limits the amount of variation that can be introduced in a model, so that the result always resembles the original. Under conservative approaches like these, the model in Fig. 33.1C cannot be said to be compatible with the model in A. In ConML, however, we prefer to be liberal regarding changes and instead introduce a collection of rules that regulate how an instance model conforming to a particular model should be reinterpreted so that it still conforms to the base model. In this manner, we allow changes that would normally break compatibility, but add some rules that help us reinterpret the result so that compatibility is maintained. In this context, *extension mechanisms* constitute those kinds of operations that we can safely perform on a model so that the result stays Liskov-compatible with the original, and *reinterpretation rules* are the associated instructions that help us to recast the associated instance models. The remainder of this section describes every single extension mechanism together with the corresponding reinterpretation rules. For this discussion, we always assume an instance model K conforming to a particular model P that has been extended from a base model B. You may want to have the online CHARM reference at www. charminfo.org/Reference handy to follow through the examples.

Adding Enumerated Types and Items

You can add enumerated types or items to a model during extension. If you add an enumerated type that specializes from another in the base model, remember that the new enumerated type may not declare root enumerated items, as described in

Chap. 10. This is not a limitation of extension, but of enumerated type generalization.

Regarding enumerated items, if you add non-root items to an enumerated type in the base model, the following reinterpretation rule applies:

RR.1

A value in K pointing at an extended non-root enumerated item in P is reinterpreted as pointing to the most immediate ancestor of said enumerated item that exists in B.

Let us use an example. Imagine that you want to extend the *Material* enumerated type in CHARM and, to this purpose, you add items *Steel* and *Bronze* under CHARM-provided *Alloy*. Values such as *Material = Bronze* in an instance model would be reinterpreted as *Material = Alloy* when interoperating with other CHARM-derived models. This makes sense, as *Alloy* is the closest abstraction of *Bronze* that exists in CHARM.

Alternatively, you may add root items to an enumerated type in the base model. In this case, the following reinterpretation rule applies:

RR.2

A value in K pointing at an extended root enumerated item in P is reinterpreted as *unknown*.

For example, imagine that we extend CHARM's *ConstructionTechnique* enumerated type by adding *3DPrinting* at root level, since there is no enumerated item with the necessary semantics to work as an ancestor for this one. Values such as *Technique = 3DPrinting* in an instance model would be reinterpreted as *Technique = unknown* when interoperating with other CHARM-derived models. This makes a lot of sense, since the semantics of *3DPrinting*, not being a descendant of any CHARM-provided enumerated items, cannot be safely inferred.

Adding Classes

You can add classes to a model during extension. Most often, you will add non-root classes, i.e. classes that specialize from other classes pre-existing in the base model. In these cases, the following reinterpretation rule applies:

RR.3

An object in K having a non-root extended class in P as type is reinterpreted to have the most immediate ancestor of said class that exists in B as type.

For example, imagine that we extend CHARM by adding a specialized *House* class under *Construction*. Objects of type *House* in an instance model would be reinterpreted as being of type *Construction* when interoperating with other CHARM-derived models. This makes sense, as *House* does not exist in CHARM, but it can be safely abstracted as *Construction* as described in Chap. 9. Another example can be found in Fig. 33.1B.

You may also add root classes during extension, that is classes that do not specialize from any other class. In cases like this, the following reinterpretation rule applies:

RR.4

An object in K having a root extended class in P as type is reinterpreted as non-existing.

A good example is shown in Fig. 33.1C. Instance models conforming to C would contain instances of *Event*, which cannot be abstracted into anything in model A. However, we can ignore them during reinterpretation so that C stays Liskov-compatible with A. In other words, *Event* objects in an instance model conforming to C would be ignored, as if they did not exist, when interoperating with other A-derived models.

Note that adding root classes during model extension is uncommon, for two reasons. Firstly, extending a model is a process during which the base model's scope and goal should be roughly maintained. Adding a non-root class, however, entails adding a new semantic field into the model, which is likely to significantly augment its scope. Consequently, root classes are rarely added. Secondly, many models are organized around a major specialization hierarchy having a very abstract root class at the top. For example, CHARM has *Entity* as its root class. This class is so abstract that almost anything can be considered to be an instance of it. In this manner, any class that we wanted to add during an extension of CHARM could be safely placed as a direct or indirect subclass of *Entity*, so the need to add non-root classes disappears.

Adding Features

You can also add attributes or associations to a model during extension, involving reused or extended classes. If they involve extended classes, you do not need to worry, as the corresponding objects will be ignored during reinterpretation. However, if the added features pertain to reused classes, then the following reinterpretation rules apply:

RR.5
A value in K having an extended attribute in P as type that belongs to a reused class is reinterpreted as non-existing.

RR.6
A link in K having an extended association in P as type that connects reused classes is reinterpreted as non-existing.

Let us use an example. Imagine that we extend CHARM's *Person* class by adding a *Gender* attribute to it. Values such as *p.Gender = Female* in an instance model would be ignored when interoperating with other CHARM-derived models. In other words, values of *Gender* would be dropped from any instances of *Person* as if they had never existed.

Modifying Packages, Enumerated Types, Enumerated Items and Classes

You can rename a package, an enumerated type, an enumerated item or a class as you wish, so that the model element better fits your terminological preferences. When doing this, the following reinterpretation rule applies:

RR.7
An object in K referring to a renamed package, enumerated type, enumerated item or class in P as type is reinterpreted as referring to the original model element in B.

For example, imagine that we extend CHARM and rename the *ManifestationOfExpressiveDesign* class as "CommunicativeEvent". Any instances of *CommunicativeEvent* in a particular model would be reinterpreted as instances of *ManifestationOfExpressiveDesign* for the sake of interoperability.

Modifying Features

You can rename features in a particular model in the same manner that you can rename other kinds of model elements, as described in the previous section. The same reinterpretation rule applies.

In addition, you can change some properties of attributes and semi-associations in a model during extension by using the redefinition mechanism described in Chap. 18. For example, you could extend CHARM by adding a *ResearchPaper* subclass under *ResearchValorization*, and then redefine the *Name* attribute as *Title*, also changing its cardinality from 0..* to 1.

Feature redefinition is a standard part of ConML, so no specific extension mechanisms or reinterpretation rules apply here. Also for this reason, feature redefinition is the simplest and safest way to modify features in a particular model.

Hiding Attributes

You can hide an attribute in a particular model if you can guarantee that every of its instances will always have the same value. To do this, you annotate the attribute to be hidden and specify the default value to use. For example, imagine that you have an *Address* class in the base model having attributes such as *Street*, *PostCode*, *Town* and *Country*. If you are certain that your particular model will only be used to describe things in Brazil, for example, then the Country attribute becomes super-fluous, so you can hide it by annotating it in the particular model with the default value *Country = Brazil*. When doing this, the following reinterpretation rule applies:

> **RR.8**
> An object in K having a class in P as type for which an attribute has been hidden is reinterpreted as having the specified default values in P for said attribute.

In the previous example, instances of *Address* in the particular model will not show values for *Country*, since it has been hidden by assuming that we work only in Brazil. However, when these instances are reinterpreted to conform to the base model, then the specified default value *Country = Brazil* is assumed.

Deleting Enumerated Types or Items

You can delete an enumerated type during extension if you have also deleted every class (see below) that contains attributes of that type. And you can delete enumerated items during extension without any limitations. No reinterpretation rules apply.

For example, imagine that you extend CHARM and delete every class related to stratigraphic entities, as you are not interested in them. In this case, you could also delete the *TemporalOrder* enumerated type, because no other classes refer to it.

Deleting Classes

You can delete a class during extension if:

1. You delete every one of its descendant classes. That is, if you delete a class, then you must delete the whole specialization hierarchy rooted in the class, if any.
2. No classes are kept in the model having semi-associations pointing to the deleted class with a minimum cardinality greater than zero. That is, you can delete a class if it is not referenced by other (non-deleted) classes with a minimum cardinality greater than zero.
3. The class is not an aspect class (subjective or temporal) or, if it is, there are no features in the model marked with the corresponding aspect. In other words, you cannot delete an aspect class if the model contains features marked with that aspect.

For example, in a CHARM extension, we could easily delete the *TangibleEntity* class if we also deleted all of its descendants (as per point 1 above), as well as *NamedMeasure*, since this contains a semi-association with cardinality 1 towards *TangibleEntity* (as per point 2 above). We could not, however, delete *Occurrence*, since it constitutes the temporal aspect of the model and there are features marked as temporal (as per point 3 above). Similarly, we could delete *NamedMeasure* and *Measure*, plus all its descendants, if we were not interested in measuring things, but we could not delete *TangibleEntity* and keep *NamedMeasure*, as the latter points to the former through an association with cardinality of 1.

No reinterpretation rules apply.

Deleting Features

You can delete a feature during model extension only if it has a minimum cardinality of zero. In the case of associations, you can delete a complete binary association if both semi-associations have minimum cardinalities of zero. When doing this for attributes, the following reinterpretation rule applies:

RR.9
An object in K having as type a reused class in P from which an attribute has been deleted is reinterpreted as having a value with null contents for that attribute in B.

For example, we may delete the *EvaluableEntity.Name* attribute when extending CHARM, as it has 0..* cardinality. Any instances of *EvaluableEntity* in an instance model conformant to the resulting particular model would be seen as having *Name = null* for the sake of interoperability with CHARM.

In the case of associations, no reinterpretation rules apply.

Worked Example

So far, we have stated the extension mechanisms and associated reinterpretation rules that can be used to construct particular models. Let us now use an example.

Creating a Particular Model

Imagine that we want to extend CHARM for a research project involving Iron Age hillforts in Atlantic Europe. We are interested in documenting the archaeological features (such as walls and ramparts), the associated pottery finds and the location of everything by using coordinates. We are not interested, however, in recording measurements, managing valorizations or documenting other kinds of things such as occurrences, agents or performative entities. The resulting particular model would look like that in Fig. 33.2.

Let us look at the figure in detail. To start with, it is evident that this model is much smaller than CHARM; it contains only 24 classes as opposed to over 160. Most of the classes in CHARM have been deleted because they are not relevant to our purpose. In particular, all classes in the agents, performative, manifestations, occurrences, abstract, valorizations and derived hierarchies have been deleted. The only classes that we have kept are those related to tangible entities and absolute locations, as these comprise the model's scope. Then, a few classes have been added to capture the specificity of our project, shaded in grey in the figure. These include *Hillfort* and *House* as subtypes of *Construction*, *Wall* and *Rampart* as subtypes of *ConstructiveElement*, and *Find* and *PotteryFind* under *ObjectEntity*. We have decided to place *Wall* and *Rampart* under *ConstructiveElement*, rather

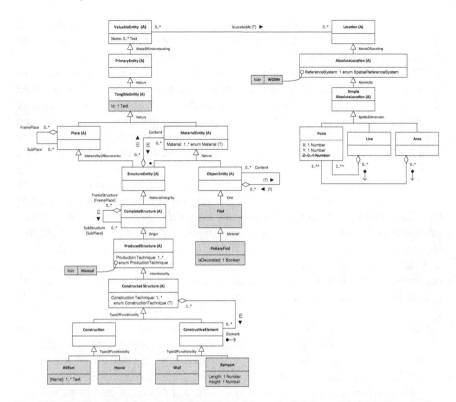

Fig. 33.2 Particular model for Iron Age hillfort study, extended from CHARM. Grey shading indicates model elements that have been added or changed as part of the extension process. Strikeout text indicates deleted elements

than *Construction*, by reading the definitions of *ConstructiveElement* and *Construction* in CHARM, and realizing that walls and ramparts do not provide a direct functionality to their end users but are components of larger structures. As always, the semantics of subtyping must be carefully observed. In relation to *Find*, you may wonder why it is necessary, as it contributes no features to the model and only has one subclass. Indeed, we may have omitted *Find* and placed *PotteryFind* right under *ObjectEntity*; however, we decided to add the apparently superfluous *Find* for two reasons. From an ontological perspective, the word "pottery" in "PotteryFind" is an adjective, indicating that pottery finds are one particular kind of finds (which is exactly what we have reflected in the model). From a more practical perspective, having the *Find* class in the model means that adding other kinds of finds such as lithics or bone in the future is very easy; we would only need to add classes such as *LithicFind* or BoneFind under *Find*. If we did not have *Find*, we would need to add it whenever we needed these additional find kind classes. This improves the quality of the model lowering the effort needed to make changes in the future, as described under the "Proportion" quality criteria in Chap. 31.

In addition to deleting many classes and adding some new ones, we have carried out other changes to CHARM during extension. For example, we have hidden the *AbsoluteLocation.ReferenceSystem* attribute by specifying a default value of *WGS84*. By doing this, absolute locations such as points and areas would not need to incorporate the reference system they are employing, as WGS84 will be assumed throughout. Similarly, we have hidden *ProducedStructure.ProductionTechnique* by specifying a default value of *Manual*, as we assume that every construction and constructive element that we will document in relation to hillforts will have been built manually rather than industrially. Also, note that we have deleted the *Point.Z* attribute, as we are only interested in 2D coordinates for location purposes in our project. We have also added an *Id* attribute to *TangibleEntity* in order to capture the fact that every tangible entity documented during the project will be assigned a text identifier. You may challenge this decision as not too ontologically solid, as tangible entities do not have an id of themselves, as described in the previous chapter. However, we will accept the *Id* attribute for pragmatic reasons in this case.

Finally, note that we have added no new associations. How are we going to document the fact that finds appear inside houses or next to walls, or that walls are part of houses, and houses and ramparts part of hillforts? We do not need to add anything to the model to support this; the associations provided by CHARM by default work perfectly. For example, we can document the fact that a house is part of a hillfort by using the whole/part self-association in *CompleteStructure*, inherited by *Hillfort* and *House*. Likewise, we can document the fact that a wall is part of a house by using the whole/part association from *ConstructedStructure* and *ConstructiveElement*, which is similarly inherited. Inheritance also helps with the location of entities. Note that every class under *ValuableEntity* inherits the *IsLocatedAt* semi-association towards *Location*; this means that we can document the location of any valuable entity no matter what kind it is. For example, we could document the area coordinates for a hillfort or the point coordinates for a pottery find.

Using the Particular Model

Let us imagine now that we use the particular model in Fig. 33.2 to document a few hillforts. Figure 33.3 depicts a sample instance model showing this. According to the figure, the Wide Fields hillfort is located in an area described by three points and consist of two rubble stone houses, one of which is named a workshop, as well as a 12-m-long rampart. Two pottery finds have been documented inside the workshop house. A few aspects of this instance model are worth mentioning. First of all, note that, despite conforming to a CHARM-extended particular model (see Fig. 33.2), the concepts being employed in this instance model ('hillfort', 'rampart', 'pottery find', etc.) are specific to the task at hand. The complexity of CHARM is barely appreciated here, as the instance model focusses on the specific classes that are relevant to the project. Most of these classes have been added by us during

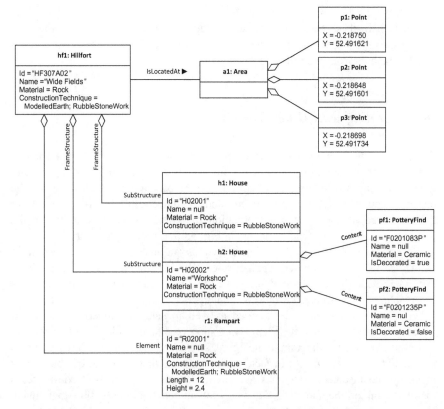

Fig. 33.3 Instance model conforming to the type model in Fig. 33.2, describing an Iron Age hillfort plus related entities

extension, such as *Hillfort* or *Rampart*, but others are reused straight from CHARM, such as *Point* or *Area*. Similarly, some attributes have been added during extension, such as *Rampart.Length* or *PotteryFind.IsDecorated*, while others are reused from CHARM, such as *ConstructionTechnique* or *Material*. This show how extension allows you to reuse whatever is relevant from the base model and add the missing detail to make the model work for your particular needs.

Secondly, note that this is a very small and simple instance model. A realistic one would probably contain many more elements with many more attribute values and links. Also, a realistic model is likely to incorporate extended enumerated types, something that we have not shown in this example for the sake of simplicity. For example, we could have extended the *Materials* enumerated type in CHARM to add our own kinds of rock that are relevant to documenting the walls and ramparts of the hillforts in the project. Finally, and as we have pointed out before, note that drawing a diagram of an instance model such as that in Fig. 33.3 is not the best option to represent large and complex data sets. If we had documented dozens of hillforts having hundreds of houses and thousands of finds, a diagram would be impractical. In these cases, a database, perhaps complemented by a geographical information system, would be a better option. Chapter 34 describes how to construct databases from type models.

Interoperating with Other Models

We said at the beginning of this chapter that the goal of model extension is interoperation and that, for this purpose, instance models confirming to a particular type model can be reinterpreted to conform to the base model. So, how would the instance model in Fig. 33.3 be reinterpreted to conform to CHARM? To answer this, we need to apply the reinterpretation rules that we have described in the previous section to the model elements in Fig. 33.3. For example, every instance of *Hillfort* in Fig. 33.3 must be reinterpreted as an instance of *Construction* in CHARM, as per the reinterpretation rule RR.3. In the case of object *hf1* in Fig. 33.3, its type in P is *Hillfort*, and the most immediate ancestor in B is *Construction*. Therefore, *hf1* would be reinterpreted as an instance of *Construction*. Other rules would need to be applied as well to cater for added and removed features, hidden attributes, etc. Figure 33.4 shows the final result of reinterpretation.

Let us examine the diagram in the figure. At a first glance, its structure resembles that of Fig. 33.3 very much; in fact, it is easy to see that the mesh of objects that make up the instance model has not changed. This is good, as it constitutes a manifestation of the fact that we have not altered the information that much. However, the types and contents of individual objects have been slightly altered. For example, the classes being used as types are now those of CHARM, such as *Construction*, *ConstructiveElement* and *ObjectEntity*, rather than *Hillfort*, *House*, *Rampart* and *PotteryFind*. Similarly, the attributes that had been added during the extension process are now gone, and the attributes that we had hidden reappear with their default values, such as *ReferenceSystem* and *ProductionTechnique*.

There are several consequences to reinterpretation. Firstly, the information in the reinterpreted model is more abstract than it was in the source model (see Fig. 33.3). This is logical, as reinterpretation always takes information expressed in terms of a particular model and recasts it in terms of a more abstract base model. In other words, we are losing some details by reinterpreting. For example, we are losing the identifiers of things, the dimensions of ramparts and whether pottery finds are decorated or not. Also, we are losing specificity with regard to what things are. For example, *hf1*, *h1* and *h2* are described as being all constructions in Fig. 33.3, but were differentiated as hillforts and houses in Fig. 33.4. This information loss is what allows us to move from a more concrete to a more abstract level of description.

A second consequence is that the instance model in Fig. 33.4 is clearly CHARM-conformant. This means that anyone who is familiar with CHARM can read and understand the model, even if they are not aware of the particular model

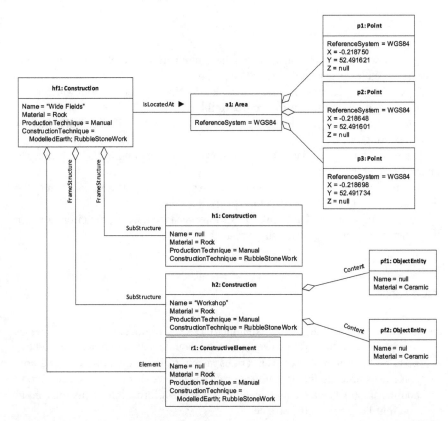

Fig. 33.4 The instance model from Fig. 33.3, after being reinterpreted to conform to CHARM

that we have used in our project. Think about this. We constructed a particular model for a project by using CHARM as a base, and then, we employed this particular model to document some entities. And now we are saying that anyone who is familiar with CHARM can understand our data, even if they are unfamiliar with our project. This is a very powerful consequence of extension and reinterpretation at work.

Finally, imagine that other people are creating their own particular models by extending CHARM like we did, each for a different purpose, scope and approach. Some may be documenting the folklore associated with traditional settlements, some may be studying the reuse processes of monuments in urban areas, and some may be looking at museum visitors. No matter what, all their instance models would be reinterpretable as CHARM-conformant, like we did in our example. And all the reinterpreted models would be understandable by all parties, no matter how specific the particular models were. In other words, anyone would be able to read, understand and reuse the information from any project, and integrate or compare it with their own. This is exactly what we mean by interoperation.

Summary

A type model can be extended to obtain a **particular model** that contains the necessary detail for a specific project or purpose.

A particular model remains **interoperable** with the base model from which it has been extended, thanks to **Liskov compatibility**.

During extension, you can **add** new model elements as well as **modify**, **hide** or **delete** existing ones.

There are some rules that you must follow when extending a model in order to guarantee interoperability.

An instance of a particular model can always be reinterpreted to conform to the base model by following some **reinterpretation rules**.

By applying reinterpretation rules to various instance models, the information in them can be easily integrated and compared.

Exercises

54. Create a particular model by extending CHARM to document reuse processes of urban spaces such as town squares. You should make sure that the model can describe the different uses that various agents make of urban spaces, and how some uses produce the appearance or disappearance of other uses. Feel free to add the necessary elements to capture whatever information seems relevant to you, but keep the model simple.
55. Use the type model created in the previous exercise to document the fact that the overtaking of a particular town square by teenager groups for evening recreational purposes has displaced its use as an improvised parking lot. Draw the corresponding instance model.

Chapter 34
Developing Database Systems

Abstract In this chapter, we focus on what is likely to be the most common and demanded application of conceptual modelling: that of the development of database systems. We start by introducing databases for those who are not familiar with them and especially relational databases. We introduce the notions of tables, columns, rows, primary keys, foreign keys and relationships and provide some examples of how a simple relational database works. Then, we provide a comprehensive list of *mapping guidelines* that can be used to construct a relational database from a conceptual model. Ten different mapping guidelines are provided, to implement enumerated types and items, classes and attributes, specialization hierarchies and associations. Finally, a worked example is provided to illustrate how a relational database is constructed from a simple type model.

Databases have been used to store and manage information since the 1960s and have become so mainstream that practically every digital device, from large server clusters to hand-held devices and mobile phones, uses databases today. From an intuitive point of view, a database is simply an organized collection of data. The specific manner in which data is organized is important, since different approaches to do it yield different limitations and capabilities regarding retrieval, querying, alteration and reporting. Since the late 1970s, the most widespread and popular approach to organize databases is the relational approach. Despite what many believe, "relational" in "relational database" does not refer to the relationships that exist between data items; to the contrary, it is a vestige of the mathematical underpinnings of what was called the "relational model" in the 1970s. According to this model, a "relation" is a collection of data rows having the same structure; in other words, relational databases are so called because they work on relations, or lists, of data rows. Other approaches exist to database organization; in fact, the last few years have seen an increase of non-relational approaches. Still, the relational approach is by far the most used today and is likely to stay like this for decades. In this chapter, we will assume the relational approach for our discussion.

Discussing databases assumes that data resides on a computer, rather than on paper or other medium. In addition, it is often assumed that this computer also

© Springer International Publishing AG 2018
C. Gonzalez-Perez, *Information Modelling for Archaeology and Anthropology*,
https://doi.org/10.1007/978-3-319-72652-6_34

contains software that is capable of manipulating the data in the database according to some specific rules. The software systems designed to manage databases are called (not very originally) database management systems, or DBMSs for short. Many relational DBMSs (RDBMSs for short) are available in the market, and you may have heard of, or even used, products such as Microsoft Access, MySQL, FileMaker Pro, Microsoft SQL Server or Oracle. Some of these systems, such as Access, can run on a personal computer, while others such as Oracle are designed for larger servers that attend many users simultaneously. Practically, all modern RBDMSs employ the Structured Query Language (SQL) to provide instructions to the system. Decades ago, it was expected that database users would learn SQL and issue SQL commands to the computer to query or modify the data. Today, this is not so anymore, and databases are rarely exposed directly to end users except for small personal ones or for learning purposes. Instead, databases are usually employed today as back-end systems that are accessed by software applications that provide a friendly user interface so that common operations on the data can be easily carried out. As a consequence, you do not need to learn SQL to use databases anymore. In fact, you probably use many databases every day without even realizing, through mobile apps or interactive systems on your computer, mobile phone, smart TV or the Web.

In any case, databases are excellent at storing and managing data, even very large amounts of it. As we have stated in a few occasions before, instance models are a poor solution when you want to document a large number of entities; in cases like this, you should put your data into a database. A database like this will be an implementation, in the terms described in Chap. 32; in other words, you will construct your database by using a conceptual model for guidance.

This chapter starts with a brief summary of how relational databases work, which you can skip if you are already familiar with them. Then, it provides some guidelines to construct databases from conceptual models.

Notions of Relational Database Systems

Tables

A relational database is, roughly speaking, a collection of *tables*, not very different to what you see when you use a spreadsheet application such as Microsoft Excel. Since a database usually contains many tables, each one has a name. Often, each table is designed (and named accordingly) to store data about a particular category in the world; in this manner, we may have tables named *Sites*, *Finds* and *Excavations* in a database for archaeology.

Tables are composed of columns and rows. However, and as opposed to a spreadsheet, columns and rows in a relational table work in very different ways. In a spreadsheet, columns and rows are interchangeable; that is, you can easily transpose data and use the horizontal and vertical directions as you please. For example, you could list some finds data in a spreadsheet by using a row for each find and each column for a particular data item of the find, such as its material or dimensions. But you could do it the other way around: you could lay out the data for each find vertically, in a column, and use rows for each data item. The layout is a matter of convenience. In the relational world, however, columns and rows are not interchangeable, as we describe below.

Columns

A *column* in a table corresponds to an item of data that you want to record, such as someone's first name or the latitude (or longitude) of a location. Each column has a name, such as *FirstName* or *Latitude*. Columns in a table are fixed, in the sense that you must know what columns a table has and what their names are. You can add and remove columns while constructing or modifying a database, of course, but usually you do not modify a table's columns during regular use.

A column, in addition, has a *data type*, which indicates what kind of data items can be stored under this column. Common data types supported by most RDBMSs include Booleans, integer numbers, decimal numbers, dates and times, or texts of various maximum lengths. Each RDBMS has its own particular data types; for example, Microsoft Access differentiates between Short Text and Long Text, calls Yes/No to Boolean and distinguishes between six kinds of numeric data types depending on their maximum number of digits, precision and other characteristics. In some systems, columns are called "fields".

Technical
The variety of data types in RDBMSs may seem overwhelming at first, especially as compared to the simple ConML data types. The reason why RDBMSs offer such a variety of data types is performance. First of all, some data types take more storage space in the database than others. For example, storing a number as single floating point takes 4 bytes, whereas storing it as double floating point takes 8 bytes. When you are storing millions of rows, this difference may amount to megabytes in storage space. In principle, you should always choose the "smallest" data type that satisfies your requirements. For example, double floating point offers more precision (roughly, more decimal places) than single floating point. Use single if you do not need the extra precision and double if you do.

Secondly, some data types are faster than others when performing searches, comparing or carrying our computations on the data. Some even may restrict what kinds of operations are possible. For example, you may sort a table on a column of the Short Text data type, but you cannot sort a table on a column of the Long Text data type in Microsoft Access. However, Short Text can store text strings up to 255 characters long, whereas Long Text has no upper limit. You should choose Short Text for the sake of sorting, unless you need the extra maximum length offered by Long Text.

At this point, you may have observed many similarities between database columns and ConML attributes. Both have a name and a data type, although ConML data types are fewer and much simpler than the data types of a typical RDBMS. In fact, database columns are a natural implementation mechanism of ConML attributes, as we will describe in the next section.

Rows

A *row* in a table contains the data items that, collectively, describe a given entity. For example, imagine a *Sites* table in an archaeological database, having columns such as *Name*, *Location* and *Dating*. Each row in the table would correspond to a particular site and would describe it through its name, location and dating. Figure 34.1 shows an example. In this example, the *Sites* table includes three columns of textual data types and contains four data rows. The top data row, for example, refers to the Monte Albán site in Oaxaca, and the second describes the Skara Brae site in Orkney. Here, we show rows alphabetically sorted by *Name*, although tables are not intrinsically sorted in a relational database; you can sort your data in any way you please when you retrieve it.

Note also the *null* value for Stonehenge's dating. In the world of databases, *null* means that data does not exist, without any indication of what this may be so. As opposed to conceptual modelling, databases do not distinguish between ontological and epistemic absence of data (see Chap. 14). In other words, table in Fig. 34.1 states that there is no dating information for Stonehenge, but it does not say whether this data does not exist or we are not aware of it.

Fig. 34.1 A very simple *Sites* table containing three columns and four rows

Sites

Name	Location	Dating
Monte Albán	Oaxaca, Mexico	Classic American
Skara Brae	Orkney, UK	Neolithic
Stonehenge	Wiltshire, UK	(null)
Troy	Çanakkale, Turkey	Bronze Age

Databases and Models

The example above shows an important fact of relational databases: tables and columns determine the *structure* of your data, whereas rows *are* your data. In other words, tables and columns play a role similar to that of type models in conceptual modelling, while rows are analogous to instance models. In the same manner that columns and attributes have commonalities, rows and objects are similar as well: each row represents an entity in the world and is arranged in a manner that is established by the pre-existing structure of the table columns; in the world of conceptual modelling, each object represents an entity in the world and is arranged in a manner that is established by the pre-existing structure of its type class. By following this reasoning, we may say that Fig. 34.1 shows the database equivalent of having a *Site* class with *Name*, *Location* and *Dating* attributes, and four *Site* instances with the necessary values. Note, however, that tables are usually named in plural (as in "Sites"), to reflect the fact that they constitute collections of rows; this is opposed to classes, which are named in singular. A bigger difference between classes and tables is that classes represent categories in the world, whereas tables are just lists of rows. In fact, a table may store data for a category in the world, but it does not have to. Some tables store auxiliary or implementation data that does not clearly correspond to any relevant category, and this is fine.

The similarities described above may make you think that relational databases are somehow equivalent to conceptual models or that they can replace them. This is not the case, because databases and conceptual models work at very different levels of abstraction, as described in Chap. 32 when discussing implementations. Using a construction metaphor, a conceptual model corresponds to the plans that the architect produces, and the house that is constructed from them corresponds to the database. Constructing a house without a clear design and the necessary plans would be a bad idea; in the same manner, constructing a database without a clear design and the necessary conceptual model is a bad idea. You need conceptual modelling as a tool to determine what you are going to store in your database and what structure it will have. This idea is the focus of the next section. But, before, we will explore some additional basic notions of relational database systems.

Primary Keys

We said above that every row in a table describes a particular entity in the world. In conceptual modelling, we had an object's identifier as a way to distinguish one object from others. In the relational database world, we have a similar construct: the primary key. A *primary key* is a data item in each row having the purpose to uniquely identify it and distinguish it from other rows in the same table. Imagine a

(A)

Sites	
Name	Short Text
Location	Short Text
Dating	Short Text

(B)

Sites		
Id	AutoNumber	PK
Name	Short Text	
Location	Short Text	
Dating	Short Text	

Fig. 34.2 The structure of the *Sites* table from the previous example. In **A**, the table as it was defined. In **B**, a primary key column has been added

Persons table with columns *FirstName*, *LastName* and *Age*. It is perfectly possible that we have two rows with identical values, because two different people may share the same name and age. The primary key would allow us to tell the two rows apart and know which one represents which person.

Sometimes, the primary key is defined through regular columns in the table. For example, we could say that the primary key of our *Sites* table above corresponds to the *Name* column. No two sites in the table share the same name, so this primary key would work fine. However, it is possible (although perhaps unlikely) that we add a new site row at a later stage having a name that clashes with an existing site in the table; this would cause a problem as we would have two rows with identical primary keys, which cannot be. To avoid situations like this, it is highly recommended that primary keys are defined in terms of an artificially introduced column that has no real-world semantics. By "real-world semantics", we mean data that describes some observable characteristic of the entities being described, such as a person's name or a site's location. A good primary key, in this manner, is similar to an object's identifier, being external to the entity and purely assigned by us for data management purposes. A good primary key can be a sequential number, a random string of characters or any other thing. Consider the example in Fig. 34.2. In Fig. 34.2A, the structure of the *Sites* table is described by listing its columns, each one with its name and data type. In B, a new *Id* column has been added with the AutoNumber data type and marked as "PK" (primary key) to make up the table's primary key. The AutoNumber data type in Microsoft Access is an equivalent to Integer, but it makes the system to generate sequential numbers every time you add a new row to the table, making it a perfect choice for primary key columns. Of course, you can use other data types for your primary keys if you want. Other RDBMSs do not have an AutoNumber data type, but may have an equivalent one.

Having a primary key in each table is generally not compulsory. However, it is necessary for certain operations, as we describe below. Since the cost of adding it is small, we recommend that you always add a primary key to your tables and that you define it in terms of an artificially added column as described above, using an self-numbering data type if available.

Relationships and Foreign Keys

In the same way that classes can be connected through associations in conceptual modelling, tables in a database can be connected through relationships. A *relationship* is a formal connection between a column in one table and the primary key of another. For example, imagine a database with a *Sites* table, as described above, plus a *Finds* table. This is shown in Fig. 34.3. As it is, the database would allow us to store sites data as well as finds data, but there is no way to record in the database which site each find was found in. To do this, we need to establish a relationship from *Finds* to *Sites*. We do this by adding a new column to *Finds* that can store the *Id* of the corresponding row in *Sites*. Figure 34.4 shows the result. Here, we have added a *SiteOfOrigin* column to the *Finds* table, with an Integer data type so that it can store the same information as *Id* on *Sites*. In addition, we have marked this column as a foreign key to the *Sites Id* column. A *foreign key* is a column that, precisely, is expected to store values that can be found in another table's primary key, thus "pointing" at it. Figure 34.5 shows some sample data for this. Here, the *SiteOfOrigin* column in *Finds* stores values taken from the *Sites* primary key column, that is *Id*. You can interpret this as a pointer or reference. For example, the *Finds* row with *Id* 19 is a pottery vase fragment found in site 312, which is Monte Albán. Note that multiple rows in *Finds* may point to the same row in *Sites*, allowing for multiple finds per site. In fact, finds 19 and 28 are recorded as coming from site 312. However, we can only have one site per find, since the *SiteOfOrigin* column can only store one integer value. This asymmetry is the reason why you always must place your foreign key in the table from which you need to look up a single row on another table. This is akin to establishing a one-to-many association

Sites			Finds		
Id	AutoNumber	PK	Id	AutoNumber	PK
Name	Short Text		Material	Short Text	
Location	Short Text		Description	Long Text	
Dating	Short Text		Width	Integer	
			Length	Integer	
			Height	Integer	

Fig. 34.3 Sample *Sites* and *Finds* tables

Sites			Finds		
Id	AutoNumber	PK	Id	AutoNumber	PK
Name	Short Text		Material	Short Text	
Location	Short Text		Description	Long Text	
Dating	Short Text		Width	Integer	
			Length	Integer	
			Height	Integer	
			SiteOfOrigin	Integer	FK Sites

Fig. 34.4 The database from Fig. 34.3 after adding a relationship from *Finds* to *Sites*

Sites

Id	Name	Location	Dating
312	Monte Albán	Oaxaca, Mexico	Classic American
319	Skara Brae	Orkney, UK	Neolithic
320	Stonehenge	Wiltshire, UK	(null)
335	Troy	Çanakkale, Turkey	Bronze Age

Finds

Id	Material	Description	Width	Length	Height	SiteOfOrigin
19	Pottery	Vase fragment	7	11	30	312
20	Pottery	Vase fragment	6	30	21	335
26	Stone	Kitchen utensil	9	28	20	319
28	Pottery	Unidentified fragment	11	64	42	312

Fig. 34.5 Sample data for *Sites* and *Finds* table. Note the foreign key *SiteOfOrigin* in *Finds* storing values from the *Sites* primary key

between classes in conceptual modelling; you need to place the foreign key on the table corresponding to the "many" side of the association. Also, note that we may use *null* values to state that a find has no assigned site. For example, we could replace the value 312 under *SiteOfOrigin* for find 19 with *null*; this would mean that find 19 has no assigned site.

Having a foreign key like *SiteOfOrigin* in the example usually means that the RDBMS that you use will enforce *referential integrity* on the column. This means that you will not be able to enter any value under this column, but only values that can be found under the referenced primary key column. For example, you could not enter 318 under *SiteOfOrigin* in the previous example, as there is no row in the Sites table with this id. Referential integrity is an excellent mechanism to make sure that your data stays consistent. Some RDBMSs apply referential integrity as soon as you define a foreign key, while others let you decide whether you want to use it or not. It is always a good idea to use it unless you have a very good reason not to, which should happen very rarely.

We have said above that a foreign key points to another table's primary key. This is usually so, but it also may be the case that a foreign key points to the primary key of the same table. This is analogous to self-associations as described in Chap. 8 and allows us to connect rows in a table to other rows in the same table. These foreign keys are sometime called *self-foreign keys*. We will see practical applications of this mechanism in the next section.

Now, what if we wanted a many-to-many connection between tables? Imagine that we add a *Persons* table to the database to keep track of who worked on each site over time. We would like to connect this table to *Sites* in such a manner that every person may be assigned to multiple sites and every site may have multiple people assigned. We cannot achieve this by adding a foreign key as described above; we need to add a relationship table instead. A *relationship table* is a database table that has the only purpose to connect two other tables and bears no actual data but only foreign keys. Figure 34.6 shows an example.

Persons

Id	AutoNumber	PK
GivenName	Short Text	
FamilyName	Short Text	

Sites

Id	AutoNumber	PK
Name	Short Text	
Location	Short Text	
Dating	Short Text	

PersonsInSites

Person	Integer	FK Persons
Site	Integer	FK Sites

Fig. 34.6 Database structure having *Persons* and *Sites* tables, plus a *PersonsInSites* relationship table to connect the two

Here, a *PersonsInSites* relationship table has been added. This table contains foreign keys to both *Persons* and *Sites*, the two tables that we want to connect. Note that the columns are named after the associated tables. The relationship table does not contain any other columns, not even one for a primary key. Each row in a relationship table like this will store a pointer to rows in each of the related tables and in our case, Persons and Sites. Figure 34.7 shows some sample data. In this example, *PersonsInSites* stores values taken from the primary keys of *Persons* and *Sites*, the tables that we want to connect. Like any other foreign keys, these values must be interpreted as pointers or references to the corresponding rows. For example, the data in *PersonsInSites* indicates that person 8 (Aspen) has worked on sites 319 (Skara Brae) and 335 (Troy) and that person 19 has worked on site 319 only (Skara Brae). We can also use the relationship table the other way around, to look up what people have worked on a given site. For example, it is easy to see that site 319 (Skara Brae) has been visited by persons 8 (Aspen) and 19 (Gertraud).

Fig. 34.7 Sample contents of the database in Fig. 34.6. Note the foreign keys in *PersonsInSites* pointing at primary keys in *Persons* and *Sites*

Persons

Id	GivenName	FamilyName
8	Aspen	Schwarz
17	Zeinab	Carbone
19	Gertraud	Kuijpers

Sites

Id	Name	Location	Dating
312	Monte Albán	Oaxaca, Mexico	Classic American
319	Skara Brae	Orkney, UK	Neolithic
320	Stonehenge	Wiltshire, UK	(null)
335	Troy	Çanakkale, Turkey	Bronze Age

PersonsInSites

Person	Site
8	319
8	335
19	319
17	335
17	312

When using relationship tables, you do not need to use *null* values to indicate missing data; you just simply omit the necessary row. For example, according to the example above, nobody has ever worked on site 320 (Stonehenge), because no row in the *PersonsInSites* table contains 320 under *Site*.

Additional Database Concepts

Relational databases are a very mature technology, and some RDBMSs are rich in features that you may never use to their full extent. Also, we cannot cover much more in this brief introduction to database systems. We will only mention two additional concepts that may be useful to you.

When you foresee that a column will be used very often to carry out searches or sortings, you may want to index it. An *index* is a data structure that accompanies a table and which pre-computes the necessary information so that searches and sortings on the indexed columns are much faster. For example, you may want to index the *Name* column of *Sites* if you think you will often search sites by name or sort sites on their name. Of course, you can index many columns, even all of them, for better performance. But bear in mind that as indexes improve performance when searching or sorting, they decrease it when adding new rows or modifying or deleting existing ones. Often, you will need to do some trial-and-error testing to find a good compromise. In any case, primary keys are always indexed automatically by the system. Foreign keys are not automatically indexed, but you may want to index them because they are often employed to look up rows.

A second interesting concept is that of constraints and validation rules. Most RDBMS let you assign constraints to a column in order to limit what values may be stored there. The simplest and most common kind of constraint, supported by virtually every RDBMS, is nullability. This involves specifying whether data for a column may be *null* or not. Usually, columns that must always hold a value should be defined as not nullable, whereas columns that may hold values but may also be blank should be defined as nullable. Nullable columns are usually labelled as such next to their data type specification.

Other kinds of constraints are possible, although they vary a lot between RDBMSs. Most let us establish a maximum length for text columns, in order to limit the amount of data that can be entered. Also, some RDBMSs support user-defined constraints. For example, you may add a constraint under *Age* in *Person* stating that its values must be between 18 and 99, to minimize spurious data or typos. You could also add a constraint to make sure that values under *GivenName* and *FamilyName* use initial capitals. Constraints are often useful to validate data, although they are rarely enough to ensure data quality overall.

In this section, we have discussed the very basics of relational databases. The following section uses the concepts introduced here to describe how databases can be designed and constructed from conceptual models.

Mapping Guidelines

As we have explained elsewhere, one of the frequent purposes of a conceptual model is to document relevant entities. In these cases, you construct a type model that describes the categories of things that you are interested in, and then, you create an instance model to represent actual things conforming to this type model. A database is an ideal device to store and manipulate large or complex instance models. However, you cannot put an instance model directly into a database, because the relational world organizes data in tables, columns and rows, and an instance model needs objects, values and links. Fortunately, we can "translate" between the object-oriented paradigm of conceptual models and the relational paradigm of databases. This is achieved through mapping guidelines, which describe how to implement each kind of conceptual modelling construct in terms of database constructs. In this section, we provide some mapping guidelines that will allow you to create relational databases from conceptual models. These guidelines are not set in stone, and you may find different approaches to implementation from different sources. The guidelines that we present here have been used by the author for some time and are often employed for teaching and research purposes. However, please bear in mind that these are just guidelines, not strict rules, and other options are indeed possible.

The first mapping guideline is very simple.

MG.1
A type model is implemented as a database structure. An instance model is implemented as the database contents.

This means that you can implement a whole type model as a database structure, that is a collection of tables. It also means that an instance model conforming to that type model will be implemented as the data contents of that database. If you want to implement multiple instance models conforming to the same type model, you will need to make copies of the database structure.

Implementing Enumerated Types and Items

All the enumerated types and items in your type model can be easily implemented as a single table.

MG.2
Create a table *EnumeratedItems* if there are enumerated types in the model. Add an *Id* column for the primary key, a text *EnumeratedTypeName* column

for the enumerated type name, a text *Name* column for the enumerated item name and a nullable integer *Parent* column as a self-foreign key.

For example, imagine that we have the following enumerated types in a model:

```
WorldRegions:    Europe
                   France
                   Germany
                   Spain
                 Asia
                   China
                   Japan

Colours:         Red
                 Green
                 Blue
```

According to MG.2, your database structure would look like that in Fig. 34.8. Now, you would populate this table with the data from the two enumerated types defined above, as shown in Fig. 34.9. The *EnumeratedItems* table is generic; that is, it can store any enumerated types, plus their items, that you may have in your model. Also, if you add new enumerated types or items in the future, or want to change the existing ones, you do not need to alter the database structure: you simply add new rows to the table or modify the existing ones.

Note in Fig. 34.9 that every row corresponds to an enumerated item, no matter what type it belongs to. Correspondingly, each enumerated item has its own primary key as provided by the *Id* column. The *EnumeratedTypeName* stores the name of the enumerated type each item belongs to, repeating values as much as necessary. The *Name* column stores the enumerated item name. Finally, the *Parent* column

Fig. 34.8 Database structure implementing generic enumerated types and items

EnumeratedItems

Id	AutoNumber	PK
EnumeratedTypeName	Short Text	
Name	Short Text	
Parent	Integer (null)	FK EnumeratedItems

Fig. 34.9 Enumerated type and item contents for the *WorldRegions* and *Colours* enumerated types

EnumeratedItems

Id	EnumeratedTypeName	Name	Parent
1	WorldRegions	Europe	(null)
2	WorldRegions	France	1
3	WorldRegions	Germany	1
4	WorldRegions	Spain	1
5	WorldRegions	Asia	(null)
6	WorldRegions	China	5
7	WorldRegions	Japan	5
8	Colours	Red	(null)
9	Colours	Green	(null)
10	Colours	Blue	(null)

works as a self-foreign key, storing the id of each item's parent item. For root items, this column stores a *null* value, since root items do not have a parent.

In this manner, we can store enumerated items in the database and keep a unique identifier for each of them that we will use later.

Implementing Classes and Attributes

In general, you will need to create a database table for each class in your model and a column for each attribute. This may change slightly for classes involved in specialization hierarchies, as we discuss below.

> **MG.3**
> Create a table for each class, named after the class but using the plural. This is called a *class-table*. Add an *Id* column for the primary key and a column for each single-valued attribute declared by the class, choosing the appropriate data type and nullability.

For example, imagine that we have the class shown in Fig. 34.10 in our type model. According to MG.3, your database structure would look like that in Fig. 34.11. In class-tables like this, each row corresponds to an instance of the associated class, *Building* in our example. Also, each column stores the value for the corresponding attribute in the class. For example, the *Height* column will store values for each instance's height in our example.

The choice of data type can be tricky. As we described in the previous section, RDBMSs often provide a wide range of data type options. You will need to evaluate the semantics and expected values for each attribute and select the best

Fig. 34.10 Sample class to be implemented in a database

Building
Height: 1 Number Style: 0..1 enum Styles Description: 0..1 Text

Fig. 34.11 Database structure implementing the *Building* class in Fig. 34.10

Buildings		
Id	AutoNumber	PK
Height	Integer	
Style	Integer (null)	FK EnumeratedItems
Description	Long Text (null)	

database data type. For example, if you are using Microsoft Access, Integer would look like a good option for *Height*, as it can store numbers without decimals in a more than acceptable range. Similarly, Long Text looks like a good option for *Description*; Short Text would not be suitable, as it is limited to 255 characters of text, and we know that building descriptions may well go above this. In any case, attributes having a zero minimum cardinality, such as *Style* or *Description* in the example, must be implemented as nullable columns, since instances may have no values for them; correspondingly, attributes having greater than zero minimum cardinality, such as *Height* in our example, must be implemented as not nullable columns in order to avoid blanks.

Look now at how we have implemented the *Style* enumerated attribute in Fig. 34.11. We have chosen an Integer data type, as the column is defined to be a foreign key to the *EnumeratedItems* table that we created earlier. This establishes a relationship between the *Buildings* table and *EnumeratedItems*, so that the values under *Style* in Buildings will correspond to enumerated item ids. Consider the example in Fig. 34.12. In this example, the *EnumeratedItems* table stores data for the *Styles* enumerated type. The *Buildings* table, in turn, contains data for two buildings. The first one, with *Id* 4, is an 11-m-high Baroque old town hospital, and the second one, with *Id* 5, is of Romanesque style. Note how each value under *Style* refers to a row in the *EnumeratedItems* table. This manner to implement enumerated-typed attributes can be summarized as an additional mapping guideline:

> **MG.4**
> Implement enumerated-typed attributes as an Integer column in the class-table, defined as a foreign key to the *EnumeratedItems* table.

Note that all the attributes in the example above have a maximum cardinality of 1. In other words, they are not multi-valued. This makes database implementation straightforward, as they can be implemented as columns in the corresponding table. But what if our model contains multi-valued attributes? In this case, we cannot use a column as above, since a column can only store one single value.

Fig. 34.12 Sample data content for the *Buildings* and *EnumeratedItems* tables

EnumeratedItems

Id	EnumeratedTypeName	Name	Parent
15	Styles	Romanesque	(null)
16	Styles	Baroque	(null)
17	Styles	Neoclassical	(null)

Buildings

Id	Height	Style	Description
4	11	16	Old town hospital.
5	8	15	(null)

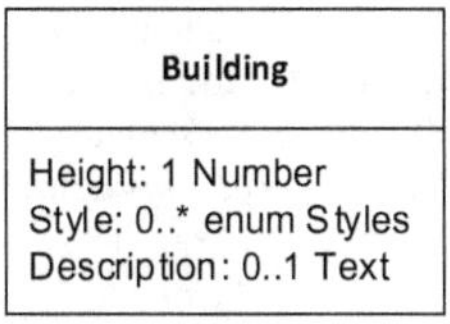

Fig. 34.13 The *Building*
class from Fig. 34.10 after
changing the *Styles* attribute
to become multi-valued

Building
Height: 1 Number Style: 0..* enum Styles Description: 0..1 Text

MG.5

For each multi-valued attribute in a class, add a new table named after the associated class and attribute. This is called an *attribute-table*. Add a column named after the class of Integer type and defined as a foreign key to the associated class-table, plus a not nullable column named after the attribute, choosing the appropriate data type.

For example, imagine that we modify the previous sample class to incorporate a multi-valued attribute, as shown in Fig. 34.13. Incorporating MG.5, your database structure would look like that in Fig. 34.14. Here, the *Buildings* class-table implements most of the *Building* class, but leaves out the *Style* attribute, as it has a greater than zero maximum cardinality. There is a specific attribute-table, named *Buildings_Style*, to do this. In this table, each row represents a particular style of a given building. The *Building* column stores the associated building id, and the *Style* column stores the id of the corresponding enumerated item. Figure 34.15 shows some sample data. In this case, note that the *Buildings* table does not hold any information about the buildings' style. This is stored separately in the *Buildings_Style* table. Here, building 4 (the old town hospital) is stated to have styles 16 (Baroque) and 17 (Neoclassical), and building 5 is stated to be of style 15 (Romanesque).

When using attribute-tables like this, the choice of data type for the attribute being implemented follows the same rules as we described for class-tables. In our example, we implemented the *Style* attribute as an Integer plus a foreign key to

Buildings		
Id	AutoNumber	PK
Height	Integer	
Description	Long Text (null)	

Buildings_Style		
Building	Integer	FK Buildings
Style	Integer	FK EnumeratedItems

Fig. 34.14 Database structure implementing the *Building* class in Fig. 34.13

Fig. 34.15 Sample data content for the *Buildings, Buildings_Style* and *EnumeratedItems* tables

EnumeratedItems

Id	EnumeratedTypeName	Name	Parent
15	Styles	Romanesque	(null)
16	Styles	Baroque	(null)
17	Styles	Neoclassical	(null)

Buildings

Id	Height	Description
4	11	Old town hospital.
5	8	(null)

Buildings_Style

Building	Style
4	16
4	17
5	15

EnumeratedItems, which is the best option for enumerated attributes. However, and as opposed to regular class-tables, you never use nullable columns in attribute-tables, since the absence of data is not indicated by *null* values but by not entering any rows in the attribute-table.

Implementing Specialization Hierarchies

Most classes in a type model are likely to be involved in a specialization hierarchy. The guidelines that we gave above to implement classes should be applied as a general case, but they need to be slightly altered for classes having generalized or specialized classes. There are three approaches to implementing a specialization hierarchy in a relational database:

1. **Single table**. You create a single table to implement all the classes in the hierarchy, with columns for all the attributes together.
2. **One table per leaf class**. You create a table for each class in a leaf position in the hierarchy, with columns for each owned or inherited attribute.
3. **One table per class**. You create a table for each class in the hierarchy, with columns for each declared attribute.

We describe the details of each approach below, including its pros and cons in relation to the others.

Single table. In this approach, you create a single table to implement all the classes in the specialization hierarchy.

MG.6

Create a table for all the classes in the hierarchy, named after the root class but using the plural. Add an *Id* column for the primary key, a *Type* column for the row type and a column for each single-valued attribute declared by the class or any of its descendants, choosing the appropriate data type and nullability.

For example, imagine that we have the specialization hierarchy shown in Fig. 34.16 in our type model. According to MG.6, your database structure would look like that in Fig. 34.17.

In tables like this, each row corresponds to an instance of the root class in the hierarchy, *Building* in our example. Since the root class has a number of subclasses, the instances of *Building* that we will document by using this model are going to be

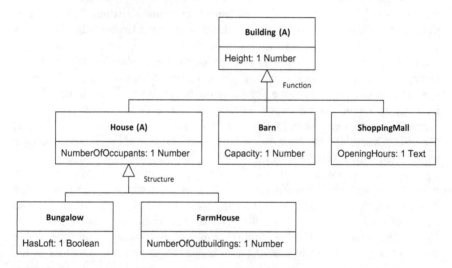

Fig. 34.16 A specialization hierarchy to be implemented in a database

Fig. 34.17 Database structure implementing the specialization hierarchy in Fig. 34.16 using a single table

Buildings		
Id	AutoNumber	PK
Type	Short Text	
Height	Integer	
NumberOfOccupants	Integer (null)	
Capacity	Integer (null)	
OpeningHours	Short Text (null)	
HasLoft	Yes/No (null)	
NumberOfOutbuildings	Integer (null)	

Buildings

Id	Type	Height	NumberOfOccupants	Capacity	OpeningHours	HasLoft	NumberOfOutbuildings
4	Bungalow	5	3	(null)	(null)	true	(null)
5	ShoppingMall	13	(null)	(null)	9:00 to 19:00	(null)	(null)
6	Barn	7	(null)	8500	(null)	(null)	(null)
7	FarmHouse	8	5	(null)	(null)	(null)	3

Fig. 34.18 Sample data content for the *Buildings* table in Fig. 34.17

not just buildings but, more specifically, bungalows, farm houses, barns or shopping malls. Consequently, different rows in the *Buildings* table will correspond to buildings of different types: one row may be describing a bungalow, the next row a shopping mall, the next a farmhouse, etc. The *Type* column has the purpose of, precisely, recording what kind of building each row is. See Fig. 34.18. Here, the building with *Id* 4 is a bungalow, as indicated by the value "Bungalow" under *Type*. However, the building with *Id* 5 is a shopping mall, and the one with *Id* 6 is a barn. In this case, we have decided to implement the *Type* column as having a text data type, so that we can store the name of the class corresponding to each row. This is a clear but not very optimal way to implement this column, as texts take a lot of storage space in the database. If you are planning to store a large number of rows in your database, you may want to implement *Type* as an integer column and keep some encoding that allows you to distinguish rows according to their type. For example, you could decide that *Type* 1 means *Bungalow*, *Type* 2 means *FarmHouse*, etc. In any case, the Type column dictates how the rest of the columns in the table should be interpreted. For example, note that row with *Id* 4 in the example above, corresponding to a bungalow, has values for *Height*, *NumberOfOccupants* and *HasLoft*, which is what we would expect from the type model from which the table was implemented. Other columns such as *Capacity* or *OpeningHours* do not make sense for bungalows, since they belong to other classes in the model, and for this reason, they hold *null* values in the table. The row with *Id* 5, for example, corresponds to a shopping mall, so it has values for *Height* and *OpeningHours*, as dictated by the model, but does not have values for *NumberOfOccupants* or *HasLoft*. In this manner, when retrieving data from a table that implements a complete specialization hierarchy, you must always look at the value under *Type* before you attempt to interpret what is stored under other columns.

In addition, note that all the columns corresponding to attributes in descendant classes have been defined as nullable in Fig. 34.17, regardless of their minimum cardinality. This is necessary to allow *null* values in rows of various types, as described above.

This approach to implementing specialization hierarchies is simple and neat, as it concentrates all the information in a single table. It also allows for the easy retrieval of rows that correspond to any particular class in the hierarchy. For example, if you wanted to get all the buildings in the database, you would just query for all the rows in *Buildings*. If you only wanted the farmhouses, you would query the table with a filter on *Type* = "*FarmHouse*". If you wanted all houses, you would query the table with a filter on *Type* = *"Bungalow"* OR *Type* = *"FarmHouse"*. This approach, however, has the disadvantage that it generates a lot of *null* values, as illustrated in Fig. 34.18. Depending on the RDBMS that you use, this may result in lower performance and wasted storage space. It also generates a single set of identifiers (primary keys) for all buildings, regardless of their type. This may be good or bad depending on how you plan to use your database.

One table per leaf class. In this approach, you create a table for every class in a leaf position in the specialization hierarchy.

> **MG.7**
> Create a table for every leaf class in the hierarchy, named after the class but using the plural. In each table, add an *Id* column for the primary key and a column for each single-valued attribute owned or inherited by the class, choosing the appropriate data type and nullability.

We will use the specialization hierarchy depicted in Fig. 34.16 to illustrate this approach. According to MG.7, your database structure would look like that in Fig. 34.19.

As opposed to the previous approach, here we do not need a *Type* column, since each row is placed in a table that corresponds to its particular type. All bungalow rows are stored in the *Bungalows* table, all barn rows in the *Barns* table, etc. We only need to create tables for leaf classes because non-leaf classes are abstract, and therefore, they cannot have direct instances.

One big advantage of this approach is that it is highly optimal regarding data storage. However, it has the drawback that it becomes harder to query the database for information related to non-leaf classes. For example, if we wanted to retrieve all the houses in the database, regardless of whether they are bungalows or farmhouses, we would need to retrieve all bungalows and then all farmhouses and then consolidate the results. Retrieving all buildings that match some criteria (e.g. that are over 10 m high) is even less optimal, as you would have to apply the filter to each individual table and then consolidate the results. Many RDBMSs support *union queries*, which allow you to perform the consolidation in the database itself. In any

Bungalows				FarmHouses		
Id	AutoNumber	PK		Id	AutoNumber	PK
Height	Integer			Height	Integer	
NumberOfOccupants	Integer			NumberOfOccupants	Integer	
HasLoft	Yes/No			NumberOfOutbuildings	Integer	

Barns				ShoppingMalls		
Id	AutoNumber	PK		Id	AutoNumber	PK
Height	Integer			Height	Integer	
Capacity	Integer			OpeningHours	Short Text	

Fig. 34.19 Database structure implementing the specialization hierarchy in Fig. 34.16 using one table per leaf class

case, be aware that this approach generates separate sets of identifiers (primary keys) for each leaf class-table, so that you may end up having a bungalow with *Id* 4 and a barn with *Id* 4 as well. This means that you will need to introduce a discriminant when consolidating data from multiple tables, either manually or on a union query if supported.

One table per class. In this approach, you create a table for every class in the specialization hierarchy.

MG.8

Create a table for every class in the hierarchy, named after the class but using the plural. For the table corresponding to the root class, add an *Id* column for the primary key; for the other tables, add an *Id* column for the primary key and make it a foreign key to the table corresponding to the generalized class. Then, for each table, add a column for each single-valued attribute declared by the class, choosing the appropriate data type and nullability.

Like in the previous case, we will use the specialization hierarchy depicted in Fig. 34.16 to illustrate this approach. According to MG.8, your database structure would look like that in Fig. 34.20.

This approach resembles the previous one, but goes one step beyond to implement a table for every class in the hierarchy, including abstract classes. Also, the tables are related through foreign keys reproducing the generalization relationships in the model. The table corresponding to the root class, *Buildings* in our example, has a regular *Id* column as primary key, defined as AutoNumber as usual. However, tables corresponding to subclasses of the root, such as *Houses*, do not incorporate an AutoNumber primary key; rather, they use a non-automated Integer column that links back to the primary key in *Buildings*. In this manner, a row in *Houses* would have a corresponding row in *Buildings*, connected through a common *Id*. Figure 34.21 shows an example. Here, note that the data for every building is scattered across multiple tables. For example, the data for the bungalow with *Id* 4 is distributed between the *Buildings* table (which stores the height), *Houses* (which stores the number of occupants) and *Bungalows* (which stores whether there is a

Buildings				Houses		
Id	AutoNumber	PK		Id	Integer	PK, FK Buildings
Height	Integer			NumberOfOccupants	Integer	
Bungalows				**FarmHouses**		
Id	Integer	PK, FK Houses		Id	Integer	PK, FK Houses
HasLoft	Yes/No			NumberOfOutbuildings	Integer	
Barns				**ShoppingMalls**		
Id	Integer	PK, FK Buildings		Id	Integer	PK, FK Buildings
Capacity	Integer			OpeningHours	Short Text	

Fig. 34.20 Database structure implementing the specialization hierarchy in Fig. 34.16 using one table per class

Fig. 34.21 Sample data content for the tables in Fig. 34.20. This is the same data as in Fig. 34.18, but laid out in a different fashion

Buildings	
Id	Height
4	5
5	13
6	7
7	8

Houses	
Id	NumberOfOccupants
4	3
7	5

Bungalows	
Id	HasLoft
4	true

FarmHouses	
Id	NumberOfOutbuildings
7	3

Barns	
Id	Capacity
6	8500

ShoppingMalls	
Id	OpeningHours
5	9:00 to 19:00

loft). Each non-root table traces back to the previous through its *Id*. For example, note that there is a row with *Id* 4 in the three tables mentioned; this means that these rows pertain to the same entity; in other words, they collectively hold data that describes the same thing in the world.

An advantage of this approach is that no redundancy exists. Attributes that belong to abstract classes in the model, such as *Height*, are implemented in one place only, rather than in multiple tables as in the previous approach. Avoiding redundancy like this improves modularity and hence quality. However, this results in data for every instance being scattered across multiple tables, which makes retrieval much more difficult than with previous approaches. For example, if you wanted to retrieve all bungalows in the database, you would need to retrieve all the rows in the *Bungalows* table and then the rows in *Houses* and *Buildings* with matching ids and then consolidate the results. This is often carried out through a database mechanism called a *join*, and most RDBMSs support joins as part of their query facilities.

Implementing Associations

There are many kinds of associations as we described in previous sections. However, all of them are implemented in very similar ways when constructing a relational database. There are two approaches to consider:

1. **One-to-many**. Associations having a maximum cardinality of 1 in at least one direction are implemented as a column.
2. **Many-to-many**. Associations having maximum cardinalities larger than 1 in both directions are implemented as a relationship table.

We describe the details of each approach below.

One-to-many. Use this approach when the association to be implemented has at least one semi-association with a maximum cardinality of 1.

MG.9

Find the table that implements the class in the "many" side of the association. Add a column named after the corresponding semi-association or its role, and make it a foreign key to the table corresponding to the "one" side of the association.

For example, imagine that we have the type model shown in Fig. 34.22. According to MG.9, your database structure would look like that in Fig. 34.23.

Most of the database structure here has been implemented by following MG.3 above. However, look at the new column *Location* in the *Buildings* table. This column implements the *IsLocatedIn* association in Fig. 34.22. Following MG.9, the table corresponding to the class in the "many" side of the association is *Buildings*. The new column has been named after the role in the semi-association pointing at the "one" table, and it has been made a foreign key to this table. In this manner, each row in *Buildings* not only contains data about the building's height and description; now, it also points to the row describing the city where the building is located. Since the cardinality for this semi-association is 0..1, we have defined this column as nullable, in order to allow for buildings that are not located in any city.

Traversing the association in the opposite direction can be done in an indirect manner. Imagine that you want to know what buildings in your database are located in a particular city. Since there is no column in *Cities* pointing at *Buildings*, you would need to query the *Buildings* table for all those rows having *Location* equal to the id of the city you are interested in.

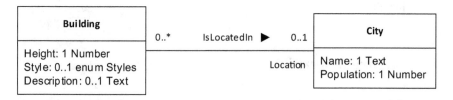

Building						City
Height: 1 Number Style: 0..1 enum Styles Description: 0..1 Text	0..*	IsLocatedIn ▶	0..1	Location		Name: 1 Text Population: 1 Number

Fig. 34.22 Sample model to be implemented in a database

Fig. 34.23 Database structure implementing the model in Fig. 34.22

Buildings		
Id	AutoNumber	PK
Height	Integer	
Description	Long Text (null)	
Location	Integer (null)	FK Cities

Cities		
Id	AutoNumber	PK
Name	Short Text	
Population	Integer	

Finally, there is an uncommon situation that you should be aware of. Sometimes, we have one-to-one associations, that is associations with maximum cardinality of 1 in both directions. This is rare, but can occur. In these cases, you apply MG.9 equally, but since there is no "many" side to the association, you can place the implementation column in either table. Do not place a column in each table to obtain a "double link", because this produces a redundant situation that is difficult to maintain.

Many-to-many. Use this approach when both semi-associations in the association to be implemented have a maximum cardinality greater than 1.

MG.10

Create a table for the association, named after the involved classes and the association itself, using the plural. Add two columns to this table, named after each of the involved classes or the associated semi-association roles, and make them foreign keys to the corresponding tables.

For example, imagine that we have the type model shown in Fig. 34.24. According to MG.10, your database structure would look like that in Fig. 34.25.

Like in the previous case, the *Buildings* and *Organizations* tables in this example have been created by applying MG.3 above. The *Organizations_Use_Buildings* relationship table, however, has been created by following MG.10. Note that it has been named after the association being implemented plus the corresponding classes. Also, note that it contains two columns defined as foreign keys to the classes connected by the association. The *Organization* column may have been named *User* instead, as this is the role name employed by the corresponding semi-association in the model. Rows in this table store pairs of ids describing links between a building and an organization. If you want to link a building to multiple organizations, you will need to enter the id of the building in multiple rows, each of them having a different organization id. And vice versa, if you want to link an organization to multiple buildings, you will need to enter the id of the organization in multiple rows, each of them having a different building id.

No matter what approach you use to implement an association, you will always need tables in the database corresponding to the classes to be connected. If these classes are involved in a specialization hierarchy, you may not have implemented tables for them; for example, look at MG.6 above and Fig. 34.17. If you want to implement an association involving a class for which no table has been created, you

Fig. 34.24 Sample model to be implemented in a database

Fig. 34.25 Database structure implementing the model in Fig. 34.24

Buildings		
Id	AutoNumber	PK
Height	Integer	
Description	Long Text (null)	

Organizations		
Id	AutoNumber	PK
Name	Short Text	

Organizations_Use_Buildings		
Organization	Integer	FK Organizations
Building	Integer	FK Buildings

will need to add the table to the database. For this reason, it is a good idea to consider whether classes in a specialization hierarchy are involved in associations before you decide on an approach to implement them. The example in the next section shows this in practice.

Worked Example

Let us develop a complete worked example. Imagine that we have the type model shown in Fig. 34.26 and that we want to implement it as a relational database.

The model is composed of a small specialization hierarchy rooted on *Archaeological-Element*, plus an associated *Site* class. First of all, we have an enumerated type in the model, *Materials*, so we will need an *EnumeratedItems* table. We might use a single table approach to implement *ArchaeologicalElement* plus descendants, but this would be a bad idea, since *Find* is involved in an association, which means that we will need a table for *Find*. The one table per leaf class approach would not work either, as we will need a table for *ArchaeologicalElement* as it is also involved in associations. For this reason, we choose a one table per class approach. Note also that the *ArchaeologicalElement. Material* attribute is multi-valued, so we will need an attribute-table for it. Finally,

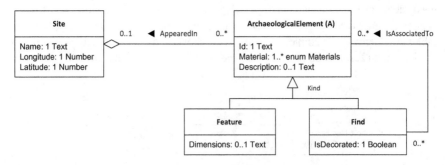

Fig. 34.26 Sample model to be implemented in a database

EnumeratedItems		
Id	AutoNumber	PK
EnumeratedTypeName	Short Text	
Name	Short Text	
Parent	Integer (null)	FK EnumeratedItems

Sites		
Id	AutoNumber	PK
Name	Short Text	
Longitude	Decimal	
Latitude	Decimal	

ArchaeologicalElements		
Id	AutoNumber	PK
Description	Long Text (null)	
AppearedIn	Integer (null)	FK Sites

ArchaeologicalElements_Material		
ArchaeologicalElement	Integer	FK ArchaeologicalElements
Material	Integer	FK EnumeratedItems

Features		
Id	Integer	PK, FK ArchaeologicalElements
Dimensions	Long Text (null)	

Finds		
Id	Integer	PK, FK ArchaeologicalElements
IsDecorated	Yes/No	

Finds_AreAssociatedTo_ArchaeologicalElements		
Find	Integer	FK Finds
ArchaeologicalElement	Integer	FK ArchaeologicalElements

Fig. 34.27 Database structure for the model in Fig. 34.26

the *AppearsIn* association, being one-to-many, will be implemented as a column, whereas *IsAssociatedTo*, being many-to-many, will need a relationship table. Figure 34.27 shows the final database structure.

Summary

Databases constitute an excellent technology to store and manipulate large collections of data.

The **relational paradigm** to databases organizes data in terms of tables, columns and rows.

A relational database can be a very good way to store your instance models.

The structure of your database will be constructed after your type model. The contents of the database will correspond to an instance model.

There are some **mapping guidelines** to help you construct a database based on a type model.

Enumerated types and items are implemented as a single generic table.

Usually, you will have one table per class in the model and one column per single-valued attribute.

Multi-valued attributes need each a special table.

Specialization hierarchies can be implemented as a single table, as one table per leaf class or as one table per class. Each approach has some pros and cons.

One-to-many associations are implemented as a column in the table for the "many" side.

Many-to-many associations are implemented as a relationship table.

Exercises

56. Look at the type model below. Create the structure for a relational database
    mapping the model.

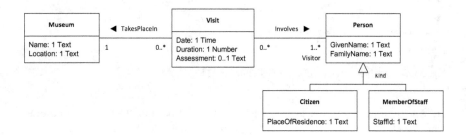

Part 5
Recap of Part V

This is the end of Part V. In this part, we have explored some topics about the application of conceptual modelling techniques to real-world situations, including modelling patterns, quality issues, the modelling process, model extension and the construction of relational databases from models. Although most of these themes have been discussed introductorily, you now have the basis to explore them in greater depth if you are so inclined.

It is worth mentioning here that most of the contents in this part have been presented in the form of guidelines or recommendations to construct better models. Patterns are a proven approach to reusing established knowledge, and the incremental and iterative process described in Chap. 32 is based on well-tested methodological solutions that are common in information systems development. This emphasis on quality is not gratuitous, as there is a big difference between knowing how to model and knowing how to model well. Most texts on computing or information technologies for the humanities describe the basics, but few address the necessary concerns to go beyond those basics and pave your way towards professional competence.

This is also the end of the book. If you have reached this far, you are probably better at conceptual modelling now than many software engineers. If you manage to apply your newly gained skills to archaeology, anthropology and other humanities related to the cultural heritage, then this book has fulfilled its goal.

Solutions to Exercises

This section contains proposed solutions to the exercises suggested along the book. Please bear in mind that most exercises don't have a single correct solution; in modelling, one problem usually has multiple valid solutions depending on your purpose, situation and even personal preferences. Take the following solutions as a guide rather than absolute answers.

1. Find a picture of the painting *Automat* by Edward Hopper on the web. Imagine you want to describe the painting to someone who doesn't know about it. Draw a diagram showing three objects that represent entities in the painting. Don't forget to give the objects meaningful identifiers and categories.

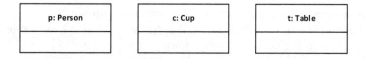

2. Complete the objects from Exercise 1 by adding some values to them. Focus on values related to the appearance of the entities in the painting. You can make up some characteristics if you want. Remember that objects of the same category must be described having the same list of value names.

3. Further complete the previous model by adding links between the objects. You may add as many links as needed. Focus on the physical and spatial relationships between entities in the painting.

© Springer International Publishing AG 2018
C. Gonzalez-Perez, *Information Modelling for Archaeology and Anthropology*,
https://doi.org/10.1007/978-3-319-72652-6

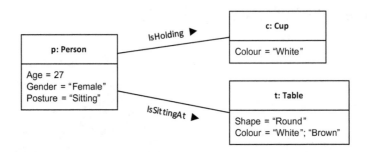

4. Imagine that you want to study how buildings are organized to make up towns. Draw a diagram showing two or three classes that describe this situation. Give the classes good names, and define them. Add some properties to the classes to represent the relevant characteristics.

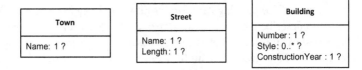

A **town** is an aggregation of buildings that make up streets.
A **street** is a space within a town that organizes buildings along a line.
A **building** is a construction in a town.

5. Look again at the diagram you created for Exercise 4, and convert as many properties into attributes in it. Use the best data types and re-think the cardinalities.

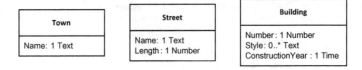

6. Draw a diagram showing some objects instantiated from the classes in the previous exercise for some particular town that you are familiar with.

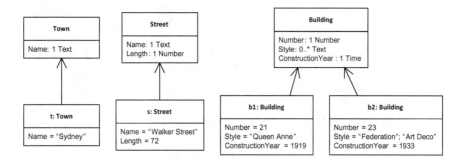

7. Look back at the diagram you created for Exercise 6 and add an attribute to describe the style of the buildings, if you don't have it yet. Use an enumerated type for this attribute, and update the corresponding values. Document the enumerated items separately.

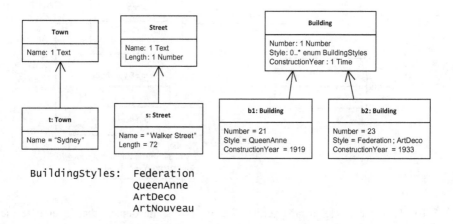

8. Look back at the classes in the diagram that you created for the previous exercise, and add as many associations between them as you need in order to represent the relationships between buildings and other entities. Use adequate names, cardinalities and roles. Use plain associations or whole/part associations if needed.

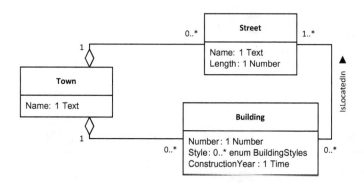

9. Working on the previous model, add an association to represent the fact that some buildings can be seen from other buildings.

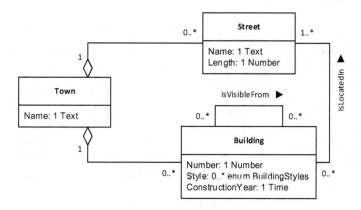

10. Take the model from Exercise 9 and draw some objects that instantiate the classes in it for a town you are familiar with. Include the necessary values and links, as dictated by the attributes and associations.

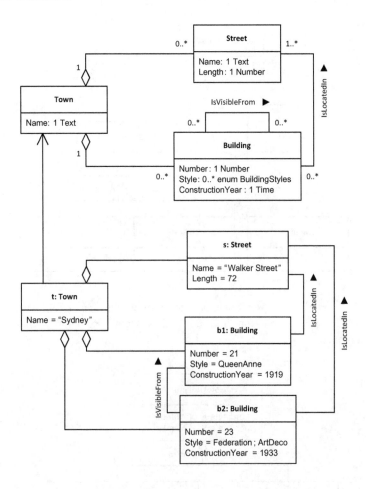

Note. The instantiation arrows for *s, b1* and *b2* have been omitted for the sake of clarity.

11. Create a type model containing an *ArchaeologicalSite* class plus classes to represent tumuli, hillforts and villages. Use generalization relationships with the necessary discriminants.

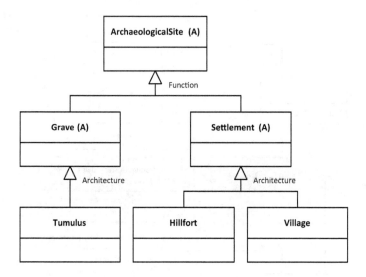

12. Add attributes to the previous model to represent the sites' coordinates and the estimated population for hillforts and villages. Remember the rule of inheritance.

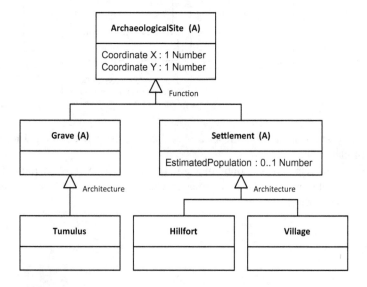

13. Draw an instance model with some objects for the *Village* class in the previous type model. Give them the necessary values.

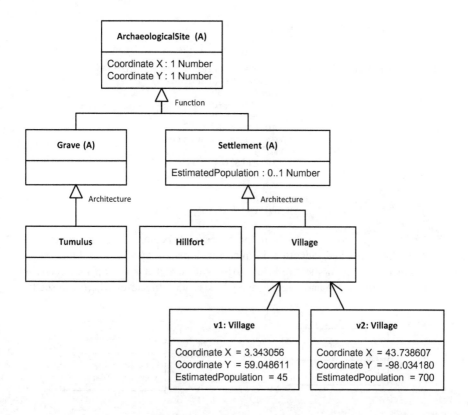

14. Imagine that you need to develop an urban planning model for a town council. In the council, overall, buildings are simply categorized as residential, commercial or industrial. However, the council planning department needs additional detail, having types such as detached house, factory, mall, or apartment block. Create two enumerated types linked by a generalization/specialization relationship and having the necessary items. Add extra items that you can think of if you wish.

```
BuildingKind:        Residential
                     Commercial
                     Industrial
PlanningBuildingType (specialized from BuildingKind):
                     Residential (inherited)
                        House
                           AttachedHouse
                           DetachedHouse
                        ApartmentBlock
                     Commercial (inherited)
                        Mall
                        RetailShop
                     Industrial (inherited)
                        Factory
                        Yard
```

15. Create a type model to represent the concept of 'person', including a person's phone numbers and jobs. Bear in mind that a person may have multiple phone numbers such as home, work, etc. Also consider that a person may have, at most, a primary job and a secondary job. Use sorted features where you see fit.

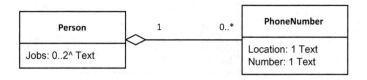

16. Create a type model to represent the fact that heritage elements may be assessed over time by different people, each assessment being about one particular heritage element. Include in your model classes for heritage elements, assessment, and people. Mark which semi-associations are strong.

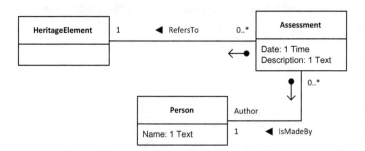

Consider the definition "an **assessment** is an interpretive statement made by an author about a heritage element". This means that the definition of the *Assessment* class depends on those of *HeritageEement* and *Person*.

17. Imagine that you are studying a group of artists and their works. Some artists may have met others during their life; also, some artists may have studied under other artists. Create a type model for the concept of 'artist' and include associations for the two situations described above. Use symmetric self-associations where suitable.

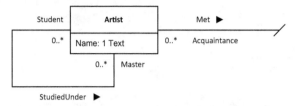

18. Imagine that you are surveying an area and recording archaeological sites and the associated material. Each archaeological site is located at a particular place, and each find corresponds to a particular site. Draw a diagram for this situation, including classes to represent sites, places and finds. Use compact notation for associations where appropriate.

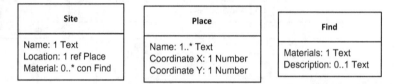

19. Imagine that you are given a model having an *Event* class to describe things that happen in a particular time and place, as well as a *Group* class to describe groups of people. You need to introduce a new class to represent social acts such as people going to church or having a party. Use multiple generalization and/or associations to connect the new class to the existing ones.

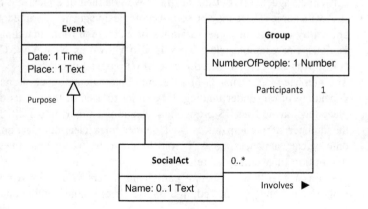

20. Take the model in Fig. 14.1 as a basis, and complete it by adding a *Team* class to represent the teams that carry out interventions, as well as a *Report* class to represent the documents generated by these teams. Put these classes in an existing package or create a new package if you think it's necessary.

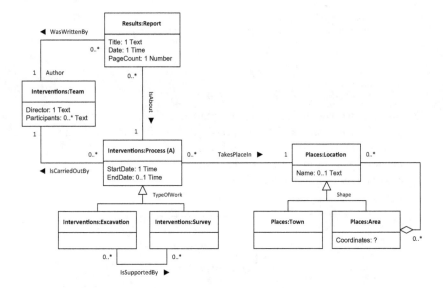

21. Below you can find a list of characteristics. For each of them, state whether it admits ontological vagueness, epistemic vagueness, none, or both.

Every characteristic admits epistemic vagueness. Regarding ontological vagueness, see the following list.

- A building's height. No ontological vagueness. We can be more or less accurate when measuring or reporting a building's height (which relates to epistemic vagueness), but the height is well defined in a clear-cut manner.
- A town's name. There may be some ontological vagueness. Some towns are known by a range of name variations of a common root, including abbreviations. For example, New York is also known as New York City and NYC. This can be considered a case of ontological vagueness.
- The number of participants in an event. Ontological vagueness may exist depending of our understanding. If we refer to each of the events that take place (such as in 'the US presidential election of 6 November 2012'), then the number of participants is well defined in a clear-cut fashion, so no ontological vagueness exists. If, on the contrary, we refer to the abstract description of a family of related events (such as in 'the US presidential elections'), then the number of participants refers to an approximation of what is usual and/or expected; in this case, there is considerable ontological vagueness.

- The starting date of a war. There is ontological vagueness. A war is a complex and diffuse process that does not start at any particular instant, but usually has a wide array of underlying causes. The transition from 'not being at war' to 'being at war' is gradual, and therefore we can say that there is some ontological vagueness. However, this vagueness may be removed if we consider the official date on a declaration of war document.
- The entities affected by a social change process. There is ontological vagueness. The concept of 'affected by' is quite imprecise, and there are many degrees of something affecting something else, from the most direct and obvious to the most indirect and questionable. For this reason, the collection of entities that are affected by a social change process is ontologically vague.

22. Create a type model to represent the fact that events happen at a particular place and time, and involve a number of people. Pay special attention to feature cardinalities, which will determine what features may take a *null* value. Then create an instance model based on the former, to represent the event of the writing of the Voynich manuscript.

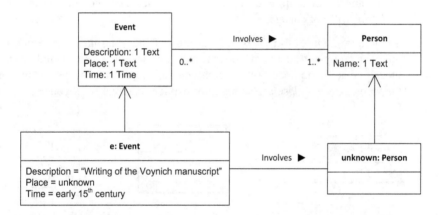

23. Modify the type model from the previous exercise with extra attributes to represent the ontological imprecision of the time when events occur.

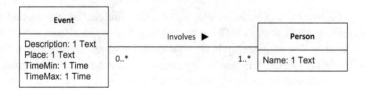

24. Below you can find a list of characteristics. For each of them, state whether it should be modelled as constant, variable or temporal. Assume that we are trying to represent the internal workings of a museum.

Please bear in mind that whether you model something as constant, variable or temporal is strongly influenced by your particular interests and the model's purpose. You may not agree with the answers below.

- The museum's name. This should be variable, because although it may change over time, we are not interested in keeping track of the different names that the museum had over time.
- The museum's inauguration date. This should be constant, because the museum's inauguration date, once happened, cannot change.
- The items on display as part of the permanent collection. This should be temporal, because although the collection is permanent, new items may be added to it at any time, and old items retired. It would be interesting to keep track of what items were in the collection when, so this feature should probably be modelled as temporal.
- The number of visitors recorded each year. This should be constant. Once the number of visitors for a year has been calculated and documented, this figure will not change.

25. Create a type model to represent archaeological sites and their occupation by different groups of people at different moments in time. Also, include in the model the ability to document the archaeological features found on the sites as they are excavated. Use aspect-based or explicit temporality as you see fit.

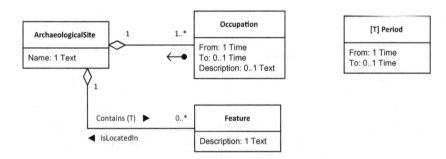

The relationship between sites and occupations has been modelled by using explicit time attributes on *Occupation*, since this is a class with strong temporal semantics. The relationship between sites and features, however, is modelled by using aspect-based temporality, because *Feature* has no time semantics, and still it's interesting to know when each feature as found within a site.

26. Using the model from Exercise 25 as a basis, create an instance model representing the following situation. The hillfort of Baroña was occupied between the 1st century BCE and the 1st century CE. It was excavated for the first time in 1933 and a large rampart was documented. Then it was excavated again between 1980 and 1984 and two roundhouses described.

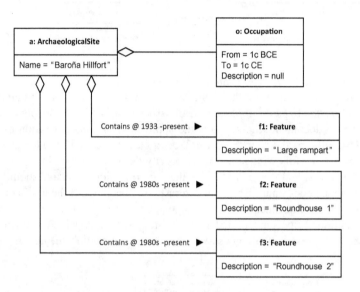

27. Below you can find a list of characteristics. For each of them, state whether it should be modelled as objective or subjective. Assume that we are trying to represent the internal workings of a museum.

- The museum's inauguration date. This should be objective, because the museum's inauguration date, whatever it is and whether different people know about it or not, is an established fact.
- The quality of the lighting conditions in the exhibition halls. This should be subjective, because different people may hold different judgments about how well lit the exhibition halls are. This is especially so if the people being considered through the subjective aspect class include museum visitors.
- The estimated dating of each item in the permanent collection. This should be objective, because the creation or construction date of an object is an established fact. Usually we employ estimates to describe these dates, but the fact that we cannot determine the dates with accuracy does not mean that the creation date of an object constitutes a judgment or an opinion.
- The maximum allowed number of visitors that can be inside the museum at any given time. This should be objective, especially if the museum capacity is regulated by law.

28. Create a type model to represent the archaeological impact and correction work done a team during the construction of a pipeline. Pay special attention to the impact assessments and corrective measures that should be taken. Use aspect-based or explicit subjectivity as you see fit.

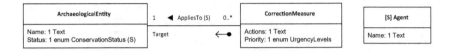

The *ArcheologicalEntity.Status* attribute has been modelled as subjective in order to capture the different views of agents. Similarly, the *CorrectionMeasure.AppliesTo* semi-association has been modelled as subjective to document who supports the application of what correction measures.

29. Using the model from Exercise 28 as a basis, create an instance model representing the following situation. A heavily deteriorated tumulus is found during the works, and the team decides that no correction measures should be taken given its poor status. This is in contrast with the views of the local council, who issues an assessment by which signalling and documentation is required. In addition, some unidentified features are discovered, which seem to be well enough preserved as to deserve a quick excavation documentation.

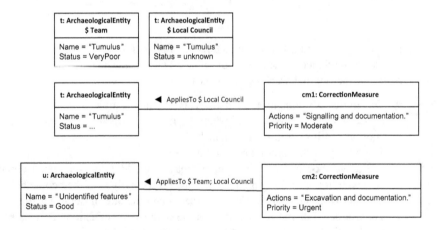

30. Imagine that a study is to be carried out on how the people from a neighbourhood use some specific buildings over the day. The following model states that, for the purposes of the study, every person may be using a building at any point in time. Taking this model as a basis, add the necessary classes, attributes and associations to reflect the fact that there are two kinds of buildings to be considered in the study: houses, where people live, and factories, where people work. Use feature redefinition wherever necessary.

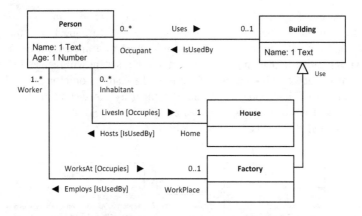

31. Below you can find a list of characteristics. For each of them, state whether it constitutes metainformation or regular information.

- A book's author in a model describing a library. This is regular information, because the entities being described by the library model are presumably books, and a book's author is a characteristic of the book.
- The architect who designed a building in a monument management system. This is regular information, because the entities being described by the monument management model probably include buildings, and a building's architect is a characteristic of the building.
- The author of a photograph of a building in a monument management system. This is metainformation, because the entities being described by the monument management model would include buildings but not photos. In this model, photos constitute information about the buildings, so a photo's author constitutes information about information, and hence metainformation.
- The author of a photograph in a historical documentation management system. This is regular information, because the entities being described by the historical documentation management model would probably include historical photographs, and a photo's author is a characteristic of the photo.
- The date when a ritual was first performed in a particular country. This is regular information if we assume that we are studying rituals, because the date when a ritual was first performed is a characteristic of the ritual.
- The date when a ritual was first documented in a particular country. This is metainformation if we assume that we are studying rituals, because the date when a ritual was first documented is not a characteristic of the ritual, but of the information about it, and hence metainformation.

32. Create two type models, one for the following scenario, and one for the necessary metainformation that would be necessary to collect. A study is to be carried out to analyse the feedback of visitors to a museum. For each visitor willing to participate in the study, a museum assistant will record their personal details, together with the date of the visit, the visitor's opinion about the quality of the exhibition, and an optional comment by the visitor. It is necessary to document when each visit was recorded and who did it.
The model for the scenario is as follows.

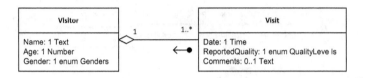

The model for the required metainformation is as follows.

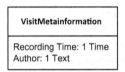

33. Using the models from the previous exercise as a basis, create an instance model plus the associated metainformation objects to describe the following situation. Alice, 54, visits the museum on 11 March 2016 and agrees to participate in the study. Bob is the assigned museum assistant who interviews her. Alice states that she found the collection to be of average quality and makes no further comments.

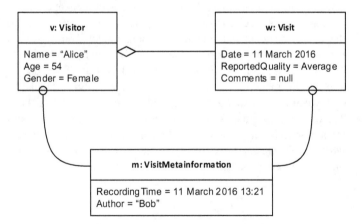

34. Below you can find a list of entities. For each of them, state what CHARM class of those described in this chapter would be more suitable to model it.

- The oldest member in a family. This is an agent.
- A period of abandonment of a settlement. This is an occurrence.
- A voodoo ritual performed in Limbé, Haiti on 22 June 1972. This is a manifestation.
- A leaf in a book. This is a tangible entity.
- Feminism. This is an abstract entity.
- A rocky outcrop. This is a tangible entity.
- The Klondike gold rush in the late 19th century. This is an occurrence.
- The obligation to pilgrimage to Mecca in some Islamic societies. This is an abstract entity.
- The Rolling Stones. This is an agent.
- A recording in a vinyl LP. This is a virtual entity.
- The Chinese New Year festival celebrated all over the world. This is a performative entity.

35. Create a CHARM-compliant instance model to describe the following situation. In 1979, a ceremonial pool measuring 2.5 m by an estimated 1.8 m was found inside a crypt, which is built between 0.6 and 1.1 m below the ground surface. This crypt is located in the outskirts of the town of Scheden in Germany.

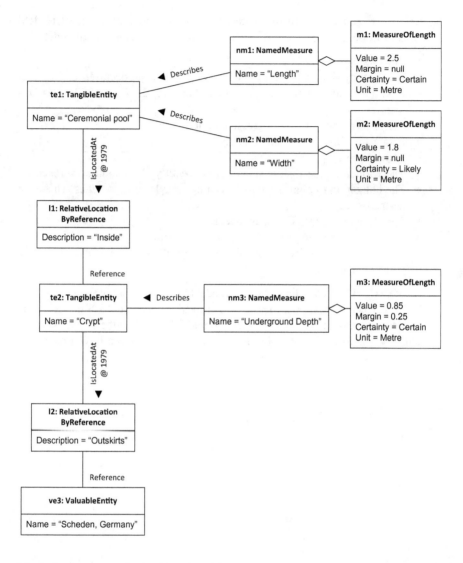

36. Below you can find a list of entities. For each of them, state what CHARM class of those described in this chapter would be more suitable to model it.

- A cave. This is a natural structure.
- The paintings in the cave. This is a material aspect.
- A sacred tree. This is probably best modelled as a natural structure, although it may be modelled as a natural object as well.
- A clay pot. This is an intentional object.
- The lid of the clay pot. This is an intentional object too. The fact that it is a component of a larger object does not mean it's not a complete and intentional object.

- A mill stone that is being reused as part of a paving. This is a complete object. The fact that it is being reused as a part of a structure does not affect this.
- The materials of a collapsed wall as found during excavation. This is a deposit.
- A set of Galician bagpipes. This is an intentional object.
- A river. This is a non-material place.
- A gate in a cattle pen. This is a constructive element.

37. Create a CHARM-compliant instance model to describe the following situation. The Dombate dolmen in Galicia, Spain consists of a polygonal chamber formed by seven vertical granite slabs, covered by a single capstone and protected by a tumulus made of rocky fragments and compacted dirt. All the vertical slabs have been decorated with geometric paintings. A small idol was found inside the dolmen.

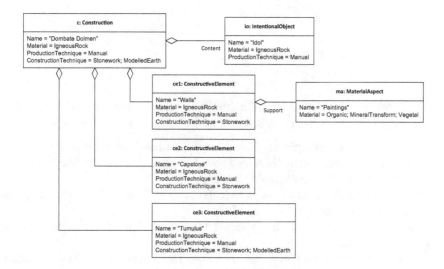

38. Below you can find a list of entities. For each of them, state what CHARM class of those described in this chapter would be more suitable to model it.

- The winner of a yearly sporting competition. This is an agent role, since it constitutes a recognized "label" that different people "play" over time.
- The members of a Quaker meeting for worship. This is an organization.
- A person who reports relevant information about their community. This would be best modelled as an informant, linked to a person.
- The Russian people. This is a community.

39. Create a CHARM-compliant instance model to describe the following situation. A family belonging to a large group has a representative in a government

council. In April 1911, this person dies, and a new individual is chosen as a representative.

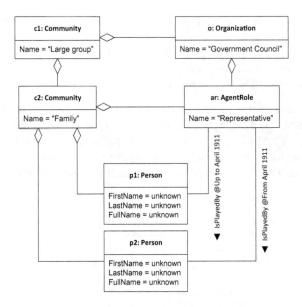

40. Below you can find a list of entities. For each of them, state what CHARM class of those described in this chapter would be more suitable to model it.

   • An opera performance. This is a manifestation of combined expressive design, since it includes at least sound (the music), language (the lyrics), and gestural (the choreography) components.
   • The lyrics of *Wuthering Heights* by Kate Bush. This is a language expressive design.
   • The name "Uluru" as spoken by a tourist. This is a manifestation of toponym.
   • The well-known thumbs-up hand sign. This is a gestural expressive design.
   • The way in which craftsmen construct Galician bagpipes. This is a knowledge.
   • Flamenco. This is a combined expressive design.
   • A jazz jam session. This is a manifestation of social act.

41. Create a CHARM-compliant instance model to describe the following situation. In 1991, the relics of Russian monk St. Seraphim of Sarov were rediscovered after being hidden in a museum for a long time. This was received with awe in post-Soviet Russia, so a procession was formed to take the relics from Moscow to the St. Seraphim-Diveyevo convent in the town of Sarov

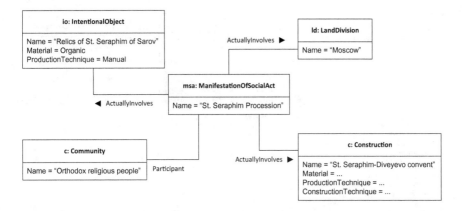

Note that an important aspect of the manifestation of social act that is central to this model, namely the moment when it happened, cannot be documented by using the CHARM classes described so far. Further chapters will allow for this.

42. Below you can find a list of entities. For each of them, state what CHARM class of those described in this chapter would be more suitable to model it.

- The time span between 8 June 2001 and 19 January 2002. This should be a time span.
- The period of time that a concentration camp survivor spent there. This is a phenomenon.
- The refurbishment an old house. This is a modification change.
- The 14th century. This is a point in time.
- The inter-war period of 1918–1939 in Europe. This is a phase starting and ending at particular points in time.
- The sinking of the Titanic. If you consider that the Titanic was destroyed at this event, then it should be modelled as a destruction change. Alternatively, you can model it as a modification change if you consider the underwater wreck still to be the Titanic.
- The construction of the Great Pyramid of Giza. This is probably best modelled as a project.

43. Create a CHARM-compliant instance model to describe the following situation. An archaeological excavation takes place between June and September 2013. As a consequence of it, an old wall is exposed and heavily altered by wind erosion over the following months.

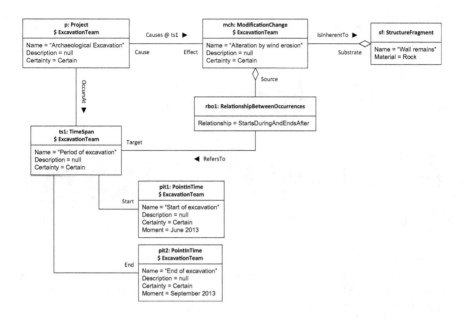

44. Below you can find a list of entities. For each of them, state what CHARM class of those described in this chapter would be more suitable to model it.

- The exchange of cards in business meetings. This is a convention.
- The heraldry conventions of canting arms. This is a language encoding.
- Marxism. This is a belief.
- The preference for male rather than female children in some cultures. This is a value.
- The entitlement to keep what one has inherited. This is a right of ownership.
- The set of race and ethnicity labels used by the US Census. This is a category system.

45. Create a CHARM-compliant instance model to describe the following situation. A historical map of North-East Hokkaido is to be exhibited at a museum. In order to protect the map, a replica is made and exhibited instead of the original.

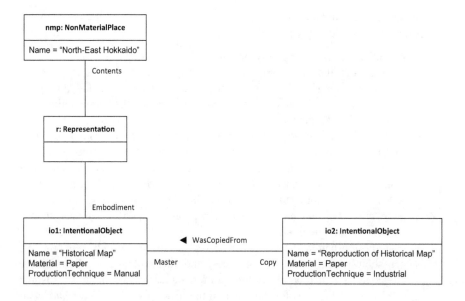

46. Below you can find a list of entities. For each of them, state what CHARM class of those described in this chapter would be more suitable to model it.

   - The decision of a Heritage Department to strongly limit the materials and colours that can be used to construct new houses in a traditional neighbourhood. This is a use valorization.
   - The disagreement of part of the local population with that decision. This is a community valorization.
   - The admiration that the beautiful and tidy neighbourhood evokes in tourists and visitors. This is an external valorization.
   - The report of the Heritage Department assessing the negative effects of ongoing unkempt construction in the neighbourhood. This is an impact valorization.

47. Below you can find a list of entities. For each of them, state what CHARM class of those described in this chapter would be more suitable to model it.

   - The Early Neolithic period in Europe. This is a cultural classification.
   - The "Extraterrestrial Highway" in Nevada, United States. This is a cultural landscape.
   - Machu Picchu in Peru. This is a site.
   - The sacred kondō in a Buddhist temple. This is a community derived entity.
   - The romantic literature of the 18th-19th centuries. This is a style.
   - A collection of Yoruba masks in a museum. This is an object collection.

48. Below you can find a list of modelling situations. For each of them, state what pattern you would apply, if any.

   - A family tree including only parent-child relationships. This can be modelled as a recursive decomposition pattern, since all the instances in the hierarchy belong to the same category and can be modelled through a *Person* class. A self-association would implement the parent/child relationship between persons.
   - The fact that archaeological sites may be excavated or not, and when. This can be modelled as a state pattern. The category being described would be *ArchaeologicalSite*, the state class would be *ExcavationStatus*, and there would be subclasses such as *Excavated* and *Non-Excavated* for each of the states. The whole/part association between *ArchaeologicalSite* and *ExcavationStatus* should be temporal in order to capture when each state is current for any given site.
   - A study of urban landscapes where cities are considered to be composed of neighbourhoods, and these or areas, and these of streets. This can be modelled as a taxonomic decomposition pattern, since there are distinct names and definitions for the ranks in the hierarchy. *City*, *Neighbourhood*, *Area* and *Street* would be necessary classes. Specific whole/part associations between each class pair would implement the connections.
   - The description of author's marks on artworks, which may be placed on the artwork itself or on a previous mark. This can be modelled as an inverted composite pattern. The composable category would be *Mark*, the non-composable would be *Artwork*, and the abstract category would be, for example, *ArtisticElement*. A whole/part association would connect *ArtisticElement* to *Mark*.
   - The composition of a thesaurus of traditional trades to tag a collection of literary works that may mention them. This can be modelled as a reference subtyping pattern. The different traditional trades could be listed as enumerated items in a *TraditionalTrades* enumerated type and arranged hierarchically as necessary.

49. Below you can find a list of modelling situations. For each of them, describe the three quality factors that you consider the most important, and in what order.

   - A model for a short research project involving only one person. This would need correctness in the first place, because correctness cannot be compromised for anything else. Then, it would probably need robustness, since research projects tend to reveal parts of the world that were not too well known in advance, and the model should work even in situations that deviate slightly from its original design. Finally, it would need usability to make its application easier.
   - A shared model to be implemented as a database in a large company for a wide range of projects. This would need correctness in the first place, for the reason stated above. Then, usability would be necessary to maximize acceptance

across the different members of the company. Finally, efficiency would be necessary to make the database implementation as smooth as possible.

- A large model intended as a reference for anyone in a given country doing archaeological fieldwork. Once again, correctness would be the top priority. Them, usability would help the many users to adopt the model easily. Finally, maintainability would be necessary to support the evolution of the model in the long term, since an investment like this should be expected to persist for a long time.

50. Look at the diagram below. What changes would you make in order to improve the model's quality in relation to the different quality factors?
Several changes are applicable:

- The *SocialPractice.Name2* attribute is difficult to understand. To improve readability and maintainability, it should be renamed to something else. For example, if it is meant to capture an alternative name for social acts, then *AlternativeName* would be better.
- Also in relation to the *SocialPractice.Name* and *Name2* attributes, there might be a correctness or robustness issue here. If social acts are known to have one or two names at most, then the model may work as it is, but it would not be very robust, since finding a social act with more than two names would be make it difficult to document. A better way to solve this would be to use a single *SocialPractice.Name* attribute with 1..* cardinality.
- The *SocialPractice.Type* attribute is redundant with the generalization/ specialization relationship of *SocialPractice*, which hinders efficiency and maintainability. If any social practice is documented as either a demonstration, a ritual or a sports event, then we don't need to state its type through an attribute, because the instantiated class already expresses that information. For this reason, the *SocialPractice.Type* attribute should be removed.
- Similarly, the *Participants* attribute in each of the three specialized classes are also redundant, which hinders efficiency and maintainability. Since all the subclasses of *SocialPractice* have the same attribute, it can be easily moved to the superclass.
- Also in relation to the *Participants* attributes, it is not very readable. Are we supposed to describe who participates in the social practices, or just state the number of participants? Since the attribute data type is Number, it would seem the latter. A better name for the attribute would be *NumberOfParticipants*.

51. Consider a model containing the classes listed below. Describe how you would group these classes into modules, and explain why.
The classes can be modularized as follows:

- *Barn*, *Farm*, *House*, *TraditionalSettlement* and *Well* are kinds of constructions. *Forest*, *Orchard* and *Stream* are natural places. All of them may be organized as a module describing places and physical structures, as well as the spatial relationships between them.

- *FamingActivity*, *FishingActivity* and *HuntingActivity* are kinds of activities that people may carry out in different places. They could be grouped into a separate module that describes what kinds of activities are carried out in which places from the previous module.
- Finally, *FarmAnimal* doesn't seem to have a tightly coupled relationship with any of the other classes, so it would remain by itself, or in a separate module just in case that other classes are added later to the model to represent things that may be in places and involved in activities, such as tools or utensils.

This arrangement would allow a model user to understand how places are represented by looking at the first module, and activities by looking at the second. Also, each module can be extended with new classes (such as *City* in the first or *MiningActivity* in the second) independently from each other.

52. Construct a type model from the text below, using the word highlighting technique.

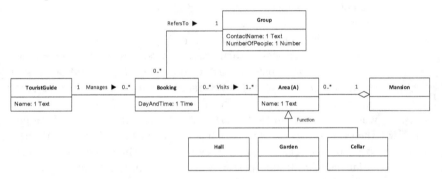

53. Below you can find a list of concerns that are likely to come up during the modelling of a museum collection. For each of them, state whether it is a genuine conceptual concern that should be captured in a model or, to the contrary, it is an implementation issue that should be left out of the model and tackled only during implementation.

- The name given to each artefact in the collection, such as "Lithic arrow head". An artefact's name does apply to the artefact even in the absence of a model, so this should be part of the conceptual model.
- The number of decimals to use when stating artefact dimensions. The number of decimals to use to state a number is an information storage and/or display concern; as such, it doesn't apply to the associated artefact, but to its management within an information system. This should not be part of a conceptual model.
- The id assigned to each artefact sample by museum technicians. Samples are entities that are methodologically constructed, and therefore it is common to assign ids to them. From this perspective, a sample's id does apply to the sample even in the absence of a model, so it should be part of a conceptual model.
- The sections of the museum web where each artefact is to be shown. The museum web is an implementation, and therefore any reference to it should not be part of a conceptual model of the museum collection.

54. Create a particular model by extending CHARM to document reuse processes of urban spaces such as town squares. You should make sure that the model can describe the different uses that various agents make of urban spaces, and how some uses produce the appearance or disappearance of other uses. Feel free to add the necessary elements to capture whatever information seems relevant to you, but keep the model simple.

In the following diagram, model elements shaded in grey have been added during extension.

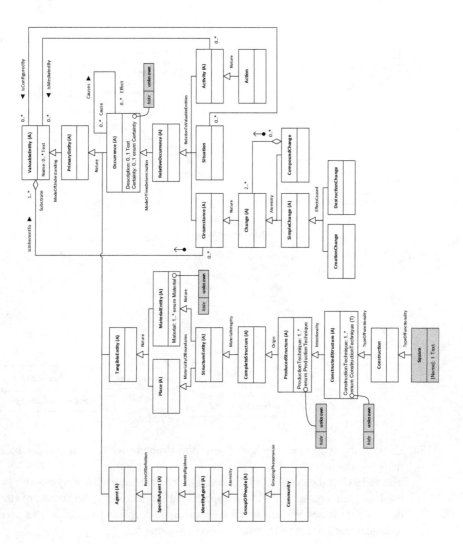

55. Use the type model created in the previous exercise to document the fact that the overtaking of a particular town square by teenager groups for evening recreational purposes has displaced its use as an improvised parking lot. Draw the corresponding instance model.

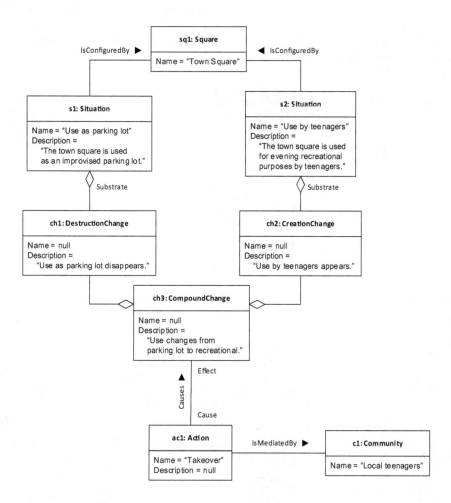

56. Look at the type model below. Create the structure for a relational database mapping the model.

The following database structure is suggested. The single table approach was used to implement the *People* specialization hierarchy, as none of the descendant classes are involved in associations. A relationship table was used to implement the many-to-many *Involves* association.

Museums

Id	AutoNumber	PK
Name	Short Text	
Location	Short Text	

Persons

Id	AutoNumber	PK
Type	Short Text	
GivenName	Short Text	
FamilyName	Short Text	
PlaceOfResidence	Short Text (null)	
StaffId	Short Text (null)	

Visits

Id	AutoNumber	PK
Date	Date/Time	
Duration	Integer	
Assessment	Long Text (null)	
TakesPlaceIn	Integer	FK Museums

Visits_Involve_Persons

| Visit | Integer | FK Visits |
| Person | Integer | FK Persons |

References

1. Partridge C, Gonzalez-Perez C, Henderson-Sellers B (2013) Are Conceptual Models Concept Models? In: Ng W, Storey VC, Trujillo JC (eds) Conceptual Modeling, vol LNCS 8217. Springer, pp 96–105. https://doi.org/10.1007/978-3-642-41924-9_9
2. Ackoff RL (1989) From Data to Wisdom. Journal of Applied Systems Analysis 16: pp. 3–9
3. Stanford University (2015) Stanford Encyclopedia of Philosophy. Center for the Study of Language and Information. http://plato.stanford.edu/. Accessed 23 July 2015
4. Stead S, Doerr M, Bruseker G, Daskalaki M (2016) Is that a good concept? Paper presented at the Computer Application and Quantitative Methods in Archaeology (CAA) 2016, Oslo (Norway),
5. Olivé A (2007) Conceptual Modeling of Information Systems. Springer. https://doi.org/10.1007/978-3-540-39390-0
6. Gonzalez-Perez C, Henderson-Sellers B A Representation-Theoretical Analysis of the OMG Modelling Suite. In: Fujita H, Mejri M (eds) The 4th International Conference on Software Methodologies, Tools and Techniques, Amsterdam, 28–30 September 2005 2005. Frontiers in Artificial Intelligence and Applications. IOS Press, pp 252–262
7. Partridge C (2005) Business Objects: Re-Engineering for Re-Use. 2nd edition. The BORO Centre,
8. Gruber T (1993) A Translation Approach to Portable Ontology Specifications. Knowledge Acquisition 5 (2):199–220
9. Gonzalez-Perez C (2017) How Ontologies Can Help in Software Engineering. In: Cunha J, Fernandes J, Lämmel R, Saraiva J, Zaytsev V (eds) Grand Timely Topics in Software Engineering. GTTSE 2015. Lecture Notes in Computer Science, vol 10223. Springer, Cham
10. Lakoff G (1990) Women, Fire, and Dangerous Things. University of Chicago Press,
11. Fowler M, Kendall S (2000) UML Distilled. Object Technology Series, Second edition. Addison-Wesley, Reading, MA
12. OMG (2006) Unified Modelling Language Specification: Infrastructure. version 2. Object Management Group,
13. Blanco Rotea R (2015) Arquitectura y Paisaje. Fortificaciones de Frontera en el Sur de Galicia y Norte de Portugal. UPV/EHU, Vitoria-Gasteiz
14. Parthenios P (2012) Using ConML to Visualize the Main Historical Monuments of Crete. Paper presented at the Computer Applications and Quantitative Methods in Archaeology (CAA) 2012, Southampton, UK,
15. Martín-Rodilla P, Gonzalez-Perez C, Mañana-Borrazás P (2016) A Conceptual and Visual Proposal to Decouple Material and Interpretive Information about Stratigraphic Data. In: Campana S, Scopigno R, Carpentiero G, Cirillo M (eds) Keep the Revolution Going: Proceedings of the 43rd Annual Conference on Computer Applications and Quantitative Methods in Archaeology. Archaeopress, pp 201–211

16. Pavlidis M, Mouratidis H, Gonzalez-Perez C, Kalloniatis C (2016) Addressing Privacy and Trust Issues in Cultural Heritage Modelling. In: Lambrinoudakis C, Gabillon A (eds) Risks and Security of Internet and Systems. LNCS, vol 9572. Springer, pp 3–16. https://doi.org/10. 1007/978-3-319-31811-0_1

17. Gonzalez-Perez C, Blanco-Rotea R, Mato C, Camiruaga Osés I (2010) A Formal Language for the Description of Historical Architectural Elements. In: Contreras F, Farjas M, Melero FJ (eds) Proceedings of the 38th Annual Conference on Computer Applications and Quantitative Methods in Archaeology, CAA2010 Amsterdam University Press,

18. Gonzalez-Perez C, Martín-Rodilla P, Parcero-Oubiña C, Fábrega-Álvarez P, Güimil-Fariña A Extending an Abstract Reference Model for Transdisciplinary Work in Cultural Heritage. In: Dodero JM, Palomo-Duarte M, Karampiperis P (eds) 6th Metadata and Semantics Research Conference (MTSR 2012), Cádiz (Spain), 2012. vol Communications in Computer and Information Science 343. Springer, pp 190–201. https://doi.org/10.1007/978-3-642-35233-1_20

19. Cobas Fernández I (2016) El concepto de paisaje cultural como recurso para la educación patrimonial en la educación secundaria, vol 37. Cadernos de Arqueoloxía e Patrimonio (CAPA). Incipit CSIC,

20. CIDOC (2011) The CIDOC Conceptual Reference Model. http://www.cidoc-crm.org/. Accessed 26 November 2012

21. ISO (2014) Information and documentation—A reference ontology for the interchange of cultural heritage information. 2 edn. International Organization for Standardization, Geneva

22. Binding C, May K, Tudhope D (2008) Semantic Interoperability in Archaeological Datasets: Data Mapping and Extraction Via the CIDOC CRM. In: Christensen-Dalsgaard B, Castelli D, Jurik BA, Lippincott J (eds) Research and Advanced Technology for Digital Libraries. LNCS, vol 5173. Springer, pp 280–290. https://doi.org/10.1007/978-3-540-87599-4_30

23. Doerr M (2003) The CIDOC Conceptual Reference Module. An Ontological Approach to Semantic Interoperability of Metadata. AI Magazine 24 (3):75–92

24. Gonzalez-Perez C, Martín-Rodilla P (2015) Integration of Archaeological Datasets through the Gradual Refinement of Models. In: Giligny F, Djindjian F, Costa L, Moscati P, Robert S (eds) 21st Century Archaeology: Concepts, Methods and Tools - Proceedings of the 42nd Annual Conference on Computer Applications and Quantitative Methods in Archaeology. Archaeopress, pp 193–204

25. Coad P, Yourdon E (1990) Object Oriented Analysis. 2nd Edition edn. Prentice-Hall,

26. Harnad S (2005) To Cognize is to Categorize: Cognition is Categorization. In: Lefebvre C, Cohen H (eds) Handbook of Categorization: Summer Institute in Cognitive Sciences on Categorisation. Elsevier,

27. McGinn C (2015) Philosophy of Language: The Classics Explained. The MIT Press,

28. Liskov B, Wing JM (1994) A Behavioral Notion of Subtyping. ACM Transactions on Programming Languages and Systems 16 (6):1811–1841

29. Guarino N (1998) Some Ontological Principles for Designing Upper Level Lexical Resources. In: Rubio, Gallardo, Castro, Tejada (eds) Proc. of First International Conference on Language Resources and Evaluation. Granada,

30. Rosch E (1978) Principles of categorization. In: Rosch E, Lloyd B (eds) Cognition and Categorization. Lawrence Elbaum Associates,

31. Gonzalez-Perez C, Martín-Rodilla P (2015) Teaching Conceptual Modelling in Humanities and Social Sciences. Paper presented at the II Congreso Internacional de Humanidades Digitales Hispánicas, Madrid, 5–7 October 2015

32. Incipit (2016) ConML Technical Specification. version 1.4.5. Incipit, CSIC,

33. World Wide Web Consortium (2004) RDF/XML Syntax Specification (Revised). World Wide Web Consortium,

34. Snodgrass RT, Ahn I (1986) Temporal Databases. Computer 19 (9):35–42

35. Svinterikou M, Theodoulidis B (1999) TUML: A Method for Modelling Temporal Information Systems. In: Jarke M, Oberweis A (eds) Advanced Information Systems Engineering. Lecture Notes in Computer Science, vol 1626. Springer, pp 456–461

36. Gonzalez-Perez C, Martín-Rodilla P, Blanco-Rotea R (2015) Expressing Temporal and Subjective Information about Archaeological Entities. In: Traviglia A (ed) Across Space and Time: Proceedings of the CAA 2013 Conference. Amsterdam University Press,

37. Gonzalez-Perez C (2013) Modelling Temporality and Subjectivity in ConML. In: Wieringa R, Nurcan S (eds) 7th IEEE International Conference on Research Challenges in Information Science (RCIS 2013). IEEE Computer Society, Paris (France), pp 1–6

38. Henderson-Sellers B (2011) Bridging Metamodels and Ontologies in Software Engineering. Journal of Systems and Software 84 (2):301–313. https://doi.org/10.1016/j.jss.2010.10.025

39. Atkinson C, Kühne T, Henderson-Sellers B (2000) To Meta or Not To Meta - That Is the Question. J OO Prog 13 (8):32–25

40. Gonzalez-Perez C, Henderson-Sellers B (2008) Metamodelling for Software Engineering. Wiley, Chichester (UK)

41. Gonzalez-Perez C, Martín-Rodilla P (2017) An Alternative Approach to Metainformation Conceptualisation and Use. In: Mayr HC, Guizzardi G, Ma H, Pastor O (eds) Conceptual Modeling (Proceedings of the 36th Int.Conf. ER 2017, Valencia, Nov. 6–9, 2016). Springer,

42. Gonzalez-Perez C (2012) A Conceptual Modelling Language for the Humanities and Social Sciences. In: Rolland C, Castro J, Pastor O (eds) Sixth International Conference on Research Challenges in Information Science (RCIS), 2012. IEEE Computer Society, pp 396–401. https://doi.org/10.1109/RCIS.2012.6240430

43. Henderson-Sellers B, Gonzalez-Perez C, McBride T, Low G (2014) An ontology for ISO software engineering standards: 1) Creating the infrastructure. Computer Standards & Interfaces 36 (3):563–576. https://doi.org/10.1016/j.csi.2013.11.001

44. Gonzalez-Perez C, Henderson-Sellers B, McBride T, Low G, Larrucea X (2016) An ontology for ISO software engineering standards: 2) Proof of concept and application. Computer Standards & Interfaces 48:112–123. https://doi.org/10.1016/j.csi.2016.04.007

45. Bendix R (2009) Heritage between Economy and Politics: An Assessment from the Perspective of Cultural Anthropology. In: Smith L, Akagawa N (eds) Intangible Heritage. Routledge, pp 253–269

46. Munjeri D (2004) Tangible and Intangible Heritage: from Difference to Convergence. Museum International 56 (1–2):12–20. https://doi.org/10.1111/j.1350-0775.2004.00453.x

47. Kirshenblatt-Gimblett B (2004) Intangible Heritage as Metacultural Production. Museum International 56 (1–2):52–65

48. Kirshenblatt-Gimblett B (1995) Theorizing Heritage. Ethnomusicology 39 (3):367–380

49. Dicks B (2000) Heritage, Place and Community. University of Wales Press,

50. Byrne D, Brayshaw H, Ireland T (2003) Social Significance: a Discussion Paper. NSW National Parks and Wildlife Service,

51. Smith L (2006) Uses of Heritage. Routledge,

52. Waterton E, Smith L (2009) There is No Such Thing as Heritage. In: Waterton E, Smith L (eds) Taking Archaeology out of Heritage. Cambridge Scholars Press, pp 10–27

53. Vecco M (2010) A Definition of Cultural Heritage: From the Tangible to the Intangible. Journal of Cultural Heritage 11 (3):321–324

54. ICOMOS (1964) International Charter for the Conservation and Restoration of Monuments and Sites.

55. Tainter JA, Lucas GJ (1983) Epistemology of the Significance Concept. American Antiquity 48 (4):707–719. https://doi.org/10.2307/279772

56. Avrami E, Mason R, de la Torre M (2000) Values and Heritage Conservation. The Getty Conservation Institute,

57. Turnpenny M (2007) Cultural Heritage, an Ill-Defined Concept? A Call for Joined-up Policy. International Journal of Heritage Studies 10 (3):295–307. https://doi.org/10.1080/1352725042000234460

58. Mason R (2004) Fixing Historic Preservation: A Constructive Critique of "Significance".
     Places 16 (1):64–72
59. Smith L (2004) Archaeological Theory and the Politics of Cultural Heritage. Routledge,
60. UNESCO (1972) UNESCO World Heritage Convention. UNESCO, Paris (France)
61. Mason R (2002) Assessing Values in Conservation Planning: Methodological Issues and
     Choices. In: de la Torre M (ed) Assessing the Values of Cultural Heritage. The Getty
     Conservation Institute, pp 5–30
62. Lipe WD (1984) Value and Meaning in Cultural Resources. In: Cleere H (ed) Approaches to
     the Archaeological Heritage. Cambridge University Press, pp 1–11
63. Garden MCE (2006) The Heritagescape: Looking at Landscapes of the Past. International
     Journal of Heritage Studies 12 (5):394–411. https://doi.org/10.1080/13527250600821621
64. Gonzalez-Perez C, Parcero Oubiña C (2011) A Conceptual Model for Cultural Heritage
     Definition and Motivation. In: Zhou M, Romanowska I, Wu Z, Xu P, Verhagen P
     (eds) Revive the Past: Proceeding of the 39th Conference on Computer Applications and
     Quantitative Methods in Archaeology. Amsterdam University Press, pp 234–244
65. World Archaeological Congress 30th Anniversary Plenary (2016) Resolution 11. WAC,
     Kyoto
66. Incipit (2016) CHARM White Paper. version 1.0.6. Incipit, CSIC,
67. Smith B, Varzi AC (2005) Fiat and bona fide boundaries: Towards an ontology of spatially
     extended objects. In: Hirtle SC, Frank AU (eds) Spatial Information Theory: A Theoretical
     Basis for GIS. LNCS, vol 1329. Springer, pp 103–119. https://doi.org/10.1007/3-540-63623-
     4_45
68. Alexander C (1975) The Oregon Experiment. Oxford University Press, New York
69. Alexander C, Ishikawa S, Silverstein M (1977) A Pattern Language. Oxford University
     Press, New York
70. Alexander C (1979) The Timeless Way of Building. Oxford University Press, New York
71. Gamma E, Helm R, Johnson R, Vlissides J (1995) Design Patterns: Elements of Reusable
     Object-Oriented Software. Addison-Wesley,
72. Meyer B (1997) Object-Oriented Software Construction. 2nd edition. Prentice-Hall, Upper
     Saddle River, NJ

List of CHARM Model Elements

© Springer International Publishing AG 2018
C. Gonzalez-Perez, *Information Modelling for Archaeology and Anthropology*,
https://doi.org/10.1007/978-3-319-72652-6

Index

© Springer International Publishing AG 2018

445

C. Gonzalez-Perez, *Information Modelling for Archaeology and Anthropology*,
https://doi.org/10.1007/978-3-319-72652-6